Hafiz and
His Contemporaries

'Understanding Hafiz's exquisite *ghazals* has never been easy through the ages, although he is one of the central figures in the canon of classical Persian poetry. Taking a holistic approach, Dominic Brookshaw has produced an erudite and readable study of the poet, his age and oeuvre. We learn about Hafiz's life and achievement in the broader literary and cultural context of medieval Iran, and also pick up virtually all the indispensable tools to understand Persian *ghazals* such as the role of performance, intertextuality, poetic imagery, and the fine line between mystical and profane. This book should be the starting point for anyone who is interested in any aspect of Persian poetry.'

Sunil Sharma, Professor of Persian and
Comparative Literature, Boston University

'This excellent book sets a new measure for historically contextualized appreciation of Hafiz and classical Persian poetry. Grounded in prodigious knowledge of sources, Brookshaw's argument is exemplary for its directness and clarity. All too often in prior discussions of Hafiz's poetry, claims of exceptionalism have had the effect of smothering the man and his work. In Brookshaw's absorbing narrative, we see Hafiz as a poetic virtuoso situated in a milieu host to worthy associates and rivals, such as 'Ubayd Zakani and Jahan-Malik Khatun. Intermeshed with the work of his predecessors and contemporaries, Hafiz's poetry exemplifies the richness of the tradition he inherited, moulded, and influenced for centuries to come. Brookshaw's exceedingly sympathetic, yet always perceptively critical, treatment of the subject marks *Hafiz and His Contemporaries* as the state of the art in Persian and Islamic literary history.'

Shahzad Bashir, Director, Middle East Studies and Aga Khan
Professor of Islamic Humanities, Brown University

"Brookshaw's comprehensive study of the poetry of Hafiz and his contemporaries provides us with an excellent map through which both specialists and amateurs are offered the opportunity to travel across time to discover the breadth of the literary and cultural richness of 14th-century Iran. Thanks to its carefully crafted arguments and analyses, this book opens multiple windows into historical events, lyric celebrations of the encounter between urban and natural spaces, nostalgic reminiscences of princely ideals, and the constant wandering of poets and verses across courts, monasteries, gardens, markets, taverns, and secluded spaces of affection and desire."

Domenico Arturo Ingenito, Assistant Professor of Classical
Persian, University of California, Los Angeles.

Hafiz and His Contemporaries

Poetry, Performance and Patronage in Fourteenth-century Iran

DOMINIC PARVIZ BROOKSHAW

I.B.TAURIS
LONDON • NEW YORK • OXFORD • NEW DELHI • SYDNEY

I.B. TAURIS
Bloomsbury Publishing Plc
50 Bedford Square, London, WC1B 3DP, UK
1385 Broadway, New York, NY 10018, USA

BLOOMSBURY, I.B. TAURIS and the I.B. Tauris
logo are trademarks of Bloomsbury Publishing Plc

First published in Great Britain 2019
Paperback edition first published 2020

Cover design: Arianna Osti

A catalogue record for this book is available from the British Library.

A catalog record for this book is available from the Library of Congress.

ISBN: HB: 978-1-84885-144-3
PB: 978-0-7556-3834-5
ePDF: 978-1-78673-588-1
eBook: 978-1-78672-588-2

Typeset by Integra Software Services Pvt. Ltd.

To find out more about our authors and books visit
www.bloomsbury.com and sign up for our newsletters.

For Naseem

Contents

Acknowledgements

Any academic publication marks the culmination point in a long process of research, writing, rewriting and conversation. I have had many great conversations over the years about Hafiz, about the way I see his poetry and about the approaches others take to him. Those conversations, whether formal, in the context of scholarly conferences and seminars, or informal, with students and colleagues, have all helped make this book what it is and I am grateful for each and every one of them. As a graduate student, I had the bounty of travelling a number of times to Iran to discuss my research with pre-eminent scholars of Persian literature and Iranian history, some of whom are no longer with us. At Stanford, where I began to work on this book in earnest, I benefited greatly from the creative intellectual energy of colleagues in my home department, Comparative Literature, in the broader Division of Literatures, Cultures and Languages, in the History and Religious Studies departments and in the Iranian Studies programme. At the Oriental Institute, I began a Hafiz reading group with my students in which we read the *ghazal*s one-by-one, week-by-week, exploring a range of interpretative approaches. Here, at Oxford, I would also like to acknowledge those colleagues both within the Faculty of Oriental Studies and at Wadham College who have been constant in their support and encouragement.

I should mention several people by name, each of whom has played a significant role in bringing this book to light: firstly, I must thank Julie Scott Meisami and Geert Jan van Gelder under whose supervision I wrote the doctoral thesis that formed the springboard for this book. I would also like to thank Iradj Bagherzade and Joanna Godfrey at I.B. Tauris for their constant enthusiasm and the reviewers for their constructive criticism of an early version of the manuscript. More recently, a number of dear friends have read drafts of part or all of the manuscript and provided me with invaluable feedback. They are: Vincent Barletta, Robert Crews, Domenico Ingenito, Nasrin Rahimieh, Sahba Shayani and Farzin Vejdani. I cannot thank each and every one of you enough. Needless to say, all errors of translation and interpretation are my own, as are all infelicities in use of grammar and style of expression.

Finally, I would like to thank my family: my parents for supporting me in what was, in their eyes, an unconventional career choice; my sister-in-law and my brother for always encouraging me in my research, even though it could not be more different to their own field of specialization; and Valiyeh and Nuriyeh for trying to understand that Baba has to spend lots of time at his *daftar* when actually all they want is for me to stay at home and play. Most of all, I would like to thank my wife, Naseem Alizadeh, for her belief in this book and in my ability to write it, which was especially important at those times when I had faith in neither. Thank you for being my critical non-specialist reader and thank you for going above and beyond with the girls when I had to work on weekends and come home late at night. Thank you for your love and your laughter – always.

A note on transliteration, dates and abbreviations

All systems of transliteration have their critics. I have omitted diacritical marks in names of people, places and literary works and have only retained the use of macrons to differentiate between short and long vowels when transliterating Persian and Arabic terms. I realize that my decision not to provide comprehensive transliteration will upset some, but I believe it makes the book easier to read. I have provided dates in the text in Common Era form unless the AH year was vital to the meaning. All of the translations in the text are my own unless noted otherwise. I have aimed to produce translations that are readable and, as far as is possible, close to the original. Wherever I could, I have preserved the semantic integrity of the hemistich. In the bibliography you will find a number of eloquent translations of Hafiz listed by name of translator/s. The following abbreviations are used in this book:

H279 = Hafiz Shirazi (1999), *Divan*, eds Qasim Ghani and Muhammad Qazvini. Tehran: Quqnus, *ghazal* number 279.

J1365 = Jahan-Malik Khatun (1995), *Divan-i kamil*, eds Kamil Ahmadnizhad and Purandukht Kashani-Rad. Tehran: Zavvar, *ghazal* number 1365.

U99 = 'Ubayd Zakani, Nizam al-Din (1999), *Kulliyat*, ed. Muhammad-Ja'far Mahjub. New York: Bibliotheca Persica Press, *ghazal* number 99.

K55 = Abu Nuwas, al-Hasan b. Hani (2003a), *Diwan Abi Nuwas* vol. III, ed. Ewald Wagner. Damascus: al-Mada, *khamrīya* number 55.

♂35 = Abu Nuwas, al-Hasan b. Hani (2003b), *Diwan Abi Nuwas* vol. IV, ed. Gregor Schoeler. Damascus: al-Mada, *mudhakkara* number 35.

♀47 = Abu Nuwas, al-Hasan b. Hani (2003b), *Diwan Abi Nuwas* vol. IV, ed. Gregor Schoeler. Damascus: al-Mada, *mu'annatha* number 47.

Individual lines of poetry are referred to thus: H105:1 = Hafiz, *ghazal* 105, line 1.

A glossary of literary terms

bayt the unit of poetry in Persian; a line or distich consisting of two hemistichs.

dīvān the collected poems of a single poet, normally subdivided according to form and arranged within sections by rhyme and *radīf*.

fakhr self-boasting in poetry which is often combined with the *takhallus* in the last or penultimate distich.

ghazal a short, monorhyme poem with double rhyme in the opening line. The Persian *ghazal* is broadly amorous but is also used for panegyric and homiletic purposes.

istiqbāl a blanket term in Persian poetics for imitation.

javāb a response poem in which the rhyme, metre, diction and semantic meaning of the model poem is imitated.

madh praise as expressed in poetry.

mamdūh 'object of praise', the patron.

mathnavī poetic form in which the two hemistichs of each line are rhymed. This form is used for long compositions, including epics and romances.

matla' the opening distich of a lyric poem.

misrā' hemistich, which in Persian poetry generally has semantic coherence.

qasīda multi-sectional, often lengthy monorhyme poem primarily used for panegyric in Persian.

qit'a monothematic, monorhyme poem, which is normally shorter than a *qasīda*.

radīf a word or phrase that can be added somewhat like a refrain after the rhyme.

rubā'ī 'quatrain,' a monorhyme poem composed of two distichs.

takhallus the poet's pen name (such as Hafiz, 'Ubayd, Jahan) which is normally included in the last distich of the *ghazal*.

talmīh allusion in poetry to a historical person or a character from the mythological, literary or religious past that is used to elucidate a truth in the present.

tazmīn verbatim quotation of a hemistich or a distich by other poets, often past masters.

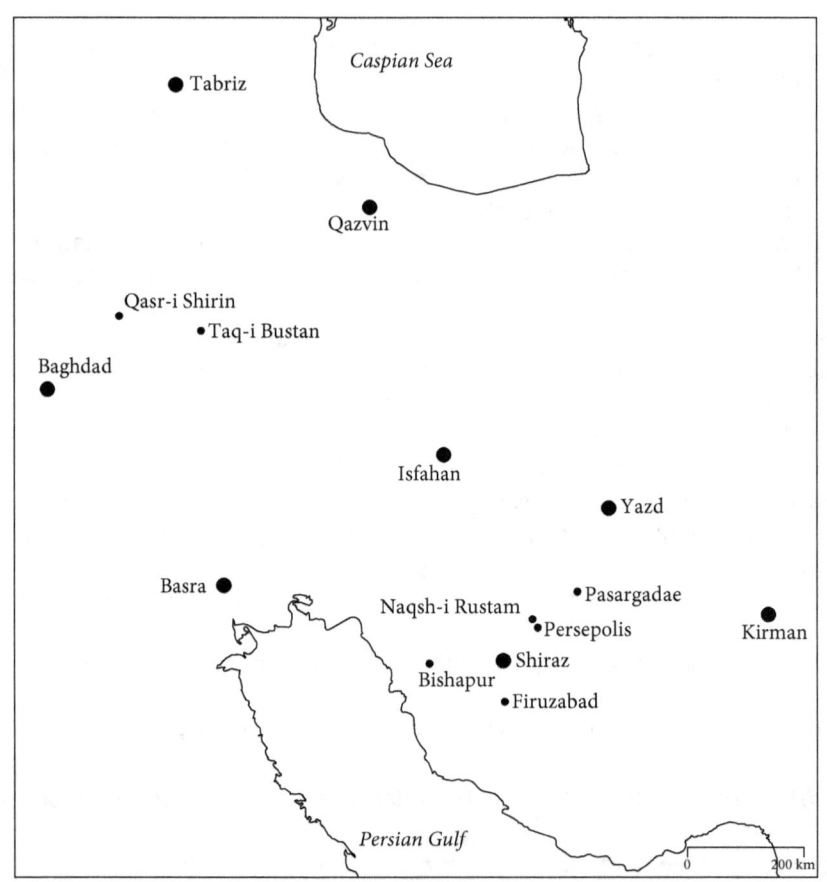

Major centres of Persian poetic activity in fourteenth-century Iran and Iraq.

Chronological list of poets

Arranged by year of death, with pen names in bold.

Thirteenth-century
Kamal al-Din Isma'il Isfahani (d. ca 1237).
Majd al-Din **Hamgar** Yazdi (d. 1287).
Fakhr al-Din **'Iraqi** (d. 1289).
Musharrif al-Din Muslih **Sa'di** Shirazi (d. 1292).

Fourteenth-century
Sa'd al-Din **Nizari** Quhistani (d. 1320).
Awhad al-Din **Awhadi** Maragha'i (d. 1338).
Shams al-Din **Shams-i Fakhri** Isfahani (d. 1348).
Kamal al-Din **Khvaju** Kirmani (d. 1352 or 1361).
Jalal al-Din 'Adud Yazdi (d. ca 1357).
Ruh-i 'Attar Shirazi (d. after 1369).
Nizam al-Din **'Ubayd**ullah Zakani (d. 1371).
'Imad al-Din Faqih Kirmani (d. 1371).
Jamal al-Din **Salman** Savaji (d. 1376).
Nasir Bukhara'i (d. 1377).
Mu'in al-Din **Junayd** Shirazi (d. after 1389).
Shams al-Din Muhammad **Hafiz** Shirazi (d. 1390).
Jahan-Malik Khatun (d. after 1391).
Sharaf al-Din **Rami** (d. 1392).
Haydar Shirazi (d. ca 1393).
Kamal al-Din Khujandi (d. ca 1400).
Bushaq At'ima Shirazi (d. 1423 or 1427).

Introduction

Dubbed an inimitable genius by literary critics of the past and held up by scholars of the present as a poet who defies comparison with others, Shams al-Din Muhammad Hafiz Shirazi (d. 1390) remains an elusive, opaque character for many. The rarefication of Hafiz began in earnest in the early to mid-1400s when either the poet and/or his poems started being referred to as *Lisān al-ghayb* ('Tongue of the Unseen').[1] As early as 1421, Hafiz's *ghazals* (short, monorhyme, broadly amorous lyric poems) were being lauded as the 'envy of the source of eternal life' endowed with the power to revive the expired heart like the breaths of Christ; the sprinklings from his pen could perform Mosaic miracles with speech.[2]

To look behind the hyperbole that surrounds Hafiz's poetry and penetrate the quasi-hagiographical film that obscures the poet himself, this book adopts a comparative approach, one rarely adopted by scholars of Persian poetry, many of whom still favour in-depth studies of individuals. What I hope to impress upon those who study the Persian *ghazal* and Hafiz scholars in particular, is both the need for and value of the analysis of Hafiz's poetry comparatively against texts composed by those working alongside him in the highly competitive, close-knit, profoundly intertextual environment of fourteenth-century Shiraz. Hafiz and his contemporaries imitated one another's poems, responded to each other repeatedly in verse and vied to outdo one another in the hope of securing lucrative patronage. Their poetry demands to be analysed in tandem; no longer can Hafiz be placed on the pedestal of incomparability.[3]

This is a study of Persian poetry at a specific historical juncture, in a particular place: post-Mongol Shiraz, a city of approximately 60,000 people that had immense cultural reach. The analysis of Hafiz and his peers in Shiraz is presented not only with respect to its local literary framework, but as part of a transregional network of poets active in the major cities of Iran and Iraq who shared a common poetic koine. My methodology is inspired by research that works to locate texts within specific social sites to uncover, in particular, the political and social pressures and impulses that create moment-specific cultural discourse.[4] By focusing on some key topoi shared by *ghazal*s produced by a network of poets that were active circa 1330–1390 across Shiraz, Kirman, Yazd, Baghdad and Tabriz, I re-read and re-evaluate Hafiz through a sober lens and with keen attention to his contemporary literary context, rather than in splendid isolation, as is all too often the case. I view Hafiz as part of a larger, organic whole, not as an exceptional figure who demands a singular reading.

I was initially inspired to undertake this study after reading one foray into the contextualization of Hafiz in particular, Annemarie Schimmel's chapter on Hafiz in the *Cambridge History of Iran*, from which the main part of the title of this book is borrowed.[5] As a comparatist, I have elected to bring Hafiz into productive, detailed dialogue with two of his less-studied peers: 'Ubayd Zakani (d. 1371), the sparkling litterateur-wit and Jahan-Malik Khatun (d. after 1391), an Injuid princess and the most prolific premodern Persian woman poet. Reading Hafiz comparatively alongside a liminal and somewhat counterhegemonic figure such as the sharp-tongued 'Ubayd and the marginalized Jahan who, despite the quality of her poetry and the clear imprint it bears of intertextual exchange with her male contemporaries, has been almost wholly ignored by the scholarship, disrupts our received understanding of this most iconic of stages in the development of the Persian short lyric, thereby creating space for new avenues of literary criticism in the field.

I have examined my three core figures in tandem with their colleagues and foes who were co-members of the thriving, vibrant, poetic community in Shiraz and the cities within its immediate political orbit. Looking beyond southern and central Iran in the interests of a fuller contextualization, I have also incorporated analysis of poetry composed in Baghdad and Tabriz, Shiraz's most significant cultural and political competitors. To add depth to this literary contextualization and to recognize the poets' own profound interaction with the tradition, relevant poems from previous periods – most substantially those of Sa'di Shirazi (d. 1292) and other Salghurid poets, but also canonical texts by foundational figures, in particular Firdawsi Tusi (d. 1020), Nizami Ganjavi (d. 1209) and the early Abbasid poet Abu Nuwas (d. ca 814) – have been brought to bear to demonstrate how the poets of fourteenth-century Shiraz did not simply see themselves as representatives of a local tradition of lyric poetry. Another comparative feature of this study which addresses the generic experimentation the *ghazal* underwent during the post-Mongol period, is the discussion of *ghazal*s alongside other lyric poems (most particularly *qasīda*s [long, polythematic, monorhyme lyric odes], but also *qit'a*s [short, monothematic lyric poems] and *rubā'ī*s [quatrains composed of two distichs]) and other genres (chiefly epic and romance *mathnavī*s [lengthy poems made up of rhyming couplets]), as well as works of prose, prosimetrums and other belle-lettristic texts, in addition to local and dynastic histories. It is only through comparative textual study that is at once loco-specific, transregional and intergeneric and which encompasses discrete historical periods, that a nuanced, altogether more balanced picture of Hafiz the poet will emerge. This study embraces the conscious and deliberate hybridity, ambiguity and polysemy of the Persian *ghazal*. Though my emphasis is on the courtly and profane, I in no way seek to deny the mystical depth of the *ghazal*. That said, it must be recognized that Hafiz, whether we wish to label him as a panegyrist or a professional poet or not, was a major player within Shiraz's socio-political fabric who enjoyed largely nourishing relationships with a long line of local rulers and their chief courtiers.

In this study, poetry is read with profound regard for the social, political, literary and broader cultural contexts that it helped both to construct and make sense of. Here, the poems of Hafiz and his peers are seen not simply as texts, but as experiences lived in a specific cultural moment.[6]

The poem itself is the event, not the representation of one.[7] The poetry examined here is viewed as performative in that it accomplished (or sought to accomplish, perhaps through repeated evocation) what it described:[8] by depicting an ideal poet–patron relationship, for example, the poet hoped to realize such an intimate bond for him/herself. A product of its context, poetry has a social role in that it affects the worldview, imaginative capacities and inter-relationships of those who listen to it.[9] We do damage to lyric poems in particular if we neglect the historical particularities of the era in which they were composed.[10] Lyric poetry deserves to be read with due attention to the social conditions in which it was performed.[11] My analysis here is inspired by the belief in texts as 'societal products'[12] and my understanding of poetry as a socially embedded activity.[13] Following Spiegel, I see texts as agents that work not only to mirror, but also to generate, social realities.[14]

Shams al-Din Muhammad Hafiz Shirazi

Very little reliable information exists about Hafiz's life. Born around 1320 in Shiraz to a local mother and a father of Isfahani stock, Hafiz appears to have received a solid education in the Islamic sciences, thereby earning the right to use the title *hāfiz* ('one who has memorized the Qur'an by heart') in his youth,[15] hence his pen name (*takhallus*; although there is a typically Hafizian ambiguity even in his pen name, since *hāfiz* also means a professional musician or singer).[16] Hafiz died in Shiraz in 1390 without having prepared a definitive edition of his own poems;[17] these were collected into a *dīvān* (volume of collected poems) only in the early fifteenth century, possibly up to a generation after his death.

It is clear that Hafiz was intimately involved in courtly life; abundant references and allusions to persons of political or social importance prove this. His many panegyrics also suggest he was dependent on the patronage of royals and influential members of the ruler's circle.[18] Hafiz's career began at the Injuid court, possibly in his early twenties under Jahan's father, Jalal al-Din Mas'ud Shah (killed 1342).[19] From that early start, Hafiz rose in status as a poet and served a long line of Shiraz's rulers and their viziers, managing to navigate between competing dynasties and feuding members of the same house. The poet also looked beyond Fars, primarily to Baghdad, but possibly also to the Persian Gulf coast and even India for recognition, if not direct patronage. Hafiz maintained a productive relationship with the court at Shiraz up until his death, enjoying royal patronage for the best part of five decades (although he is believed to have fallen out of favour with Shah Shuja', his most significant patron, for up to a decade [ca 1366–1376] during which he perhaps spent time in Isfahan and Yazd).[20]

Although we cannot be absolutely sure that all Hafiz composed has survived, we also have little evidence to the contrary. In the fifty years or so that he was active as a poet, Hafiz most likely did not produce many more *ghazals* than the number that have survived him, which probably means he did not produce much more than one *ghazal* or thereabouts per month.[21] This is interesting when we consider that Khvaju Kirmani (d. 1352 or 1361), who produced many panegyric *qasidas* for Injuid, Muzaffarid and Jalayirid patrons as well as a quintet of *mathnavi*s after the model of Nizami,[22] left almost twice as many *ghazals* for posterity, while Tabriz's Kamal Khujandi (d. 1401) and Jahan who, like Hafiz, focused almost exclusively on the short lyric, penned more than 900 and 1,400 *ghazals* respectively. Shafi'i-Kadkani believes Hafiz was perpetually refining his poetic craft for aesthetic considerations and to conform to the socio-political strictures he faced.[23] For these reasons, perhaps, Hafiz edited, amalgamated and repurposed many of his *ghazals*, which goes some way to explaining the large number of variants in the manuscript tradition.[24]

Hafiz was a well-known poet in his own day.[25] In an anthology of lyric poetry produced most likely in Shiraz perhaps only a year or so before the poet's death,[26] Hafiz's *ghazals* appear together with poems by earlier poets and a good number of his peers, including Awhadi Maragha'i (d. 1338), Jalal Yazdi (d. ca 1357), Nizari Quhistani (d. 1320) and Salman Savaji (d. 1376) as well as poems by two contemporary royals, Shah Shuja' (d. 1384), and Sultan Ahmad b. Shaykh Uvays (d. 1411), and one Injuid vizier, 'Amid al-Mulk.[27] The anthologist (who hints that he was personally acquainted with Hafiz)[28] deliberately included an equal number of *ghazals* by Hafiz and Jalal (fifty each). This suggests the anthologist (or the person who commissioned the anthology) viewed Hafiz and Jalal, contemporaries at the court of Shah Shaykh Abu Ishaq, as equal in poetic stature.[29]

In the fifteenth century, the foundations of Hafiz's lasting fame were firmly laid.[30] Hafiz was gradually brought out of the margins surrounding his peers and severed from the intertextual framework he had shared with them through the compilation of his *dīvān* and its repeated copying, distribution and ultimate fetishization as an object imbued with other-worldly powers. By 1500, Hafiz's *dīvān* had become a 'mass product' which was already widely used for consulting omens and popular fortune-telling.[31] In 1486, Dawlatshah Samarqandi hails Hafiz as 'the one initiated in the divine mysteries' (*mahram-i rāz-i hazrat-i bī-niyāz*);[32] he describes Hafiz's poetic style as *bī-takalluf* ('unfussy', 'without unnecessary ornament') and *sāda* ('plain').[33] Writing just a year after Dawlatshah, the poet 'Abd al-Rahman Jami (d. 1492) claims that Hafiz almost achieves *i'jāz* ('wondrous inimitability'), a term that is most frequently associated with the text of the Qur'an.[34] Dawlatshah characteristically plays down Hafiz's interaction with royals and other men of power[35] and 'Ali-Shir Nava'i, writing a few years later, says Hafiz's poems are enjoyed by all levels of society. In Nava'i's assessment, Hafiz's *dīvān* is as famous as the *Gulistan* and *Bustan* of Sa'di;[36] so famous, it would appear, that some Timurid anthologists felt no need to cite examples from Hafiz's poetry when discussing the poet in their works.[37]

Nizam al-Din 'Ubaydullah Zakani

'Ubayd Zakani (pen name 'Ubayd, lit. 'little slave', 'small servant') is universally acknowledged as medieval Iran's pre-eminent satirist. 'Ubayd expressed profound social critique in often obscene poetry and prose,[38] the popularity of which has caused his courtly poetry to be largely overlooked.[39] Born around 1300 into a family of scholars in the region of Qazvin, by 1329 'Ubayd had accrued enough social capital to be hailed by Hamdullah Mustawfi as a talented poet and a skilled writer of treatises.[40] For reasons that are not completely clear, at some point in the mid-to-late 1330s, 'Ubayd moved south and ultimately sought the patronage of the Injuids at Shiraz, in whose honour he went on to compose many panegyric *qasīda*s.[41] As panegyrist to Shah Shaykh Abu Ishaq,[42] 'Ubayd would most likely have had personal dealings with Hafiz who, it is believed, began his poetic career around 1340. 'Ubayd is said by Dawlatshah to have engaged in 'poetic contests and debates' (*mushā'ara u munāzara*) with Jahan and (erroneously) to have lampooned her in two vulgar, one-line poems (*mufradāt*).[43]

'Ubayd left Shiraz around 1353 in the wake of the overthrow and flight to Isfahan of Shah Shaykh Abu Ishaq. The poet eventually found his way to Baghdad and, most likely with the help of his new-found friend, Salman

Savaji, chief panegyrist to the Jalayirds,[44] gained access to the glittering circle of Sultan Uvays (r. 1356–1374).[45] Near the end of his life, 'Ubayd successfully solicited Muzaffarid patronage and returned to Shiraz where he is believed to have died.[46] 'Ubayd provides a fascinating point of comparison with Hafiz because he did not focus obsessively on the *ghazal*. 'Ubayd's poetic output is varied and includes a large number of *qasīda*s and strophic poems, as well as *ghazal*s, *qit'a*s, *rubā'ī*s and *mathnavī*s. 'Ubayd's *ghazal*s demonstrate much of the flare and vibrancy of Hafiz's more playful amorous, bacchic or socially critical *ghazal*s, though, because 'Ubayd produced numerous panegyric *qasīda*s, he did not generally use the *ghazal* to praise his patrons.

Jahan-Malik Khatun

As has been the fate of many fourteenth-century Persian poets, Jahan-Malik Khatun (pen name Jahān, lit. 'world'), premodern Iran's most prolific woman poet, has been overshadowed by Hafiz, perhaps even more so than others because of her sex.[47] That Jahan, a literate, elite woman, wrote poetry is neither surprising nor without precedent. Jahan was not a freakish anomaly. As she demonstrates in the preface to her *dīvān*, writing poetry is something women of her social class do! Like Hafiz, Jahan's primary focus was the *ghazal* in which she displays a noticeable affinity with Hafiz.[48] Though Jahan disguised neither her name nor her gender identity,[49] it is only occasionally that one senses a feminine poetic voice in her *ghazal*s.[50] Jahan plays with the gender of the lyrical 'I',[51] but, with almost implacable consistency, she conforms to convention: she assumes a male homoerotic posture.[52] In addition to her more than 1,400 *ghazal*s, Jahan wrote two panegyric *qasīda*s, over 350 *rubā'ī*s and a handful of other poems. Jahan was the only child of Jalal al-Din Mas'ud Shah to survive to adulthood and was the niece of the last Injuid, Shah Shaykh Abu Ishaq, who most likely encouraged her to write poetry and host private literary salons (*majālis*). As with other premodern women poets, Jahan could only have excelled in poetry to the extent that she did with support from within her literary community.[53] On her mother's side, Jahan was a direct descendent of the Ilkhanid vizier, Rashid al-Din Fazlullah (d. 1318);[54] her stepmother, Sultanbakht Khatun, was a Chupanid princess and the sister of Dilshad Khatun (d. 1351), the Jalayirid queen of Baghdad who was a generous patron to both Salman and Khvaju.[55]

Born after 1324, Jahan died no earlier than 1391. She is believed to have married Amin al-Din Jahrumi, boon companion (*nadīm*) to her uncle[56] and is introduced in later anthologies as one of Shiraz's famous poets. She did not shy away from taking on 'Ubayd in poetry competitions and is said to have met Hafiz in person.[57] Jahan prefaced a fine copy of her *dīvān* (one that she is thought to have gifted to the Jalayirid prince-litterateur, Sultan Ahmad b. Shaykh Uvays),[58] with a fascinating introduction in which she speaks of her anxieties vis-à-vis the propriety of her recording her poetry as a woman. In defence of her literary activities,[59] Jahan invokes the memory of earlier female predecessors in her art, thereby tapping into a 'sisterhood of poetry'.[60] Among the poets Jahan mentions in her preface are two royals: Qutlughshah Khatun,[61] a wife of the Mongol ruler Öljeitü (d. 1316) and the formidable Padishah Khatun, who ruled independently in Kirman from 1292 until she was killed three years later.[62] In the world of literature, Padishah Khatun is best remembered for her stridently feminine self-praise poetry.[63] Interestingly, Shah Shuja' was distantly related to Padishah Khatun through his mother.[64]

Only four manuscripts of Jahan's *dīvān* (or selections therefrom) are known: two kept at the Bibliothèque Nationale in Paris (one a complete copy of Jahan's *dīvān* produced during her lifetime; the other a selection of her poetry, copied possibly in Herat around 1460);[65] one at the Topkapı Palace Library in Istanbul (the second most complete manuscript copy of Jahan's *dīvān* to have survived) dated to 1437;[66] and the fourth, a short selection of Jahan's poems with a preface in praise of Shah Shuja' dating to 1618 that belonged to Browne and is now kept at the University Library in Cambridge.[67] Since the first and only publication of Jahan's *dīvān* in 1995, an additional thirty-six *ghazals* have been uncovered in three Timurid anthologies.[68]

In the thirteenth and fourteenth centuries, the cultural, religious and political spheres of life in Shiraz felt the impact of several powerful royal women. In the Salghurid period, the key female political figures were: Shiraz's queen regent, Turkan Khatun (r. 1260–1262); the independent and then de facto ruler of Fars, Abish Khatun bint Sa'd (d. 1286); and her daughter (and Padishah Khatun's sister-in-law), Kurdujin (d. 1338).[69] In the Injuid period, significant contributions to the development of local shrines and investment in the production of fine Qur'an manuscripts were made in the 1340s by Tashi Khatun,[70] the mother of Shah Shaykh Abu Ishaq and by his sister, Fars-Malik Khatun.[71] However, Jahan's impact was on Shiraz's literary scene: as poet, host of well-attended literary salons[72] and sparring partner in verse for male (and, possibly, female) peers.[73]

Blair reads the depiction of elite, economically powerful women in the arts of the late thirteenth to early fourteenth century as a reflection of their changing status under the Mongols and their immediate successors.[74] Building on Blair's interpretation, perhaps we should see Jahan's audacity in compiling her own *dīvān* as a literary manifestation of that same Mongol effect. That said, we are hampered in attempts to contextualize Jahan within contemporary gynocentric poetic networks by the simple fact that insubstantial evidence of the poetry produced by women in her period remains, presumably having suffered more from neglect than that of men because of society's anxieties around the dissemination and recording of women's compositions in written form.[75] But it would seem that there were other women in the period who were producers of literary culture. There is anecdotal evidence of Bibi Hayat, wife of the Injuid vizier Qavam al-Din Hasan (d. 1353), who is said to have lampooned Jahan in verse and there is also the Jalayirid poet, Afaq, sister of Hasan-i Buzurg (d. 1356).[76] But what astonishes in the case of Jahan's poetry is not its large volume (impressive as it is) but that in terms of quality it is comparable to that of the professional male poets of her day. Jahan's eloquent *ghazals* not only belie her extensive training in the poetic arts and her deep knowledge of the tradition, they also open a window onto the hidden world of private literary salons, hint at the sophistication in poetic practice and appreciation among the elite classes from which patrons were sought and testify to the very high level of education open to some women in Injuid and Muzaffarid Shiraz.

The *ghazal*

Originating in Arabic as an amorous poetic mood and developing in the course of the first centuries of Islam into a standalone, monorhyme, predominantly heteroerotic love poem with a courtly spirit,[77] the *ghazal* eventually acquired a fixed form in Persian, along with a squarely homoerotic focus and distinct motifs and imagery. From Persian, the form moved into other great literatures of the Muslim world (Chaghatai, Ottoman Turkish and Urdu) that used the Persian *ghazal* as the model for their own.[78] The *ghazal* (defined by a set of prosodic rules almost identical to the *qasīda*, but shorter in length) perhaps first appeared in Persian as a text to be sung. Appropriate for memorization and preferably composed in metres suitable for singing, by the close of the tenth century, *ghazals* were already closely linked to the manners and protocols of the courtly *majlis* and its entertainments: wine-drinking, musical performance and erotic flirtation.[79] The normative form and standard formal features achieved by the Persian *ghazal* in addition to monorhyme include the *radīf* (an independent word, phrase or particle added repeatedly to the rhyme) which provides a degree of semantic coherence[80] or infuses the poem with a common dynamic.[81] The *ghazal* also has internal rhyme in the *matla'* (opening line); in Persian, it carries the poet's *takhallus*, an almost ubiquitous feature of the form by the end of the thirteenth century which is normally found in the final line, though it can be moved to the penultimate line to add emphasis to the formal naming of the patron.[82] The poet uses the *takhallus* to appear to speak to or about him/herself in the second or third person. It is in combination with the pen name that typically we find *fakhr* ('self-boasting') about the poet's literary talents, eloquence and/or fame (often in combination with the solicitation of monetary reward or some other favour from the addressee).[83] Persian *ghazal*s can vary in length, but the majority of those from the fourteenth century are made up of 7–10 lines.

According to Persian mystical terminology, the *ghazal* deals with two kinds of love: *majāzī* ('metaphorical'): earthly love and *haqīqī* ('real', 'true'): love for God. The connection between the two is both intimate and many-sided;[84] even in so-called mystical *ghazal*s the sensual and spiritual coexist as analogues, rather than alternatives.[85] By definition, a *ghazal* has love as its main subject,[86] though very early on in its development in Persian, bacchanalian topics were added, followed by didactic and mystical themes.[87] In panegyric *ghazal*s, the beloved (*ma'shūq*) becomes identified with the patron (*mamdūh*), who thereby becomes the focus of both desire and praise.[88] The use of the *ghazal* for panegyric was facilitated by the homosocial performance contexts of lyric poetry and normatively homoerotic desire that pervades Persian lyric poetry.[89]

The unit of Persian lyric poetry is the *bayt* ('line', 'distich') which consists of two *misrā*'s ('half-lines', 'hemistichs'). As a rule, each line (sometimes each half line) contains a complete, albeit pithy, statement which is not only syntactically but also semantically independent.[90] Much ink has been spilt over the unity or connectedness between the individual *bayt*s in the Persian *ghazal*, in particular the Hafizian short lyric. Bausani sees each *bayt* as a 'closed unit, only slightly interconnected with the others' and each poem as an assemblage of a multiplicity of motifs 'only lightly tied together'.[91] Except for the coherence provided by metre, monorhyme and (where present) *radīf*, some detect little formal unity, particularly in Hafiz's *ghazal*s.[92] I neither demand unity between the lines of a *ghazal*, nor do I fetishize the absence of an obvious coherence. Hillmann concluded that a portion of Hafiz's *ghazal*s exhibit 'palpable superficial unity', but even this assessment is tentative since it would appear that the poet was not particularly wedded to the finality of the number or order of the *bayt*s, most probably for reasons related to recitation or performance to musical accompaniment.[93]

Mystical or profane?

By the end of the thirteenth century, *ghazal*s fell into two broad categories: mystical in tendency or predominantly profane.[94] Here, my primary focus is the non-mystical aspects of the post-Mongol *ghazal*, though I do not deny the form's mystical stratum in this period, nor do I wish to present a dogmatically secularized reading of Hafiz. The thirteenth and fourteenth centuries witnessed the pinnacle in the development of the Persian *ghazal*, first at the hands of Sa'di and then Hafiz, who are universally recognized as the pre-eminent masters of the form,[95] the embodiment of Shiraz's poetic 'genius'.[96] As such, their poetry possesses a certain cachet which has contributed to their overshadowing of all their respective contemporaries.[97] Sa'di championed the amorous *ghazal*,[98] a style with limited scope for mystical interpretation.[99] Hafiz developed the polysemic *ghazal*,[100] at once amorous, socio-political, mystical and panegyric, a style that has been called *ghazal-i talfīq* ('the composite *ghazal*'). The chief practitioners alongside Hafiz of *ghazal-i talfīq* were Khvaju, 'Imad Kirmani (d. 1371) and Salman.[101] In the fourteenth century, addressing a multiplicity of themes in a single *ghazal* became prevalent[102] and in the output of some, such as Hafiz, the norm. By the last quarter of the fourteenth century, this style of *ghazal* would have been expected (and demanded) by audiences in Shiraz and elsewhere.

Though a mystical reading of Hafiz's *ghazal*s aimed at uncovering the poet's 'erotic spirituality' is possible,[103] it must be acknowledged that the form's links with the profane were never completely severed.[104] But a prominent characteristic of Hafiz's *ghazal*s, one that makes overly Sufistic or religiose interpretations of his lyrics problematic, is the inclusion of consistent, unforgiving jibes against the popular preacher, the ascetic and other 'pretenders of piety' in Shiraz's religious establishment; the guardians and judges of moral rectitude who are despised by Hafiz for secretly practising the transgressions they publically exhort others not to commit.[105] Hafiz associates latent hypocrisy with false piety and hollow asceticism.[106] Arguably the most outlandish hypocrites of his world are: the *vā'iz* ('[popular, public] preacher') and the *zāhid* ('ascetic').[107] Hafiz rebukes and ridicules the *vā'iz*, ordering him to cease his preaching, while setting himself up as an alternative source of authority.[108] Hafiz similarly sees himself in opposition to the dry *zāhid*: he attacks the sham ascetic for his deficient mystical insight, misplaced conceit, thin piety and superficial understanding of reality.[109]

But Hafiz's moral project goes beyond doing battle with the 'sterile pietism' of the *zāhid* and the 'sanctimonious counsel' of the *vā'iz*: the poet's real targets are religious dogmatism and authoritarianism.[110] For Hafiz, the Sufi is himself two-faced in his piety and is deceitful. Often alongside the *zāhid*, the Sufi forms the object of Hafiz's scorn and mistrust.[111] Hafiz lambasts the Sufis' materialistic and corrupt establishments,[112] though he does hint that they might be redeemed through consumption of and devotion to wine.[113]

Yarshater argues that a failure to realize the intensity of Hafiz's passionate animosity towards these figures is a failure to appreciate much of his poetry; a fair point given that attacks against this 'impious clique' are found in around one-third of his *ghazal*s.[114] Although Hafiz is most closely associated with this motif, it is also found in the *ghazal*s of 'Ubayd, who riles against hypocritical actions that he often associates with Sufis and ascetics[115] and who dismisses the preacher and his moralistic gatherings.[116] Two other contemporaries, 'Attar Shirazi (d. after 1369) and Junayd Shirazi (d. after 1389) also sneer at the same motley crew.[117] It would appear that the anti-Sufi/anti-clerical taunt was a distinguishing feature of the post-Mongol Shirazi *ghazal*.

For Shamisa, Hafiz's *ghazal*s are characterized by an earthly, amorous and often panegyric 'vertical axis' to which mystical elements are attached horizontally.[118] This is what Moayyad has called the *ghazal*'s 'vertical harmony' which creates coherence through an interdependence of ideas.[119] A vertical link binding successive lines in a cohesive, monothematic direction is detectable in many of Sa'di's *ghazal*s, but the relationship between lines in a typical Hafizian *ghazal* is difficult to sense, often being so nuanced as to be barely detectable.[120]

That Hafiz succeeded in firmly establishing the *ghazal* not only as a suitable, but an efficacious, vehicle for praise, through a seamless blending of the imagery and diction of the amorous and the panegyric, is an intergeneric triumph.[121] Hafiz is the master of the *ghazal-i qasīda-gūna* ('*qasīda*-esque *ghazal*')[122] and he used it to deliver both explicit and veiled panegyrics.[123] Even when he does not name the patron in a *ghazal*, Hafiz makes his panegyric intent clear through topical allusions and historical references that point to the identity of the addressee[124] or by imitating the diction (and sometimes the form) of the *qasīda*.[125] It is oft repeated that the panegyric *qasīda* went into decline in the Mongol period and that the last great panegyrist was Kamal Isfahani (d. ca 1237).[126] This claim is unfounded, given the many polished Salghurid, Injuid, Muzaffarid and Jalayirid praise odes produced after Kamal's death. Critics who take a more measured view hail Salman as the last great *qasīda* poet.[127] Although it is an exaggeration to say that the *ghazal* had largely displaced the *qasīda* as the preferred vehicle of Persian lyric expression by the end of the thirteenth century,[128] this became a reality by the close of the fourteenth, due in large part to Hafiz's obsessive relationship with the short lyric.

Intentionally ambiguous?

Hafiz's poetry enjoys a direct relationship to its milieu of composition,[129] a fact most evident in his panegyrics. Those who ignore the Sitz im Leben of Hafiz's poems as if they were conceived in a transcendental vacuum or timeless void misunderstand, misinterpret and misrepresent them. Although they defy definition as 'plain' or 'secular'[130] to ignore or downplay the non-mystical, this-worldly aspects of Hafiz's love lyrics in favour of amplifying their mystical dimension is to miss the crux of the poet's aesthetic project. Ambiguity is at the heart of the Hafizian *ghazal* and we must resist attempts to simplify it to any one of its constituent layers.[131] As Lewis says, Hafiz transformed the *ghazal* into a 'deep, complex meditation, at once carnal, socio-political, and mystical'.[132]

There is an impetus in some scholarship to attempt a division of the mystical from the non-mystical in Hafiz's poetry, thereby creating a dichotomy that is inauthentic and alien. The medieval Iranian court was itself a mystically charged nexus, a fact that complicates readings that downplay the so-called secular dimensions of Hafiz's poetry. Unlike some of his contemporaries (such as Kamal Khujandi and 'Imad Kirmani) who had strong ties to Sufi orders and lodges,[133] Hafiz appears to have avoided organized forms of mysticism.[134] Hafiz's bacchanalia and eroticism cannot be reduced to mere mystical connotations.[135] By the Timurid period, the mystical interpretation of lyric poems had already become an obsession;[136] Yarshater does well to remind us that Hafiz's cultural climate was itself saturated with mystical thought, but that the currency of such ideas and expressions 'did not entail a deliberate attachment to Sufi tenets or practices'.[137] We must also acknowledge that Hafiz and his contemporaries wrote with a variety of contexts in mind and that their sophisticated audiences were capable of understanding a given poem on many levels.[138]

The political landscape of post-Mongol Iran and Iraq

As Mongol rule weakened, Iran and Iraq fractured into smaller administrative units governed by multiple local successor dynasties, many of which were drawn from families who had served the Ilkhanid state (ca 1256–1335).[139] Three local dynasties competed for control of the cities inhabited by our poets: the Injuids (1325–1353), who secured Shiraz as their powerbase, but also enjoyed intermittent control of Isfahan and Luristan;[140] the Muzaffarids (ca. 1314–1393),[141] who established themselves first in Yazd and Kirman and, later, in the former territory of the Injuids; and the Jalayirids (late 1330s to 1432), who ruled in Baghdad and then also in Tabriz (definitively from 1359).[142] These rival dynasties fought over control of key cities on the Iranian plateau, at times ruled significant tracts of former Ilkhanid lands, made alliances with one another (which they frequently broke) and were connected by blood ties and through marriage. The complex relationships between and within these warring houses are not easily untangled. For example, the Muzaffarid Shah Shuja' fought against his brother, Shah Mahmud (d. 1375), an ally of the Jalayirds who was married to a daughter of Shaykh Uvays.[143] When Shah Mahmud discovered that his Injuid wife, Jahan's cousin, Khan Sultan (whose father, Ghiyath al-Din Kay-Khusraw, had himself helped the Muzaffarids take Yazd),[144] had been clandestinely supporting Shah Shuja',[145] Shah Mahmud rewarded her treachery with execution.[146]

In 1343, Shah Shaykh Abu Ishaq gained control of Shiraz and ruled for a decade marred by unsuccessful and costly campaigns aimed at wresting Yazd and Kirman from the Muzaffarids.[147] By all accounts, Shah Shaykh Abu Ishaq's generous patronage saw the city flourish and restored Shiraz's reputation as a haven for poets,[148] as it had been under the Salghurids.[149] Just as the Injuids, Muzaffarids and Jalayirids did battle by the sword, so did their poets in pen by critiquing, lampooning and, occasionally, expressing admiration for one another. Following the collapse of Mongol rule, the subsequent reconfiguration of patronage networks served to tip the balance in favour of poets, as numerous flourishing local courts with imperial aspirations vied to attract the best.[150] Local kings needed eloquent poets to spread positive images of them abroad, so considerable resources were made available to eulogists.

The fourteenth century was a period of intense cultural exchange between the city-states of Iran and Iraq. There was increased mobility among poets, with the cultural pull of Shiraz and Baghdad being strongest. 'Ubayd moved from Qazvin to Shiraz to Baghdad and back again to Shiraz; Khvaju, originally from Kirman, spent time in Baghdad and Isfahan, before settling in Fars; Salman moved from Sava (located between Qazvin and Qum) to Baghdad; Hafiz flirted with a move westwards to join him.

The reign of the first Muzaffarid king of Shiraz, the reportedly severe and strictly pious Mubariz al-Din Muhammad (r. 1353–1358), is not thought to have been particularly favourable for Persian letters,[151] though a good amount of poetry in praise of this supposedly despised Muzaffarid has survived. In contrast, the long rule of his son, Shah Shuja' (r. 1358–1364 and 1366–1384), fostered an atmosphere conducive to the arts and the king built upon the cultural foundations laid by Shah Shaykh Abu Ishaq.[152] It is worth noting that Shah Shuja' was not only a connoisseur of poetry, but also a poet of some talent himself. In post-Ilkhanid Iran and Iraq, many royals were skilled amateur versifiers and astute critics of poetry;[153] perhaps this encouraged poets to attribute a portion of their eloquence and literary success to their special relationship with their royal patron.[154] Hafiz, 'Ubayd and Jahan all produced panegyric poetry for Shah Shuja'. When he died in 1384, Hafiz would have been more than sixty years old. Nevertheless, the seasoned court poet sought out new patrons, most notably the nephews of his late master, Shah Yahya (who ruled from Yazd) and Shah Mansur in Shiraz.[155] Both were eventually executed by Timur in 1393, shortly after Hafiz's own death.[156]

Patronage

Poetic patronage is a form of social and economic exchange that serves to nurture and encourage poets.[157] In Persian, patronage is often called *tarbīyat*,[158] which also means 'training' or 'educating'. Premodern court poets in the Islamicate world exchanged their loyalty and literary services for their patron's 'favours' (in Persian, *ni'mat, an'ām, mavāhib*)[159] in the form of protection, regular stipends and/or one-off payments.[160] The professional poet strove to establish and maintain a 'bond of clientage' with the royal patron he flattered,[161] thereby accruing socio-cultural recognition and literary capital.[162] In pre- and early modern contexts, poets might be associated with a specific court or move within a more 'diffuse' patronage matrix.[163] Poets and other writers who became disenchanted in one city would move on elsewhere in search of a more favourable reception. This mushrooming of local royal patronage nodes encouraged mobility in some poets and helps explain the large amount of court poetry produced circa 1330–1390.[164] The ruler as chief benefactor of poets could make or break the panegyrist's career through the granting or withholding of generosity.[165] In Muslim societies, the patron's largesse conferred prestige upon him/herself;[166] the patronage of literary culture being emblematic of good governance.[167] Royal patrons sought immortality for their name and were prepared to provide handsome rewards to poets who might preserve their good reputation for posterity.[168] As Sharlet has demonstrated, relations between poets and patrons were 'fraught with risk', not least because of the competitive, precarious environment in which they were nurtured and the disparity in the status of the two parties.[169] In Persian panegyrics, the poet–patron relationship is often depicted using the language of love and motifs of desire; the poet–lover seeks to foster intimacy with, and elicit favour from, the distant patron–beloved.[170] The poet as the best servant/slave and the patron as the exemplary king/master, forms the basis of many a popular trope.[171]

Injuid, Muzaffarid and Jalayirid patrons

The poets studied here composed many panegyrics for royals, viziers and other courtiers. Some poets also penned posthumous elegies in memory of dead patrons, often tinged with nostalgia. Most of these praise poems are in *qasīda* form though, as one would expect in this period, a good number are *ghazal*s (there are also *qit'a*s and some strophic poems). From the table below it is not only possible to see which individual poets wrote for which patrons, but also which clusters of poets worked alongside one another, often in heated competition for the same patrons' attention.

Injuid

Jalal al-Din Mas'ud Shah d. Mahmud Shah (Jahan's father; r. 1336–1339)	Hafiz;[172] Khvaju;[173] Nasir.[174]
Ghiyath al-Din Kay-Khusraw b. Mahmud Shah (Khan Sultan's father; d. 1338)	Khvaju.[175]
Jamal al-Din Shah Shaykh Abu Ishaq b. Mahmud Shah (Jahan's uncle; r. 1343–1353)	Hafiz;[176] 'Ubayd;[177] Khvaju;[178] Salman;[179] 'Imad;[180] Jalal.[181]
Rukn al-Din 'Amid al-Mulk (vizier)	'Ubayd;[182] Khvaju.[183]
Hajji Qavam al-Din Hasan Tamghachi (close adviser to Shah Shaykh Abu Ishaq; d. 1353)	Hafiz.[184]
'Imad al-Din Mahmud Kirmani (vizier to Shah Shaykh Abu Ishaq)	Hafiz.[185]

Muzaffarid

Shah-i ghazi Amir Mubariz al-Din Muhammad (d. 1363)	Hafiz;[186] Khvaju;[187] 'Imad;[188] Jalal.[189]
Abu l-favaris Jalal al-Din Shah Shuja' b. Mubariz al-Din (r. 1358–1364, 1366–1384)	Hafiz;[190] 'Ubayd;[191] Jahan;[192] 'Imad;[193] Salman.[194]
Qutb al-Din Shah Mahmud b. Mubariz al-Din (r. 1364–66)	Salman.[195]
Sharaf al-Mulk Shah Muzaffar b. Mubariz al-Din	'Imad.[196]
Nusrat al-Din Shah Yahya b. Muzaffar b. Mubariz al-Din (r. 1387–1391)	Hafiz;[197] Haydar.[198]
Shuja' al-Mulk Shah Mansur b. Muzaffar b. Mubariz al-Din (r.1391–1393)	Hafiz;[199] Jahan.[200]
Burhan al-Din Fatullah (vizier to Mubariz al-Din; d. 1358)	Hafiz;[201] Khvaju;[202] 'Imad.[203]
Khvaja Qavam al-Din Muhammad Sahib-'Ayyar (vizier to both Mubariz al-Din and Shah Shuja'; d. 1363)	Hafiz;[204] 'Imad;[205] 'Attar Shirazi.[206]
Khvaja Jalal al-Din Turanshah (last vizier to Shah Shuja')	Hafiz.[207]

Jalayirid

Shaykh Hasan-i Buzurg (husband of Dilshad Khatun; r. 1340–1356)	Salman.[208]
Dilshad Khatun (mother of Sultan Uvays; d. 1351)	Khvaju;[209] Jalal;[210] Salman.[211]
Mu'izz al-Din Shaykh Uvays b. Shaykh Hasan (r. 1356–1374)	'Ubayd;[212] Salman;[213] Nasir.[214]
Jalal al-Din Shaykh Husayn b. Shaykh Uvays (r. 1374–1382)	Salman;[215] Khvaju;[216] Nasir.[217]
Ghiyath al-Din Sultan Ahmad Bahadur b. Shaykh Uvays (r. 1382–d.1410)	Hafiz;[218] Jahan.[219]

Intertextuality

This book examines poets in Shiraz and in rival cultural hubs across post-Mongol Iran and Iraq who worked within localized, yet interconnected, networks of composition, performance, reception and transmission. These environments were highly competitive; poets continually played off one another, all the while treading the fine line between plagiarism, flattering *imitatio* and slavish mimicry. They strove to not only outdo one another in eloquence, but also to negotiate a foothold for themselves in the tradition by asserting their status as rightful heirs to the poetic past. The chief way in which such rivalries were worked out was through poetic imitation, the practice of 'reciprocal validation and authorization of the imitated and the imitator'.[220] It is through imitation (of both dead and living poets) and mastering the canon and its generic conventions,[221] that the successful poet made a lasting name for him/herself. Just as with other competitive pre- and early modern poetry environments, this one was highly self-reflexive.[222] But the poets of Shiraz, though locked in intense local competition, were also players within a transregional intertextual poetic network established in the mid-thirteenth century which incorporated cities near and far: Yazd, Kirman, Baghdad and Tabriz.[223]

In Persian, poetic imitation (formal, lexical, syntactic and semantic) is known by various names, including: *istiqbāl* ('welcoming'), *tatabbu'* ('pursuit'), *iqtifā* ('following'), *javāb-gūʾī* ('answering,' 'dialoguing') or *nazīra-gūʾī* ('composing parallel or companion poems').[224] Poetic response (which normally involved the adoption of the formal features of the model poem and often featured direct quotation [*tazmīn*] of a line or a key phrase from it) was not considered plagiarism, but rather borrowing.[225] When a poet engages in *istiqbāl*, a demand is made that the new poem be read in dialogue with its source. In such imitation, Losensky says, we witness the 'conscious remaking of the literary past'.[226] But the towering genius of a canonical poet could, if not negotiated wisely, stifle the talent of an aspiring one, which meant that imitation could only be embarked upon with a deep knowledge of literary heritage.[227] Imitation was permissible, even desirable, as long as the responding poet proved a worthy imitator.[228] In imitation, intertextual acknowledgement of poetic prowess is coupled with an implicit challenge to the poet whose words are being reworked: the imitator presents him/herself as an equal, equipped with the necessary literary skills not only to imitate, but also to interpret and, potentially, better the work of his predecessor or contemporary.[229]

A junior or less famous poet could, through imitating a recognized past master or a more famous peer, appropriate something of that poet's fame and gain recognition for his/her own new poem. Poetic imitation was an initiating test of technical skill used to define one's own generic affiliation: a successful imitation proved that a poet belonged to the tradition.[230] When contemporaries engage in imitation, the directionality of the modelling is not always clear and it is often assumed, perhaps mistakenly, that the younger or less famous poet in the pair is the imitator. For *javāb*, the active cooperation of a competent listener is required, one whose literary connoisseurship allows him/her to recognize and appreciate the intertextual allusions in the response.[231] Such social intercourse assumes that the poet and the consumer belong to a single 'textual community'.[232] The practice of responding to predecessors and contemporaries via *javāb-gūī* also has a diachronic value in that it has the potential to create a transhistorical chain of intertextual replies.[233]

Since Hafiz was writing with a backdrop of at least three centuries of the development of the written Persian *ghazal* behind him, it comes as no surprise that it is almost impossible to detect any element in his *ghazal*s that cannot be attested in the works of previous poets.[234] Hafiz's *ghazal*s are replete with evidence of mutual intertextual engagement with his peers in Shiraz (most notably 'Ubayd, Jahan, Khvaju, 'Imad and Haydar Shirazi [d. ca 1393])[235] and his contemporaries elsewhere (Salman, Kamal Khujandi, Awhadi and Nasir Bukhara'i [d. 1377]).[236] Such intense patterns of mutual imitation between peers contributed to the false attribution early on of Hafiz's *ghazal*s to others or the confusion of theirs with his.[237]

Responding to past masters

As underlined by Lewisohn,[238] the poets of fourteenth-century Shiraz strove to outdo the great poets of the past. Hafiz's commitment to imitating past masters bordered on the excessive[239] and the poet responds in verse to many great poets of the Persianate world, including: Rudaki Samarqandi (d. 941),[240] Amir Mu'izzi (d. 1125),[241] Anvari (d. 1189),[242] Zahir Faryabi (d. 1201),[243] Kamal Isfahani,[244] Fakhr al-Din 'Iraqi (d. 1289),[245] Nizari Quhistani (d. 1320)[246] and, most substantively, Sa'di.[247] Composing responses to Sa'di or quoting his poetry verbatim was, unsurprisingly, a prominent feature of fourteenth-century Persian lyric poetry, both inside and outside Shiraz.[248] Beyond mere quotation, deference is shown to earlier poets through the living poet's unflattering comparison of his/her own poetry to that of a recognized master.[249] More often than not, though, irreverence is displayed as post-Mongol poets claim eloquence and fame superior to that of canonical poets.[250]

Competing with peers

Premodern Persian poets were highly conscious of the poetry being written by others. Often composing for the same patrons, they engaged in repeated allusion to one another with the goal of 'self-aggrandizement, paying homage, or simply catering to the audience's taste'.[251] In addition to polite expressions of professional rivalry,[252] poets also engaged in the derision and ridicule of their contemporaries. Three celebrated examples are: the misogynistic attacks on Jahan in the form of vulgar, invective 'one-liners', in which Jahan's *ghazal*s are reviled for their feminine stench and the poet's sexual propriety is questioned;[253] the Baghdad-based Salman's ridicule of 'Ubayd's village origins;[254] and Haydar's disparagement of Khvaju whom he calls a fake poet who steals from Sa'di,[255] a 'gypsy thief' and a 'Kirmani spy'.[256] In milder tone, poets might criticize their competitors' *ghazal*s for being too long, substandard or too wordy;[257] they might also bemoan the general quality of contemporary poetry and complain that the court is overcrowded with poets.[258]

When asked to pronounce on the comparative eloquence of Hafiz and Salman, 'Attar Shirazi gives a balanced, diplomatic assessment of their merits. This suggests that the two great poets were ranked equally by contemporary audiences.[259] Since Salman is regarded essentially as a court poet and panegyrist,[260] for him to be compared to Hafiz in this manner means that this is how Hafiz was perceived by 'Attar and his Shirazi circle. Manuscripts produced in the last few decades of the fourteenth century and the first few decades of the fifteenth show that Hafiz's *ghazal*s were read side-by-side with those of his contemporaries. In a manuscript from 1379, a single *ghazal* by Hafiz appears alongside three others, including one by Jalal and another by Salman.[261] In another manuscript from 1407, *ghazal*s by Hafiz are inscribed in the margins with Salman's poetry as the central text.[262] One of the earliest almost complete copies of the *dīvān* (containing over 450 *ghazal*s) is found in a *majmū'a* ('literary anthology') dating to 1411 which contained thirty-two full works or excerpts from the poetry of several of Hafiz's contemporaries: 'Imad, Salman and Kamal Khujandi.[263] A manuscript from 1421 contains 428 *ghazal*s by Hafiz and Muhammad Gulandam's preface, as well as Jalal's *dīvān* and a selection from that of Kamal Khujandi.[264]

Bushaq Shirazi (d. 1423 or 1427), a younger contemporary of Hafiz whose poetry displays a disregard for mystical pretensions,[265] parodies more than twenty of Hafiz's *ghazal*s in satirical gastronomic *javāb*s. Reading Bushaq's *javāb*s, we gain a sense as to which of Hafiz's *ghazal*s enjoyed the greatest popularity in Shiraz at the dawn of the fifteenth century.[266] Bushaq's playful responses to Hafiz appear alongside similar *javāb*s to *ghazal*s by several of Hafiz's contemporaries: 'Imad, Salman, 'Ubayd, Khvaju, Jalal and Kamal

Khujandi. Bushaq's *dīvān* and the manuscripts discussed above evoke the deep influence contemporary poets affected upon one another[267] and the interwovenness shared by pairs or chains of poems composed in the fourteenth century.[268]

The structure of this study

These introductory comments have set the scene of the competitive, intertextual, imitative environment within which Hafiz, 'Ubayd, Jahan and their peers worked. My book is divided into two parts each consisting of three chapters. In Part One the concerns are primarily contextual, whereas in Part Two the focus is textual. Part One explores the political, social and cultural contexts and settings of the production and performance of the poetry under examination. Chapter 1 roots the poetry temporally and geographically in the political networks of post-Mongol Shiraz and uncovers the poets' intimate and productive relationship with their Injuid and Muzaffarid patrons. In this chapter, the literary supremacy of Shiraz in the fourteenth century, the poets' attachment to and disaffection with the city, and the city both as beloved and the abode of the beloved are also studied. Chapter 2 investigates the social and aesthetic dimensions of the primary context for the performance of poetry in the premodern Iranian world, the *majlis-i sharāb* (wine symposium). The multifarious *majlis-i sharāb* was also the forum for activities considered taboo or of dubious moral status in orthodox readings of Islam: wine-drinking, musical performance, singing, dancing and flirtatious revelry. The stamp of the *majlis-i sharāb* on the Persian *ghazal* is unmistakable and here I explore the ways in which the poets present an ideal image of the royal wine symposium to inspire a change in the reality of their performance and reception settings. Chapter 3 scrutinizes the poets' depiction of the omnipresent beloved, the focus of earthly, normatively homoerotic desire and the chief metaphor for the patron and/or Divine. In this chapter, we witness the intertwining of performance and patronage.

Part Two is an extended exploration of the use of one key rhetorical device: *talmīh* (poetic allusion). Derived from the Arabic root *L-M-H* which bears connotations of gazing briefly, perhaps surreptitiously, *talmīh* means: 'intimation', 'indirect reference', 'hint' and 'suggestion'. In rhetoric, *talmīh* denotes a brief, deliberate, tacit allusion to a person, place, story or event (fictitious or actual) in Islamic or non-religious literature and lore.[269] Allusions are often used to add semantic and cultural density and/or topicality to a poem.[270] Concise allusions functioning on several levels simultaneously allowed Persian lyric poets to point with brevity (with minimal information and often through one crucial phrase) to broader, pre-existing narratives without mentioning the full details of a given episode,[271] thereby avoiding weariness in their listeners.[272] Through the lens of *talmīh*, Chapters Four, Five and Six explore how the poets, by drawing on a communal understanding of the past, reconfigured tales of kings and heroes from the Iranian tradition, lovers from Persian romances, and prophets from the Qur'an and non-canonical Islamic texts, to make sense of the present. In Chapter 4 we see how the poets used *talmīh* to articulate Shiraz's deep connection to a distant past which they saw as being attached to local *lieux de mémoire* and mystically charged objects that they associated with their living patrons. In Chapter 5, by alluding to stories of archetypal lovers, we witness the representation of an ethical model for princes to follow in the post-Mongol present, in particular in relation to their performance of patronhood and their responsibilities towards the poets in their care. Chapter 6 looks at the poets' ability to utilize sacred narratives not necessarily for mystical purposes, but in the service of two broad aims: the bolstering of their image of the patron as being divinely guided and ultimately triumphal and in the expression of hope in the context of a turbulent age.

Reading Hafiz comparatively as I have here without regard for the supposedly inferior literary calibre of those of his contemporaries alongside whom I have chosen to study him, disrupts our received notions of the canon of premodern Persian poetry as laid out in the Timurid period, reinforced through the Safavid/Mughal, Zand and Qajar periods by countless anthologists and solidified in the late nineteenth and early twentieth centuries by Riza-quli Khan Hidayat, Shibli Nu'mani, E.G. Browne and others. A great poet like Hafiz did not cut himself off from other poets because they wrote for a rival court, because they excelled in a different genre or because they enjoyed less fame than he; nor should we when studying him.

1

Evocations of Place

This chapter explores the attachment of the poets of post-Mongol Shiraz and their immediate predecessors to the city in which they built their careers and eulogized their patrons. The poetry produced in Shiraz in this century and a half is rooted in a specific time and place and it is through topographical allusions to localities in and around Shiraz couched in extravagant praise, that the poets manifest their patriotic attachment and local pride. These loco-descriptive poems are infused with an intense love of place, demonstrating a dynamic, productive connection between spaces evoked in poetry and the reality of the politico-cultural situation the poets worked to fashion. The contextualizing effect of toponyms in localized poems of place is discussed here alongside the panegyric and political functions of allusions to metropolitan Shiraz, its gardens, meadows and pleasances, and Shiraz's competitive relationship to rival cities of Iran and Iraq and regions of the broader Persianate world.

The fabric of a city, its palaces, parks and other created landscapes can be read collectively as a stage for conveying regal power.[1] In addition to shaping Shiraz's built environment, its rulers displayed their power through patronizing panegyrics that conveyed Shiraz's intoxicating allure, presented it as a welcoming abode of perfect bliss and established it once and for all as the source of the finest Persian poetry. In the fragmented political landscape of post-Mongol Iran, identification of the ruler with the city (and not a wider empire) led to a greater focus on Shiraz and its dependent territories as a 'micro-state' (not wholly dissimilar to the city-state in ancient Greece or Renaissance Italy).[2] As Ingenito has argued, when poets mention their city in verse, they engage in 'a speech act normally implying an encomiastic or celebratory function'.[3] Persian poetry was largely produced in an urban environment where the city served as the pivotal platform of culture and hosted a nexus of patronage networks.[4]

When the poets studied here wrote about Shiraz, they did so deliberately and with the intention of conveying a particular impression about the city.[5] When read with sensitivity to the political and patronage-related functions of evocations of place, seemingly hyperbolic or esoteric imagery can be deciphered to show how Persian lyric poetry of the period circa 1240–1400 actually contributed to the creation of its environment; poets chose to present Shiraz and the region of Fars, both to those attached to the local court and to those at rival cultural centres, as an earthly paradise at the heart of the Iranian world.[6] How the poets achieved this goal and what the construction of such an image of Shiraz afforded them, are the chief topics discussed here.

Shīrāzīyāt: A local poetics of place

As city-based regimes, unlike the empires that had come before, the importance of the urban centre was proportionally greater in the post-Mongol context. Cities such as Shiraz lay at the centre of fragmented decentralized polities; each local ruler was a world-king and each regional capital was the seat of a court with imperial aspirations. Accordingly, each provincial court and its poets drew on local cosmological and mythical associations attached in the minds of their city's inhabitants to nearby ancient ruins that functioned as *lieux de mémoire* or 'sites of memory' (see Chapter 4). Shiraz, unlike its chief rival, Baghdad, was largely spared the ravages of the Mongols and appears to have flourished for much of the thirteenth century. The Salghurids (1148–1282) nurtured local poets and provided refuge to literati such as Shams-i Qays-i Razi fleeing from Mongol attacks.[7]

From the Salghurid period on, poets produced a series of eulogies in praise of Shiraz in which the city, its environs and its inhabitants are extolled. These stand-alone lyric poems in praise of Shiraz the 'city of knowledge' (*dār al-'ilm, madīna-yi 'ilm*)[8] can be called *Shīrāzīyāt*.[9] Poets also incorporated topophilia into their praise odes, often in the form of a Shiraz-focused amorous introit (*taghazzul*). The poets' explicit use of a set repertoire of topographical allusions forged intertextual bridges linking poems from distinct historical periods, resulting in time in a harmonized vision of Shiraz as the ideal city. Shiraz can stand for the city proper, the urban conglomeration, its suburbs, dependent villages, extramural garden belt and its rural, bucolic hinterland or even the whole realm of Fars.[10] Praise for Shiraz may at first seem hyperbolic until we consider what travellers and geographers had to say about the city. In the twelfth century, Tusi praised Fars as a 'blessed, fortunate, and flourishing clime' (*iqlīmī-st mubārak u farkhunda u 'āmira*); a land that boasts 'abundant bounties' (ni'mat-hā-yi farāvān).[11] And in the thirteenth century, al-Qazwini (d. 1283) praised Shiraz for its 'healthy air, fresh water, many good things, and abundant agricultural products'.[12] The famous North African traveller, Ibn Battuta (d. 1377) visited Shiraz twice, first in 1327 and then again in 1347 during the reign of Shah Shaykh Abu Ishaq. Ibn Battuta remarks how well-built and superbly planned Shiraz is, how pious and chaste the city's inhabitants are (in particular the women) and he rates Shiraz second only to Damascus among cities of the Islamic east in terms of markets and orchards. Ibn Battuta also mentions the sweetness of the water of the Ruknabad canal and the comeliness of Shiraz's inhabitants.[13]

Writing in 1340, Hamdullah Mustawfi describes the city as 'exceedingly pleasant' (dar ghāyat-i khushī).[14] He mentions the mild climate and Shiraz's excellent grapes, fine cypress trees and the 'lean' (lāghar), 'dark-skinned' (asmar) majority Sunni populace. Mustawfi also notes that most of Shiraz's wealthy 'are outsiders' (gharīb-and).[15]

This admiration for Shiraz expressed in travelogues and local histories dovetails neatly with much of what we find in Shīrāzīyāt. Shiraz is one of those cities whose charm inspires attachment, pride and personal loyalty[16] and the loco-centric poems produced in the city more than six or seven centuries ago still dictate how Shiraz is memorialized and imagined today. The most famous fourteenth-century Shīrāzīya is this poem by Hafiz:[17]

خداوندا نگه دار از زوالش
که عمر خضر می بخشد زلالش
عبیرآمیز می آید شمالش
بجوی از مردم صاحب کمالش
که شیرینان ندادند انفعالش
چه داری آگهی چون است حالش
دلا چون شیر مادر کن حلالش
که دارم خلوتی خوش با خیالش
نکردی شکر ایام وصالش

خوشا شیراز و وضع بی مثالش
ز رکن آباد ما صد لوحش الله
میان جعفرآباد و مصلی
به شیراز آی و فیض روح قدسی
که نام قند مصری برد آنجا
صبا زان لولی شنگول سرمست
گر آن شیرین پسر خونم بریزد
مدار از خواب بیدارم خدا را
چرا حافظ چو می‌ترسیدی از هجر

Blessed be Shiraz and its peerless situation!
O God, protect it from all deterioration!
May God protect our Ruknabad a hundred times
For its crystal waters bestow the life of Khizr.
Between the Ja'farabad quarter and Musalla promenade
Blows her north wind, mixed with perfume.
Come to Shiraz and, from its excellent inhabitants,
Seek the bounty of the Holy Spirit.
Whoever carried the name of Egyptian sugar there
Without being shamed by its sweet beauties?
O gentle breeze, of that giddy, drunken gypsy

What news do you have? How is he faring?
O heart, if that sweet boy should shed my blood,
Make it as lawful for him as his mother's milk!
For the sake of God, do not waken me from this dream
For I am enjoying a private audience with his spectre!
Why, Hafiz, when you were fearing separation from him
Did you not give thanks for the days of union?

Hafiz's *ghazal* opens with a benediction for the city and a 'prayer for its good fortune' (*du'ā*), the kind of blessing one expects to find dedicated to the patron at the close of a panegyric *qasīda*. In the opening line, Hafiz stresses Shiraz's uniqueness through the adjective *bī-mithāl* ('peerless') that he uses to describe its 'goodly situation'; a feature of all great cities.[18] Hafiz extends the *du'ā* into the second line where he mentions Ruknabad, a subterranean canal carrying fresh spring water for drinking and irrigation from the mountains ten kilometres northeast of Shiraz built by the Buyid Rukn al-Dawla in 949.[19] Hafiz claims magical properties for Shiraz's water through an allusion to the mysterious figure Khizr and his successful quest for the water of everlasting life (*āb-i hayāt, āb-i hayavān, āb-i zindagānī*). Hafiz thus associates Shiraz's ruler with Khizr and his magical liquor (see Chapter 4). As we shall see, the Ab-i Ruknabad or Ab-i Rukni is one of three iconic loci alluded to in *Shīrāzīyāt* that evoke pleasure-seeking and poetry performance.[20]

The other two loci repeatedly invoked in Shiraz panegyrics are the Musalla meadow and Ja'farabad, a small settlement to the southeast famed for its cluster of suburban gardens, estates and orchards fed by the manmade Ab-i Rukni and Ab-i Zangi.[21] To borrow terminology from Snir, Ruknabad, Musalla and Ja'farabad can be called Shiraz's three chief 'icons' and they anchored the city's identity.[22] Shirazis frequented all three loci in pursuit of earthly delights[23] and they provided the core sensory stimuli for Shiraz-centred topophilia. In the poetry, Ruknabad, Musalla and Ja'farabad frequently combine to form an image of Shiraz as an Elysium; a place of total bliss.[24]

Having introduced Shiraz's magnetism in the first three lines of his poem, Hafiz addresses those who reside elsewhere and entreats them to come to the city. As a poet with strong ties to the court, Hafiz worked to promote abroad a superior image of his patron and city. Line four, in which the poet takes a somewhat pietistic stance, includes praise for Shiraz's inhabitants who he describes as *sāhib-kamāl*, that is, endowed with all human accomplishments and distinctions. In line five we encounter a subtle instance of self-boasting on behalf of the city: Shiraz is a greater source of sweetness (a standard metaphor for both physical beauty and literary eloquence) than Egypt, a major producer of sugar and home to the captive and then triumphant Joseph; the epitome of ideal, youthful male beauty (see Chapter 6).

Hafiz's prayer for Shiraz's good fortune combined with his praise for the city's paradisiacal allure serve to foreground a lament for an absent beloved, which underscores the link between the city and the human object of desire. It is as though Hafiz, by starting with praise and moving to erotic longing, has inverted the conventional order of the panegyric ode. As with almost all Persian lyric poetry, the love object longed for here is a young male and the desire expressed is male homoerotic. By eulogizing a 'gypsy' (*lūlī*), Hafiz casts this absent beloved as a local, rather than exotic, boy. As we shall see, gypsy beloveds crop up in a number of erotic *ghazals* with strong Shirazi overtones. This object of desire is a blood-thirsty 'sweet boy' (*shīrīn-pisar*), an appellation that, as shall be borne out in Chapters 3 and 5, points to the patron as an all-powerful beloved, the pivotal amorous topos of the panegyric *ghazal*. In line eight, Hafiz takes a step back from the eroticism of the previous two lines by claiming existence in a dream state. The conventional mentioning of the poet's pen name in the final line is coupled with regret that union with the beloved was not celebrated while it lasted.

Hafiz and his contemporaries inherited an established tradition of local topological praise poetry chiefly from Sa'di via the following poem with its rhyme, – *āz* that is modelled on the name of their city:[25]

رسیده بر سر سر الله اکبر شیراز	خوشا سپیده دمی باشد آنکه بینم باز
که بار ایمنی آرد نه جور قحط و نیاز	بدیده بار دیگر آن بهشت روی زمین
که تختگاه سلیمان بدست و حضرت راز	نه لایق ظلماتست بالله این اقلیم
که کعبه بر سر ایشان همی کند پرواز	هزار پیر و ولی بیش باشد اندر وی
بحق روزبهان و بحق پنج نماز	بذکر و فکر و عبادت بروح شیخ کبیر
ز دست ظالم بددین و کافر غماز	که گوش دار تو این شهر نیکمردان را
که دار مردم شیراز در تجمل و ناز	بحق کعبه و آن کس که کرد کعبه بنا
بریده باد سرش همچو زر و نقره بگاز	هر آن کسی که کند قصد قبة الاسلام
که شهرها همه بازند و شهر ما شهباز	که سعدی از حق شیراز روز و شب میگفت

Blessed be that dawn when once again I will see
Shiraz having reached the Allāhu Akbar pass!
My eyes will gaze once more upon that Paradise on earth
Which offers safety, not the harshness of famine and need.
By God, darkness does not befit this clime
For it was the seat of Solomon's throne and the court of mysteries.
In it more than a thousand sages and saints are buried
From above whose heads the Ka'ba continually takes flight.
Through invocation, meditation and devotion; by the soul of Ibn Khafif;
By the truth of Ruzbihan, and that of the five daily prayers –
Protect, God, this city of righteous men
From the hand of the irreligious tyrant and the slanderous infidel!
By the truth of the Ka'ba and its builder, Abraham

Keep the people of Shiraz in splendour and pride!
Whosoever heads for Basra, the Dome of Islam,
May his head be lobbed off like gold or silver by tongs!
For Sa'di would say day and night in praise of Shiraz:
All other cities are hawks, and ours is the royal falcon!

The connection between Hafiz's poem and Sa'di's is to be found in the very first word of both: *khushā* ('blessed be ... ', 'how fine is ... '). Hafiz made it clear by opening his *ghazal* with the same word that he intended it to be read against that of the master poet of Salghurid Shiraz. This is a singular example of a dialogic device we find employed in the poetry of Shiraz: intertextual allusions to 'predecessor poems' that reference a genre history or textual community that both poet and audience share.[26] After the first word, though, similarities between Sa'di's poem and H279 become more subtle. Unlike Hafiz who speaks from within the city, Sa'di speaks at a distance from his home town and, consequently, his poem is tinged with a longing to return (residual elements of this nostalgic sentiment were possibly incorporated by Hafiz into his longing for reunion with the absent gypsy boy). The poet imagines viewing Shiraz from the vantage point of the Allāhu Akbar Gorge which overlooks the city from the north. What Sa'di sees is Paradise on earth and a place of safety.

In line three, Sa'di too alludes to Khizr's quest in the darkness of the underworld. The allusion to Shiraz as the former 'seat of Solomon's throne' (*takhtgāh-i Sulaymān*) speaks to the fact that from the early thirteenth century, Fars was referred to in poetry, prose and official inscriptions as *mulk-i Sulaymān*, the 'Realm of Solomon' (see Chapter 4). Some have interpreted the phrase *hazrat-i rāz* ('court of mysteries') found in line three esoterically.[27] Conversely, I believe this phrase is an expression of belief in the cosmic, transformative nature of Iranian kingship.[28] The term *hazrat* is used in Persian praise poems to refer to the hallowed royal presence, as are *hurmat* ('inviolability'), *harīm* ('sacred precinct') and *haram* ('sacred sanctuary').[29]

From line four, Sa'di adopts a pietistic tone, one that promotes Shiraz's moral economy. The poet sings of the city's 1,000 or more saints whose combined holiness gives strength to the Ka'ba, Islam's most revered shrine. Perhaps borrowing from local history writing, Sa'di hints at the profound correlation between the physical city and the spiritual state of its denizens.[30] Sa'di's statement here reflects the importance of Shiraz as a centre for shrine visitation in this period (one of Shiraz's epithets being *Burj-i 'awliyā* ['Tower of Saints']).[31] Cities such as Shiraz derived devout power from the large-scale veneration of saintly bodies buried within them.[32] A saint's tomb was visited because it was believed that it retained the miracle-working power of the long-deceased saint.[33] The associated social, cultural and commercial benefits of such large-scale shrine visitation should not be ignored.

Sa'di continues to place emphasis on piety in line five where he invokes the memory (and associated 'holy blessing' or *baraka*) of two of the city's most celebrated mystics with whom he perhaps felt a close personal connection.[34] Poets and their patrons derive glory from the achievements of these individuals and a pious gravitas attached to the physical location of their sacralizing remains in the city.[35] In the medieval Christian context, association with tombs and holy relics served to reinforce a ruler's power by proxy.[36] It is likely the same was true for the rulers of premodern Shiraz.

Line six opens with a two-line *du'ā*, in which Sa'di calls on God via Abraham and his Ka'ba, to protect his city of 'righteous men' (*nīk-mardān*) from all oppressors (the 'slanderous', 'flirtatiously untrustworthy' infidel [*kāfir-i ghammāz*]; perhaps an allusion to the Mongol threat). Sa'di's wish that the people of his city continue to live in a state of 'splendour and pride' (*tajammul u nāz*) is perhaps not so different from the tone of Hafiz's poem, since *tajammul* also means to beautify oneself or to live in luxury; *nāz* can mean the feigned disdain and coquetry of the recalcitrant love object.

Salghurid Shiraz invites chauvinistic comparisons with rival cities and in the last two lines of his poem, Sa'di threatens anyone who would turn his back on his city and head for Basra (or perhaps Baghdad).[37] While incorporating his *takhallus*, the poet ostensibly quotes himself to say that Shiraz is superior to all great cities (his use of *shahbāz* ['royal falcon'] as a metaphor for Shiraz adding a panegyric touch). In the prologue to the *Gulistan*, Sa'di expresses a similar hope that God will preserve the 'pure land of Shiraz' and that its Salghurid ruler will protect Fars from the 'injuries of fate'. The poet prays to God to protect the realm from the 'wind of sedition.'[38]

A contemporary of Sa'di, Majd al-Din Hamgar, in a lengthy panegyric *qit'a* with the same rhyme scheme as Sa'di's poem, embeds a similarly religiose encomium for Shiraz:[39]

حبّذا بام مسجد شیراز   روضهٔ مشهد ارچه روحانیست

در فضای تو می کند پرواز   زه زهی کعبه ای که مرغ دلم

جسد مرده روح یابد باز   گر بیاید نسیم جان بخشت

Although the shrine of Mashhad is holy,
How fine is the roof of Shiraz's mosque!
An excellent Ka'ba, such that the bird of my heart
Takes flight within your precincts.
If your life-giving breeze were to blow,
The dead body would find life once more.

Moving to the early fourteenth century, we encounter a two-line poem in Zarkub's *Shiraznama* that incorporates phrases borrowed from Sa'di (indicated in italics in my translation) and which shares the same metre and rhyme. This short poem commemorates the return to Shiraz from Luristan in 1342 of Jalal al-Din Mas'ud Shah, Jahan's father:[40]

خدیو مملکت آرا شه غریب نواز   سپاس و شکر خدا را که میر فرّخ بخت

به تختگاه سلیمان رسید دیگر باز   بسال هفت صد و چل با سه در تجمل و ناز

Gratitude and thanks be to God that our fortunate prince,
The realm-adoring ruler, the king who showers strangers with kindness
In the year seven-hundred and forty-three *in splendour and pride*
Has once again reached *the seat of Solomon's throne!*

This fragment tells us something about the popularity of Sa'di's city panegyric in the decades after his death; it also supports a kingly (rather than purely mystical) interpretation of the model poem's Solomonic allusion. A senior contemporary of Hafiz, Jalal al-Din 'Azud Yazdi, has a panegyric *ghazal* for Shah Shaykh Abu Ishaq in which the immediacy of the relationship between praise for the city and adulation of the king is underscored. Here are the first three lines of Jalal's *Shīrāzīya*:[41]

بزم بیارا به سان جنّت اعلی   خیز که شب رفت و صبح کرد تجلّی

نکهت فردوس یا هوای مصلّی   روضهٔ خلد است یا مدینهٔ شیراز

سرو خرامان شکست رونق طوبی   باغ سبق برد از حظیرهٔ فردوس

Arise for night has gone and dawn has appeared!
Adorn the banquet like the exalted Paradise garden!
Is this the Paradise garden or the city of Shiraz?
Is this the scent of Paradise or the breeze of Musalla?
The royal garden has surpassed the enclosure of Heaven;
The strutting cypress has spoiled the splendour of Tuba.

The third ode to Shiraz we will examine in full is by 'Ubayd and it imitates the rhyme and the metre of Sa'di's and can be considered a *javāb* to the master's poem. In his poem, 'Ubayd appears to be in competition with Sa'di spurred on by a desire not only to imitate, but to outdo.[42] As with all great response poems, though, 'Ubayd invokes enough of the earlier poem to garner attention for his own, whilst penning a masterful challenge to it. 'Ubayd's celebration of his adoptive town is counter-pietistic. But, like Sa'di, he speaks at a distance from Shiraz; U95:

مرا دلی است گرفتار خطهٔ شیراز

خوش ایستاده و با لعل دلبران در عیش

گهی به کوی خرابات با مغان همدم

گهی مقامر و گه زاهد و گهی فاسق

همیشه بر در می خانه می کند مسکن

به روی لاله رخانش گمان های نکو

شده برابر چشمی همیشه گوشه نشین

امیدوار چنانم که آن خجسته دیار

معز دنیی و دین تاجبخش ملکستان

عبیدوار هر آن کس که هست در عالم

ز من بریده و خو کرده با تنعّم و ناز

طرب گزیده و با وصل شاهدان دمساز

گهی به صومعه با جمع صوفیان همراز

گهی معاشر و گه رند و گاه شاهدباز

مدام بر سر می خواره می کند پرواز

به زلف سروقدانش امیدهای دراز

مدام در خم محراب ابرویی به نماز

به فرّ دولت سلطان اویس بینم باز

خدایگان جهان پادشاه بنده نواز

دعای دولت او می کند به صدق و نیاز

I have a heart that is taken with the city of Shiraz
That has forsaken me and become accustomed to ease and coquetry
It stands cavorting with the ruby lips of heart-stealers;
It has chosen excitement and enjoys intimate union with beauties
Sometimes it consorts with the Magi in the lane of taverns;
Sometimes it shares in the mysteries of the Sufis in their hermitage
At times it is a gambler, an ascetic, a sinner;
At others it is a convivial companion, a libertine, a lover of boys
It always resides at the door to the tavern
And it continually takes flight above the head of the wine-bibber
It gazes on tulip-cheeked ones and thinks pleasant thoughts
It has high hopes when spying the locks of cypress-statured boys
It sits continually in the corner, gazing into the beloved's eyes
Constantly at prayer in the curve of the niche of that eyebrow
I am still hopeful that, by the glory of Sultan Uvays
I shall see once again that blessed land
The crown-bestowing, all-conquering Mu'izz–i Dunya va Din,
The servant-nurturing king, sovereign of the whole world!
Just like 'Ubayd, all those who inhabit this world
Pray for his good fortune with sincerity and in supplication

In the first line, there is obvious, possibly satirical, imitation of Sa'di's phrase *tajammul u nāz*: 'Ubayd speaks of his heart becoming accustomed to *tana''um u nāz* ('ease and coquetry'). In line two, 'Ubayd's counter-pietistic view of the city comes into full view: Shiraz offers (and is emblematic of) the good life in all its erotic splendour. Contrary to Sa'di's pious whitewashing of the city, 'Ubayd presents us with balance: his heart associates with the Magi in the wine taverns as well as with the Sufis in their lodge. Ultimately, though, the poet promotes an antinomian perspective that finds its crescendo in line five: whereas Sa'di depicts the Ka'ba taking flight above the hallowed tombs of Shiraz's innumerable saints, his fourteenth-century imitator depicts his intoxicated heart flying from above the head of the wine-bibber! In lines six and seven we find homoerotic imagery not dissimilar to Hafiz's. In the *ghazals* of Shiraz, the eroto-panegyric is seldom absent.

Of the three *Shīrāzīyāt* discussed in full so far, 'Ubayd's is the only one with a clearly demarcated formal praise section (lines eight and nine). 'Ubayd dedicates his poem not to the king of Shiraz, but to the Jalayirid ruler of Baghdad, Sultan Uvays (r. 1356–1374) and it is through the 'divinely-gifted authority' (*farr*) possessed by him that 'Ubayd hopes, one day, to return to Shiraz. Line eight ends with *bīnam bāz* ('I shall see once again') lifted from the opening half-line of Sa'di's poem, but more intriguing is the link between U95 and a fifteen-line *qasīda* by 'Ubayd in praise of Shah Shaykh Abu Ishaq which shares the same rhyme and metre.[43] This poem opens with praise of the 'servant-nurturing king' (*pādishāh-i banda-navāz*) and Shiraz as 'Paradise on earth' (*bihisht-i rū-yi zamīn*).[44] 'Ubayd most likely repurposed this *qasīda* into the panegyric *ghazal* for Sultan Uvays after the execution of Shah Shaykh Abu Ishaq in 1357.

Two further *Shīrāzīyāt* are found in the *dīvān* of Haydar Shirazi, a junior contemporary of Hafiz. In one, Haydar imitates the rhyme scheme of Sa'di's poem although, unlike 'Ubayd, he alters the metre. Haydar's poem opens with these three lines:[45]

خاک شیراز مگر کعبهٔ عالم شد باز   که برین خاک نهادند همه روی نیاز

باغ فردوس که مرد از هوشش میمیرد   خوش عروسی است ولی رشک برد از شیراز

این هم از لطف خداوند جهاندار بود   خلق شیراز به شادی همه در نعمت و ناز

Has the land of Shiraz once more become the world's Ka'ba?
Is this why all have turned their faces towards this land in supplication?
The Paradise garden, longing for which causes men to die,
Is a comely bride, but even she is envious of Shiraz.
All of this stems from the grace of the world-ruling Lord:
Shiraz's people live ever happy, surrounded by ease and glory.

In the third line, the phrase *ni'mat u nāz* (translated here as 'ease and glory') is a nod to Sa'di's 'splendour and pride' (*tajammul u nāz*). Haydar's phrasing could also be read as a riff on 'Ubayd's statement that his heart has become infatuated with Shiraz and thereby accustomed to 'ease and coquetry' (*tana''um u nāz*). This exact phrase is also found in two panegyric *qit'as* with a Fars or Shiraz focus by Hamgar.[46] Derived from the Arabic root N-'A-M, the words *ni'mat*, *na'īm* and *tana''um* denote 'bounty', 'ease', 'comfort' and 'luxury' and they evoke the Qur'anic Paradise: *Jannāt al-na'īm* ('The gardens of bliss').[47] Sa'di refers to Shiraz and its immediate surroundings as an earthly abode of 'bliss' (*na'īm*) inhabited by 'paradisiacal beauties' (*lu'batān-i bihishtī*).[48] For 'Ubayd, Shah Shaykh Abu Ishaq's audience hall is the true locus of *nāz* and *na'īm*.[49]

Haydar, however, moves in this poem from praise of Shiraz to praise of the beloved as Hafiz does in H279. In both poems, the equation of the beloved with the patron is deliberate. Haydar likens his devotion to the beloved to Ramin's love for Vis and Mahmud's for Ayaz (see Chapter 5) and styles his beloved as his *qibla* (see Chapter 3).

Haydar's other *Shīrāzīya*, although it has a different rhyme and *radīf*, shares its metre with the poems by Sa'di and 'Ubayd discussed above:[50]

که به ز خطهٔ مصر و دمشق و بغدادست	دلم ز خطهٔ شیراز و قوم او شادست
به هر کجا نگرم لعبتی پری زادست	به هر طرف که روم دلبری شکردهن است
که همچو کعبه عزیز و لطیف بنیادست	طواف خطهٔ شیراز می کنم شب و روز
به لاله زار خرامم که جنّت آبادست	چو یار حوروشم با شراب دست دهد
ببین که لاله عذارم چو سرو آزادست	در آ به باغ ملک بند غم ز دل بگشا
ببین که باغ ارم باغ جعفرآباد است	بیا که جنت و کوثر مصلی و رکنی است
که شور شکر شیرین ز سوز فرهادست	مگر که خسرو شیرین دهن نمی داند
که خاکساری من در هوای او بادست	در آب و آتش عشقش چگونه خاک شوم
دلش به شادی وصل تو در جهان شادست	نمی خورد غم دنیا و آخرت حیدر

My heart is gladdened by Shiraz's environs and its people
For Shiraz is superior to Egypt, Damascus and Baghdad!
In every direction I go there is a sugar-mouthed beloved;
Wherever I look there is a fairy-born doll.
Night and day I circumambulate around Shiraz
For, like the Ka'ba, it is both mighty and elegant.
When my houri-like beloved and wine are at hand,
I strut through the tulip swathe, for it is a paradisiacal place.
Enter the royal garden and loosen grief's bond from your heart;
See how my tulip-cheeked beloved is like a tall, straight cypress!
Come, for Musalla is Paradise and the Rukni canal is Kawthar;
See that the Ja'farabad garden is in fact the Garden of Iram.
Does the sweet-mouthed Khusraw really not know that
The passion in Shirin's sugar derives from Farhad's burning heart?
How can I humble myself in the water and fire of his love
When my humiliation through desire for him is worthless?
Haydar grieves neither for this world nor for the next;
His heart derives worldly joy from the felicity of reunion with you.

In the opening line, Haydar links the city, its people and felicity, recalling the opening of Sa'di's poem as imitated by Hafiz. The boastful tone (reminiscent of the final line in Sa'di's poem) serves to elevate Shiraz above rival cities both near and far: the reference to Baghdad encompasses an allusion to the Jalayirids; the mention of Egypt evokes the sugar trade alluded to in H279. Haydar's opening line recalls that of a *ghazal* by Awhadi Maragha'i in which his city has been transformed into the 'Damascus of passionate love' and the 'Egypt of beauty' by a horde of

Turkic lovelies.[51] In line two, Haydar depicts Shiraz teeming with beauties in every direction; connecting human beauty and the city is commonplace in Shirazi lyric poetry. The circumambulation (*tavāf*) of Shiraz as Ka'ba evokes Sa'di's assertion that the Ka'ba takes flight from above the heads of the many saints buried there and Haydar's own depiction of the city as a 'new Ka'ba'.

In lines four, five and six, Shiraz's pleasances and the good life foci of Musalla and Ruknabad are collectively presented as the Paradise to come. It is in Haydar's Shiraz that the promised Kawthar stream and the ethereal Iram garden – built by king Shaddad to rival paradise only to be destroyed by God for the pride shown by the ruler and his wayward people[52] – are made manifest. From the 'royal garden' (*bāgh-i malik*; perhaps a contemporary garden in Muzaffarid Shiraz) Haydar switches into eroto-panegyric mode and alludes to his patron as that 'sweet Khusraw' (*Khusraw-i shīrīn*) and casts himself as the dejected Farhad (see Chapter 5). The poem ends with an expression of devotion to the patron-beloved and the yearning for an earthly reunion (and an implied rejection of a mystical or heavenly focus for the poem).

Shiraz as paradise on earth

The late Ilkhanid chronicler Vassaf (d. 1329) hails Shiraz as the 'promised Paradise' (*bihisht-i maw'ūd*) and the 'prototype of the pleasure-ground of the exalted Paradise' (*nuskha-yi nuzhat-i firdaws-i barīn*).[53] In the early 1340s, Ahmad b. Abi al-Khayr Zarkub Shirazi wrote the *Shiraznama*, a topographical work on the 'superior merit' (*maziyat*), the 'eminence' (*fazilat*) and the 'blessed', 'auspicious', nay 'sacred' (*mubārak*) nature of Shiraz and its environs.[54] Inspired by unabashed enthusiasm for the city, Zarkub composed his work in prose with interpolated verse. The *Shiraznama* is dedicated to Hajji Qavam al-Din Hasan,[55] senior adviser to Shah Shaykh Abu Ishaq. Borrowing almost verbatim from Vassaf,[56] Zarkub declares Shiraz the 'cream' (*zubda*) of all lands[57] and the 'prototype of the pleasure-script of Paradise' (*nuskha-yi nuzhat-nāma-yi bihisht-i barīn*).[58] If the Paradise garden can be found on earth, it is Shiraz.[59] Zarkub also repurposes lines from a poem by Vassaf in praise of Sultaniya to exalt Shiraz:[60]

شهر شیراز تو گویی که سپهریست برین   یا بهشتی است مشکل شده بر روی زمین

شهری آراسته چون کارگه انگلیون   خاصه چون باغ شود از رخ گلها رنگین

> You would say that the city of Shiraz is the highest heaven
> Or else the Paradise garden formed upon the earth?
> It is a city adorned like a workshop where iridescent silk is woven
> Especially when the gardens are coloured by the cheeks of roses

Poets attribute the flourishing of Shiraz, the security maintained in the province of Fars[61] and the renewed God-given *farr*[62] not only to the grace of God,[63] but also to the justice of the royal patron[64] and his good deeds.[65] Hamgar writes this in praise of his Salghurid patron:[66]

خاک او یافت بوی خلد برین   تا تو بر پارس سایه افکندی

شد نسیم صبای او شیرین   گشت آب و هوای او جانبخش

When you cast your shadow over Fars
Its soil acquired the scent of Paradise
Its climate became life-bestowing
Its messenger breeze turned sweet

Hamgar says that every night there passes through Fars a 'caravan of prayers to the highest heaven' (*kārvān-i du'ā bi 'illiyīn*) thereby suggesting a special relationship between the people of Shiraz and the Divine. Discussion of the transformative power of the beneficent patron to which the current agreeable and prosperous atmosphere in Shiraz must be attributed adorns the opening lines of two *qasīda*s by 'Ubayd in praise of Shah Shaykh Abu Ishaq. The alignment of good governance and urban vitality when positioned at the start of a poem serves to colour the whole:[67]

بهشت روی زمین است خطهٔ شیراز   به یمن معدلت پادشاه بنده نواز

By the good fortune of the justice of the servant-nurturing king,
The city of Shiraz has transformed into Paradise on earth.

And:[68]

خوشتر ز صحن جنت و خرم تر از بهار   شد ملک پارس باز به تأیید کردگار

Once again, through the confirmations of God, Fars
Has become finer than Paradise's plot and more verdant than spring

'Ubayd characterizes the royal audience hall as a micro paradise (*firdaws, khuld-i barīn*), situated within the broader bliss that is the city and its hinterland.[69] Poets often sought to focus the gaze of their listeners toward the outskirts of Shiraz and beyond, into the surrounding countryside in a kind of bucolic vision. As noted, there are allusions in the *ghazal*s of this period to the garden of Iram.[70] Although the primary purpose of these allusions may be to evoke the legendary garden of Iram, they may also allude to an historical garden in Shiraz, the Bagh-i Iram. The age of modern Shiraz's Bagh-i Iram has yet to be established conclusively, though some believe it to have a pre-Safavid foundation.[71] In a lengthy *qasīda* in praise of a Salghurid *atābak*, Hamgar engages in protracted *ubi sunt* in which he laments the sorry state of the ruins at Persepolis and the barrenness of a place he calls the Bagh-i Iram whose soil produces neither rose nor sweet basil.[72] Ultimately, Shiraz outdoes any Edenic bliss: for Haydar, the true 'Garden of Iram' is Bagh-i Ja'farabad.[73] Hafiz asserts that Shiraz is the ethereal made tangible; H65:4:

جز طرف جویبار و می خوشگوار چیست   معنی آب زندگی و روضهٔ ارم

What is the meaning of 'Water of Life' and 'Garden of Iram'?
What more are they than the riverbank and delicious wine?

It is not entirely clear why in *ghazal*s Injuid and Muzaffarid poets generally refrained from focusing on locations within Shiraz's urban fabric since the description of royal palaces form the focus of a number of 'Ubayd's *qasīda*s and *qit'a*s in praise of Shah Shaykh Abu Ishaq.[74] Suffice it to say that in the lyric poetry of this period, Shiraz – the walled, built-up urban centre plus its outlying satellite villages, meadows and gardens – is praised as a coherent unit.[75] Praise for one part is praise for the whole.

The pull of Ruknabad, Musalla and Ja'farabad

As noted previously, Shiraz's paradisiacal charms are concentrated in three iconic sites: the Ruknabad channel, the Musalla meadow and the gardens of Ja'farabad. These three act as emotive loci that arrest the poets and prevent them from leaving or else draw them back to Shiraz through their amorous magnetism. Ruknabad, Musalla and Ja'farabad act as markers of a pragmatic, local *carpe diem* attitude: they fuel Shiraz's trans-regional pull and excite passionate attachment in locals and outsiders alike. The fixed association of these toponyms and their repeated and significant use across multiple poems penned by a series of Shiraz-based poets, their would-be colleagues and literary rivals, facilitated their functioning in a not dissimilar way to *utamakura* in Japanese poetry. *Utamakura,* or place names, act as 'nodes within a poem through which the maker of that poem reaches out to make contact with other poems (or poetic moments) and thereby complicate or enrich the signifying process of that poem as a whole'.[76] With *utamakura*, the reiteration of toponyms not only evokes the physical features of the named places, but also, as Kamens says, calls to mind 'any or all of the agglutinated associations (derived from history, lore or prior literary usage) adhering to the place'.[77] In my assessment, Ruknabad, Musalla and Ja'farabad are akin to *meisho utamakura*: places that are famous precisely (though, not exclusively) because of their roles in poetry.[78] As noted in my discussion of H279, the Ruknabad channel and its sweet water are shorthand for the Shirazi good life as experienced or longed for. These three loci, though all on the edge of the city proper, constitute the poetic heart of Shiraz. In the fourteenth century, these sites, located in Shiraz's 'garden city',[79] provided seclusion and were the settings for wine drinking and amorous trysts. It is to these emotive icons that poets turn with greatest frequency when broadcasting the unique attraction offered by Shiraz.

The *Shiraznama* is in part Zarkub's response to having been chided in Baghdad for praising his home town.[80] Zarkub likens the taste of the Ruknabad to the Salsabil spring and Kawthar river of the Islamic Paradise: it is 'aromatic and perfumed' (*mutayyib u mu'attar*) like heaven's Tasnim fountain. If it is not Kawthar, Zarkub asks, how come the water of eternal life flows through it? And if it is not of the same substance as the Salsabil and Tasnim, how come it is the cause of 'delight' (*tafrih*) and 'comfort' (*tan'im*)?[81] Zarkub couples praise for contemporary Shiraz with reflections upon local history, an approach towards praise of the city that helps mitigate the esoteric and the temporal. Zarkub displays a fascination with the ancient sites of Fars that was typical in the thirteenth and fourteenth centuries (see Chapter 4).

Hafiz's best-known twin evocation of the Ruknabad channel and the Musalla meadow appears in his well-known 'Turk of Shiraz' *ghazal*; H3:2:

کنار آب رکن آباد و گلگشت مصلا را   بده ساقی می باقی که در جنت نخواهی یافت

Wine server! Give the eternal wine, for in Paradise you will not find
The banks of the Ruknabad channel and the Musalla flower meadow.

Here Hafiz ranks Shiraz's earthly, tangible pleasances above the promised Paradise garden. The wine served is referred to as *may-i baqi*, here translated as 'eternal wine', although 'remaining wine' is a possible alternative: the dregs of the patron's wine being superior to that promised in the afterlife. This couplet comes directly after the *matla'* in which Hafiz says he would give away the Central Asian cities of Bukhara and Samarqand for the *khal-i Hindu* (the 'Hindu' or 'Indian' [i.e. jet-black] beauty spot) on his beloved Turk's white cheek. The naming of two locations within the environs of Shiraz (those with which his audience would have enjoyed intimate familiarity) immediately following the mention of two distant cities focuses the listeners' attention on the local and, in the process, on the here and now. In this poem (and many others by Hafiz and 'Ubayd) there is an undercurrent of a preference for the local beloved over an exotic love interest. Belief in Shiraz's superiority over Samarqand is manifested by both Vassaf and Zarkub who claim that the freshness of Shiraz's meadows consigns the Central Asian city to the 'corner of the shelf of oblivion' (gūsha-yi tāqcha-yi nisyān).[82]

Elsewhere, Hafiz responds to lines one and three from Sa'di's famous Shīrāzīya; H39:7–8:

عیش مکن که خال رخ هفت کشور است　　شیراز و آب رکنی و این باد خوش نسیم

تا آب ما که منبعش الله اکبر است　　فرق است از آب خضر که ظلمات جای اوست

Shiraz with its Rukni water and this sweet, scented breeze
Criticize it not, for it is the beauty spot of the seven climes
There is a difference between Khizr's water from the dark underworld
And our water, which springs from Allāhu Akbar!

Here Hafiz ranks Shiraz's present over the ethereal. The 'seven regions' (haft kishvar) or 'seven climes' (haft iqlīm; overlapping but not identical topographical schemes) are the usual geographical divisions of the world in the Iranian tradition.[83] In his qasīdas, 'Ubayd hails Shiraz's ruler as 'king' or 'sun' of the seven climes/regions; that is, king of the whole world.[84] Through stressing the centrality of Ruknabad and its associated pleasure grounds, Hafiz reorientates his listeners' attention away from pious nexuses towards foci of both earthly and erotico-mystical arousal. The phrase Allāhu akbar here is an allusion to the gorge through which the Ruknabad channel flows.[85]

There is little evidence that Hafiz spent any time away from Shiraz. He uses an allusion to the pull of Shiraz's emotive loci to excuse his inertia; H101:9:

نسیم باد مصلا و آب رکن آباد　　نمی دهند اجازت مرا به سیر سفر

The sweet breeze of Musalla and the water of Ruknabad
They do not give me permission to wander and travel!

The poet is trapped in an amorous entanglement with the city. Although he is believed to have travelled extensively in the Islamic world, Sa'di expresses a similar sentiment, though he casts Shiraz in the subservient role of the plaintive lover unable to detach from the departing beloved:[86]

خاک شیراز و آب رکن آباد　　دست از دامنم نمی دارد

The soil of Shiraz and the water of Ruknabad
They will not let go of the hem of my robe!

Wherever Sa'di travels, the hem of his robe still carries the scent of Shiraz's perfumed earth and the life-giving properties of its fresh water. Elsewhere,

Sa'di describes the pull to return to Shiraz from Damascus like that of Khusraw who left Shikar out of longing for Shirin.[87] In yet another *ghazal*, Sa'di paints a dramatic image of the city's captivating powers:[88]

هر که را در وی گرفت آرام نیست   باد صبح و خاک شیراز آتشیست

The morning breeze and the soil of Shiraz constitute a fire;
Whomsoever they entrap has no hope of respite.

'Ubayd was an outsider who made his literary career in Shiraz. In premodern times, patriotism was a local sentiment: love of *terra patria* or natal land.[89] 'Ubayd, like other migrant poets,[90] alludes to his 'temporary sojourn' in Fars[91] and speaks of himself as an 'outsider' (*gharīb*) who is far from his home town. But for 'Ubayd, Musalla and Ruknabad more than compensate for his alien status; U45:1:

غریب را وطن خویش می برد از یاد   نسیم باد مصلّی و آب رکن آباد

The sweet breeze of Musalla and the water of Ruknabad
Remove any thought of home from the stranger's memory.

Poets had a professional need to belong. Of course, 'Ubayd must stress he belongs in Shiraz because, to be a great Persian poet in the fourteenth century, one either had to hail from Shiraz, serve Shiraz's court or – if you were based at another court or hailed from another town – imitate Sa'di and/or his most celebrated successor: Hafiz. As Ingenito has shown, being Shirazi by birth or association (through shared patronage or intertextually via imitation) was considered a pre-requisite for poetic eloquence and authority.[92] 'Imad employs references to Shiraz's famed loci in the opening lines of an amorous *ghazal*:[93]

که مفرّح دل و مقوّی جان باد   خوشا هوای مصلی و آب رکن آباد
چو قد دوست همه سروهای او آزاد   چو باغ روضه همه حوض های او کوثر
مناسب است که رسم طرب کنم بنیاد   بیا که موسم نوروز خاصه در شب عید

Blessed be the breeze of Musalla and the water of Ruknabad
For they exhilarate the heart and restore the soul
Like the Paradise garden each of its pools is a Kawthar
Like the beloved's stature, each of its cypresses stands tall
Come, for at Nawruz, especially on the eve of 'Id-i Fitr,
It is fitting that I lay the foundation for merry-making

'Imad not only equates Shiraz's verdant environs with Paradise, he also presents them as locations for the royal celebrations of the spring equinox festivities and the feast to mark the end of Ramadan. In the first word of the poem, *khushā*, ʿImad invokes Saʿdi's famous *Shīrāzīya*, as perhaps he does H279, if ʿImad's poem was composed after it. In content, though, ʿImad follows the counter-pietistic mode of city panegyric typified by ʿUbayd. As noted above, Haydar composed a number of poems in praise of Shiraz. In one, he appears to quote verbatim from ʿImad (see the italics in my translation):[94]

خوشا نگار گل اندام و باغ نوروزی   خوشا هوای مصلی و آب رکن آباد

Blessed be the rose-limbed beloved and the Nawruz garden!
Blessed be the breeze of Musalla and the water of Ruknabad!

Interestingly, it is not only in the *ghazals* of poets based in Shiraz that we find allusions to Ruknabad. An intriguing *ghazal* attributed to the Jalayirid poet Salman and quoted in full below,[95] bears a striking similarity to H81 in which Hafiz depicts the devoted nightingale and the coquettish rose, alludes to the Garden of Iram and references objects associated in the popular imaginary with Fars's ancient past: the 'throne of Jamshid' and the 'world-seeing cup':[96]

همی نالید و با گل راز می کرد   سحرگه بلبلی آواز می کرد
نیازش می شنید و ناز می کرد   نیاز خویش با معشوق می گفت
مرا با خویشتن دمساز می کرد   بهر آهی که می زد در غم یار
دلم دیوانگی آغاز می کرد   نسیم زلف دلبر می شنیدم
هوای خطهٔ شیراز می کرد   خیال آب رکن آباد می پخت

At dawn a nightingale began to sing
It lamented and confided in the rose
It spoke of its needs to the beloved
Who listened and showed coquettish disdain
The sigh it uttered in longing for its beloved
Caused me to become its intimate confidant
I smelled the sweet scent of the beloved's locks
And my heart began to turn crazed with love
It longed for the water of Ruknabad
And desired the environs of Shiraz

By evoking Shiraz in this manner, the Baghdad-based panegyrist hints that his lot might be better in Fars. Salman penned at least two *qasīdas* in praise of Shah Shujaʿ[97] and (as noted in the Introduction) there is good evidence both that Salman's poetry enjoyed critical acclaim in Muzaffarid Shiraz[98] and that his *ghazals* were read alongside those of Hafiz in the early Timurid period. As Salman's poem demonstrates, Shiraz inspired a similar reaction in poets based beyond the territory of Fars.

Jahan's tempered praise for Shiraz

Jahan alludes with far less frequency to Shiraz. This absence is not dictated by form or genre and, given that the evocation of Shiraz constitutes a normative feature of *ghazal*s produced in the city in the fourteenth century, the paucity of imagery in Jahan's *ghazal*s requires some thought. There are two possible reasons for this: (i) the trauma Jahan endured following the overthrow and execution of her uncle; and (ii) the reputedly harsh reign of his Muzaffarid executioner which followed. Moreover, given that praise of Shiraz is found in panegyrics intended for performance at court, the fact that Jahan's poetry contains few examples of such praise for the city suggests she may have had comparatively less access to the royal *majlis* than her male counterparts. That said, in one *ghazal*, Jahan gives what appears to be a mystical spin to the Ruknabad/Musalla trope. Having called on God to maintain the 'palace of loving kindness' (*sarā-yi mihrabānī*), Jahan ends her poem thus; J78:7:

غذای روح ما اندر مصلی   ز آب سرو رکن آباد بادت

May the nourishment of my soul in Musalla
Be from the water of the cypress of your Ruknabad.

Given its well-established paradisiacal associations, here Ruknabad could be read as emblematic of the Paradise garden itself, rather than the matchless earthly pleasance. This more pious reading is further facilitated by the word *musallā*, which also means 'place of prayer', 'oratory'. A notable exception to the almost complete absence of allusions to Shiraz in Jahan's poetry is a *rubā'ī* in which her positivity for the city can be read as nostalgia for the Injuid past or, perhaps, as a celebration of the coming to power of Shah Shuja', for whom she penned a panegyric *qasīda*:[99]

شیراز خوش است خاصه در فصل بهار   و آنگه لب جوی و لب جام لب یار
آواز دف و چنگ و نی و عود و رباب   اینها همه با نگارکی شیرین کار

Shiraz is fine, especially in the spring season
Beside the stream, with the lip of the cup and the beloved's lips
The melody of the tambourine, harp, flute, lute, and *rubāb*
All of these, with a sweet-mannered young beauty.

The opening hemistich of Jahan's quatrain is reminiscent of a half-line by Sa'di with which it shares an allusion to Shiraz at springtime and some shared words.[100]

Shiraz as beloved and as abode of the beloved

Hafiz says one must not find fault with Shiraz for it is the 'beauty spot on the cheek of the seven climes' (*khāl-i rukh-i haft kishvar*).[101] In this eroticized topophilia, Shiraz's peerless beauty is expressed in the same language used to depict the coquettish boy or handsome royal patron.[102] In U95, 'Ubayd speaks of losing his heart to Shiraz and its environs just as a lover falls for his beloved. Like Florence for Dante (d. 1321), Shiraz for Hafiz and his contemporaries is an emotional object of desire.[103] The seductive allure of the city complements that of the ruler and reinforces the connection made by Persian poets between beauty and kingship.[104] For Sa'di, Shiraz's enticing aroma evokes that of his beloved:[105]

این نسیم خاک شیراز ست یا مشک ختن   یا نگار من پریشان کرده زلف عنبرین

Is this the scent of Shiraz's earth, or of musk from Khutan?
Or else has my beloved dishevelled his ambergris-perfumed hair?

The city's scent infuses the outlying meadows with a musky perfume when the Nawruz breeze wafts over the city.[106] The scent of Shiraz, carried on the breeze, mingles with that of the beloved who resides there and, as these combine, they make the beloved and his city an inseparable whole; H333:7:

هوای منزل یار آب زندگانی ماست   صبا بیار نسیمی از خاک شیرازم

The breeze of the stopping-place of the beloved is our Water of Life
O messenger breeze! Bring me a sweet breeze from the dust of Shiraz.

Here Hafiz speaks at some distance from Shiraz (perhaps from Yazd),[107] having undertaken a journey (hence the allusion to the 'stopping place' [*manzil*]). Haydar opens a *ghazal* with a commentary on the effect the return of the beloved to Shiraz has on the lover:[108]

تا به شیراز نگارم ز سفر باز آمد   راحت روح من خسته جگر باز آمد

When my beloved returned to Shiraz after his journey
Solace returned once more to my heart-sore soul

Perhaps written to celebrate a royal triumph or a processional entry into the city by the returning ruler, Haydar suggests that, for the welfare of the poet, the patron should never leave (the departure of the beloved from Shiraz being the impetus for mournful poetry).[109] In a similar vein, Sa'di fuses his beloved and his home town thus:[110]

آخر ای باد صبا بویی اگر می آری   سوی شیراز گذر کن که مرا یار آنجاست

In the end, O messenger breeze, if you are to bring a scent
Pass by Shiraz, for there resides my beloved.

There is an implied ambiguity here:[111] *ma-rā yār ānjā-st* can be read as 'there resides my beloved' or 'that place [Shiraz] is my beloved'.[112] Shiraz is worthy of praise simply because it is the beloved's abode. The eroticization of the city is a logical extension of the conceit that layers patron over beloved in Persian lyric poetry. This is not dissimilar to the treatment of the *qibla* (the direction to which Muslims turn in prayer) and the Ka'ba (the cube-shaped structure in Mecca that is the focal point of the Hajj) as metaphors for the beloved and patron as objects of worship and adoration (see Chapter 3).[113]

Persian poets also speak of *ghurbat*, an emotionally charged term that means distance from home, alienation, exile and the condition of being a stranger.[114] In his desperation, Hafiz seeks union with his beloved through *ghurbat*; H313:6:

من کز وطن سفر نگزیدم به عمر خویش   در عشق دیدن تو هواخواه غربتم

I who have never elected to travel from my homeland in my lifetime
In my ardent desire to see you, am longing for exile.

Given a political reading, we detect a further layer of signification here: if we read constancy in attachment to the home town as loyalty to the local ruler, then willingness to give up that attachment for another beloved might signal the poet's flirtation with a move to a rival court or the solicitation of alternative sources of patronage.

But Shiraz's emotional hold over the poet does not simply stem from the fact that it is the patron's domicile. The city is home to innumerable beauties whose appeal trumps that of the lovelies of exotic locales. Interestingly, Ibn Battuta praises the inhabitants of fourteenth-century Shiraz for their attractive appearance and cleanliness.[115] Aesthetic beauty surrounds our poets and their interlocutors. In Khvaju's estimation, Shiraz has become a 'Turkistan' because of the presence of many fine Turks ('beautiful youths').[116] For Hafiz, the city should be exploited for aesthetic pleasure; H444:1:

شهریست پر ظریفان وز هر طرف نگاری   یاران صلای عشق است گر می کنید کاری

It is a city filled with refined people; everywhere a beauty
It is an invitation to love passionately, if you will act.

Shiraz produces and provides a multiplicity of beloveds and, with them, a myriad of erotic possibilities;[117] H338:5–7:

شیراز معدن لب لعل است و کان حسن   من جوهری مفلسم ایرا مشوشم

از بس که چشم مست در این شهر دیده ام   حقا که می نمی خورم اکنون و سر خوشم

شهریست پر کرشمهٔ خوبان ز شش جهت   چیزیم نیست ورنه خریدار هر ششم

Shiraz is the mine of ruby lips and the quarry of beauty
I am a penniless jeweller, that's why I am disturbed
I have gazed into so many drunken eyes in this city
That truly, having drunk no wine, I am light-headed
It is a city filled with coquettish beauties in all six directions
I have nothing to my name; otherwise, I would buy all six!

Hafiz adopts an intemperate tone in these lines which contrasts with the chaste praise for Shiraz voiced by Sa'di. Elsewhere, Hafiz portrays himself as an aroused vagabond-drunk who is unable to afford the abundant delights his city has to offer; H46:9:

میخواره و سرگشته و رندیم و نظرباز   وآن کس که چو ما نیست در این شهر کدام است

We are wandering winebibbers, libertines, and we ogle boys
Who is there who is not like us in this town?

'Ubayd expresses the desire of the rindān ('libertines') who will spare no expense in their quest to secure the affections – however temporary – of the city's beaus; U114:1:

ما که رندان کیسه پردازیم   کشتهٔ شاهدان شیرازیم

We who are free-spending, generous libertines,
Are murdered by the pretty youths of Shiraz!

'Ubayd uses kushta ('killed', 'murdered') and shāhidān (pretty young males whose beauty bears 'witness' [shahid] to that of God) in the phrase 'we are murdered by the pretty youths of Shiraz'. The poet makes a subtle link here between the shahīd, the 'martyr' who dies for love, and the etymologically related shāhid (see Chapter 3). Sa'di also uses the term shāhid to praise the physical attractiveness of Shiraz's inhabitants:[118]

خاک شیراز چو دیبای منقش دیدم   وان همه صورت شاهد که بر آن دیبا بود

I saw the land of Shiraz like embroidered brocade
And how many images of pretty youths were on that brocade!

The Shiraz painted in these poems is a city populated by wandering winebibbers and libertines who lust after local lads. In the poetry, the urban zone associated with seductive *shāhid*s is the *kharābāt* – the ruins on the periphery of the city that exist both physically and morally on the edge of society. The *kharābāt* signify liminal, counter-hegemonic spaces on the margins of polite society where non-Muslims run wine taverns in the ruined quarters abandoned by the new city.[119] The depiction of a city brimming with *shāhid*s (and the erotic energy they arouse) conflicts with celebrations of Shirazi piety and the morally conservative tone of contemporary texts such as Junayd's catalogue of the city's numerous shrines (although even Junayd penned erotic *ghazal*s that he presumably used when preaching to excite his listeners and maintain their attention).[120] Hafiz, 'Ubayd, 'Imad and Haydar all engage in counter-pietistic readings of Shiraz that serve to highlight the multiple layers of this sophisticated regional metropole with a population not dissimilar in size to contemporary London before the Black Death struck in 1348.[121] Such a reading of Shiraz is informed by the belief that great cities are complex moral and physical entities.[122]

Given devotion to the patron is expressed in the poetry in amorous terms, allusions to irresistible Shirazi *shāhid*s can be read as allusions to the local ruling class who patronized the arts, the most significant patron being the ruler himself. The physical beauty of Shah Shuja' is celebrated in *qasīda*s, contemporary histories and works of prose literature;[123] his reputed good looks, combined with his part-Turkic heritage, have led some to interpret Hafiz's *Turk-i Shīrāzī* as an allusion to him (or else his son, Zayn al-'Abidin). The overlap between patron (*mamdūh*) and beloved (*ma'shūq*) is particularly strong in Hafiz's *ghazal*s but, since we also find this overlap in *ghazal*s written by the poet's peers, it should be recognized as a feature common to many fourteenth-century Shirazi *ghazal*s.

As noted already, medieval Shiraz was a major centre for shrine visitation: the city boasted hundreds of shrines of greater or lesser sacred importance (as enumerated in Junayd's Arabic language guide completed in 1389,[124] better known in his son's Persian translation under the title *Tadhkira-yi Hizar mazar*). The sacralization of Shiraz as a transregional centre for shrine visitation lends weight to the metaphorical equation of the beloved with the *qibla*; U21:1–3:

توتیای دیده خاک پای توست	قبلهٔ دل روی شهرآرای توست
از فریب نرگس شهلای توست	عربده در شهر و فتنه در جهان
از بلای هجر جان فرسای توست	غلغل خلق و فغان عاشقان

The *qibla* of my heart is your city-adorning face
The collyrium of my eyes is the dust beneath your feet
The scuffles in the town and the disturbance in the world
Come from the deceptive enchantment of your dark, narcissus eyes
The commotion of the people and the cries of the lovers
Are caused by life-sapping separation from you.

The description of the beloved's face or his person as 'city-adorning' (shahr-ārā) stresses the urban identity of the one praised in the poetry.[125] In the poetry studied here, we encounter no rural beloveds, though a bucolic film is discernible when urban beloveds are transposed to extra-mural locations. The presence of the beloved within the city is a cause of instability, unrest and even upheaval. The chief source of this commotion being his extraordinarily captivating looks; U16:1:

از جهانی مرد و زن و زن آشوب و افغان برنخاست   تا نقاب از روی شهرآرای جانان برنخاست

Until the veil was lifted from the city-adorning face of the beloved
Neither commotion nor cries had risen up from the world of men and women.

'Ubayd's beloved, like Joseph – the archetype of perfect human beauty – arouses the sexual appetite of men and women alike (see Chapter 6). The beloved is 'city-disturbing' (shahr-āshūb), a term also used to denote a subgenre of the Persian lyric often focused on beautiful young men of the bazaar.[126] The tumult caused by the beloved's beauty is labelled fitna ('sedition'), qiyāmat ('upheaval') and ghawghā ('turmoil') – the same terms used to describe political strife or social upheaval. Haydar speaks in similar terms to 'Ubayd about the broad impact of the beloved's destructive allure:[127]

مه خورشید رخ موی میان می گذرد   بت شکر سخن پسته دهان می گذرد

کآفت مرد و زن و پیر و جوان می گذرد   خلق شیراز بدانید و نظر باز کنید

The sugar-speaking, pistachio-mouthed idol is passing by
The sun-cheeked moon with its hair-thin waist is passing by
O people of Shiraz! Know well, and open your eyes,
For the calamity of men and women, of old and young is passing by!

The poets warn of the disruption that Shiraz and the region of Fars will endure due to the beloved's attractiveness:[128]

ترسم که آشوب خوشت بر هم زند شیراز را   شیراز پر غوغا شدست از فتنه چشم شوخت

Shiraz is in tumult from the sedition caused by your playful eyes
I fear that your sweet disturbance might throw Shiraz into commotion.

And:[129]

مگر ز چشم تو برخاست فتنه در شیراز   چه شد که ملک دل عاشقان مشّمر شد

What has occurred to cause commotion in the realm of the lovers' hearts?
Can it be that your eyes have caused sedition in Shiraz?

Jalal warns that the full disclosure of the Shirazi beloved's alluring features could cause upheaval as far away as Jalayirid Tabriz:[130]

ترسم آشوب رخش بر هم زند تبریز را   گر ز پیش چهرهٔ زیبا براندازد نقاب

> If he were to remove the veil from his beautiful countenance
> I fear the riot of his face would trigger turmoil in Tabriz!

The single factor that can disrupt this order, is the beloved's unsettling allure:[131]

بیمست که برخیزد از حسن تو غوغایی   در پارس که تا بودست از ولوله آسودست

> As long as Fars has existed, it has been free of tumult
> The fear is that from your beauty commotion will rise up.

The beloved has the potential to eradicate all trace of the famed purity and chastity of Shiraz's inhabitants:[132]

دگر نبینی در پارس پارسایی   اگر تو روی نپوشی بدین لطافت و حسن

> If you do not cover your face, with this grace and beauty
> You will no longer see any purity in Pars.

There is a pun in the second hemistich on the name of the region, Pars and *pārsā'ī* ('purity').

Shiraz and poetry

The city's hold over poets

Hafiz was bound to Shiraz and the patronage network the city afforded him. Couched in the language of romantic devotion, the poet muses on his relationship with his patron; H32:7:

به خنده گفت که حافظ برو که پای تو بست   ز دست جور تو گفتم ز شهر خواهم رفت

> I said: 'I will leave this city because of your cruelty.'
> Laughing, he said: 'Go ahead Hafiz! Who tied your foot?'

The court poet, by definition, is tied to the royal circle within which he has gained status and the patron from whom he receives his stipend. A professional poet would only leave a city if forced to do so or if lured away by a better deal. The poetry of Hafiz – a local poet in the employ of patrons with non-Shirazi roots – bridged a gap between Shiraz's royal outsiders, long-established elite families from the wider region and indigenous middle-to-lower classes.[133] Hafiz only ever left Shiraz temporarily and against his will.[134] Born and raised there, Hafiz enjoyed an almost constant affinity with the city; H448:7:

نام نیک ار طلبد از تو غریبی چه شود   تویی امروز در این شهر که نامی داری

> If through you a stranger seeks a good name what does it matter
> To you, who today has earned a good name in this city?

'Ubayd was an outsider and he left Shiraz after the overthrow of the Injuids, only returning in the last years of his life, midway through the reign of Shah Shuja'. 'Ubayd's four *qasīda*s in praise of Shah Shuja' bear witness to the poet's tenacity in re-cultivating royal favour after a considerable period of absence, much of which was spent in Jalayirid Baghdad. The thought (or reality) of leaving Shiraz is too much for 'Ubayd to bear. In a heartfelt *ghazal*, he depicts his involuntary departure from the city, alluding to the fear that the separation will spell his professional downfall; U107:

وه کز این رفتن ناچار چه خونین جگرم   رفتم از خطهٔ شیراز و به جان در خطرم
زین سفر تا چه شود حال و چه آید به سرم   می روم دست زنان بر سر و پای اندر گل
گاه چون غنچه دلتنگ گریبان بدرم   گاه چون بلبل شوریده در آیم به خروش
من از این کوی اگر بر گذرم در گذرم   من از این شهر اگر بر شکنم در شکنم
ای رفیقان بگذارید که من بی خبرم   خبر راه مپرسید و مرا به سر راه
می روم وز سر حسرت به قفا می نگرم   بی خود و بی دل و بی یار از شیراز بیرون
خبر از پای ندارم که زمین می سپرم   قوت دست ندارم که عنان می گیرم
قول ناصح نکند چاره و پند پدرم   این چنین زار که امروز منم در غم عشق
می کشد دهر به زنجیر قضا و قدرم   ای عبید این سفری نیست که من می خواهم

> I have left Shiraz and, by my life, I am in danger
> Oh, how my liver bleeds at this unavoidable departure!
> I go beating my hands on my head, dragging my feet in the mud
> What will happen in this journey? What will befall me?
> At times I cry out like an impassioned nightingale
> At others I tear my collar, like a lovesick rosebud.
> If I quit this city, I will be crushed;
> If I venture from this lane, I will expire.
> Do not ask me about the path, my friends
> Just set me on my way for I am uninformed of what will come!
> Out from Shiraz, without self, heart, or beloved
> *I go, and I look back longingly in regret.*
> I have no strength in my hands to take the reins;
> *I cannot feel my feet as they tread the ground.*

I am so distraught today, afflicted by love sickness
that neither the counsellor's words nor those of my father have effect.
O 'Ubayd! This is not a journey I wish to take
Fate is dragging me by the chains of decree and destiny!

Here 'Ubayd inserts two verbatim quotations from a long *ghazal* by Sa'di (indicated in my translation in italics).[135] By quoting Sa'di in this mournful piece about his flight from Fars, perhaps 'Ubayd sought to underline his literary credentials and his ties to this preeminent city of poets. For a remunerated poet, leaving the king's circle might not only spell financial ruin, but could also potentially compromise the poet's safety as he would now fall outside the patron's protective sphere. Of course, mobility did not always result in a failed career: some poets moved between courts without too much disruption to their livelihoods, so Hafiz's own largely sedentary professional life should be viewed as an exception to the norm. For a biting satirist such as 'Ubayd, an outsider who maligned many,[136] the risks associated with a move to another court were great. But 'Ubayd was also a prolific panegyrist who managed to balance biting satire with saccharine praise. The poet's ability to adapt quickly to new social environments and to integrate himself within new patronage systems saved him from ruin. 'Attar Shirazi echoes 'Ubayd's complaint about the alienation caused by changed circumstances. He indexes 'Ubayd's *Shīrāzīya* by incorporating the terms *nāz* and *tana''um* from it in this line:

غريب و عاشق و مسكين و بيقرار تو كردى   به شهر خويش مرا بود عيش و ناز و تنعّم

In my own town I enjoyed the good life, coquetry and ease
It was you who made me alienated, amorous, unfortunate and unsettled.

Shiraz as the bastion of fine poetry

By the close of the thirteenth century, Shiraz had become synonymous with fine poetry in the collective Persianate imaginary. As noted in the Introduction, all the great poets of the immediate post-Mongol period either hailed from the city, spent part or the entirety of their career there and/or connected their poetry intertextually with that of preeminent Shirazi poets, particularly Sa'di. In such lyrical encounters within a transregional network of dense intertextual relationships that included poets in Shiraz, Yazd, Kirman, Baghdad and Tabriz, younger poets attempted to forge a direct link with Sa'di's canonical lyric legacy aimed at eliciting a favourable comparison in the minds of their listeners between their poetry and his.[137] Post-Mongol poets underscored the symbolic association between Shiraz, Sa'di and great poetry,[138] an association promoted by the poet himself:[139]

ز لطف لفظ شکربار گفتهٔ سعدی   شدم غلام همه شاعران شیرازی

By the grace of the sugar-shedding words of Sa'di's verses
I have become the devoted slave of all Shirazi poets.

The poets of fourteenth-century Iran and Iraq sought to appropriate something of Sa'di's fame whilst promoting the idea that they were the true inheritors of his style. One of the earliest examples of such posturing (that may even be contemporary with the master himself) can be found in a *ghazal* by Awhadi (d. 1338) who had Isfahani ancestry:[140]

قصهٔ اوحدی از راه سپاهان شنو   همچو آوازهٔ سعدی که ز شیراز آید

Listen to Awhadi's tale from the Isfahan road;
Just like Sa'di's fame that arrives from Shiraz.

There is a secondary pun here on the musical mode *Isfahān*. The Kirmani poet, 'Imad, a panegyrist to both Injuids and Muzaffarids, tempers his self-boasting in the following manner:[141]

مشهور شد بنظم روان در جهان عماد   لیکن بگرد سعدی شیراز کی رسد

'Imad has become famous in the world for his flowing verses
But, how can he ever hope to match the dust beneath Sa'di's feet?

And in a panegyric *ghazal* for Shah Shaykh Abu Ishaq,[142] 'Imad inserts a *tazmīn* from Sa'di as he repurposes a one-line *du'ā* from a *qasīda* by the master.[143] In another *ghazal*, 'Imad addresses himself in a self-important tone claiming he has reached a level in poetry akin not only to that of Sa'di, but also 'Attar of Nishabur (d. 1220):[144]

نه بازارت کم از بازار سعدی است   نه دکانت کم از دکان عطار

Your market is no less than Sa'di's market;
Your apothecary is no less than 'Attar's apothecary.

Although he spent the bulk of his career in serving Shiraz's rulers, 'Imad hailed from Kirman, so it is unsurprising that he expresses in some of his poems a desire to be taken for Shirazi (or desiring to be considered as eloquent as a poet born and raised there). In a *qasīda* in praise of Mubariz al-Din, 'Imad declares that, even though he is a 'follower' of Sa'di he is not, in fact, Shirazi.[145]

Evidence of the equation between Shiraz, fine poetry and Sa'di is also found in the works of poets who did not make their careers in Shiraz, such as Kamal Khujandi (d. 1400). When Kamal invokes the memory of Sa'di, his tone is often haughty. In a *ghazal* written in imitation of one by Sa'di which ends with a half-line quoted verbatim from the model poem, Kamal declares his response poem to be no less eloquent than Sa'di's original.[146] Kamal boasts that if Sa'di had been alive in his day, he would have wiped clean his poetry notebook upon hearing his subtle sayings.[147] Elsewhere, Kamal suggests that his poetic genius is fed by Sa'di's:[148]

کمال ار بشنود سعدی دو بیتی زین غزل گوید   که خاک باغ طبعت برد آب بوستان من

Kamal, if Sa'di were to hear just two lines from this *ghazal* he would say:
'The dust of the garden of your genius has syphoned the water from my fragrant plot'
(*būstān*)

The 'fragrant plot' alluded to here is Sa'di's monumental *Bustan*. Kamal claims he has mastered Sa'di's 'delicate poetic skill' (*lutf-i tab'*) such that no one believes he is from Khujand and not Shiraz.[149] Kamal also declares himself the 'Sa'di of the age' due to his fine poetry and prose.[150] Kamal quotes directly from Sa'di and claims that his own verses are so sweet they will attract sugar from Egypt and Sa'di from Shiraz.[151] The Tabriz-based poet says that, because of him, Khujand, which was previously considered inferior to Shiraz, has now gained some honour.[152] As we shall see below, Kamal's poetry also bears the mark of interaction with that of his most significant Shirazi contemporary, Hafiz.

Moving beyond Shiraz

As a poem spread, so did the fame of the poet and his/her patron.[153] With the spread of loco-specific poetry, the renown of the patron's city was also propagated far and wide. This intertwining of the fame of patron, poet and city helps explain why allusions to Shiraz and Fars regularly appear alongside bursts of *fakhr*. Hafiz, in praising his own natural poetic ability and the popularity of his poetry, indirectly praises Shiraz and its ruler. An integral part of Hafiz's self-boasting is the claim that his *ghazal*s are appreciated well beyond the confines of Fars, not just in other cities of post-Mongol Iran and Iraq, but much further afield; H429:12:

حافظ حدیث سحر فریب خوشت رسید   تا حد مصر و چین و به اطراف روم و ری

Hafiz, your beautiful, magic-defying words have reached
To the borders of Egypt and China, and the environs of Anatolia and Rayy.

Shafi'i-Kadkani believes *ghazal*s composed in Shiraz in this period travelled orally (via performance and recitation) within even a single month to Central Asia and Northern India.[154] According to Gulandam's preface to the *dīvān* of Hafiz (composed not later than 1421), within his lifetime or very soon after, Hafiz had accrued considerable fame, his poetry having spread to Central Asia, India, Mesopotamia and northwest and central Iran.[155] Hafiz claims it is through his poetry that Fars is in dialogue with its regional neighbours: he has 'conquered' Fars and 'Iraq' (here, western and central Iran, including Isfahan and its immediate surroundings) and now his eyes are set on the Jalayirid realm. Regional political and cultural rivalries are evoked in the poetry; H41:7:

عراق و فارس گرفتی به شعر خوش حافظ   بیا که نوبت بغداد و وقت تبریز است

> You've captured Iraq and Fars with sweet poems, Hafiz.
> Come, for it is Baghdad and Tabriz's turn!

Hafiz may be hinting here that he is contemplating leaving Shiraz, while boasting of the reception his poetry will soon enjoy alongside that of Salman in Baghdad and Kamal in Tabriz. Here, poetic ambition and military posturing work in tandem as Muzaffarid imperialist ambitions are voiced by the court's propagandist. In a long, posthumous, elegiac *qit'a* for Mubariz al-Din, Hafiz extols the conquests that were achieved shortly before the ruler's demise:[156]

عاقبت شیراز و تبریز و عراق   چون مسخّر کرد وقتش در رسید

> Finally, when Shiraz, Tabriz, and Iraq
> He had conquered, his time was up!

It is difficult to know the exact extent to which Hafiz's poetry had spread during his lifetime, but it is reasonable to assume that it was not only known to the Jalayirids, but also performed at their *majālis*. Hafiz's *ghazal*s would have spread to other Persian-speaking courts along the same routes taken by itinerant Sufis, pilgrims, preachers, merchants, musicians and other entertainers who passed through Shiraz having intersected the elite and non-elite networks in which Hafiz's *ghazal*s circulated. Evidence of Hafiz's impact well beyond Fars within his lifetime (or shortly after) is found in Kamal Khujandi's poetry in the form of verbatim quotation and literary critique.[157] In one *ghazal*,[158] Kamal reassures his Tabrizi audience that, for their sake, he will not express a desire to travel to Shiraz (and will not, therefore, seek Muzaffarid patronage). Elsewhere, Kamal engages in imitation of and response to Hafiz's *ghazal*s[159] and he also parodies H41:7:[160]

من که خوارزم گرفتم بسخنهای غریب   نبود میل عراق و هوس تبریزم

Having conquered Khvarazm with my extraordinary words
I had no interest for Iraq, and no desire for Tabriz.

Whatever the medium (war, trade, diplomacy, wandering Sufis, travelling musicians, itinerant poets), Hafiz's poetry exported his fame and that of his patrons far beyond Shiraz without him leaving the city for any significant amount of time. As discussed in the Introduction, Hafiz's popularity was consolidated in the Timurid period with the compilation, voracious copying and wide dissemination of his *dīvān*.[161] Timurid fascination with Hafiz is manifest in Bushaq Shirazi's humorous *javāb*s to over twenty of Hafiz's *ghazal*s[162] and in Jami's liberal quotation from and imitation of Hafiz in his own poetry.[163] Jami's poetry was popular across the full span of the Persianate world by the close of the fifteenth century.[164] Given his deep intertextual dialogue with Hafiz, perhaps Jami should be credited with solidifying his posthumous popularity. The power of imitation, evocation and invocation for the dissemination of a poet's works must not be underestimated.

Puns on musical modes with topographical names are also used by Hafiz to allude to his popularity outside of southern Iran; H259:7:

فکند زمزمهٔ عشق در حجاز و عراق   نوای بانگ غزلهای حافظ از شیراز

The loud melody of the *ghazal*s of Hafiz from Shiraz
Has cast the murmuring of love into Hijaz and Iraq.

The toponyms *Hijāz* and *'Irāq* are also the names of two Persian musical modes. Hafiz claims his verses have enlivened those modes with songs of love that have carried his poetry as far as the geographic regions of Iraq (here, Mesopotamia) and the Hijaz. *'Irāq* was a mode played at midnight and is, therefore, evocative of nocturnal poetic performance. Night time musical modes also evoke what Lewis has termed 'alba *ghazal*s', in which refrains such as *imshab* ('tonight') or allusions to the breaking of the nightly veil and the coming of dawn feature heavily.[165]

Just as his Muzaffarid patrons cause a stir in the region's political life, so Hafiz has penetrated the literary salons of rival dynasts with his poetry. Hafiz looks eastwards and claims that the beauties of Kashmir and Samarqand dance to his poetry; H440:8:

به شعر حافظ شیراز می رقصند و می نازند   سیه چشمان کشمیری و ترکان سمرقندی

To the poems of Hafiz of Shiraz they dance and flirt,
The black-eyed beauties of Kashmir, and the Turks of Samarqand.

The beauties alluded to here could be the ruler of Samarqand (i.e. Timur) and the king of Kashmir (a shah of the Shah Mir dynasty), the poets they patronize or the entertainers who perform at their courts. The allusion to Samarqand might also contain a subtle jibe at Kamal, whose roots were in Khujand and who claimed great popularity for his own poetry in Transoxiana. Another possible interpretation is that, rather than being about the geographical spread of the poetry, Hafiz is alluding to dancers brought to Shiraz from India and Central Asia or to local dancers who, because of their dark complexion or the whiteness of their skin, evoke Indian and Turkic beauties. The allusions in H440 are analogous to those to Bukhara and Samarqand in H3: the mentioning of exotic counterparts to Shiraz serves to raise the status of the local court by drawing comparisons (and hinting at possible connections) with courts in distant regions of the Persianate sphere, especially those already under Timurid control.

In Persian poetry, the 'parrot' (tūtī) is a standard metaphor for the poet and sugar candy for poetry:[166]

ببوستان سخن طوطیان شکرخای   ز شور شکر شعرم نوای عشق زنند

From the sugary insanity of my poetry the sugar-crunching parrots
Play the melody of passionate love in the fragrant garden of words.

Translated here as 'insanity', shūr denotes derangement caused by frantic love, but shūr also means 'salty'; this contrast intensifies the sweetness (i.e. eloquence) of Khvaju's words. The 'fragrant garden of words' (būstān-i sukhan) is perhaps another allusion to Sa'di's poem. Hafiz's most famed reference to India is commonly read as an allusion to the reception (actual or potential) of his poetry at the court of Sultan Ghiyath al-Din in Bengal;[167] H225:3:

زین قند پارسی که به بنگاله می رود   شکر شکن شوند همه طوطیان هند

They'll crack sugar, all the parrots of India
From this Persian candy that travels to Bengal!

Hafiz boasts his sweet poetry will be 'crunched' (imitated and/or responded to) by the poets of India, whether they be Iranian émigré or indigenous. As with the claim that his poetry has already reached Egypt, Anatolia and Central Asia, Hafiz's suggestion that his poetry will soon reach India should perhaps be interpreted as aspirational or visionary, rather than reflective of a reality he witnessed. It is believed that in the thirteenth century there was a trade network that linked Shiraz with India.[168] These mercantile corridors may have facilitated the migration of Hafiz's ghazals eastwards in the 1300s,[169] but there is literary chauvinism at play here too: the poetry of Fars is far superior to the Persian poetry produced in all other regions, including India.

Hafiz says his poetry is Persian rock candy ready for export. Sa'di went even further when he drew a parallel between himself and cane sugar, Egypt's chief luxury export:[170]

هر متاعی ز معدنی خیزد   شکر از مصر و سعدی از شیراز

Every valuable commodity springs from a single source:
Sugar from Egypt and Sa'di from Shiraz.

The assertion is that his poetry is as vital to the economic well-being of Shiraz as sugar is to Egypt.[171] It is, of course, impossible to quantify the value of Sa'di's writings to his home town in the way that one might assess the importance of sugar to the Mamluk economy but, as Sa'di's poetry spread, so did the fame of Salghurid Shiraz. This would have encouraged outsiders to travel to the city, a process that would have enhanced long-distance trade between Shiraz and other major Islamic cities, bringing economic benefit to Fars. Sa'di travelled far and wide in the Muslim world, including to Egypt (a fact which lends a layer of the real to his Egyptian sugar metaphors). Khvaju responds to Sa'di in this line:[172]

شکر از گفتهٔ خواجو بسوی مصر برند   گرچه کس قند بسوی شکرستان نبرد

They shall take sugar from Khvaju's words towards Egypt
Even though no one ever takes candy to the sugarcane field!

Kamal penned an even more direct response to Sa'di's saccharine *fakhr*, which ends with these two lines (the last hemistich of the poem being a *tazmīn* from Sa'di; see the italics in my translation):[173]

در شکر ریز فکر خویش کمال   قند هر یک سخن مکرّر ساز
تا بیاید به چاشنی گیری   شکر از مصر و سعدی از شیراز

Pour your thoughts into the sugar, Kamal
And refine the candy content in each word
So that, in order to sample it, will come
Sugar from Egypt and Sa'di from Shiraz.

The phrase translated here as 'refine the candy content in each word' is *qand-i har yik sukhan mukarrar sāz*. *Qand-i mukarrar* means 'refined sugar' and the word *mukarrar* alone means 'repeated', 'reiterated' (perhaps even 'reworked') so there is a sense in these lines that Kamal believes that his poetry constitutes a polished version of Sa'di's, recapitulated for a new audience. Equating a Shirazi poet's writings to exportable luxury goods does not always bear a western-orientated bias:[174]

شنیده ای که مقالات سعدی از شیراز   همیبرند بعالم چو نافۀ ختنی

Have you heard that they export Sa'di's writings from Shiraz
Throughout the world, as they do Khutanese musk?

Translated here as 'writings', *maqālāt* can mean 'treatises', 'discourses'; here it is possibly an allusion to Sa'di's prosimetrum, the *Gulistan*. The fact that Sa'di travelled widely serves to cloak his topographical allusions with verisimilitude; there is some evidence to suggest that his works were popular beyond the Iranian plateau during his lifetime.[175] Elsewhere, Sa'di depicts the spread of his poetry north-eastwards:[176]

شعرش چو آب در همه عالم چنان شده   کز پارس میرود بخراسان سفینه ای

His poetry has flowed like water all over the world to such an extent
That a 'ship' can now travel from Pars to Khurasan.

In mentioning Khurasan, Sa'di means to challenge the lyric giants of the formative period of Persian poetry. There is a pun here on the word *safīna*. Translated here as 'ship', *safīna* also means 'book of poetry', more specifically a notebook of oblong shape, which accounts for the idea of a barge. *Safīna* can also refer to an anthology or miscellany, so Sa'di might be alluding to his collected works.

Ghazals are texts that travel easily between multiple performance contexts, both within and across sites of production. In the case of poets such as Sa'di and Hafiz, their *ghazals* travelled to rival courts dotted across large swathes of the Persianate world. Praised by the poets of the thirteenth and fourteenth centuries, Shiraz subsequently transformed into a poetical image for later Indo-Persian poets in particular, who considered Shiraz 'the true home of classical Persian lyrics, the ideal city of the purest literary tradition'. As Schimmel argues, to state that one's heritage was Shirazi, 'was to claim spiritual and linguistic nobility'.[177]

Shiraz's rivals

Injuid and Muzaffarid poets claimed Shiraz was located at the heart of the 'seven climes' or 'seven regions' that made up the world, and that the ruler of Shiraz was not simply the king of Iran, but rather the king of the world (see Chapter 4). Between them, the Injuids and the Muzaffarids ruled Yazd, Kirman, Isfahan and (briefly) Tabriz, but the axis of their political and cultural power was Shiraz. It therefore follows that Shiraz's poets would engage in the articulation of long-held city-based animosities when presenting their town's inherent superiority over rival cultural nodes both near and far. Shirazi *fakhr* needs to be understood in light of the rivalry that existed among the successor city-states, in particular the jockeying for political and cultural pre-eminence between Shiraz and Baghdad.

Baghdad

Sa'di's direct contemporary, al-Qazwini, praises Baghdad's air, water, soil and breeze in terms as superlative as those used by Persian poets to laud Shiraz. For al-Qazwini, Baghdad is 'the Paradise Garden on earth'. The city's climate is more pleasant, its water sweeter, its soil more perfumed and its breeze gentler than those of any other city.[178] Writing in the first decades of the fourteenth century, Vassaf praises the Tigris for its sweetness,[179] equates the river with Khizr's water of life, says it shames the Nile, that silver-skinned Turks crowd its banks and that the surrounding meadows in springtime are so bedecked with flowers that they resemble the gardens of Paradise.[180]

Fourteenth-century Shiraz's rivalry with Baghdad stems in large part from the fact that it served as the Jalayirid capital. Shiraz-Baghdad rivalry is also found in the monarchic poetry of the day, most specifically in an amusing and somewhat vulgar poetic exchange between Shah Shuja' and Sultan Uvays.[181] Hamgar apostrophizes Baghdad and suggests a love connection between Iraq and Fars.[182] Elsewhere, Hamgar engages in nostalgic reminiscence of Baghdad's gardens, suggesting he may have spent time in the city.[183] Under the Jalayirids (in particular Hasan-i Buzurg [r. 1336–1356] and his influential wife, Dilshad Khatun [d. 1351]), Baghdad enjoyed a degree of material and cultural rejuvenation and the city became a thriving base for Persian poets. Salman served as panegyrist to the Jalayirids and wrote in praise of Baghdad in a fashion not dissimilar to that in which Hafiz lauded Shiraz. In one such poem, Salman declares Baghdad a 'perfumed tract of land' that humbles both Tabriz and Egypt.[184] Salman opens another *qasīda* by depicting a dawn drinking bout on the banks of the Tigris in which the royal wine and wine cup evoke ancient Iran.[185] In two *ghazals* with the rhyme scheme *–āz* (one of which shares its metre with Sa'di's celebrated *Shīrāzīya*), 'Attar Shirazi couples Baghdad and Fars by saying that, if he continues to shed floods of tears, the Tigris will change course and flow in Shiraz, or Shiraz will be transformed into a Tigris.[186]

In the prologue to his *Shiraznama*, Zarkub says that he composed his work in response to arguments made by certain individuals he encountered in Baghdad who claimed superiority for their city over Shiraz.[187] Hafiz mentions Shiraz alongside Baghdad in a number of poems in which he expresses a desire to leave his home town, the impetus for the departure being perhaps disaffection or professional disappointment;[188] H190:8:

خرم آن روز که حافظ ره بغداد کند   ره نبردیم به مقصود خود اندر شیراز

> We have not reached our desired goal in Shiraz
> Blessed be that day when Hafiz heads for Baghdad.

And similarly, in a panegyric *ghazal* for the Jalayirid ruler of Baghdad, Ahmad Bahadur b. Shaykh Uvays, Hafiz says in H472:8:[189]

حبّذا دجلهٔ بغداد و می ریحانی   از گل پارسی ام غنچهٔ عیشی نشکفت

> From my Persian rose, not one bud of pleasure bloomed
> How excellent are Baghdad's Tigris and the city's sweet-smelling wine!

Given the belief current among Hafiz's primary interlocutors that their city was superior to Baghdad, the poet's threat to desert his home town for its perceived inferior would have been provocative. Hafiz's hint that he is considering relocating to the Jalayirid court signals the degree of his dissatisfaction at home.[190] Such disaffection with Shiraz stands in stark contrast to the devotion to the city he expressed elsewhere. Allusions to Shiraz and/or Fars are also paired with allusions to Baghdad that place them on a more equal footing; U115:4:

ما جمری بغدادیم ما بکروی شیرازیم   زین پیش کسی بودیم و امروز در این کشور

> Before this, we were somebody, and now, in this land
> We are the base ones of Baghdad; the heavy drinkers of Shiraz.

'Ubayd is suggesting that his lot was better in his native Qazvin. The poet had first-hand experience of all three cities, so was in a position to compare them. In an expression of love-stricken grief, Hafiz confronts both Fars and Baghdad; H250:4:

دیده گو آب رخ دجلهٔ بغداد ببر   سینه گو شعلهٔ آتشکدهٔ فارس بکش

> Tell the breast: 'Extinguish the flames of the fire temple of Fars'!
> Tell the eyes: 'Shame the Tigris of Baghdad with your tears'!

As noted earlier, Hafiz's *ghazals* contain allusions to the musical mode *'Irāq*. These often appear in stylized asides to the *mutrib* or musician-singer; H138:8–9:[191]

که بدین راه بشد یار و ز ما یاد نکرد   مطربا پرده بگردان و بزن راه عراق
که شنید این ره دلسوز که فریاد نکرد   غزلیات عراقیست سرود حافظ

O *mutrib*, change the melody and play in *'Irāq*!
For that's where our beloved went, and made no mention of us
The songs composed by Hafiz are *'Irāqī ghazal*s
Whoever heard this heart-burning tone without wailing?

Here, Hafiz identifies his poetry with either 'Iraq-i 'Ajam (central and west Iran) or, perhaps 'Iraq-i 'Arab (Mesopotamia). Perhaps Hafiz is saying that, once set to music, his poems blend the styles of both Fars and Iraq; H460:11:

به شعر فارسی صوت عراقی   بساز ای مطرب خوشخوان خوشگو

Sing, o eloquent, sweet-voiced minstrel
An *Irāqī* song (*sawt*) with *Fārsī* lyrics (*shi'r*)!

Jahan has two intriguing *ghazal*s in which she employs the refrain, *Baghdādī pisar* ('Baghdadi boy', 'boy from Baghdad').[192] Given Jahan's familial ties to Baghdad and its Jalayirid overlords and the fact that her *dīvān* contains a *qasīda* in praise of Sultan Ahmad b. Shaykh Uvays who first ruled Baghdad from 1382 to 1393[193] and again from 1405 until he was killed in 1410, we can read her Baghdadi boy poems as subtle panegyrics composed for that same Jalayirid prince; J763:

آشفته و سرگشته ام در کوی بغدادی پسر   چون زلف سودایی شدم بر روی بغدادی پسر
آرد نسیمی صبحدم از سوی بغدادی پسر   بر روی خط و عارضش جان را کنم ایثار اگر
محراب هردو چشم من ابروی بغدادی پسر   روی تو چون برگ سمن قد تو چون سرو چمن
صد جامهٔ جان بر درم بر روی بغدادی پسر   بویی که آرد صبحدم از زلف یارم دم به دم
از خود ندارم من خبر از خوی بغدادی پسر   بدخویی دارم چو خور کز وی شود خیره بصر
کاشفته گردد همچو دل گیسوی بغدادی پسر   بر روی چون ماه چگل بر قامت رعنا مهل
دارد دلم بس آرزو بر روی بغدادی پسر   دارم همه کام جهان دانی چه خواهم این زمان

I am crazed like the hair that frames the face of that Baghdadi boy
I am disturbed and wandering in the lane of that Baghdadi boy
For the scent of his down and cheek I will offer up my soul,
If at dawn there wafts a sweet scent from that Baghdadi boy
Your face is like a jasmine petal; your frame like the garden's cypress
The prayer niche of my eyes is the eyebrow of that Baghdadi boy
The scent that wafts bit by bit from my beloved's locks at dawn
Makes me tear a hundred robes of my soul when I sense that Baghdadi boy
I have an ill-mannered, sun-like one who causes my eyes to be transfixed
I have lost all sense of self because of the nature of that Baghdadi boy
Do not dismiss that moon-like, Turkic face and that graceful form
For distressed they will become – like my heart – the locks of that Baghdadi boy
I possess all I could desire of this world, but you know what I want now
My heart so yearns for the face of that Baghdadi boy!

Jahan objectifies the *Baghdādī pisar* for his physical beauty and bewitching charms; in line four there is an oblique allusion to the story of Joseph. Jahan speaks as the lustful Zulaykha, although here it is the robe of her own soul that she tears a hundred times, rather than Joseph's shirt (see Chapter 6). The Baghdadi boy's jasmine-like complexion (line 3) and the comparison of his countenance (line 6) to a 'moon from Chigil' (a town in Turkistan famed for its beautiful youths), suggest the arresting beauty of a Turk. In J762, Jahan employs the terms *yaghmā* ('pillage') and *ghawghā* ('tumult') to describe the intensity of the beloved's effect on the lover. Both terms similarly suggest the love object is a violent, bawdy Turk. Given the Turk can stand for a wealthy, powerful beloved, perhaps Jahan's Baghdadi boy is a possible source of patronage. If we entertain this interpretation, the boy transforms into a suitable object for a princess's desires. The exoticism of the alien boy creates in these *ghazals* a kind of erotic topographic rivalry, a provocative amorous transgression, especially when compared to Hafiz's and 'Ubayd's express desire for a Shirazi beloved (whether a local Turk or a gypsy boy from Fars).

Yazd

Given the proximity of Yazd to Shiraz, the protracted, fierce military conflict between the Injuids and the Muzaffarids for control of the city and the fact that it was from Yazd that Mubariz al-Din launched his decisive attack on Shiraz in 1353, one might expect to find more allusions to Yazd in the *ghazals* of fourteenth-century Shiraz. 'Ubayd and Jahan do not allude to Yazd and Hafiz's *ghazals* contain just two obvious allusions to the city that date from the period (possibly up to two years)[194] Hafiz spent in Yazd in the service of Shah Yahya. In one allusion to Yazd, Hafiz expresses his eagerness to return to the 'Realm of Solomon', a typical allusion to Fars; H359:3:

رخت بربندم و به ملک سلیمان بروم   دلم از وحشت زندان سکندر بگرفت

My heart grew weary with the horrors of Alexander's Prison
I'll pack up and head for the Realm of Solomon.

Hafiz dubs Yazd 'The Prison of Alexander' (*zindān-i Iskandar*) and there stands a building in Yazd today that locals call by that name.[195] H359 appears to be a *javāb* to a similarly despondent *ghazal* by Khvaju in which the poet expresses the desire to leave Kirman in pursuit of his beloved.[196] The contrast between the negative light in which Hafiz portrays Yazd and the positivity associated with Shiraz in this poem is stark. The other overt allusion to Yazd found in Hafiz's *ghazals* is similarly negative; H12:11:

کای سر حق ناشناسان گوی چوگان شما　　　　ای صبا با ساکنان شهر یزد از ما بگو

O messenger breeze, tell the inhabitants of Yazd this on my behalf:
May the heads of the ungrateful be the balls to your polo sticks!

This *bayt* has been interpreted as a castigation of Yazd penned by Hafiz out of his frustration at the miserliness of the town's inhabitants.[197] In a *ghazal* that was possibly written in Yazd, Hafiz expresses his 'alienation' (*gharībī*) and his 'nostalgic longing' (*ghurbat*) for Shiraz; H337:1–2:

چرا نه خاک سر کوی یار خود باشم　　　　چرا نه در پی عزم دیار خود باشم

به شهر خود روم و شهریار خود باشم　　　　غم غریبی و غربت چو بر نمی تابم

Why should I not seek to set out for my own home town?
Why should I not be the dust at the end of my beloved's lane?
When I cannot bear the sorrow of alienation and nostalgic longing
I should return to my own city and become my own king!

Hafiz is said eventually to have escaped Yazd for Shiraz in the company of the Muzaffarid vizier, Jalal al-Din Turanshah.[198]

Isfahan

Hafiz alludes to the city of Isfahan in at least three *ghazal*s and suggests that he had personal experience of the city. One might expect to find more allusions to Isfahan in the *ghazal*s composed in Shiraz during this period, given the relative geographical proximity of Isfahan and the fact that the city was, like Yazd, under the control of the Muzaffarids for many years and had been controlled for a time by the Injuids before them. It is possible that the *ghazal*s by Hafiz that bear allusions to Isfahan, were composed there. Hafiz's allusions to Isfahan, unlike his allusions to Yazd, are positive. Perhaps Hafiz was influenced by the rich body of poems in praise of paradisiacal Isfahan, its life-giving river and sumptuous gardens produced in the centuries before him.[199] Shah Shuja' spent a period of time in Isfahan after he was temporarily ousted from Shiraz by his rival brother, Shah Mahmud, so these poems may date from that interlude period.

Hafiz pines for two of Isfahan's most celebrated locales: the city's river (here called Zinda-rud, rather than the now conventional Zayanda-rud) and the adjacent Bagh-i Karan,[200] a large garden on the city's periphery (originally planned out by the Saljuq ruler, Malikshah [r. 1072–1092]); H103:5:

زنده رود باغ کاران یاد باد　　　　گرچه صد رود است در چشمم مدام

Even though a hundred rivers flow constantly from my eyes,
Long live the memory of the Zinda-rud and the Bagh-i Karan!

Writing during the reign of Malikshah, al-Mafarrukhi says the Bagh-i Karan boasts two pavilions: one looking over the river, the other towards the great square.[201] As late as the mid-fourteenth century, the Bagh-i Karan served as a popular locus for *majālis*;[202] it is possible that Shah Shuja' himself drank wine on the banks of the Zinda-rud.[203] Hafiz may have employed these allusions to Isfahan to recall Shah Shuja''s victory over Shah Mahmud and his subsequent triumphal return to Shiraz.[204] The *radīf* fulfils a nostalgic function; by repeating *yād bād* ['long live the memory of!'], the poet instructs his audience to memorialize.

In another *ghazal*, Hafiz depicts Isfahan as the setting for a raucous *majlis*; H460:3:

خرد در زنده رود انداز و می نوش   به گلبانگ جوانان عراقی

Cast reason into the Zinda-rud and drink wine
To the excited cries of Iraqi youths!

Hafiz's 'Iraqi youths' (beautiful young men from either Persian or Arab Iraq or, specifically, from Isfahan)[205] evoke Jahan's erotic exuberance for her Baghdadi boy. Junayd, too, depicts a spring *majlis* on the banks of the Zayanda-rud with music played on the Iraqi *nay* and the 'lute' (*rūd*, a word that also means 'river').[206] Allusions to Isfahan and to its Iraqi youths can also be read musically, given that *Isfahān* and *'Irāq* are musical modes.[207] In a *qasīda* penned in praise of Shah Shaykh Abu Ishaq, Hafiz alludes to the Injuids' control over the city of Isfahan[208] and their ambition to conquer the entirety of 'Iraq-i 'Ajam through punning on the same musical modes:[209]

نوای مجلس مارا چو بر کشد مطرب   گهی عراق زند و گاهی اصفهان گیرد

When the musician draws out the melody of our *majlis*
At times he strikes *'Irāq*, at others he takes *Isfahān*.

Kamal Khujandi makes similar use of the dual meaning of these toponyms to suggest the superiority of his Tabrizi poetry over that of 'Iraq-i 'Ajam, while also alluding to its performance to musical accompaniment:[210]

شوند اهل سپاهان غلام طبع کمال   گر این دو بیت سرایند مطربان به عراق

The people of Isfahan will become slaves to Kamal's poetic talent,
If these two lines were sung by the minstrels in *'Irāq*!

Elsewhere, Kamal mentions the city of Isfahan when comparing his literary genius to that of the sometime panegyrist to the Salghurids, Kamal Isfahani. Kamal of Khujand boasts he is unparalleled in composing *ghazal*s today just as Kamal of Isfahan was unmatched as a writer of *qasīda*s in his day; there being no more than a whisker between them.[211] The Tabriz-based poet also claims to have surpassed the eloquence of his celebrated namesake.[212] In a more corporeal version of the above conceit, Jalal claims to be the return of Kamal Isfahani.[213]

Asserting the superiority (or exceptionalism) of one's metropolis over others is common to much Persianate city poetry.[214] A straightforward, rather blunt comparison between Isfahan and Shiraz is made by Hafiz; H419:10:

اگرچه زنده رود آب حیات است   ولی شیراز ما از اصفهان به

Even though the Zinda-rud is the Water of Life
Our Shiraz is simply better than Isfahan!

There is possibly a pun in this line on *bih* to mean not only 'better', but also 'quince' – the most prized of Isfahan's fruits.[215] Hafiz's praise for Isfahan's river echoes his acclaim of Shiraz's Ruknabad canal. The Zinda-rud (whose name translates as 'live river') provides, as al-Qazwini noted, the lifeblood for the city and its surrounding gardens, orchards and agricultural lands.[216] Declaring Isfahan's river to be the *āb-i hayāt* is high praise, although, even with such adulation, Isfahan cannot outdo Shiraz.

Hafiz's insistence on Shiraz's superiority over Isfahan may also carry a non-geopolitical dimension: in the fourteenth century, Shiraz surpassed Isfahan in the quality of its cultural production, both poetic and artistic (in particular as a centre for manuscript illustration and fine calligraphy).[217]

Qazvin

Unsurprisingly, allusions to Qazvin are found in the poetry of 'Ubayd, who was originally from Zakan, a small town fifteen kilometres northwest of Qazvin. 'Ubayd mentions Qazvin overtly in two *rubāʿī*s, ranking his adoptive city above his home town:[218]

گر یک عالم ز من بنفرین آید   حاشا که ز چون منی کنون این آید

شیراز رها کند به قزوین آید   بر هشت بهشت دوزخی بگزیند

Even if am cursed by a whole world
Heaven forbid someone like me would do this
He chooses Hell over Paradise
Who leaves Shiraz and comes to Qazvin

'Ubayd appears to allude to his family situation when he describes the only circumstances under which he would consider returning to Qazvin:[219]

از خانه بدر آمده ام یک چندم   امروز ز من دور شده فرزندم

در آرزوی خانه و هم فرزندم   ور باز به قزوین سفر افتاد مرا

> Today my child is distant from me
> It has been some time since I left my home
> If at some point I were to travel back to Qazvin
> It would be in longing for my home and my son.

'Ubayd was an itinerant, some might argue opportunistic, poet. Throughout his career he remained an outsider and, as such, his position would have been precarious, whether at Shiraz or Baghdad. We also encounter disaffection with Qazvin in 'Ubayd's humorous anecdotes in which he shames its men for their innate stupidity.[220] 'Ubayd also pokes fun at his hapless compatriots for their penchant for pederasty, the most characteristic element in modern jokes about adult males from Qazvin.[221] 'Ubayd's denigration of Qazvin and its population was a mechanism he employed to assert his bond with Shiraz and his loyalty to the local ruling family.

Criticizing Shiraz

One aspect of the poetry studied here that highlights its temporal and spatial specificity is the criticism of Shiraz it contains and the associated voicing of complaint by the poets.[222] Frustration with patrons and the inconsistent support they provided could lead poets to turn on the city they had once praised. As noted above, Hafiz and 'Ubayd both threatened to leave Shiraz to pursue their poetic careers elsewhere (Hafiz left only briefly, whereas 'Ubayd was absent for a decade or so). Critiques of Shiraz and its inhabitants bear witness to the fact that poets in the Injuid and Muzaffarid periods used lyric poetry to comment on the reality of the world that surrounded them.

For reasons which remain unclear, Hafiz temporarily fell out of favour with Shah Shuja'. Although Hafiz subsequently re-entered the service of Shah Shuja' and went on to write poetry for the ruler's successors, it is possible that the poet never fully regained his standing at the Muzaffarid court. In H190, Hafiz suggests that he is contemplating leaving Shiraz for Baghdad, a statement Sudi Busnavi interprets as a desire (albeit unfulfilled) to join Salman.[223] This line by Sa'di bears a striking similarity to that of Hafiz:[224]

وقت آنست که پرسی خبر از بغدادم   دلم از صحبت شیراز بکلی بگرفت

I am utterly disheartened by my intimate association with Shiraz;
It is time for you to ask news of me from Baghdad.

The term *suhbat* ('intimate association', 'companionship', 'amorous intercourse')
adds a quasi-sexual energy to the intense love of the poet for his city.

Hafiz expresses a desire to leave Shiraz for another court in a poem that
may have been composed during the reign of Mubariz al-Din, when the city's
poets are believed to have witnessed a tangible downturn in their fortunes
(alluded to by Hafiz through reference to the closing of Shiraz's wine taverns);
H343:6–7:

با این لسان عذب که خامش چو سوسنم   حیف است بلبلی چو من اکنون در این قفس

کو همرهی که خیمه از این خاک برکنم   آب و هوای فارس عجب سفله پرور است

It's a shame that a nightingale like me should now be in this cage,
With this sweet tongue of mine silent like that of a lily
The climate of Fars is exceedingly good at nurturing rabble;
Where is my fellow traveller, so I can tear my tent from this land?

The straitened circumstances faced by producers of secular culture may
have included censorship, a reduction in patronage possibilities and a
restriction on performance venues.[225] Mubariz al-Din, who was dubbed
muhtasib by Hafiz, was a stern, pious, moralistic figure.[226] The criticism of
Shiraz that Hafiz expresses in H343:7 is damning. This stridently negative
depiction of Fars contrasts the poet's laudatory statements in praise of
the same found elsewhere in his poetry. We can only speculate on what
the context for so negative a portrayal of Shiraz could have been. Given
the anti-Shiraz sentiment it displays, it is possible that this poem was only
recorded when Hafiz's *dīvān* was compiled after his death. The poem may
have been composed outside Shiraz for a rival local ruler or perhaps after
the reign of Mubariz al-Din in a retrospective mode, looking back from the
reign of his poet-nurturing son (and thereby flattering Shah Shuja'). It is
also possible that the poem was composed during the reign of Mubariz
al-Din and only performed later[227] or that through these superficially anti-
Shiraz poems, Hafiz intended a provocation: by feigning disaffection with
the city and its inhabitants perhaps he hoped to receive added attention
(and augmented financial incentives) from his patrons for opting to remain
in Shiraz. In a *ghazal* that Lescot dates to Hafiz's period of 'disgrace',[228] we
read; H374:8:

بیا حافظ که تا خود را به ملکی دیگر اندازیم   سخندانی و خوشخوانی نمی ورزند در شیراز

They do not cultivate eloquence and fine singing in Shiraz;
Come, Hafiz! Let's cast ourselves into another land!

Hafiz appears to complain that his abundant literary talents are not sufficiently appreciated in his home town, compelling him to leave. Even Shiraz can fall from grace if it fails to provide a nurturing environment for skilled wordsmiths of Hafiz's calibre. The city's cultural allure is continuously negotiated and liable to fluctuation.

    Hafiz speaks in other poems of a desire to depart. Although he does not make explicit mention of Shiraz, references to 'this town' (*īn shahr*) and 'this land' (*īn diyār*), given that we know that he barely left Shiraz, function as allusions to the city and Fars respectively; H291:1:

بیرون کشید باید از این ورطه رخت خویش   ما آزموده ایم در این شهر بخت خویش

We have tested our fortune in this city
We must now extract ourselves from this perilous predicament.

The key word in the *radīf* here, *khīsh* ('self', 'oneself'), underlines Hafiz's focus on his own professional plight. As he does not mention Shiraz or Fars by name, Hafiz introduces an element of ambiguity, thereby opening a space in which he can criticize without confronting the censure of his fellow-townsmen. One of the poet's most celebrated laments bemoans the situation for poets in his day; H169:5:

مهربانی کی سرآمد، شهریاران را چه شد   شهر یاران بود و خاک مهربانان این دیار

This place was the city of friends and the land of the kind;
When did kindness cease to exist? What has happened to the kings?

Sudi understands *īn diyār* here as an allusion to Fars.[229] The poet is perhaps lamenting the overthrow and execution of his first royal patron, Shah Shaykh Abu Ishaq or Shah Shuja's brief absence from Shiraz.[230] There is a pun: *shahr-i yārān* in the first hemistich means 'the city of friends' and *shahriyārān* in the second means 'kings'. The linking of *shahr*, *yārān* and *shahriyārān* forges a connection in the listener's mind between the city, loyal friends and generous kings (who, it is suggested, no longer exist – at least not in Fars). Of Hafiz's contemporaries, it was Jahan, an Injuid princess, who perhaps had the most cause to bemoan her plight in the wake of Muzaffarid ascendancy; J1103:6:

ای دل بیا بیا که به شهری دگر رویم   چون در دیار خویش نداریم رونقی

Since I have no splendour in my own land
O heart, come, come! Let's leave for another town.

In a quatrain,[231] Jahan laments being distant from her home town, suggesting either that she was not born in Shiraz or that the city has changed such that she no longer recognizes it as her own:

از صحبت یار خویش مهجور شود   بیچاره کسی که از وطن دور شود

بی برگ و جگرخسته و رنجور شود   تنها و به دست دشمنان گشته اسیر

Woe is she who is far from her homeland
She who is separated from her beloved
She who is alone, captive in her enemies' hands
With no money, a weary heart, and sore afflicted!

The question of *in situ* poetry versus poetry composed outside Shiraz, but with a Shirazi audience in mind, is an intriguing one, in particular in relation to city panegyrics. There exist a number of anti-Shiraz statements in 'Ubayd's *ghazals*, attacks on the city that read as neither abstract nor metaphorical and which appear to relate to actual events as seen from the poet's perspective. The disgruntled tone of the following lines lends weight to the hypothesis that 'Ubayd composed them when away from Shiraz; U31:9–11:

در وی به هیچ نوع طرب را مجال نیست   از غم چنان پر است دل ما که بعد از این

شیراز جای مردم صاحب کمال نیست   جانم فدای خاطر صاحب دلی که گفت

زین بیش ای عبید مرا احتمال نیست   درویشی و غریبی و زحمت ز حد گذشت

My heart is so full of grief that, after this
There is no room therein for any kind of ecstasy.
May my life be a sacrifice to the wise man who said:
'Shiraz is not the abode of erudite men'!
Poverty, alienation and torment have exceeded all bounds
More than this, 'Ubayd, I cannot bear.

Here 'Ubayd appears to dialogue with H279:4, in which Hafiz labels Shiraz's inhabitants *sāhib-kamāl*: 'endowed with perfections', 'erudite'. 'Ubayd distorts Hafiz's positive assessment of his fellow Shirazis, recasting it in negative terms, perhaps to poke fun at (what he considers) misplaced hyperbole. Indeed, the statement 'Ubayd claims is a quotation in his *ghazal*, 'Shiraz is not the abode of erudite men', which he attributes to that 'wise, enlightened man' (*sāhib-dil*), is the poet's own; 'Ubayd is engaging in self-reflexive praise, not praise of Hafiz, whose statement, in any case, he has misrepresented. There is an implicit opposition between *sāhib-*

kamāl and *sāhib-dil* here; book-learnt knowledge as opposed to mystical enlightenment. Whatever the circumstances of the composition of 'Ubayd's poem (given that Hafiz is the younger poet, it is possible he penned his poem in response to 'Ubayd's), 'Ubayd is clearly expressing dissatisfaction with his adoptive city and its populace. In a *rubāʿī*,[232] 'Ubayd similarly laments the negative changes that have come about in Shiraz in his lifetime:

وان شاهدکان چابک بزم افروز   کو عشرت شیراز و می اندہ سوز

دوزخ باشد چنان کہ شیراز امروز   فردا بہ بہشت ار می و شادی نبود

> Where is the merriment of Shiraz and the grief-burning wine?
> And where are those nimble, feast-illuminating young beauties?
> Tomorrow, if there was no longer any wine and rejoicing in Heaven
> It would become a hell, just like Shiraz is today!

The biting tone of this anti-Shiraz quatrain suggests that it was composed for an audience that shared the poet's reading of Shiraz's situation immediately following the fall of the Injuids. The poet expresses similar sentiments in this line; U65:2:

کز ہیچ جاش ہیچ نشانی نمی رسد   زین ملک امن و راحت و شادی چنان برفت

> From this realm security, ease, and joy have so departed
> That of their marks not even a single trace remains!

'Ubayd says that his only reason to stay in Shiraz is the arresting allure of his beloved (that is, his patron); U3:5:

نتوان داشت در این شہر بہ زنجیر مرا   گر نہ زنجیر سر زلف تو باشد یک دم

> If the chains of your forelocks for one moment did not exist
> You could not keep me in this town, even with chains.

In more than one poem, 'Ubayd rails against this 'city of strangers' (*shahr-i kasan*; a riff on Hafiz's lost 'city of friends'?);[233] U109:1–3:

غریب شہر کسان وز دیار خود محروم   منم اسیر و پریشان ز یار خود محروم

نشستہ در غم و از غمگسار خود محروم   بہ درد و رنج فرو ماندہ وز دوا نومید

ز قوم و کشور و ایل و تبار خود محروم   گزیدہ صحبت بیگانگان و نااہلان

> I am captive and bewildered, deprived of my beloved
> An alien in a city of strangers, deprived of my homeland
> Fatigued by pain and suffering with no hope of a remedy
> Stalled by grief and deprived of my dispeller of cares

Having chosen the fellowship of strangers and the unsuitable
Deprived of my people, my land, my clan, and kindred.

Elsewhere, 'Ubayd laments being far from his own land,[234] Qazvin, a city that he feels both nostalgic towards and estranged from. As noted previously, 'Ubayd ridiculed his fellow Qazvinis in his prose works to ingratiate himself with his new Shiraz-based patrons and audience.[235] 'Ubayd rails against his comprehensive alienation from the people of every region and every town; U71:2:

در هیچ شهر ما را کس آشنا نباشد   در هیچ ملک با ما کس دوستی نورزد

No one is a friend to me in any realm;
I have no close acquaintances in any city.

Being *gharīb* – an alien in a foreign land – is an emotional state we also encounter in some earlier Persian poetry.[236] In 'Ubayd's poems in praise of Shah Shaykh Abu Ishaq, the poet's sense of alienation and his need to belong are mitigated by the king's generosity. In at least one poem 'Ubayd labels himself as an outsider only to underscore the fact that his royal patron is *gharīb-navāz*: 'hospitable, welcoming, and nurturing towards outsiders'.[237]

Conclusion

Praise for a city in premodern Persian poetry is praise for its ruler, his family, his ministers and all those who patronize the arts. By praising the city, the poet contributed to the ruler's popularity and ingratiated him/herself with ordinary Shirazis. As the poet's verses began to circulate in private *majālis* and other contexts not directly linked to the court, they filtered down to non-elite spaces such as the tavern and the bazaar, which meant that the poet's popularity consequently grew among the common folk. In turn, his/her status at court would have grown as he/she became seen as an important propagandistic ally. In turn, the poet would have received greater financial reward and added prestige in recognition of their poetry's currency among the ruler's subjects.

    Poems distributed beyond Fars spread the fame of the poet as well as that of the patron. It was in large part through its poetry that Shiraz came to be revered as a cultural hub, not only by those who lived in other parts of Iran and Iraq governed by rival post-Mongol successor dynasties, but also far beyond into vast regions where Persianate culture was firmly established. Boosting Shiraz's popularity outside of Fars would benefit the ruler and his administration by promoting the image of a strong, benevolent ruler and a culturally and economically productive realm. Such literary propaganda would also benefit the city as other poets, artisans and scholars would be attracted to settle there in the hope of securing similarly generous patronage. As noted above, it was not just poets who produced works in praise of fourteenth-century Shiraz: belles-lettristic works lauding the city, its inhabitants and its unique environs were also written. It therefore seems that the praise for Shiraz expressed in Injuid and Muzaffarid lyric poetry is emblematic of a vogue for local city panegyrics, one that, as demonstrated here, can trace its origins at least as far back as the mid-thirteenth century.

From the political context of the city we now zoom in on the social context of the *majlis-i sharāb*, the primary forum for poetry activities in the premodern Iranian and broader Persianate world. A (chiefly) homosocial space, the *majlis-i sharāb* was also the space within which amusements normally seen today as either in contravention of Islamic law or, at the very least, of dubious morality (drinking wine and instrumental music) were engaged in. Here, poets petitioned their patrons and both entertained and edified their audiences. The study of the *majlis-i sharāb* presented in Chapter 2 helps us understand better how the *ghazal*s of fourteenth-century Shiraz functioned *in situ* and what were the social conditions of their production, performance and reception, with the ultimate aim being to read them better in the present.

2

Evocations of Performance

Poetry not only shapes the social contexts and settings within which it is performed, it is also shaped by them and thus reflects their contemporary reality.[1] Poetic performance and reception were at the heart of cultural and social life in the premodern Iranian world. Poetry was understood as a courtly practice and was engaged with in the *majlis* (pl. *majālis*; rowdy bacchanal or more formal wine symposium), the primary context for privileged cultural life (as it had been for earlier Arabic poetry).[2] The size of these gatherings varied greatly and the term *majlis* is used in lyric poetry and other texts to denote a wide spectrum of gatherings diverse in terms of the number of participants, degree of formality and level of intimacy. This speech event involved the poet (or other verbal artist such as a singer-musician or reciter), the poem, the audience (the patron and his courtiers) and the setting.[3] Textual evidence is mustered in this chapter to argue for the recognition of the connection between the world of the lyric poem and the physical world of the performance space; worlds that work in tandem in the *ghazal*, the Persian 'performance poem' *par excellence*.[4] Texts emerge in contexts and, as de Bruijn has argued, the *ghazal* has been more impregnated by the atmosphere of the wine bout than any other type of Persian poetry and all elements of the form's 'thematical complex' are, he says, 'in one way or another related to this real background, whether they are meant in a profane or in a religious sense'.[5] In the context-sensitive reading presented here, the Persian *ghazal* is studied both as a representation of the *majlis* and an active agent in its own right that served to mould the performance act.

Drawing on Bauman's understanding of performance as 'situated within and rendered meaningful with reference to relevant contexts',[6] here the Persian *ghazal* is understood as a dynamic form that shaped the ceremonial and/or convivial space within which it was enjoyed. Accordingly, I consider Persian lyric poetry to be evocative of those social settings. The *ghazals* of fourteenth-century Shiraz are not merely tropological, figurative or clichéd. When we read them with care, we see that, for contemporary audiences, these texts communicated an image of the ideal performance and, through that communication, shaped their performance and reception settings. The present study sees context as an organic, ever-evolving space that is further complicated by variation in the constitution and size of the audience, the time of day and/or year of the performance and the staging of the setting with props and accoutrements. Here, context is understood as a process, rather than a static phenomenon.[7]

This chapter is informed by the work of Lewis who sees the *ghazal* as a 'textual representation of a performance occurring in a specific context drawing on a nexus of genres and expectations, themselves in flux'.[8] A given poem was not only performed within the *majlis* (an event Lewis likens to a theatrical performance), it was also shaped semiotically in that setting; it was through the response of the live audience to the poet, performers, attendants and other extra-textual elements that the meaning of the text was completed.[9] Audience response is a key component in the wholeness of any poem: the act of speaking is directed to the audience and must be ratified by it.[10] In this sense, as Duranti has argued, the audience shares co-authorship of the text.[11]

The court poets of Shiraz composed for sophisticated, appreciative interlocutors, a good number of whom were amateur versifiers whose refined literary interests and critical judgment would have encouraged, even demanded, a high standard of poetic production. Audience interpretation is not a passive activity, but rather a way in which listeners make sense of what they have heard through linking the text to a world they can best relate to (accordingly, as audiences shift, so do their interpretative and contextual referents).[12] Viewing poetry as an activity or process of communication,[13] we come to appreciate the importance to the poem's efficacy of the social interaction between performer and audience within the confines of the courtly literary salon. As Bauman has noted, it is through performance that 'the performer elicits the participative attention and energy' of the audience.[14]

The post-Mongol poet–audience relationship most likely shared much with that of the Abbasid period in which the audience would both laud and critique the poet who, in turn, would assume the audience's knowledge of themes and motifs, whilst testing their familiarity with the canon.[15] In her reading of the Arabic *qasīda*, Gruendler asserts that the contemporary success of a poem in part depended on the cooperation, attention and discernment of its hearers.[16] Premodern Persian poets reciting aloud before a live audience could not be indifferent to their listeners' reactions.[17]

Persian *ghazal*s when read in tandem with other forms of lyric poetry, histories and belles-lettristic texts provide an invaluable mine of information about the physical setting and social context of poetic performance. When using lyric poetry to uncover clues regarding its performance, scholars have mostly looked to the panegyric *qasīda*,[18] while the *ghazal* has been considered either too formulaic or else insufficiently time- and/or place- specific to be a source of productive information on the matter. However, Persian *ghazal*s can illuminate the nature of both the immediate settings and the broader social contexts within which they were performed.

The description of wine symposia is a major, often dominant, component of a given *ghazal*, which serves as a forum for the presentation of intrinsic components of the ideal party as aspired to by the patron-host and as experienced by the poet's audience as a whole. In this sense, the *ghazal* is itself an ideal poetic space. Because of its tendency towards abstraction, its versatility and its use for the celebration of both earthly and heavenly desire, the *ghazal* became the go-to vehicle for the reflection of the ideal *per se*. Though the royal *majlis-i sharāb* dominates, it does not necessarily follow that all *ghazal*s composed in this period were produced exclusively for courtly performance. Even while creating an urban poetry for non-royal settings within the private salons of, say, aristocrats, literati or Sufi leaders, poets persisted in using well-established, court-focused imagery and language. Some of the description of wine parties found in the poetry should be read as aspirational, in that it encourages the emulation of a courtly model.

The social context for lyric poetic performance: The *majlis*

The Arabic term *majlis* is a noun of place derived from the verb *jalasa* ('to sit') and it denotes nearly every convivial social meeting. The *majlis* can be an assembly hosted by a person of high socio-economic status (a caliph,[19] king,[20] vizier[21] or Sufi *pīr*)[22] who provides patronage to those whose verses are recited and discussed within that forum (a kind of literary 'soirée').[23] *Majālis* can be more sober gatherings convened by prominent administrative officials where scholarly questions of law, jurisprudence or doctrine are debated[24] and the guests adhere to a strict etiquette[25] or events hosted by popular preachers.[26] The term *majlis* can also be used to denote a less-formal symposium where guests engage in wine-drinking and feasting and are entertained by poets, singers, musicians and other performers.[27] These convivial gatherings are variously referred to in premodern Persian texts as *majlis-i sharāb* ('wine party'), *majlis-i uns* ('convivial party'), *majlis-i bazm* ('feasting party'), *majlis-i 'ishrat* ('pleasure party'), *nashāt-i sharāb* ('wine bout'), *'aysh u nūsh* ('merriment and drinking'), *mahfil, mihmānī* or *anjuman* ('gathering', 'party' or 'assembly').

The convivial *majlis* served as the primary forum for the performance and discussion of poetry in the Iranian and broader Islamic world throughout the premodern period.[28] In the Persianate sphere, as in many regions in the pre-modern period, convivial life was largely concentrated at court[29] and it was within the framework of the royal *majlis* that power, wealth, privileged culture and poetic imagination coalesced. The Injuid and Muzaffarid rulers of Shiraz stood at the centre of social life in south-central Iran and it was via the *majlis*, the pivot of court social life, that these patrons sought to broadcast their kingly charisma far and wide via poetry. The public display of princely magnificence channelled through literary propaganda was common in much of the late medieval world.[30]

Wine symposia formed a regular part of the daily or weekly routine of many early Muslim rulers and other members of the urban elite.[31] Many caliphs and kings surrounded themselves with small bands of 'boon companions' (sing *nadīm*) with whom they engaged in entertainment sessions.[32] The *nadīm*s, who were handpicked and enjoyed a privileged status at court, often included the patron's favourite poets. Participants' positions at the *majlis*, often dictated by the patron-host, were allotted in a hierarchical arrangement according to social rank and in accordance with refined etiquette. Some participants might be seated,[33] while others stood throughout.[34] There are hints in the poetry studied here as to the composition of contemporary audiences. Jahan, for example, frequently addresses her audience as 'Muslims'[35] and 'friends'[36] or 'intimate companions'.[37] In a handful of poems, she appears to address a mixed audience of males and females.[38]

Rulers offered sumptuous rewards to their entertainers who praised them in song and verse, although excessive praise was generally looked upon unfavourably.[39] The size of the reward granted and the manner in which it was bestowed constituted a public demonstration of generosity and formed an important theatrical element of the *majlis*.[40] Through liberality and largesse, the patron accrued prestige, demonstrated his/her discernment and manifested devotion to poetry and other prestigious manifestations of culture.[41] Royal *majālis* – in particular those of a more public nature held at the great feasts in the Perso-Islamic calendar (the spring equinox celebration, Nawruz; the autumnal grape harvest festival, Mihragan; and 'Id-i Fitr, the feast that marks the end of Ramadan) – were prime occasions for the magnificent display of kingly generosity aimed to impress.[42]

Many Injuids, Muzaffarids and Jalayirids were trained in the composition of Persian and Arabic verse,[43] a fact that adds texture to their appreciation of professional poets' talents.[44] As Toorawa reminds us, lavish patrons were not only to be found among royalty, as viziers, governors and military leaders were financially and politically able to rival royals in their provision of patronage.[45] This patronage dimension of the *majlis* is frequently alluded to,[46] and it is common for a *ghazal* to contain the poet's solicitation for a monetary reward or other tangible manifestation of generosity. Such solicitations to the patron often appear at the end of the *ghazal* in combination with the *takhallus*;[47] the request for financial reward often coupled with a lamentation on the part of the poet about their supposedly penniless, beggar-like status.[48]

High-status patrons bestowed rewards with much pomp and ceremony[49] and made a spectacle of their munificence by distributing gold,[50] showering the poet with precious coins[51] or stuffing the poet's mouth with gems and coins.[52] Poets who failed to flatter or entertain sufficiently risked forfeiting their financial rewards and, in more extreme cases, their hard-won position. For aspiring poets, admission to the privileged court circle was essential for them to demonstrate their skill and solicit (and secure) potentially lucrative patronage. In the case of professional poets such as Hafiz and 'Ubayd, we can be confident that they strove, through their poetry, to please their patrons and that this was the central motivation behind its composition. Through praise poetry, skilled poets presented an aspirational ideal of kingship to the ruler and his court, one to be modelled: poets were, in some sense, moral teachers to the king and his immediate entourage, not sycophants.[53]

The *majlis* setting (often referred to as the *bazm-gāh* ['place of feasting'])[54] could be located indoors or outdoors.[55] Such royal gatherings could be held in the audience halls of urban palaces, in kiosks constructed specifically for the staging of such events, in gardens or in the open countryside. During the more temperate months, parties were often held in meadows, beside riverbanks or in hunting lodges.[56] The materiality of the *majlis* has yet to be fully explored, but verse and prose texts suggest that spaces in which convivial gatherings were staged were bedecked with movable soft furnishings and other decorative props.[57] The beloved himself (whether ruler-patron, *sāqī* or *ghulām*) also augments the beauty of the occasion: he is *majlis-ārā* ('assembly-adorning').[58] The variability in terms of furnishings meant that no one *majlis* was like any other; the perfect *majlis* was an evolving concept, never static and, consequently, unachievable. The *bazm-gāh* could be strewn with gems and coins,[59] laden with sweetmeats, carpeted with flowers,[60] scented with scattered rose petals[61] and perfumed with fragrant substances such as musk and aloes wood[62] (which were also burnt as incense on hot coals or in censers).[63] Musk and ambergris, because of their high cost and scarcity, enjoyed a particular association with Islamic royalty.[64]

Audience chambers and pavilions were occasionally constructed from sweet-scented materials, adding another olfactory dimension to an already fragrant setting.[65] Ilkhanid palaces were decorated with the finest and most expensive materials available;[66] it is likely that the Injuids and Muzaffarids went some way to emulate this approach in the construction of their own royal buildings. Contemporary poets certainly considered the royal palace a worthy subject for a *qasīda*.[67]

The *majlis* was an aesthetic event; a multi-sensorial experience in which each participant's sight, hearing, smell, taste and touch were bombarded, enticed and aroused. The attendants, performers and guests were expected to wear fine robes,[68] perfume their hair, body and clothes with sweet-smelling fragrances[69] and behave in a refined manner.[70] There was no one experience of any one *majlis* as each participant interacted with the space and the activities engaged therein in a distinct manner dependent upon his/her social status and the role he/she played within the gathering.

Terminology used to denote the wine and poetry party

Various qualifiers are added by poets to the term *majlis* to introduce nuance to the description of the gathering. These qualifiers hint at the specific nature of the event depicted. For example, by adding *uns* ('companionship', 'fellowship') a more intimate gathering is suggested;[71] J1162:4:

تو شمع مجلس انسی به عنبر آگنده   ز وصل خویش شبستان ما معطر کن

> You are the candle of the *majlis-i uns*, packed with ambergris;
> Perfume our night chamber through union with you!

Similarly, the term *suhbat* – which conveys a range of meanings from 'company' through 'intercourse' and 'intimate association' to 'coitus' – suggests a less-formal gathering with only a handful of participants, perhaps simply the poet, the patron, a musician and a single attendant: in Jahan's *majlis*, there is no room for *suhbat* with strangers.[72] Similarly, Hafiz speaks of the 'intimate company of true friends',[73] locates the setting for *suhbat* within the garden at springtime,[74] alludes to night-time *suhbat*[75] and combines *suhbat* with *bazm* (see below).[76] Like Jahan, 'Ubayd laments his *suhbat* with unknowns[77] and yearns for the company of the winebibbers.[78] The word *khalvat* ('seclusion', 'privacy', 'private apartment') also suggests a restricted affair on a small scale.[79]

A Persian equivalent for *majlis* is *bazm* ('feasting', normally with drinking)[80] as in the term *bazm-gāh* introduced above. *Bazm* is commonly combined with *razm* to mean 'banqueting and fighting'[81] as it can indicate a feast held in celebration of victory in battle.[82] In those instances, *bazm* signals a bawdy, large-scale, drunken affair. The phrase *bazm-i dawr* refers to the practice of revellers drinking wine seated in a circle in the tavern. Once they had consumed the amount of wine they had paid for, they would leave the circle.[83] *Bazm* is also found in conjunction with *tarab*:[84] the delight, rapture or ecstasy fostered, most commonly, by music.[85]

Other terms used to designate such parties include *mihmānī* ('party' to which guests [sing. *mihmān*] are invited),[86] *mahfil* ('assembly')[87] and *anjuman* ('gathering').[88] Both *mahfil* and *anjuman* point to a somewhat more serious affair, although the evidence from the poetry is inconclusive.[89] The term *halqa* ('circle [of companions]') is employed with regularity: *halqa-yi gul u mul* ('circle of the rose and wine'); *bahth u dhikr-i halqa-yi 'ushshāq* ('discussion and remembrance in the circle of lovers'); *halqa-yi dhikr* ('circle of remembrance'); *halqa-yi rindān* ('circle of libertines'); *halqa-yi chaman* ('circle of the lawn').[90] An analogous term in the poetry is *majma'* ('assembly', 'gathering spot'): *majma'-i rindān* ('gathering place of the libertines'); *majma'-i khūbān* ('gathering place of the beauties'); and *majma'-i sāhib-nazarān* ('gathering place of those endowed with true insight'). These various terms are not used precisely enough to allow us to link them categorically to distinct subgenres of convivia. This is arguably where poetry and contemporary prose sources such as histories and belletristic works diverge.

As mentioned above, another important element of the ideal *majlis* is ecstatic emotion and intense joy (usually denoted by *tarab*).[91] The state of *tarab* is induced by the drinking of wine to the accompaniment of music and/or the recitation of poetry, both of which come under the category of 'implements [or causes] of intense ecstatic emotion' (*asbāb-i tarab*).[92] Indeed, the most commonly used word for musician, *mutrib*, literally means 'one who produces *tarab*', which shows us that *tarab* can also be used to denote music per se (as we note in the compound *tarab-khāna* for 'music room').[93] A word of Arabic origin, *tarab* originally stood for extreme positive and/or negative emotion, including intense grief or sorrow. Although these meanings are possible in Persian, they are quite uncommon. The term *tarab* can be combined with *bazm*,[94] *'aysh*[95] and *shādī* ('merrymaking').[96] The phrases 'days of ecstasy' (*ayyām-i tarab*) and the 'time' or 'season' for intense joy (*vaqt-i tarab, mawsim-i tarab*) most likely refer either to Nawruz, Mihragan or 'Id-i Fitr or to a metaphorical springtime: the social renewal ushered in by the coming to power of a sympathetic, poet-friendly ruler and the creation of a stable and vibrant patronage and performance environment; U75:6:

گل بریز که آن سرو ِ خرامان آمد   می بیارید که ایام ِ طرب روی نمود

Bring wine, for the days of ecstasy have appeared!
Scatter roses, for that strutting cypress has arrived!

At any of the major annual festivals, music and poetry would be performed
and wine consumed.[97] The 'ecstasy-proffering wine servers' would impart
merriment whilst they handed guests the 'goblet of extreme joy'.[98]

   The term 'aysh[99] which can be combined with majlis,[100] tarab,[101] nashāt
('excited enjoyment', 'wine drinking'),[102] or nūsh ('drinking') – a term that
denotes the good life as enacted through the consumption of wine[103] or a
'stage' or 'station' (maqām) on the mystical path that one must strive for[104] –
is associated with the garden[105] and is potentially eternal.[106] Consisting of
wine-drinking and other worldly pleasures, 'aysh is typically engaged in at
springtime or is evocative of it;[107] H175:1:

که موسم ِ طرب و عیش و ناز و نوش آمد   صبا به تهنیت ِ پیر ِ میفروش آمد

The messenger breeze came to congratulate the wine-selling elder
Saying: the season of joy and merriment, cavorting and drinking has come!

'Aysh can also suggest sexually charged physical encounters and/or sensual
gratification.[108] For the devoted lover, there is no enjoyment in 'aysh during
times of separation from the beloved; J1362:9:

جز وصل تو چه باشد مقصود این جهانی   تلخست کام عیشم زهرست بی تو نوشم

The palate of my merriment is bitter; without you wine-drinking is poison to me
Besides union with you, what other goal could there be in this world?

Another term linked to the majlis context is 'ishrat ('merriment', 'pleasure-
taking'). Poets refer to 'ishrat-i shabgīr ('merriment that steals the night'),
majlis-i 'ishrat, zamān-i 'ishrat ('the time for pleasure-taking'), mawsim-i 'ishrat
('merriment season')[109] and sāghar-i 'ishrat ('the wine cup of merrymaking').[110]
Like 'aysh, experience of 'ishrat is more often than not located within the
spring garden; J592:3:

که وقت عشرت و باغ و بهار ما آمد   خبر به بلبل شیدا ده ای نسیم صبا

O messenger breeze! Inform the lovesick nightingale that
Our time for pleasure, the garden, and spring has arrived.

The term nashāt denotes wine-drinking with hints of erotic physical liaisons;[111]
J592:6:

برون رویم به صحرا و خرمی و نشاط   که از سفر بت چابک سوار ما آمد

Let's go out to the meadow for pleasure-taking and enjoyment
For our swift-riding idol has returned from his journey.

The period in which pleasure and merriment can be sought and engaged in is understood to be transitory and many poems carry an admonition to the audience that they should capitalize upon, or consider as 'booty' (ghanīmat),[112] any 'opportunity' (fursat)[113] for such pleasure-taking. Injunctions to seize the moment for merriment call to mind the *carpe diem* attitude manifested in quatrains attributed to Khayyam, an essential theme not only of the *rubāʿī* but also the *ghazal*; U129:7:

صحبت یار و می صافی غنیمت دان عبید   حاضر این گنج و دولت باش کارزان یافتی

Value intimate companionship with the beloved and pure wine, 'Ubayd
Attend to this treasure and good fortune that you have found in abundance.

One of the constituent activities engaged in by guests at a garden *majlis* is *tamāshā*.[114] Related to the Arabic term *tamashshī* ('recreational walking'),[115] in premodern Persian, *tamāshā* means contemplating beauty whilst seated or strolling in the garden. The beauty contemplated can be that of the garden in full bloom or the human beloved;[116] J552:2:

کی کند بس ز تماشای گلستان رخت   خاصه کز وصل تواش بوس و کناری باشد

Who can get enough of gazing on the rose garden of your face?
Especially when, through union with you, he will receive kisses and cuddles?

In a number of fourteenth-century Shirazi *ghazal*s, one encounters concise, one-line portrayals of what makes a great wine party; H477:1:

دو یار زیرک و از بادهٔ کهن دو منی   فراغتی و کتابی و گوشهٔ چمنی

Two quick-witted lovers and two maunds of ancient wine
Some peace and quiet, a book, and the corner of a garden.

Note Hafiz's unusual use here of *kitāb* rather than *daftar* to indicate a handbook of poetry. These condensed descriptions list those elements that were thought not only desirable but rather vital for the most intimate of gatherings;[117] U78:3:

باده پیش آر که بر طرف چمن خوش باشد   مطربی چند و گلی چند و گل‌اندامی چند

Bring forth the wine, for at the side of the lawn it would be so pleasurable
With a few musicians, a few roses, and a few rose-limbed beauties.

In some portrayals of intimate parties, it is unequivocally stated that both wine *and* music must be present for true *'aysh* to occur.[118] Elsewhere it is stated that the *mutrib*, his musical instruments and the other trappings of a conventional wine *majlis* are not necessary as long as wine and an object of desire are present; U27:2:[119]

حاجت به شمع و مطرب و چنگ و رباب نیست　　　در خلوتی که باده و ساقی و شاهد است

> In a secluded place where there is wine, a *sāqī*, and a beautiful youth
> There is no need for the candle, *mutrib*, the harp, or the *rubāb*.

The term translated above as 'secluded place' is *khalvat*, possibly an allusion to the seedy wine tavern or *kharābāt* that symbolizes the permissiveness proffered by the fringes of society.[120] An allusion to the seclusion of the tavern can be read as a nod to the social taboos or official moral constraints of the time. As well as being secluded, the *majlis* setting must also be safe and secure (the security of the venue being guaranteed by the host). Hafiz speaks of a *jā-yi amn* ('a safe place'), *maqām-i amn* ('a secure spot') and *ma'man* ('a safe haven').[121]

Activities engaged in at the majlis

Some *bayt*s read as wish lists for the ideal wine party; H288:1:[122]

معاشر دلبری شیرین و ساقی گلعذاری خوش　　　کنارِ آب و پای بید و طبعِ شعر و یاری خوش

> The riverbank, the foot of a willow, poetic talent, and a pretty beloved;
> A sweet, heart-stealing companion and a fine, rose-cheeked *sāqī*.

Wine-drinking, feasting, gaming, listening to music, reciting poetry and flirting with *sāqī*s – in various combinations – constituted a *majlis*.

Wine-drinking

Allusions to wine-drinking in the poetry of Hafiz are often interpreted somewhat reductively and rigidly as narrow metaphors for the all-consuming love of God and mystical intoxication.[123] Such interpretations ignore what I believe to be Hafiz's intent: the presentation of an intentionally ambiguous blend of earthly and heavenly through vinous imagery; an endeavour in which he was not, by any means, alone. The debate over the symbolic or literal interpretation of wine and wine-drinking in Persian poetry represents a false dichotomy. As

Lewis has argued, though *ghazal* poets invested wine-drinking rituals with symbolic significance that 'transcends the actual denoted referents of the sign', they assumed the familiarity of their audience with the actual practices of the wine bout.[124]

Hafiz, in typical fashion, calls for earthly enjoyment of wine in the context of the *majlis* as well as intoxication in the Divine, as proffered by the *jām-i 'ishq* ('cup of passionate love'); H432:1:

پر کن قدح که بی می مجلس ندارد آبی   مخمور جام عشقم ساقی بده شرابی

I am drunk on the cup of passionate love. *Sāqī*, give me some wine!
Fill my cup, for without wine, the *majlis* has no lustre.

Metaphorical allusions to wine-drinking mirror the reality of wine consumption in royal circles in fourteenth-century Shiraz;[125] J899:2:

دایماً سرگشته ام در مجلس او همچو جام   چون صراحی می رود خون دلم از جور یار

The beloved's harshness makes blood flow from my heart like pure, unmixed wine
I am continually wandering dizzy in his *majlis*, like the wine cup.

The image of wandering dizzy evokes the passing round of the wine cup in the *majlis* and picks up on the opening (Arabic) hemistich of the first *ghazal* in Hafiz's *dīvān* (in particular the phrase, *adir ka'san*, 'circulate a wine cup'). There are many allusions in the poetry to the consumption of real, intoxicating wine[126] and the relationship between wine and mysticism is complicated all the more by the fact that some antinomian Sufis practised bacchanalia as part of their ritualistic behaviour.[127] Jahan plays with the prohibition on wine to complain that she does not get to enjoy what others do, for love sickness predominates; J64:4:[128]

من خورم خون و دیگران می ناب   شرط نبود که در مسلمانی

It is not stipulated in being Muslim that
I should drink blood and others pure wine.

For his part, Hafiz declares the worship of wine morally or doctrinally 'correct' or 'proper' (*savāb*)[129] and the 'blood' of the wine cup legally 'licit' (*halāl*; like that of the criminal).[130] Hafiz asserts the lawfulness of grape wine consumption despite it being outlawed in all mainstream interpretations of Islamic law. Since the vine and her grapes are inherently sinful, they too must be sacrificed in the interests of the restoration of honour and the rebalancing of society's moral equilibrium.[131]

Muslim contemporaries of the poets studied here would have considered the consumption of grape wine (khamr) to be prohibited by the Qur'an.[132] The degree to which wine was allowed to be produced, sold and consumed in any given period depended largely upon the proclivities of the ruler, his viziers and the supervisor of markets-cum-guardian of public morals (muhtasib).[133] The image of the wine-bibber being forced to drink in private because of the censure of the religiously devout and the officiousness of the muhtasib is found most frequently in the poetry of Hafiz; H350:9:

به بانگ ِ بربط و نای رازش را آشکارا کنم   ز باده خوردن ِ پنهان ملول شد حافظ

Hafiz has grown tired of drinking wine in secret
I will disclose his secret with the clamor of the lute and flute.

In light of the anxieties surrounding the consumption of wine, it is unsurprising that many of the poetic allusions to wine in the poetry are couched in metaphor. This is particularly true of Jahan's ghazals, in which, perhaps because of her gender, the poet sagaciously distances herself from wine-drinking, either by contrasting herself to those who drink wine or by resorting to puns; J794:7:

باده شوق توام در دل جامست هنوز   گر چو پیمانه شکستی همه پیمان مرا

Although you broke all your promises (paymān) to me, like a wine cup (paymāna)
There remains a goblet in my heart for the wine of your desire.

Jahan's heart is broken like the wine cup one breaks after repenting and promising to stop drinking.

Given what we know of the performance context of Persian lyric poetry, it is unsurprising that allusions to the wine's scent[134] and colour[135] feature prominently in the ghazal. The kingly appurtenances and luxurious vessels associated with its consumption are also frequently alluded to: sāghar-i zarrīn ('golden goblet'), jām-i zarrīn ('golden cup'), kāsa-yi zar ('golden bowl'), jām-i zar ('golden cup'), jām-i murassa' ('jewel-encrusted cup'), sāghar-i durr-i khushāb ('pearl-studded cup') and sarāh ('goblet').[136] The kissing of the lip of the cup is a common motif[137] and, in some poems, the lips of the sāqī and the 'lip' (i.e. rim) of the cup appear to converge.[138] In the Persian ghazal, wine is normally described as being consumed within the confines of the garden:[139] wine-drinking is accompanied by the performance of music, in the presence of the beloved[140] and as the participants gaze on something or someone of incomparable beauty.[141]

The practice of wine drinking at the royal court, its associated rituals (including banqueting), necessary accoutrements and the provenance of the wines consumed, all enjoy a strong pre-Islamic pedigree in the Iranian world.[142] The act of serving intoxicating liquor is an important aspect of wine-focused poetry: it circulates among the guests[143] and the *sāqī* is near omnipresent.[144] Indeed, the *sāqī* is the *mīr-i majlis* or 'prince of the party'.[145] Exhortations to the *sāqī* to provide (more) wine often come in the opening hemistich (thereby setting the tone for the poem)[146] or in the penultimate line (to signify a break from more serious topics and a return to the wine bout setting):[147]

H8:1:

ساقیا برخیز و در ده جام را

O *sāqī*, arise and pass around the cup!

H11:1:

ساقی به نور باده برافروز جام ما

Sāqī, illuminate our cup with the light of the wine!

H81:7:

ساقیا می ده و کوتاه کن این گفت و شنفت

O *sāqī*, pour the wine, and cut short this discussion!

H354:7:

صباح الخیر زد بلبل کجایی ساقیا برخیز

The nightingale has greeted the dawn; where are you, *sāqī*? Arise!

U7:6:

ساقیا تا کی نشینی جام جان افزا بیار

O *sāqī*, how long will you remain seated? Bring the soul-augmenting cup!

It is the *sāqī* who imparts *tarab*[148] and pours the 'joy-inducing' (*tarabnāk*) liquid.[149] And it is the *sāqī* who is most frequently the object of the participants' desire[150] or who acts as go-between in the relationship between the patron and the poet.[151]

The wine-seller (*may-furūsh*,[152] *bāda-furūsh*)[153] or vintner/taverner (*khammār*),[154] a stock character in the Arabic *khamrīya*,[155] is less frequently referred to in the Persian *ghazal*, which might suggest that wine was more readily available at court and its consumption less frowned upon, so the role of the wine-seller had diminished somewhat. That said, there is a profusion of references to the wine tavern (*may-kada*,[156] *may-khāna*,[157] *sharāb-khāna*,[158] *khum-khāna*,[159] *kharābāt*)[160] in particular in the *ghazals* of Hafiz.[161] Arguably, Hafiz's tavern has a more immediately mystical significance given the tavern is the abode of the *pīr-i mughān* (Zoroastrian elder), Hafiz's spiritual guide; H53:1:

دعای پیر مغان ورد صبحگاه من است   منم که گوشه میخانه خانقاه من است

I'm the one whose Sufi lodge is the corner of the tavern
Benediction of the Magian elder is my dawn mantra.

In Bürgel's reading, the *pīr-i mughān* constitutes the symbolic centre of Hafiz's humanistic message that 'pervades his *divan* under its surface of tavern scenes, erotic play and passion'.[162] For Hafiz, the tavern and its inhabitants symbolize sincerity and true religion,[163] in contrast to the hypocrisy of the religious establishment that he vilifies: the theological colleges and their vacuous debates;[164] the popular preachers and their empty, moralizing sermons;[165] and the Sufi *shaykh*s, their corrupt orders and their unappealing lodge;[166] H175:8:

مگر ز مستی زهد ریا به هوش آمد   از خانقاه به میخانه می رود حافظ

Hafiz goes from the Sufi lodge to the wine tavern
Has he sobered up from the stupor of false asceticism?

There are infrequent allusions to the Jewish or Zoroastrian identity of the wine producer or seller,[167] the vintner's house,[168] the money paid for wine[169] and the fact that the wine taverns were closed during certain periods (presumably during times of stricter enforcement of Islamic law, such as was apparently the case under Mubariz al-Din).[170] All this meant that wine was, on occasion, produced at home.[171] Given the Qur'anic prohibition, it is unsurprising that poets felt compelled to defend wine-drinking; by incorporating elements of religio-legal terminology, they exhort their audience to continue to drink wine.[172]

Some *ghazal*s read as 'how-to' guides for the host of a *majlis*. There are allusions to the most suitable times of day or night to drink it. The most auspicious season of the year in which to hold a party is spring, when it is well-nigh impossible to avoid its consumption (in part because of the ceremonial relationship between wine and Nawruz).[173] The age of the wine consumed is also hinted at in the poetry. Wine that is 'vintage' (*sāl-khvurda*) or 'ancient' (*kuhan*)[174] is favoured because it can dispel age-old grief.[175] Alongside vintage wine, we find wines produced from recent harvests: two-year-old wine[176] or forty-day-old wine.[177] Various strengths of wine are also mentioned in the poetry, such as wine labelled *bī-ghashsh* ('pure', 'unadulterated').[178] A variety of methods for processing wine are evoked: it is described as *pukhta* ('cooked', perhaps heated with spices) or *khām* ('raw', perhaps unadulterated or undiluted wine).[179] 'Ubayd speaks with the voice of the vintner when he suggests two uses for the grapes of the garden; U58:45:

در خم و در سبوش خواهم کرد   هرچه یابم در باغ از انگور

نیمهای پخته جوش خواهم کرد   نیمهای در شراب خواهم ریخت

Whatever grapes I find in the garden
I will place them into jars and pitchers
Half I will pour into the wine
Half I will boil with spices.

The amount of wine consumed by the participants in a given drinking session is also alluded to: one 'large cup' (ratl-i girān),[180] 'five bowls' (panj kāsa)[181] or even a whole maund.[182] Other intoxicants, such as opium (afyūn, taryāk)[183] and bang (hemp or a drink made from its leaves) are mentioned rarely; the poets are inconsistent in their praise or condemnation of these narcotics.[184]

Feasting

With drinking comes the practice of feasting,[185] the splendour of which, as Babaie has highlighted in relation to the Safavids (although the observation holds for earlier dynasties), 'had a political purpose'.[186] In the feast, the ruler displayed his authority through his peerless hospitality and generosity. There are allusions in the poetry to the consumption of wine (sharāb) along with roasted meat (kabāb). Although the primary function of such allusions is metaphorical (wine = bloody tears of the lover; roasted meat = the lover's grief-branded heart or liver), they reflect the importance of feasting within the broader framework of the bazm event; J63:4:[187]

هر دم از دیده شراب آرم و از سینه کباب   گر شبی خیل خیال تو بود مهمانم

If one night, the cavalry of your apparition were my guest
At every moment I would provide wine from my eyes and roasted meat from my breast.

It was customary at medieval Iranian symposia to serve confections such as sugar candy and candied almonds, which are standard metaphors for, respectively, the beloved's sugary sweet lips and narrow eyes; U78:4:

تا بود نقل من از شکر و بادامی چند   چشم و لب پیش من آور چو رسد باده به من

Bring your eyes and lips close when the wine reaches me
So that I will have some sugar and almonds to nibble.

In this bayt, note the allusion to Nizami's heroine, Shirin ('sweet') and her chief rival for her beloved Khusraw's affections, the courtesan Shikar ('sugar'; see Chapter 5); H46:6:

ز آن رو که مرا از لبِ شیرینِ تو کام است   از چاشنی قند مگو هیچ وز شکر

Say nothing of the taste of the candy or sugar
For I derive my satisfaction from your sweet lips.

These sugary accompaniments are collectively known as *nuql*. The poetry itself is a kind of sweetmeat to be consumed by the guests: it is the *nuql-i majlis*.[188]

Gaming

Guests at *majālis* played board games such as chess (*shatranj*) and backgammon (*nard*).[189] Jahan uses the following chess terms in her poetry: *'arsa* ('chessboard');[190] *farzīn* ('queen'),[191] *asb* ('knight'),[192] *rukh* ('rook'),[193] *pīada, sarbāz* ('pawn');[194] and *shah-māt* (checkmate).[195] Although they are used metaphorically to say that humans are merely figures on the world's chessboard caught in the game of love, their use suggests that chess was popular with contemporary audiences;[196] J112:9:

دل سرگشته ام چون فرزین است   چه کنم چون به عرصه ستمت

What should I do? For on the chessboard of your cruelty
My wandering heart is like the queen.

And J1263:7:

شاه دل من شدست ماتی   در عرصه عشقت ای جهانگیر

On the chessboard of your love, O world-conqueror
The king of my heart has been checkmated.

Here Jahan puns on her *takhallus*: the beloved is the *jahān-gīr* ('world conqueror,' 'world-taker'), he who has captured Jahan's heart. The lover can also lose her heart in the 'backgammon of ecstasy' (*nard-i tarab*); J1225:8:

با تو تا نرد طرب را باخته   جان ما در ششدر عشقت بماند

My soul was cornered on the board of your love
Until it lost the game of ecstasy to you.

The technical term translated as 'cornered' here is the *shishdar*, which signifies a position in backgammon from which one cannot extricate oneself.

Allusions to chess and backgammon also appear in 'Ubayd's *ghazal*s ('the backgammon of love' [*takhta nard-i 'ishq*])[197] and Hafiz ('the chessboard of the libertines' ['*arsa-yi shatranj-i rindān*]).[198] The reason for the greater incidence of allusions to chess and backgammon in Jahan's poetry might be her imitation of Sa'di, in which such allusions are fairly common.[199] It may also be the case that chess and backgammon (that carry strong royal connotations) were considered suitable pastimes for elite women. That said, from a devout Muslim perspective, chess and backgammon are considered to be suspect. As with the celebration of wine-drinking, with gaming too it would seem that the poets are promoting a parallel or alternate moral code for the court.

Allusions to another royal entertainment, polo, abound in *ghazal* poetry of this period.[200] We know from prose sources that a wine party might either precede or follow a hunting expedition[201] and the same may have held for polo matches. A standard image employed in the poetry is that of the lover (or the lover's heart) as a 'polo ball' (*guy*) that is struck by the beloved's stick (a metaphor for his erotically enticing arched eyebrow or curved forelock).[202] Hafiz combines metaphors drawn from both polo and hunting, that quintessential courtly activity;[203] H482:2:

باز ظفر به دست و شکاری نمی کنی   چوگان حکم در کف و گویی نمی زنی

You have the polo stick of rule in your hand and you do not strike the ball
You have the falcon of victory on your arm and you do not hunt.

Flirtation and erotic physical contact

The expression of frustrated or unrequited erotic desire is a standard motif of the Persian *ghazal*.[204] Jahan's *ghazal*s are less bawdy than those of her male contemporaries. There are in her poetry, however, occasional bursts of sensuousness. Below, Jahan puns on the word *kām*, which conveys at least three distinct meanings: 'desire', 'satisfaction' (including sexual gratification) and 'palate'; J902:1–2:

به کام دل نشستن با دل آرام   چه خوش باشد شراب وصل در جام

بده کامم که شیرین گردد کام   مرا کام دل از هجر تو تلخست

How sweet it is, with the wine of reunion in the cup
To sit to your heart's satisfaction with the beloved
The palate of my heart is bitter from your separation
Give me my desire, so that my palate may be sweetened.

Pulling or playing with the beloved's hair whilst drinking is also alluded to.[205] Jahan voices a longing to take hold of her beloved by the hair and force him to kiss her, even though she claims to be fearful of the consequences; J688:1–3:

ویا ز زلف تو تاری گرم به شست آید   مرا چو دامن وصلت شبی به دست آید

اگرچه غمزه خونریز یار مست آید   ز لعل تو بربایم به حیله بوسی چند

یقین شدم که از آن باده می پرست آید   هرآنکه چشم تو را دید و آن لب میگون

If one night I grasp the hem of reunion with you
Or if one strand of your hair falls into my grasp
I will steal from your ruby lips, by some ruse, a few kisses
Even though the bloodthirsty glance of my beloved seems drunk
Anyone who has seen your eyes and those wine-coloured lips
I am certain, will turn into a worshipper of wine through that wine.

Unlike in Abbasid lyric poetry in which the boundary between erotic and licentious verse is repeatedly blurred,[206] the Persian *ghazal* is predominantly chaste and, by convention, does not go beyond sexual suggestiveness; H42:3–4:

با تو تا روز خفتنم هوس است   شب قدری چنین عزیز شریف

در شب تار سفتنم هوس است   وه که دردانه ای چنین نازک

On such a mighty and noble Night of Power
To sleep with you until daylight, is my desire;
Oh, to pierce that finest of pearls on this,
The darkest of nights, is my desire!

Here the phrase -*am havas ast* ('is my desire/lustful wish') as repeated in the *radīf* infuses the poem with strong erotic undertones. When read alongside the bawdy prose and sexually explicit quatrains of 'Ubayd (which were produced for the same courtly audience), the subtle eroticism of Hafiz's *ghazal*s in particular comes to life.[207] A phrase found quite commonly that hints at a relationship of a more physical nature is *būs u kinār* ('kissing and embracing').[208] Allusions to all these activities are found in the poetry: kissing on the mouth,[209] kissing the beloved's *ghabghab* (the area of the neck under the chin),[210] biting his lips,[211] kissing his chest and shoulders,[212] embracing[213] or sleeping with (and holding or being held by) the beloved all night,[214] fondling the beloved and undressing him,[215] paying him for sex or company,[216] flirting with the beloved[217] and gazing lustfully upon his beauty (one of the meanings of the term *nazar-bāzī*).[218] Hafiz suggests that the ideal partner or companion is he who accompanies the lover in the private house, public baths (a homosocial and homoerotic zone) and garden.[219] The implication is that the beloved should be versatile, mobile and ever-present in his companionship.

In Jahan's poetry too, there are glimpses of erotic encounters. The line below comes from a poem that echoes the erotic undertones and rhyme scheme of a celebrated *ghazal* by Hafiz in which he revels in his status as *shuhra-yi shahr* ('talk of the town');[220] J1140:7:

با نگاری به سبزه غلطیدن   در لب جوی و پای گل چه خوشست

On the riverbank, at the foot of the rose, how pleasant it is
To roll around with an idol on the fresh, green grass.

'Ubayd infuses his depictions of such interactions with intense sensuous energy; U45:9:

بنوش بادۀ صافی و هر چه بادا باد   بگیر دامن یاری و هر چه خواهی کن

Grab the hem of a beloved and do whatsoever you desire
Drink some pure wine, and throw caution to the wind!

The physical infidelity of the fickle beloved is a common motif; J835:1:

گرفتی دیگری جز من در آغوش   چرا کردی مرا از دل فراموش

Why have you cast memory of me from your heart,
And taken someone else into your arms?

Poetry as song

In the medieval Iranian context, as had been the case in the Abbasid *majlis*, song did not compete with, but rather complemented, poetry.[221] Music was played as an accompaniment to poetry;[222] *mutrib*s might perform whole poems or select *bayt*s or sections from individual poems as songs.[223] Lewis has demonstrated (with specific reference to Hafiz's use of the word *ghazal*)[224] that the poet composed his short lyric poems with the idea that they would (or could) be sung.[225] The profusion of asides to musician-singers, and the link drawn between wine, music and poetry, suggest that many of Hafiz's *ghazal*s were intended to be sung by professional entertainers either at wine parties or with bacchanalia in mind. The interaction between poet and singer in the medieval Islamicate world deserves fuller exploration, but it seems that poets who composed verse to be sung concentrated on themes most appropriate to a courtly convivial context: the amatory, bacchic and panegyric.[226] Looking beyond those *ghazal*s composed with the express intention that they be performed to music, it is reasonable to assume that others not initially intended for musical performance may subsequently have been set to music and sung.[227]

A similar degree of connection between poetic text and musical performance can be asserted for the *ghazals* of other contemporaries.[228] In the case of Jahan, allusions to the link between poetic recitation and musical performance are less common (although in one poem, there is an allusion to a *mutrib* playing by heart).[229] The relative paucity of musical performance imagery in the poetry of Jahan may indicate that, as a woman poet, Jahan needed to establish a greater distance from music in her compositions because of moral strictures. Even so, in a few poems, Jahan alludes to the link between her written word and musical performance; J1383:8–9:

وآنچه میگوئی به نزد عاشقان با ساز گوی   مطربا در ساز کن عود و نی و چنگ و رباب

در سرابستان تو با دستان خوش آواز گوی   گر بخوانی یک دو بیتی دلپذیر از شعر من

O musician! Play the lute, the flute, the harp, and the *rubāb*
And whatever you say to the lovers, accompany it with music.
If you sing a pleasing verse or two from my poems
In your private garden, sing them with sweet melodies.

The musician-singer played the role of secondary performer of the poetry (after the poet).[230] Asides framed in direct speech and addressed to the *mutrib* complement those to the *sāqī* and in some poems they appear side by side;[231] H164:8:

چند گویی که چنین رفت و چنان خواهد شد   مطربا مجلس انس است غزل خوان و سرود

O musician! This is the convivial gathering; sing *ghazals* and songs
How long will you speak of what has passed and what is to come?

The *ghazal*'s performance context is reflected in these apostrophes:[232] Hafiz instructs the *mutrib* to play so that those present can recite poems as they dance; H374:4:

چو در دست است رودی خوش بزن مطرب سرودی خوش

که دست‌افشان غزل خوانیم و پاکوبان سراندازیم

Since you have a fine lute in your hand, musician, play a fine tune,
So that we may dance and sing *ghazals*, stamp our feet, and swing our heads.

Likewise Hafiz exhorts the minstrel:

H173:8:

مطرب از گفتهٔ حافظ غزلی نغز بخوان

Musician, sing a fine *ghazal* composed by Hafiz!

H460:11:

به شعر فارسی صوت عراقی   بساز ای مطرب خوشخوان خوشگو

O sweet-voiced, sweet-singing *mutrib*, play
An *'Irāqī* song with Persian lyrics!

H479:4:

مطرب نگاه دار همین ره که می زنی

Minstrel, maintain this tune you are playing!

It is poetry (*shi'r*, which also means 'song lyrics') that forms the basis for songs (*tarāna, surūd*) enjoyed at the wine party.[233] The term *qawl* (lit. 'speech', but in this context 'song'; perhaps more specifically Arabic poems sung to music) can also be found paired with the term *ghazal* (perhaps indicating the singing of Persian poems).[234] Within the poetic performance context, the terms *ghazal, qawl, surūd* and *tarana* enjoy semantic overlap.[235] The *mughannī* ('singer, vocalist') is less commonly evoked than the *mutrib*,[236] although he features prominently in Hafiz's wine-focused *mathnavī*.[237]

Of the poets studied here, it is Hafiz who makes the most creative use of the *takhallus* line to boast of the elegance of his verses and his all-round skill as a poet,[238] an important use of the pen name.[239] In these final or penultimate lines, the *mutrib* is frequently called upon to sing the poetry of Hafiz to the exclusion of all other poets. Coming at the end of the poem, these directives facilitate a smoother transition from the poem as a text recited by the poet, to the poem as a song, performed to music.[240]

Since one meaning of the term *hāfiz* is 'singer',[241] such addresses can be read as exhortations either to the minstrel or else to the poet himself as the performer of his own verse: 'come and sing sweetly, Hafiz/singer!'; 'Hafiz/ singer, sing *ghazals* on separation'.[242] Hafiz manifests his musical ability and intimate knowledge of musical practice in his *ghazals*.[243] It is possible that he not only recited, but also sang his poetry as he praises his singing voice in at least two poems.[244] 'Ubayd praises his own verses in a similar manner; U117:7:

مطرب غزل عبید خوانده   دل برده ز دست تیز هوشان

The musician has sung a *ghazal* by 'Ubayd
And stolen the hearts of those with sharp minds.

The verb *khvāndan* employed by 'Ubayd here is itself ambiguous since it simultaneously means to read, to recite and to sing. In some poems, it is not clear which meaning is intended. Occasionally there are even stronger hints that the poet him/herself sings his/her poetry to the accompaniment of music: 'Let's recite those stories to the sound of the harp'; 'I was singing this song while drinking pure wine'.[245] Note that the verb used here is *guftan*; the noun *gufta* denotes a 'song' or a 'sung poem'. *Gūyanda* overlaps with other terms for singer-reciter such as *qavvāl* and *khvānanda*.[246]

Well before the fourteenth century, the roles of the poet (*shā'ir*) and the minstrel (*mutrib*, *rāmishgar*, *khunyāgar*)[247] had become quite distinct.[248] It would appear that, while the *mutrib* was accompanied on occasion (perhaps vocally) by the *sāqī*,[249] most depictions of *mutrib*s in the poetry suggest an individual performer who both played instrumental music and sang.[250] Music and wine are frequently mentioned as an essential pair at the *majlis*[251] and there are allusions to the host paying for both.[252] Just as music and drinking are often paired, so too poetry recitation and wine-drinking appear side-by-side as complementary activities;[253] H246:6:

می خور به شعر بنده که زیبی دگر دهد   جام مرصّع تو بدین درّ شاهوار

Drink wine to my poetry, for this fine royal pearl
Will lend extra beauty to your bejewelled cup.

Hafiz and 'Ubayd composed a number of *ghazal*s which, based on their content, strident bacchanalian tone, simplicity, length and/or rhythm, could be categorized as drinking songs.[254] One good example is a *mulamma'a* (mixed Persian–Arabic poem) by Hafiz in which the second hemistich of each of the first two lines is written in a style reminiscent of the earlier Arabic wine poem; H13:1–2:

الصبوح الصبوح یا اصحاب   می دمد صبح و کله بست سحاب
المدام المدام یا احباب   می چکد ژاله بر رخ لاله

Dawn is breaking and the clouds have pitched their tent;
Companions drink the morning cup, the morning cup!
The dew drops are dripping upon the tulip's cheek;
Friends bring the wine, the wine!

The *ghazal* genre itself is commonly associated with the tavern and with a state of intoxication that is more this-worldly than it is heavenly; H359:6:

تا در ِمیکده شادان و غزلخوان بروم   نذر کردم گر از این غم به در آیم روزی

I vowed that if one day I escaped from this woe
I would proceed to the tavern, rejoicing and singing *ghazals*.

'Ubayd combines the celebration of wine-drinking, music and sex with antinomian flare. His poems speak to the worldly side of poetry performance in fourteenth-century Shiraz and evoke lyric poetry of the tenth and eleventh centuries in which wine consumption is celebrated freely;[255] U114:4–5:

عاشق قحبهٔ خوش آوازیم   واله دلبر شکردهنیم
همه با جام باده دمسازیم   همه با عود و چنگ هم نفسیم

We are enraptured with a sugar-mouthed beloved,
We are enamoured of a sweet-voiced whore;
We the intimate companions of the lute and harp,
We are the constant consorts of the wine cup.

The playing of musical instruments

Musical performance (as an accompaniment to singing or the recitation of poetry or to augment the atmosphere for wine-drinking) was an important component of convivial entertainment.[256] From an Islamic legal perspective, music (like wine-drinking and game-playing, though to a lesser degree) was at worst considered 'illicit' (*harām*), at best 'permissible' (*mubāh*) and, only rarely, 'licit' (*halāl*);[257] H254:6:

گوید تو را که باده مخور گو هو الغفور   می خور به بانگ چنگ و مخور غصه ور کسی

Drink wine to the harp's sound, and do not worry; and if anyone says:
'Do not drink wine!' Say, 'He is the All-Forgiving!'

It was the connection between music and *lahw* (frivolous amusement, including licentious behaviour) that was considered by Muslim scholars to be most dangerous.[258] Whereas a minority argued that the legal status of musical practices depended on their pragmatic usage (rather than a notion of inherent sinfulness),[259] many medieval religious scholars opposed music because of its link to the production of profound emotional effects on the listener and his/

her body,[260] effects that might stimulate or provoke other pursuits considered morally dubious in Islam; J289:9:

بوستان پر غلغل چنگست و عود و نای و رود   موسم گل در سرابستان یکی مستور نیست

The garden is filled with the clamour of the harp, 'ūd, flute, and lute
During the season of the rose in the palace garden, no one is chaste.

The word translated here as 'chaste' is *mastūr* which literally means 'veiled' or 'covered' and is often used in connection with female sexual propriety. Hafiz suggests a similar link between music and cavorting; H219:2:

بنوش جام صبوحی به ناله دف و چنگ   ببوس غبغب ساقی به نغمه نی و عود

Drink the morning cup to the lament of the tambour and harp
Kiss the underside of the *sāqī*'s neck to the melody of the flute and lute.

There is good evidence of serious interest in music on the part of fourteenth-century elites in Iran for whom a number of important treatises in favour of music were produced,[261] including: the *Risala-yi chang* by Saraj al-Din Qamari (d. 1334), an older contemporary of 'Ubayd who also hailed from Qazvin; the *Kitab al-advar*, Yahya b. Ahmad Kashani's Persian rendering of al-Urmawi's original, commissioned by Shah Shaykh Abu Ishaq in 1345; and the poet 'Imad al-Din Kirmani's *Tariqat-nama*, a lengthy *mathnavī* on Sufi practice with sections on *samā'* (musical performance often linked to mystical devotion) written circa 1355 and dedicated to Mubariz al-Din.[262]

To engage in music without wine is considered unthinkable by Hafiz.[263] 'Ubayd links music and wine when he rejoices that 'the days of the flute and wine-drinking have arrived'; he underscores the inseparability of the two in the intimate domain of the wine gathering which comprises him and his companions, the wine, the flute and the tambour.[264] Along with music and wine comes dancing,[265] whether by hired dancing boys,[266] lissom *shāhid*s,[267] an intoxicated Sufi,[268] the *majlis* participants[269] or the *sāqī*;[270] U93:5:

طرف کلاه کج کن و بند کمر ببند   پایی بکوب و دست بزن و کاسه بدار

Tilt the rim of your hat and tighten your waistband
Stamp your feet, clap your hands, and pour a cup of wine.

The phrase *band-i kamarband bi-band*, translated here as 'tighten your waistband', could also refer to the dancer putting on a waistband to accentuate the swaying of his hips. In the following *bayt*, Jahan alludes to a dancing boy and her use of the term *samā'*,[271] may indicate that she is alluding to a Sufi gathering, rather than a rarefied, elite gathering; J762:8:

چون بشنود گوش دلم هیهای بغدادی پسر　　　　گر در سماع آید قدش جان را بر افشانم بر او

If his slender form would sway with the music, I shall offer up my life to him,
When the ear of my heart hears the cries of the Baghdadi boy.

The practice of *samā'* had its supporters and detractors.[272] The parameters of good conduct in *samā'* were outlined: the *qavvāl* (singer) should neither be a woman nor a desirable young male (and he must have a beard); the motivation for *samā'* should be mystical, not based on worldly passion.[273] In his introduction to Hafiz's *dīvān*, Muhammad Gulandam says no Sufi *samā'* could warm up without the poet's exhilarating lyrics (just as no *majlis* of wine-worshippers passed muster without his choice words).[274]

Hafiz makes frequent allusion to musical instruments in his *ghazals*,[275] a good number of which were considered problematic from a moral standpoint because of their association with wine culture and people of corrupt morals.[276] The instruments most frequently mentioned in the poetry (and perhaps the most popular at a *majlis*) are: the *chang* (which can denote either 'harp' or 'lute'),[277] the *daff* ('tambour'),[278] the *nay* or *nāy* ('reed flute'),[279] the *'ūd* or *rūd* ('lute'),[280] the *rubāb* (a four-stringed *tār*),[281] the *barbat* (normally 'lute' but also 'harp'),[282] the *kamāncha* (a stringed instrument resembling a small, upright fiddle)[283] and the *chaghāna* (either a percussion instrument with bells or a stringed instrument that is bowed or plucked).[284] A number of these instruments were associated with wine drinking and feasting as far back as the late Sasanian period.[285] Interestingly, Jahan does not allude to the *barbat, kamāncha* or *chaghāna* in her poetry, which may indicate that these instruments are associated with musical performance within contexts considered inappropriate for women of high status.

Musical instruments are often arranged in pairs or groups of three or more in the poetry, providing a sense of the constitution of a standard musical ensemble: *chang/rubāb*;[286] *chang/nay*;[287] *chang/'ūd/nay*;[288] *chang/'ūd*;[289] *chang/daff*;[290] *chang/daff/nay*;[291] *chang/daff/nay/'ūd*;[292] *chang/daff/'ūd*;[293] *'ūd/nay*;[294] *nay/daff*;[295] *chang/chaghāna*;[296] *chang/barbat/nay*[297] and *barbat/nay*.[298] Pre-modern Persian poets also employed musical terms[299] including: *parda* ('note', 'key', 'melody'),[300] *naghma* ('melody'),[301] *navā* ('note', 'tone'),[302] *bāng* ('loud sound'),[303] *sāz* ('music', 'musical instrument'),[304] *āvāz* ('singing voice', 'song'),[305] *āhang* ('melody'),[306] *sawt* ('tone', 'song')[307] and *qawl* ('song', more specifically Arabic lyrics sung by the *qavvāl*).[308] The use of this musical terminology is more common in the *ghazals* of Hafiz, although it is also found in the poetry of both Jahan and 'Ubayd.

A feature common to a number of Jahan's *ghazal*s is the portrayal of the poet-lover as a stringed instrument which is struck mercilessly by the hand of a harsh beloved.[309] Similar depictions of complaining musical instruments are also found in the poetry of Khaqani Shirvani (d. 1190);[310] J683:1–3:

در فراق خود مرا بنشاند بر آتش چو عود   دلبر از شوخی و عیاری دل از دستم ربود

میدهد هر دم به هجران گوشمالم همچو عود   همچو چنگم میزند لیکن نوازش کمترست

چون رسیدم جان به لب زین ناله زارم چه سود   نی صفت مینالم از دست جفای هر خسی

The beloved, through playfulness and villainy, stole from me my heart
In his absence, he placed me on the fire, like aloes ('ūd)
He strikes me like a harp, although his strokes are less intense
He hits me hard at every moment with separation, like a lute ('ūd)
I cry out like a flute from the harsh hand of every mean man
Since I am now near to death, what use is there in this wretched wailing?

Here the suggestion is that the pains and trials of love produce enchanting smells, music and poetry. Jahan employs similar metaphors in this line; J1084:6:

در راه عشق تو اسرارها زدیم   چون چنگ در خروشم و چون نی زناله زار

I am warbling like a harp, and like a flute I am hoarse from crying out
In the path of your love we have played many mysteries.

The lover may also be likened to the reed flute because its tune echoes the groans and wails of heartache; H335:7:

از لب خویش چو نی یک نفسی بنوازم   همچو چنگ ار به کناری ندهی کام دلم

If you will not grant my heart's desire by embracing me like a lute,
Breathe a breath into me from your lips as you would a flute.

The mournful flute evokes the opening to Rumi's *Mathnavi*, the *Nay-nāma* or 'book of the reed'.[311] Musical instruments may also be depicted as silent: Haydar likens his 'tune-less' (*bī-navā*) state in Ramadan to that of the tambour, harp and flute that have not been played throughout the month of fasting.[312]

The poetic process and how poetry circulated

Hafiz urges his audience to commit his poems to memory; H397:12:

ز کارها که کنی شعر حافظ از بر کن   پس از ملازمت عیش و عشق مهرویان

After persevering in merriment and falling for the moon-faced ones
One of the things you should do is learn Hafiz's poetry by heart.

What role did the performance context play in the dissemination of the *ghazal*? The *majlis* was not only a forum for poetic performance, it was also the place for debates on the style and quality of poetry (*bahth-i shi'r*).[313] The role of the *rāvī* or professional reciter (sometimes an apprentice poet) in the disseminating (and, perhaps, tweaking) of the poetic text is one that requires additional exploration,[314] as does that of the poets themselves in the revision or repackaging of their own poetry during the composition process or when looking for new patrons or performance opportunities.[315] As Lewis has argued, poets and other authors 'frequently negotiated a single work through more than one public version, reworking and rewording the text'.[316]

Fourteenth-century *ghazal*s also contain allusions to the composition process, some of which indicate that certain poems may have been intended for performance at a gathering of poets, perhaps within the framework of the *mushā'ara* ('poetry competition'); U69:7:

گرش گفت توانی جواب خوش باشد   عبید این دو سه بیتک به یک زمان گفته است

'Ubayd composed these two or three verses some time back;
It would be sweet if you were able to answer them in verse.

Jahan evokes the garden as a suitable site for poetry composition; J410:1–2:

ز بوی گل به مشامم خیال یار افتاد   مرا به صبحدمی در چمن گذار افتاد

چو از هوا نظرم سوی آن نگار افتاد   گذشت یک دو سه بیتی به خاطرم به هوس

I passed across the lawn one early morning
The rose's scent in my nostrils set me to imagining the beloved;
Two or three verses passed through my mind out of love
When out of desire my eye fell upon that beauty.

Although she does not boast of her poetic talents to the same extent as her male contemporaries, Jahan reflects on the content and tone of her recorded poetry; J1372:2:

نامه جور و جفا طی کنی   گر بخوانی دفتر غمهای من

If you read the poetic notebook (*daftar*) of my woes
You will traverse a book (*nāma*) of injustice and cruelty.

Performance settings

The palace

Throughout the medieval Islamic world, royal audience chambers and pavilions served as locations for courtly conviviality,[317] though allusions to such spaces as settings for poetry and music performance or for the drinking of wine are rare in Injuid and Muzaffarid *ghazal*s. Hafiz lauds the palace as the 'alighting-place of intimacy',[318] but in the majority of allusions to palaces and/or pavilions, architectural terms are employed to metaphorical effect: *zīr-i in tāram-i fīrūza* ('under this turquoise dome'); *nuh rivāq-i sipihr* ('the nine arches of the sky'); *zīr-i tāq-i sipihr* ('under the archway of the sky'); *īn saqf-i sabz u tāq-i mīnā* ('this green ceiling and bright blue arch'); *īn gunbad-i mīnā* ('this bright blue dome'); and *īn fīrūza ayvān* ('this turquoise portico').[319] However metaphorical in their primary meaning, they evoke real performance settings: those palaces and royal pavilions of fourteenth-century Shiraz that are depicted in panegyric poetry as settings for kingly *majālis*.[320]

The terms used to allude to buildings in the poetry include: *sarā* ('palace', 'mansion'),[321] *bustān-sarā* ('large garden pavilion'),[322] *dawlat-sarā* ('royal palace'),[323] *sarā-cha* ('pavilion', 'villa'),[324] *dār al-mulk* ('royal residence', 'capital city'),[325] *qasr* ('palace', 'castle'),[326] and *kākh* ('palace').[327] Hafiz evokes a palace setting in the last line of a panegyric *ghazal* in praise of Burhan al-Din Fathallah, vizier to Mubariz al-Din; H362:16:

خالى مباد كاخ جلالش ز سروران   وز ساقيان سروقد گلعذار هم

> May the palace of his glory never be devoid of lords!
> Nor may it be empty of cypress-limbed, rose-cheeked *sāqī*s!

The royal palace – a universal symbol of dynastic legitimation, kingly power and earthly fame[328] – is likened in Persian poetry and prose to Paradise as conceptualized in the Qur'an and other Islamic texts. The palace is the *qasr-i firdaws* ('palace of Paradise'),[329] located in the 'garden of Paradise' (*bāgh-i bihisht*)[330] and populated by the dark-eyed beauties associated with the Islamic afterlife (*hūr, hūr al-'ayn*).[331] As Robinson has observed in relation to the Andalusian context, paradise is suggested as a 'referent ... for the setting in which the real-life gathering took place, i.e. the palace itself'.[332]

Smaller, separate chambers within the palace complex are alluded to in the poetry: the *tarab-sarā* or *tarab-khāna* ('music room', 'entertainment room');[333] *tamāshā-khāna* ('viewing room');[334] *khalvat-gāh* or *khalvat-sarā* ('private apartments', 'women's quarters') often qualified with *khāss* to denote those parts of the palace exclusive to the ruler's inner circle or *uns*, to stress the space's strong association with small-scale, intimate conviviality;[335] and *shabistān* ('bedchamber');[336] J256:3:

وصف نور رخش نشاید کرد   شمع ما زیور شبستانیست

It is not proper to describe the light of his face
Our candle is the ornament of a bedchamber.

A similarly secluded quarter of the palace alluded to is the *nihān-khāna* ('hidden chamber', 'private chamber'); H326:1:

در نهانخانۀ عشرت صنمی خوش دارم   کز سر زلف و رخش نعل در آتش دارم

In the private chamber of merriment I have a beautiful idol,
Whose locks and cheeks render me uneasy and perturbed.

The poets also allude to architectural features commonly associated with royal gatherings: *ayvān* ('portico', 'open veranda');[337] *shāh-nashīn* (royal seating area in a pavilion)[338] and *tāq u manzar* ('archway and viewing platform').[339] Occasional allusions are also made to calligraphic inscriptions on buildings;[340] H179:8:

بدین رواقِ زبرجد نوشته اند به زر   که جز نکویی اهل کرم نخواهد ماند

On this emerald-coloured portico they have written in gold:
'Nothing save the goodness of the people of generosity will remain.'

In two fifteenth-century texts from Yazd, it is said that quotations from poetry by Sa'di, Kamal Isfahani, Khvaju and Nizami were inscribed on pavilions constructed and/or renovated in the Muzaffarid period in the pleasure gardens that encircled the city.[341] These poetic inscriptions would have added a dialogical dimension to the poetry recited or sung within the pavilions, as did the frieze tiles decorated with verses and pictorial depictions of scenes from the *Shahnama* that adorned the Ilkhanid palace at Takht-i Sulayman (built from 1272 onwards).[342] Select story cycles from the *Shahnama* appear to have dominated the interiors of that particular palace and perhaps also the throne and banqueting halls of other contemporary royal buildings.[343] Blair has argued that such decorative schemes were aimed at legitimizing the present through identification with the past.[344] A similar argument can be made for objects such as bowls, plates, cups and ewers bearing poetic inscriptions used at the *majlis*.[345] Poems were also composed in praise of new buildings and might be inscribed upon them.[346]

Though primarily metaphorical in thrust, these architectural allusions are of value to those who wish to gain a fuller understanding of the spatial dimensions of fourteenth-century performance settings. As Losensky has argued, Persian architectural poetry is 'birthed' by buildings and it unfolds the fullness of those structures' meaning in the eyes of their beholders. This poetry documents and represents buildings' social uses that give them much of their meaning and, however metaphorical, such poetry 'provides an interpretative commentary on the built environment'.[347]

The pavilion

References to pleasure-grounds, pavilions and kiosks built in and around fourteenth-century Shiraz are found in contemporary and near-contemporary texts.[348] The kiosk-pavilion functioned as a viewing platform: raised off the ground, these structures provided elevation for guests. Many of the terms for built structures listed previously are used rather loosely in the poetry as they often are in prose texts[349] and can easily be read as alluding to pavilions and kiosks, rather than large palace complexes.

When a *majlis* is said to have been staged, 'at the centre of the garden' (*miyān-i bāgh*),[350] this can be read as an allusion to a pavilion erected at the centre of the *chahār bāgh*, the traditional Persian garden divided into four sections.[351] The main pavilion was often erected at the point at which the paths or water channels that divided the garden converged;[352] J598:3:

چو جام باده به بستان دمید و گل بشکفت   ز چارسوی چمن های و هوی نوش آمد

> When the wine cup appeared in the garden and the rose bloomed
> From the four sides of the lawn came the joyous cries of wine-drinking.

The *majlis* participants used the pavilion as their base, gazing from it at the garden beyond (and perhaps at the countryside behind the garden's walls).[353] The pavilion would provide shelter from the blistering sun or the inconvenience caused by spring showers. It was from the pavilion that the garden's beauty was admired and from which guests might set out to stroll among its flowers and scented vegetation. It is, therefore, not surprising that there is much less discussion of the pavilion or kiosk than there is of the garden itself.

The royal tent

Allusions to tents (sing. *khargāh, khayma*)[354] point to their use as improvised, mobile, impermanent venues for *majālis* held in the countryside;[355] U93:2:

از خانه دور شو که کنون خانه دوزخ است   خرگه ساز کن که بهشت است مرغزار

Distance yourself from your home, for now the house is hell
Pitch the tent, for now the meadow is a paradise.

A tent or a series of tents might also be erected as a temporary roof-top or courtyard addition to permanent edifices – a pop-up performance venue.[356] The beloved Turk is regularly associated with the space of the tent; U67:5:

خیز ای عبید مجلس ترکانه راست کن   کآن ترک خرگهیم به خرگاه می‌رسد

Arise, 'Ubayd and set up a *majlis* fit for a Turk
For that tent-dwelling Turk of mine is reaching the tent.

The addition of a tent to a garden that had no pavilion would have provided added privacy for more illicit entertainments; J1146:1:

باد نوروزی برآمد خیمه بر گلزار زن   دست دل در بوستان در دامن دلدار زن

The Nawruz breeze has arrived; pitch the tent in the rose garden
In the garden insert the hand of the heart into the beloved's skirt.

The garden

As I have demonstrated elsewhere, it is the garden – and its pleasure pavilion – that was the primary setting for poetry performance in premodern Iran.[357]

که باشد موسم گل بوستان خوش   بیا در گلستان تا گوشه گیریم
بود در پای سرو آب روان خوش   به سوی ما خرام ای جان که دانم
نگارا هست طرف گلستان خوش   به بانگ بلبل و قمری سحرگاه
نباشد هیچ بی آن دلستان خوش   نوای چنگ و عود و نالهٔ نای

Come into the rose garden so we can sit in a corner
For in the rose season the garden is so fine
Strut towards us, O beloved, for I know
Flowing water at the foot of the cypress is so fine
With the warbling of the nightingale and the turtle-dove at dawn
O my beauty, the edge of the garden is so fine
The sound of the harp and the lute, and the moan of the flute
Without that heart-grabber, not one of them is fine.[358]

Meisami has argued that the garden depicted in medieval Persian poetry should be understood as a microcosm of the world.[359] While valid, this interpretation provides only part of the picture. The age-old link between Iranian royalty and the garden-cum-earthly paradise has received keen scholarly attention.[360] Here, I re-read Persian poetry for the clues it contains to the use of gardens as focal settings for poetic performance. Descriptions of the garden (normally during springtime) are combined with descriptions of wine-drinking, intimacy with the human beloved and the performance of music and/or poetry.[361] This evidence from the poetry, when combined with anecdotal material taken from court histories and contemporary prose sources, suggests that the garden was the default setting for the elite convivial *majlis* in post-Mongol Iran. As in other premodern contexts,[362] royal gardens in the Persianate world served as open-air stages for courtly meetings and rituals. Although her reading of Hafizian garden imagery may be overly allegorical, Meisami is right to stress that the *ghazal* poetry of fourteenth-century Shiraz, 'testifies to the pervasive influence of the garden on the poets' vision of life and love'.[363] In some poems, the garden mimics (and even replaces) the human beloved.[364]

Over a period of many decades, Shiraz's successive Salghurid, Injuid and Muzaffarid rulers maintained a number of extramural gardens or garden residences, including: Bagh-i Atabak, Bagh-i Iqbalabad, Bagh-i Qutlugh, Bagh-i Takht-i Qaracha and Bagh-i Sunquri.[365] Even as late as the early seventeenth century, the number and size of Shiraz's gardens impressed visitors, as did the variety of flora (edible and ornamental) that their high, thick walls contained.[366] Fifteenth-century Yazd boasted more than thirty gardens and pleasure-grounds in and around the city that sported fine mansions and kiosks,[367] the urban fabric of the city having been much augmented in the late fourteenth century by Shah Yahya.[368] Elite individuals in Yazd and other cities frequently hosted *majālis* in private gardens, thereby providing employment for musicians, singers and other performers.[369]

Why did the garden become the primary setting for the courtly *majlis*? Fundamentally, the visually and sensually pleasing surroundings provided by the garden, especially in springtime, make it an obvious choice. Rulers may also have chosen to hold *majālis* in the garden because of the symbolic significance of the setting as an institution for the benefit of the public (not unlike a modern park) connoting prosperity and embodying the ideal values espoused by the court. Rulers typically built and maintained more than one garden and they regularly conducted their affairs from the garden: holding court there transformed it into a space of great importance to the practice of Islamicate statecraft.[370] Some rulers developed such a strong attachment to their favourite garden that they were buried there. Poets in the early Ghaznavid period composed *qasīdas* in praise of royal gardens, understanding them to be emblematic of the prosperous state.[371] The construction of a new garden was seen as a major event in the reign of a ruler: by laying out a new garden, he showed himself to be a fashioner and tamer of nature; the royal garden was an artefact often purposefully designed by the king.[372]

As with the pavilion, the terms used to signify 'garden' in the Persian *ghazal* are mostly interchangeable and largely overlap in meaning:

bāgh ('large garden', 'garden residence' or 'walled garden'),[373] frequently associated with *'aysh* and *tarab*,[374] and often named the 'world garden' (*bāgh-i 'ālam, bāgh-i jahān*).[375]

bustān ('garden', 'orchard'),[376] a place of 'hope' (*umīd*), 'beauty' (*husn*) and 'passionate love' (*'ishq*).[377] The *bustān* may not have been located within the city, which would explain the spatial dimension in the phrase *'azm-i bustān* ('heading for the garden').[378]

gulistān, gulbun, gulshan, gulzār ('rose garden', 'rose bed', 'swathe of roses') – often depicted as a convivial space[379] with kingly[380] or paradisiacal[381] associations that promises or facilitates (re-)union with the beloved (*vasl, visāl*).[382]

rawza ('garden', 'meadow') – possibly the name of an actual space in Shiraz.[383]

chaman ('lawn', 'grassed area', 'central portion of the garden'),[384] a setting for feasting and merrymaking[385] whose 'youths' are the cypress, rose and sweet basil[386] – naturalistic metaphors for the lissom serving boys and other young male attendants – and whose 'song birds' are the court poets.[387]

Jahan alludes to the *sarā-bustān*,[388] a compound of *sarā* and *bustān* that blurs the boundary between palace and garden and denotes a space adjacent to an elite residence. Given the proximity of the *sarā-bustān* to the domestic space, it is the type of garden most likely used by royal women, which might explain why the term is encountered in Jahan's *ghazals* with some frequency; J1115:6:

چون جنت فردوس است امروز سرابستان   آمد ز صبا بویی از گلشن جان باری

There came with the zephyr a scent from the rose garden of the soul
Today the palace garden is like the garden of Paradise.

The Spanish ambassador Ruy González de Clavijo tells us that some royal women in early fifteenth-century Samarqand owned private gardens to which they invited guests and in which they hosted wine parties and other celebrations.[389] Marefat has demonstrated how Timurid women accrued wealth and property and commissioned the construction not only of buildings, but also of gardens.[390] Geographically and culturally closer to the context we are focusing on here, we know of the Bagh-i Baygum owned by a royal woman in fifteenth-century Yazd.[391] It is likely that a similar pattern of female garden ownership and use existed in Injuid and Muzaffarid Shiraz.

Although they were not Turks, the Injuids and Muzaffarids were likely influenced by comparatively liberal Turco-Mongol attitudes towards royal women,[392] as a legacy of Mongol rule, the Turkmen Salghurids, and through intermarriage with local Turkic and Mongol dynasties, such as the Qarakhita'ids of Kirman, the Chupanids of Tabriz and the Jalayirids of Baghdad.[393]

The contemporary garden is paradise, here and now.[394] By associating the earthly garden with a stock of topoi linked to the Paradise garden[395] – whose denizens are depicted in the Qur'an drinking from cups served to them by beautiful young males (*ghilmān, wildān*)[396] – poets perhaps sought to distance themselves from the accusation that their poetry promoted activities not strictly licit in this life.[397] This might have been a crucial strategy for female poets in particular; J177:6:

وه وه چه خوش بود به صبوحی میان باغ   واندر کنار حور پریزاد بس خوشست

Ah, how pleasing it would be to take a morning draught in the garden
And seated at the side of a fairy-born houri, it is so fine!

The positioning of the wine party was an important decision. A location beside a source of fresh water was considered ideal: *lab-i jūy* ('beside the stream'),[398] *kinār-i jūy* ('next to the stream'),[399] *kinār-i āb* ('beside the water'),[400] *lab-i rūd* ('on the banks of the river'),[401] *lab-i āb* ('on the edge of the water'),[402] *tarf-i jūybār* ('beside the stream'),[403] *bar atrāf-i jūybār* ('on the banks of the stream'),[404] *ābī ravāna bar lab-i kisht* ('running water on the edge of the field');[405] H257:8:

میل رفتن مکن ای دوست دمی با ما باش   بر لب جوی طرب جوی و به کف ساغر گیر

Don't seek to leave, O beloved! Stay with us a while
Beside the stream seek ecstasy; take the wine cup in your hand!

Here there is a pun here on the word *jūy*, which means both 'stream' and 'seek'. Having water close at hand would have been desirable in the summer for its cooling properties. Running water evoked the streams flowing through the Qur'anic Paradise gardens.[406] Fresh running water was also prized for its soothing sound and perhaps for chilling wine or cooking the food served at a party.

One way in which the garden was enjoyed was via strolling: *tawf* ('going around', 'circling'),[407] *tafarruj* ('recreation' or 'amusement', normally including strolling)[408] and *gardīdan* ('sauntering', 'walking around').[409] The terms *tawf* and *tavāf* evoke the circumambulation of a shrine or object of religious devotion, such as the Ka'ba at Mecca. In this way, the garden acts as an alternate site of ambulatory devotion.

Where a royal garden did not boast a pavilion, a throne might be brought in and the party set up around the throne on the lawn;[410] H495:2:

لب گیری و رخ بوسی می نوشی و گل بویی   مسند به گلستان بر تا شاهد و ساقی را

Take the throne into the rose garden so that you can
Bite the *shāhid* and *sāqī*'s lips, kiss their cheeks, drink wine, and smell roses.

The fact that *majālis* were most frequently staged in gardens had a pronounced effect on the development of the language used to describe the beauty of the beloved in Persian lyric poetry, a poetic idiom that consequently employs a myriad of metaphors based on the flora and fauna of the premodern Iranian garden.[411] Medieval historians employed similar garden-related language to describe the beauty of the ruler[412] and poets would evoke the garden setting in their portrayals of sexuality; J1034:3:

بی باد هوای تو شکفتن نتوانم   من غنچه شوقم به تن باغ ارادت

I am a bud of ecstasy in the body of the garden of desire
Without the breeze of your desire, I cannot bloom.

The countryside

Parties might be held in the open countryside as entertainment for the participants before and/or after hunting outings. Extramural parties might also be held to celebrate the blossoming of the plains at springtime; U104:4:

برون رود ز خانه به عزمِ سلامِ گل   خوشوقت آن که با می و معشوق بامداد

Fortunate is he who at dawn, with wine and beloved,
Leaves his home to go to pay homage to the rose!

In the fourteenth century, the Musalla meadow (located just north of Shiraz, the location of Hafiz's own burial) was popular with locals who sought to escape the city and its restrictions.[413] Meadows and private gardens located beyond a city's limits provided a measure of seclusion for entertainments and would have been a less risky option for a *majlis* than the taverns, which regularly fell foul of the *muhtasib*.[414] It would seem that leaving the city proper, wine in hand and beloved in tow, to celebrate the blooming of the rose, was a favoured pastime; U61:8:

چو گل به باغ رود رو به خانه نتوان کرد   بخواه باده و با یار عزم صحرا کن

Ask for wine and, with the beloved, head for the plain
When the rose goes to the garden, you cannot head for home!

And H145:2:

که مرغ نغمه سرا ساز خوشنوا آورد   تو نیز باده به چنگ آر و ره صحرا گیر

You too grasp the wine and head for the meadow
For the melodious nightingale is singing a sweet tune.

In the Shirazi dialect, *sahrā*,[415] which normally denotes a 'plain', 'wasteland' or 'desert', denotes a meadow beyond the urban fabric.[416] The practice of moving from city to *sahrā* at springtime to party is reflected in the poetry;[417] U23:5:

هر کسی را هوس باغی و صحرایی هست   نرگس از غنچه برون آمد و اکنون در شهر

The narcissus has opened, and now in the city
Everyone craves a garden and a meadow.

In addition to the *sahrā*, other spaces beyond the city that were frequented during spring included the *margh-zār* ('meadow'),[418] *dasht* ('broad plain'),[419] *banafsha-zār* ('swath of violets')[420] and *lāla-zār* ('tulip field', a large bed of wild tulips).[421]

The best time of year for a majlis

Majālis were hosted in gardens and extramural meadows in the temperate months, particularly in spring; as Hafiz says, 'spring is simply no fun without wine!'[422] Audiences are urged to drink wine in the spring.[423] Many Ghaznavid panegyrics that were composed for recitation at Nawruz open with lengthy, detailed descriptions of royal gardens.[424] The poets of fourteenth-century Shiraz appear to have composed *ghazal*s specifically for performance at Nawruz (not simply evocative of the festival), often in the form of a *bahārīya* or spring song.[425] Nawruz and spring symbolize rebirth and renewal and, in poetry, can stand as metaphors for periods of political stability. Spring on the Iranian plateau is a brief season and depictions of vernal gardens would have drawn the audience's attention to the analogously fleeting nature of the good life.[426] In the opening line to this *bahārīya* presented in full here, Jahan puns on the two meanings of *naw-bahār*: (i) the first days of spring and (ii) the famed ruined Buddhist temple at Balkh; J165:

جهانی سر به سر چون نوبهارست به باغستان جان گلها به بارست

زمین همچون زمرد سبز گشته همه صحرا ز گل نقش و نگارست

همه بستان پر از گلهای رنگین هزاران بلبل اندر شاخسارست

لب جو سر به سر خیری و سوسن درخت ارغوان بس بیشمارست

ز عشق گل میان بوستانها فغان بلبل و بانگ هزارست

بیا یک دم که با هم خوش برآییم چو میدانی که عالم در گذارست

چرا از بوستان وصلت ای جان نصیب خاطر ما جمله خارست

The world, all around, is like a painted temple
In the garden of the soul, the roses are in bloom
The ground has become green like emeralds
Every plain is painted with flowers
Every garden is filled with colourful roses
Thousands of nightingales are perched on the branches
Beside the stream, wallflowers and lilies are dotted around
The Judas trees are too numerous to count
Out of love for the rose, the gardens are filled
With the cries of the *bulbul*s and nightingales
Come for one moment so we can take pleasure together
For you know that the world is a transient place
Why, O soul, from the garden of reunion
Is our share no more than a thorn?

Given the importance of the spring garden for poetry performance, it is unsurprising that Nawruz itself is so lauded in the Persian lyric;[427] J252:5:

جهان بگو ز چه خرم شود چو باغ بهشت   ز من بپرس که گویم ز باد نوروزیست

Tell me what causes the world (*jahān*) to turn verdant like the garden of Paradise
Ask me, and I will tell you that it is because of the Nawruz breeze.

It is the mild, magical, Jesus-like spring breeze that breathes new life into the garden and perfumes the world (by causing fragrant bulbs and buds to bloom).[428] The breeze 'unties the cord around the rosebud's cloak'[429] and brings wine's 'healing' (*shafā-bakhsh*) scent.[430] The first months of the Iranian year, Farvardin and Urdibihisht, are equipped with 'the instruments of ecstasy'.[431] Spring is the best time of year and the lover wishes days even better than Nawruz for the beloved.[432]

A frequent theme in Persian *ghazal* poetry is the urgency with which spring should be enjoyed, as there is no certainty that there will be another;[433] H444:5:

می بیغش است دریاب وقتی خوش است بشتاب   سال دگر که دارد امید نوبهاری

There's unadulterated wine: take it! It's a pleasant time: hurry!
Who is there who has hope of a spring next year?

The garden, first ravaged by autumn,[434] comes back to life in spring as the warmer weather brings an end to the desolation and misery brought by winter.[435] Hafiz advises his audience to conserve something of spring for the cold, gloomy months of mid-winter; H430:2:

که می‌رسند ز پی رهزنان بهمن و دی   ذخیره بنه از رنگ و بوی فصل بهار

Store up some of the colours and scents of the spring season
For the highway robbers Bahman and Day will soon arrive.

Gardens and meadows would not be used for *majālis* in the winter months, in part because of the inclement weather but also because of the lack of blooms essential for *tamāshā*. Having moved inside, *ghazal*s performed in winter would function as nostalgic musings to evoke the sights, smells and sounds of spring. When spring does return like a triumphant royal rose[436] there is only one thing to do: drink wine; H239:1:

وظیفه گر برسد مصرفش گل است و نبید   رسید مژده که آمد بهار و سبزه دمید

The good news has arrived: spring has come and the grass has sprouted
If our stipend arrives, it should be spent on roses and wine.

Spring is the best time for wine drinking.[437] It is the 'repentance-breaking' (*tawba-shikan*) season (where *tawba* = abstinence from wine drinking).[438] Hafiz suggests three months of wine drinking during the spring, followed by nine months of repentance.[439] The wine consumed at Nawruz might be that made from grapes pressed the previous Mihragan, which is marked by the culmination of the grape harvest and the pressing of the grapes for wine-making. Spring is the 'season for being a lover' (*mawsim-i 'āshiqī*),[440] the milder weather being ideal for spending time with your beloved in the seclusion of the garden;[441] H376:3:

نازنینی که به رویش می‌گلگون بنوشیم   خوش هواییست فرح‌بخش خدایا بفرست

It's fine, joy-giving weather; O God, send me a sweetheart
Face to face with whom I might drink rose-coloured wine.

In spring one must gaze upon the full beauty of both the beloved and the garden as they reflect and complement one another.[442] The lover and beloved must not be separated; U126:6:

خوش نبود میان ما فصل بهار فاصله   ای بت نازنین من دور مشو ز پیش من

O my beloved idol, do not stray far from my side
It's not nice for distance to be between us in the spring season.

The spring garden mirrors the courtly *majlis*: the flowers, trees and other plants mimic the royal patron, the *nadīm*s and the other participants, while the lawn stands for the throne or assembly room.[443] In these extended metaphors, the conceit of the garden as a microcosm of the world, or microcosm of the realm, is most clearly delineated;[444] U93:3–4:

با غنچه مصاحب شو و با یاسمن نشین   با ارغوان طرب کن و با لاله می گسار
گل ریز مطربان بنشان انجمن بساز   یا توق خواه شیره بنه جرغتو بیار

Associate with the rosebud and sit beside the jasmine
Make merry with the Judas tree, and pour wine with the tulip.
Scatter roses; seat the minstrels; set up the party
Or request firewood, place the new wine and bring the cup.

The flowers converse with one another:[445] the tulip takes up the wine cup and the narcissus is drunk[446] and bows respectfully before the cypress tree.[447] The spring blossoms are scattered before the feet of the wild rose, just as the patron might shower the performer with coins and pearls.[448]

For Jahan, merriment, the garden and springtime are interlinked. It is in spring that the world regains its youth and it is the time for pleasure-seeking;[449] J169:7–8:

بیا که موسم عیش و رواج گلزارست   رسید بوی بهار و دمید سبزه جوی
مباش غره بدان کم زرست و دینارست   به عمر نیست بسی اعتماد تا دانی

The scent of spring has arrived; fresh grass has sprouted by the stream
Come, for it is the season for pleasure and the time for the rose garden
You know that one cannot rely too much on this earthly life
Be not deceived by it; it has little gold and few silver coins.

Here Jahan implores her audience to seize the day and make merry before the physical (and political?) climate changes. This *carpe diem* attitude resonates through much of Jahan's poetry and may reflect her attitude to the political upheavals she has witnessed and of her personal trials. In the turbulent post-Mongol period, perhaps more than before, much depended on the whim of the ruler; radical changes could come into effect when power passed from father to son or from one rival house to another. For Jahan, the future was uncertain and many of her poems can be read as reflections on the pessimistic and troubled mood that prevailed; J85:6:

که را امید بقا ای عزیز بر فرداست   بیا بیا و غنیمت شمر یکی امروز

Come, come! Consider this one day a great bounty!
Who, O beloved, has hope of survival tomorrow?

The days of the rose

The brief period during which the first roses of the year bloom is presented
in the poetry as the most auspicious time for convivia. These days are alluded
to as 'the days of the rose',[450] 'the time of the rose'[451] or 'the season of the
rose'[452] – the rose itself carrying regal overtones.[453] This brief period in spring/
early summer is a metaphor for the ephemeral beauty of the youthful beloved
and the transient nature of worldly splendour.[454] It serves as a warning to the
audience through which the poet counsels them to make the most of their
current prosperity; H395:3:

ساقی به دور ِبادهٔ گلگون شتاب کن   ایّام ِگل چو عمر به رفتن شتاب کرد

The days of the rose, like life, have made haste to depart
Sāqī, hurry and pass around that rose-coloured wine!

And H162:3:

که گل تا هفته دیگر نباشد   غنیمت دان و می خور در گلستان

Appreciate this bounty, and drink wine in the rose garden
For the rose will not last into next week!

The rose is the object of the poet-lover's affections. It is the 'king' of the
flowers, before whom all the other plants and blooms of the garden prostrate.
The rose is the royal flower par excellence and a stock metaphor for the royal
patron. It is depicted as seated on its throne with the tulip-*nadīm* by its side;[455]
U104:1–2:

بگرفت گل جهان و جهان شد به کام گل   بلبل چو خواند خطبهٔ شاهی بنام ِگل
نگه چو دید چهرهٔ گل شد غلام ِگل   می کرد سرو دعوی ِآزادی ز دور

When the nightingale recited the royal sermon in the name of the rose
The rose conquered the world, and the world was as the rose desired
The cypress tree made claims of freedom from afar
But see how it became the rose's slave when it saw the rose's face.

The arrival of the rose, like the return of a long-awaited, triumphal king, is a cause for celebration;[456] H164:7:

که به باغ آمد از این راه و از آن خواهد شد   گل عزیز است غنیمت شمریدش صحبت

The rose is precious; treasure its intimate companionship
For it entered the garden here and will leave it from there.

The rose itself is also a focus of aesthetic contemplation: Hafiz urges us, 'sit not around the rose without wine, a pretty boy and the harp.'[457] The time of the rose is synonymous with wine-drinking and intimacy with close companions within the garden;[458] a time of year when repentance for the drinking of wine and other illicit activities would be a sure sign of insanity;[459] H346:2:

توبه از می وقت گل دیوانه باشم گر کنم   من که عیب توبه‌کاران کرده باشم بارها

I, who have repeatedly found fault with those who repent,
Would be crazy to give up wine in the time of the rose!

To abandon wine in this season would display deficiency of reason; H351:1:

من لاف عقل می‌زنم این کار کی کنم   حاشا که من به موسم گل ترک می کنم

God forbid that I, in the season of the rose, should give up wine
I boast of being a man of reason; whenever would I do such a thing?

Sha'ban, Ramadan and 'Id-i Fitr

In preparation for the month of Ramadan, during which wine-drinking was most likely suspended at court, Hafiz suggests imbibing wine throughout the whole of the preceding month, Sha'ban.[460] In speaking thus, Hafiz animates the antinomianism common to many forms of Persian Sufism that found expression though the intentionally provocative language of eroticized wine description.[461] Wine is also used by poets as a mark of sincerity and a counterbalance to the hypocrisy of the corrupt religious elite.[462] Hafiz alludes to drinking during the month of Ramadan itself, although he shields himself from reproach by asking for the 'wine of love' (may-i 'ishq) to be brought.[463] Risqué allusions are also made to erotic, drunken liaisons on Shab-i Qadr ('The Night of Power'), the night on which the revelation of the Qur'an is celebrated;[464] H42:3:

شب قدری چنین عزیز شریف　　　　با تو تا روز خفتنم هوس است

On such a mighty and noble Night of Power,
To sleep with you until daybreak is my desire.

The word translated as 'mighty' here is *azīz* which, as we have
noted, carries an allusion to the story of Joseph and its associated erotic
dimensions (see Chapter 6). Such erotically charged incitements are rarely
encountered in the poetry of Jahan but, in a *ghazal* in which she advocates
merry-making, she promotes engagement in wine-drinking as part of 'Id-i
Fitr; J721:4–7:

حیفست اگر نه عیش کنی با وصال عید　　　　فصل بهار و دامن گلزار و روی یار

بشنو ز بلبلان حزین وصف حال عید　　　　بنشین میان سبزه و باغ و کنار رود

در دیده هیچ نگذرد الا خیال عید　　　　در ماه روزه دل شده از ضعف سست حال

باد صبا و مقدم جاه و جلال عید　　　　چون فصل نوبهار جهان تازه می کند

Springtime, the rose garden's edge and the beloved's face
It's a pity if you do not make merry at the arrival of 'Id
Sit amidst the new grass, at the centre of the garden, beside the stream
Hear from the melancholic nightingales a description of 'Id
In the month of fasting, the heart has grown weary from weakness
In its eyes nothing passes but the spectre of 'Id
Just as the spring season refreshes the world
So does the messenger wind, and the coming of the glory of the 'Id.

The end of Ramadan allowed courtiers to celebrate the Islamic festival with
the consumption of wine.[465] 'Attar Shirazi has a lengthy panegyric *qasīda*
composed for the occasion with the refrain *may* ('wine'),[466] Hafiz congratulates
the *sāqī* on the arrival of the feast and calls on him to keep the 'promises' he
has made[467] and Haydar promotes breaking the thirty-day fast with wine.[468]
Drinking at the 'Id is a necessity in Hafiz's eyes:[469] the *sāqī* should bring wine
because the month of fasting – the season of 'honour and good name' (*nāmūs
u nām*) – has passed.[470] Since the Islamic lunar calendar is not fixed, in some
years, 'Id-i Fitr can coincide with Nawruz or Mihragan, giving added cause for
wine-fuelled revelry;[471] H246:1:

ساقی به روی شاه ببین ماه و می بیار　　　　عید است و آخر گل و یاران در انتظار

It's 'Id and the rose and the friends are in anticipation
sāqī, see the [new] moon in the face of the king and bring the wine!

The best time of day (or night) for a majlis

When poets speak of the time of day or night to gather for a wine party, it is either a nocturnal gathering[472] or a dawn bout (as the culmination of nightly revelry) that is most frequently evoked. In the following lines, Jahan depicts a night-time *majlis*, the nocturnal setting being emphasized through the refrain *ast imshab* ('[it] is tonight'). In this flirtatious atmosphere, the drunken *sāqī* is addressed and entreated to provide physical erotic gratification. The context is a wine party, rather than a furtive, clandestine lovers' tryst; J67:3–6:

گرچه آن ماه تمامم ز لبش کام نداد هر قدر لطف که فرمود تمامست امشب

خواب در دیده ما نیست نگارا شب وصل که مرا با رخ تو خواب حرامست امشب

به یکی بوسه دل خسته ما را بنواز چون تو سرمستی و انعام تو عامست امشب

دارم از دولت تو مطرب و ساقی و ندیم لب جوی و رخ دلدار مدامست امشب

> Even though that full moon gave me no satisfaction from his lips
> However much kindness he gives is complete, tonight
> On this night of union, O beauty, there is no sleep in my eyes!
> For to sleep before your face is forbidden to me, tonight
> With just a single kiss try to soothe our weary heart
> For you are drunk and your favours are free for all, tonight
> From your good fortune, I have a *mutrib*, a *sāqī*, and a *nadīm*
> The stream's edge and the beloved's cheek are constantly with me, tonight.

In the closing line of this poem, Jahan calls on her beloved to give her what her heart desires, for tonight it is her turn to be satisfied. Salman has a very similar *ghazal* with the same *radīf* that shares six rhyming words with Jahan's poem.[473] Jahan composed an additional two *ghazal*s which incorporate *imshab* into their *radīf*,[474] both of which describe a similar setting, in which the beloved is entreated to stay until dawn. The incorporation of *imshab* into a *radīf* is somewhat conventional, perhaps so much so that *ghazal*s with *imshab* in the *radīf* can be categorized as a subgenre of their own.[475] Did poets write at night because it is the time for writing/reciting poetry or because there is an established convention of poems written about the night? The two are not mutually exclusive and it is possible that such poems were composed to be recited at night ('alba' or dawn poems are, contiguously at least, also about the preceding night).[476] There is also the possibility that these poems speak to the practice of drinking wine at sunset or else at sunrise.[477]

Jahan hints that the lover and beloved might spend the whole night until daybreak together in the garden (elsewhere Jahan expresses the desire to spend a 'sweet night' [*shabī khush*] with her beloved);[478] J1114:4–5:

چه خوش باشد شبی تا روز در باغ   ندای چنگ و بانگ عندلیبان

خصوصاً وقت گل در شادکامی   نشسته روی در روی حبیبان

> How pleasant it would be to spend a night till dawn in the garden
> With the sound of the harp and the song of the nightingales!
> Especially during the time of the rose in delight,
> Seated face to face with the beloveds.

A nocturnal *majlis* is also evoked by the description of the beloved's face as so luminous that it replaces the need for a candle to light the party; J133:3:

گویند شمع نیست به مجلس چه می کنی   مهر رخ چو ماه نگارم کفایتست

> They say: 'There is no candle in the *majlis*; what will you do?'
> [I reply]: 'The sun of my beloved's moonlike face will suffice!'

Hafiz speaks of 'those who sit through the night' (*shab-nashīnān*) and 'those who keep the night alive' (*shab zinda-dārān*).[479] References to 'candles' (sing. *shamʿ*), the 'night' (*shab*), 'moonlight' (*mahtāb*) and/or the 'bedchamber' (*shabistān*) are common in Jahan's poems and are suggestive of nocturnal merriment.[480] Hafiz and 'Ubayd also allude to nighttime activities: musical performances,[481] drinking 'bright' wine in the dark night,[482] 'intimate intercourse' with one or more sweethearts,[483] anticipating reunion with the beloved under the cover of darkness[484] and lying next to him all night long;[485] U48:3:

خرم کسی که با تو روزی به شب رساند   یا چون تو نازنینی شب در کنار دارد

> Happy is he who spends a whole day with you until night,
> Or he who has a darling like you by his side at night!

After a night of revelry comes drinking at dawn, a metaphor for realization; the moment of clarity after the dark night of bewilderment;[486] U69:1:

سپیده دم با صبوحی شراب خوش باشد   نوا و نغمهٔ چنگ و رباب خوش باشد

> The break of dawn with a morning cup of wine would be sweet
> The tune and melody of the harp and the *rubāb* would be sweet.

The frequent evocations of the night in combination with the dawn suggest that all-night *majālis* were popular. Having spent the night in a garden or meadow, beside a river or stream, the revellers might start their day with a morning draught (*sabūh*), a supposedly effective cure for a hangover;[487] J750:1–2:

ساقیا برخیز و زود آن باده گلگون بیار   خوش نسیمی می وزد در صبح از بوی بهار

بشکنم در انتظار آن نگار غمگسار   تا خمار روز هجرانرا به آب سرخ می

At dawn a sweet breeze blows, bringing the scent of spring
O *sāqī*, arise and swiftly bring that rose-coloured wine!
So with crimson wine, I might break the hangover of the separation day
While waiting expectantly for that grief-repelling beloved.

Of course there is a tension between the realistic versus the conventional renderings of these images, but the evocation of the pitch-black night, which allows for the staging of the lovers' tryst away from the reproachful eyes of others, is symbolic of the night as a liminal time during which taboo activities or illicit fantasies are entertained.

Conclusion

Some of the *bayt*s discussed above can be read as asides or prompts to the *sāqī* and musician, guiding them how to sing the poetry or when to serve the wine. It would appear there are 'cues' for the creation of a poetry performance, wine party or other convivial event. It is not unreasonable to argue that these evocations reflect aspects of the reality of the contemporary contexts and settings for the performance of the poetry. The considerable overlap between evocations of performance found in the poetry and the descriptions of *majālis* encountered in contemporary histories and other prose works from the fourteenth and fifteenth centuries penned in the southern and central Iranian plateau adds weight to the argument that the *ghazal*s of this period can be read to illuminate the social environments within which these poems were originally performed.

The Persian *ghazal* is inherently suggestive, impressionistic and ambiguous; it is also malleable. Given the nature of the *ghazal*, it is problematic to argue that the evocations of performance in lyric poetry are depictions of actual, historical *majālis*. What these evocations do convey, however, is how audiences conceptualized the ideal context for the recitation and/or musically accompanied performance of poetry and what the aspirational settings were for such activities. Undoubtedly there exists an aesthetic distance between the evocation of performance and the actual staging of a poetic recital, but the links between these texts and their social contexts cannot be ignored.[488]

To understand the function of these performative and contextual evocations, much remains to be done. One preliminary hypothesis is that such references work as aides-mémoires; through evocation, the audience is reminded of the joys of spring (if the poem was composed for performance at another time of year) or entreated to recall better times; times of stability and ease – thereby raising their morale. In this sense, many Persian *ghazal*s can be read as texts of nostalgia, whose fundamental characteristics are evocative, rather than mimetic.

Spatial and temporal variations in setting and context dictated by a change of season, a change in the weather, or a change in the time of day at which a given poem was performed, would have significantly affected both the performance itself (especially in terms of the sonic environment when a move from indoor to outdoor performance occurred) and, consequently, the way in which that poem was received by the audience (keeping in mind that context is an evolving process, rather than a monolithic state). The recitation of that same poem in secondary and tertiary performance contexts (such as the private literary salon, the Sufi lodge or even the wine tavern) would have altered radically how the poem was received and interpreted within the poet's lifetime, let alone after his/her death.

We now delve deeper into the specifics of the *majlis-i sharāb* by focusing on the figure of the beloved who stands front and centre in the wine bout and the *ghazal*, the convivial poetic form par excellence. The amorous ethos of the Persian *ghazal* is normatively homoerotic and, as we shall see, the objects of male–male spectatorship (the coquettish wine-boy and the comely *shāhid*) function as metaphors for both the worldly beloved (the patron) and the other-worldly object of desire (the Divine).

3

Evocations of the Beloved

In this chapter, through focusing on evocations of the beloved, we explore further the relationship between poetic description (*vasf*) and the reality of poetry performance and reception. Descriptions of the beloved provide imitative representations of the sensory world surrounding poet, audience and patron. On one level, the poet uses description to represent this world – a project in part aimed at producing verisimilitude, albeit in a vision of an ideal rather than the strictly real.[1] Although the poet may present an imagined beloved, that form is, in many aspects, believable. Description of the beloved can be viewed as aspirational since it is used to encourage the listeners to strive for that ideal through a process of modelling. The Persian *ghazal* is a call to action and a courtly blueprint for emulation: once we have recognized this function of the form, we can appreciate how it acted to mould the contexts within which it was performed.

In the Persian mystical tradition, the lover and beloved are seen as part of a continuum;[2] both derived from love, their complementary duality is ultimately subsumed into the single reality of love.[3] In Ghazali's estimation, the beloved can only recognize the perfection of his own beauty in the mirror of the lover's full experience of passionate love and desire for him:[4] the beloved is dependent on the lover for his existence in the here and now.[5] What develops in Persian lyric poetry in particular is the idea of the supernatural, beautifying power of the beloved, what Bürgel terms the beloved's 'emanative energy', through which he bestows beauty upon other beings.[6] A description of the beloved's physical features and behavioural characteristics is an essential component of the Persian *ghazal*, as it is of *ghazal*s composed in the other major languages of the Islamic world. The beloved is the pivot of the *ghazal*, just as he is of the *taghazzul*, the erotic introit of the formal praise ode.[7]

Though the beloved of the Persian *ghazal* is not always human, it is description of the physical beauty of the human object of desire that is paramount. This description focuses on the beloved's upper body:

> It is a feature common to Persian *gazal* poetry that the description is chaste, almost entirely focusing on the beloved's face, in particular the eyes, the lips, the locks and the line (*xatt*) of the first beard; the most notable exception is the beloved's stature, 'straight' as a cypress.[8]

This emphasis on the upper body in the Persian lyric signals somewhat of a departure from its older, bawdier Arabic counterpart and, indeed, from Persian *taghazzul*s of the tenth to twelfth centuries, which can include waist-down description.[9] In the Persian *ghazal*s studied here, sexually suggestive images are rare, although some more risqué elements are detectable, such as allusions to sexual play with the youthful beloved.[10] Even the *ghazal*s of 'Ubayd (who penned some of the most sexually explicit poetry and prose of premodern Iran) are, on the surface at least, chaste. Although the majority of his *ghazal*s do not display vulgarity, we must be mindful of the intertextuality that binds the various genres of 'Ubayd's literary output. And, just as we must read across genres within the oeuvre of an individual poet, so we must read across the *dīvān*s of poets who operated side-by-side within the same patronage networks to uncover the erotic subtexts at play.[11]

From at least the time of Anvari (d. 1189), there has existed in Persian poetics a fairly clear distinction between the chaste *ghazal* and the often sexually explicit genres of *hazl* ('bawdy verse', 'facetiae') and *hajv* ('lampoon', 'mockery') in which vulgarity is employed in the service of ridicule. By contrast, when dealing with the early Abbasid short lyric it is often futile to attempt a distinction between a bawdy love or wine poem and truly licentious verse.[12] Many Persian poets wrote simultaneously in both chaste and bawdy modes to achieve the much-prized balance of *jidd* ('seriousness') and *hazl* ('humour').[13] Today we tend to classify serious and playful as opposite poles, but they were not seen as such by those who produced and consumed poetry.[14] The act of distancing the *ghazal* from obscene verse is a marked one in Persian.

The most sensual elements of the description of the beloved in the *ghazal*s examined here are evocations of the beloved's scent and the sugary taste of his mouth and lips. There is rarely any mention of the teeth (a feature found in Abbasid love poems)[15] and no direct allusion to the buttocks; the description of the roundness, fullness and sheer weight of the beloved boy's posterior being rather commonplace in Abu Nuwas's homoerotic poems.[16]

The Abbasid beloved as comparative model

Although separated by more than three centuries, early Abbasid lyric poetry (in particular the *mu'annathāt* [love poems about females], *mudhakkarāt* [love poems about young males] and *khamriyāt* [wine poems] of Abu Nuwas and his contemporaries) had a profound effect on the emergent literary Persian *ghazal* of the eleventh and twelfth centuries that ultimately found its culmination in the generic experimentation witnessed in the *ghazals* of Hafiz.[17] By comparing the Persian *ghazal* of the Mongol and immediate post-Mongol periods – the pinnacle of the development of the genre in Persian – with the Arabic *ghazal* of the eighth century, it is not my intention to suggest that all the elements of Persian description have their ultimate roots in Arabic. Indeed, some elements of description found in Abbasid love poetry may themselves have been influenced by contemporary oral New Persian poetry or else by Middle Persian material of the late Sasanian/early Islamic period (that is now lost).[18] The likelihood of Persian influence on early Abbasid poets appears plausible when we remember that Bashshar b. Burd, Abu Nuwas and others were wholly or partially of Persian stock[19] and a number of Abbasid poets inserted Persian words and phrases into their poetry or otherwise extemporised in New Persian.[20]

Many of the elements of description of the beloved in Persian are most likely transformations of metaphors commonly encountered in Arabic lyric poetry. Some transferred quite directly, retaining the same Arabic vocabulary and conveying the same meaning. An example of this being *hilāl* ('crescent moon') for eyebrow. Others perhaps transferred indirectly through translation of the Arabic into Persian: for example *māh* ('moon') to denote a beautiful beloved or his luminous face, a far more common word in Persian poetry than the Arabic loanwords *qamar* ('moon') and *badr* ('new moon'). Another example is *kamān* (rather than *qaws*) to describe the bow-like arch of the beloved's eyebrow. By translating Arabic terms into Persian or by preferring the Persian term over the Arabic loanword, poets ensured that their metaphors would be readily understood by those who did not know Arabic. It can also be argued that by coining novel Persian metaphors, poets were able to form new associations and work from something approaching a cleaner poetic slate. Since no pre-Islamic Persian love poetry has survived, it is not possible to state categorically whether or not these metaphors existed in Middle Persian before the Arab invasion although, as van den Berg has hypothesized, 'the presence of non-Arabic elements in [early New Persian] poetry fully justifies the assumption that the indigenous tradition exerted some influence'.[21]

There are other areas of description which seem to have undergone a more subtle, sideways shift. One example is the description of the beloved's torso or stature: in Abbasid poetry, it is conventionally likened to a fresh twig[22] or branch (both of which imply a lissom, sinuous body),[23] whereas in Persian the standard metaphor is the elegant 'cypress' (*sarv*). Perhaps Persian poets favoured the cypress as it was ubiquitous on the Iranian plateau and an integral element of the ideal garden; it therefore served as a more suitable metaphor for the beloved's tall, slender stature.[24]

There are also differences in descriptive focus between the Arabic and Persian *ghazal*. For example, the 'sweetness' or 'sugariness' of the beloved's breath, saliva, mouth, lips and physical movements are typical motifs in Persian, whereas they are of only secondary significance in Arabic. These hypotheses are presented here with the caveat that additional qualitative and quantitative research needs to be done before we can ascertain at what points specific Arabic elements were incorporated, whether directly or via translation, into the Persian *ghazal* and at what points other elements of description were dropped or remoulded.

Structuring the description of the beloved

Persian readily creates compound nouns and adjectives and it is common for two or more verbal and/or non-verbal components to be combined to create words not frequently encountered outside poetic or other lyric contexts. Some examples are:

> *majlis-ārā*: '*majlis*-adorning' (the noun *majlis* + the present stem of the verb *ārāstan*, 'to adorn': *ārā*);
> *gul-andām*: 'rose-limbed' (the noun *gul*, 'rose' + the noun *andām*, 'limb'); and
> *sīmīn-bar*: 'silver-chested' (the adjective *sīmīn*, 'silvery' + the noun *bar*, 'chest').

The Persian *ghazal* is an exercise in concision. Compounds are economical and allow the poet to describe more using fewer words. Most Persian *ghazal*s are short (on average consisting of seven to nine lines) so description of the beloved is normally clustered in no more than two lines.[25] It is unusual for more than one line to be dedicated to the description of any single body part, physical feature or behavioural characteristic. Notable exceptions are *ghazal*s which feature the name of a body part in the *radīf*.[26] In such poems, a single physical feature might be described throughout the poem cumulatively, from line to line.

Description can come in the form of similes, where comparison is signalled by the insertion of *chu* or *chun* ('like'), *hamchu* ('just like') or *mānand-i* ('resembling', 'similar to'). Persian poets developed an extensive, ready stock of largely stereotypical expressions;[27] a rich lexical repertoire of concise, fixed metaphors organized within a highly structured system which they used to describe the 'conventionalized' human beloved,[28] such as: 'cypress' for his erect, elegant frame and 'moon' for his luminous, beardless complexion. When these shorthand forms are added to poetic compound adjectives and/or nouns, the combinations can strike the untrained ear as unusual: *sarv-i gul-andām* ('rose-limbed cypress'),[29] *sarvi qabā-pūsh* ('a cloak-wearing cypress'),[30] *māh-i sarv-qadd-i gul-andām* ('cypress-statured, rose-limbed moon'),[31] *gul-'izār-i sīm-andām* ('rose-cheeked, silver-limbed one').[32]

Some *ghazals* open with lines that read like an abbreviated *taghazzul*;[33] J161:1–3:

رخش چو آتش و لبها چو قندست   سهی سرو مرا بالا بلندست

بر آن آتش دل و جانها سپندست   رخش چو آتش و لب پر از قند

دل مسکین چو مرغی پایبندست   در آن زلفین پیچاپیچ یارم

> My straight, upright cypress is tall and high
> His cheeks are like fire and his lips like sugar
> His cheeks are like fire and his lips full of sugar
> Upon that fire, hearts and souls burn like wild rue
> In those twisting, curled locks of my beloved
> My wretched heart is trapped like a tethered bird.

In these mini *taghazzuls*, description of the beloved morphs into that of the garden, the wine party hosted within it and the bacchanal accoutrements. A *ghazal* might open with an apostrophe to the beloved and a plea for favour.[34] This address can take the form of a cluster of invocations, reminiscent of the 'devotional invocations' (*munājāt*) of Khvaja 'Abdullah Ansari (d. 1088);[35] J52:1:

دلبرا حوروشا لاله رخا گلبویا   صنما سنگ دلا سروقدا مه رویا

> O idol! O stone-hearted one! O cypress-statured one! O moon-faced one!
> O heart-taker! O houri-like one! O tulip-cheeked one! O rose-scented one!

And J1186:1:

مه رخ شکرلب شیرین دهن   ای بت سنگین دل سیمین بدن

> O stonehearted, silver-bodied idol!
> Moon-faced, sugar-lipped, sweet-mouthed one!

Clusters or strings of descriptors can run to two or more *bayts*. These lines by 'Ubayd have a rhythmic, song-like quality; U137:3–4:

بالا بلندی گیسو کمندی   سلطان حسنی فرمان روایی
ابرو کمانی ناز کمیانی   نامهربانی شنگی دغایی

You are tall, your locks are like lassos; you are the king of beauty, you are the one who
    rules.
Your eyebrows are like bows, your waist is narrow; you are unkind, playful, and deceitful.

Whole lines can be packed with description of the beloved; H287:3:

شیوه و ناز تو شیرین خط و خال تو ملیح   چشم و ابروی تو زیبا قد و بالای تو خوش

Your gestures and coquetry are sweet; your down and beauty spot are elegant.
Your eyes and eyebrows are beautiful; your stature and height are fine.

And H282:2:

نگاری چابکی شنگی کله دار   ظریفی مهوشی ترکی قباپوش

You are a nimble, playful, crowned beauty;
You are a delicate, moonlike, tunic-wearing Turk.

Non-human objects of desire

Non-human beloveds function in the Persian *ghazal* as metaphors for the
human beloved, acquiring anthropomorphic qualities.

Wine

In the Abbasid short lyric, description of the beloved's beauty often combines
or becomes conflated with that of the wine.[36] The beloved's face and the cup
together shine like the full moon,[37] the beloved's cheeks and the wine are
both 'rosy' (*muwarrad*),[38] the boy's saliva is itself wine[39] and he has 'wine' in
his eyes.[40]

In the Persian *ghazal*, the beloved's face finds perfect reflection in the wine
cup;[41] H11:2:

ما در پیاله عکس رخ یار دیده ایم   ای بیخبر ز لذت شرب مدام ما

We have seen the beloved's face reflected in the wine cup
O you who are unaware of the pleasures of our continual drinking!

The wine cup can be likened to a mirror because of the reflective quality of the surface of the liquid it contains.[42] When the winebibber is intoxicated, the surface of the wine seems to come alive with the face of his beloved; H111:3:

یک فروغ رخ ساقیست که در جام افتاد   این همه عکس می و نقش نگارین که نمود

All these reflections in the wine and these beauteous forms
Are from a single flash of light from the *sāqī*'s cheek that has fallen into the cup

Taken more metaphorically, this reflection might be shorthand for the exposure of the true character of those who give themselves over to wine drinking. The replication of the beloved's face in the wine marries the deep red colour of the wine with that of the beloved's ruby lips and ruddy cheeks. The hue of the wine is reflected in the beloved's moonlike, unblemished countenance; H14:5:

همچو برگ ارغوان بر صفحهٔ نسرین غریب   می نماید عکس می در رنگ روی مهوشت

The reflection of the wine in the hue of your moonlike cheeks
appears as strange as a Judas tree leaf upon the surface of the wild rose.

The wine and the wine cup take on the form of the beloved's facial features: the 'rim' (*lab*) of the goblet acts like the beloved's 'lips' (*lab*), as it both smiles and contorts in laughter.[43] Anthropomorphization of the wine and the cup (and the linking of both to the beloved) is a feature of Hafiz's *ghazals* in particular.

The daughter of the vine

In Persian lyric poetry, wine is called the 'daughter of the vine' (*dukhtar-i raz*) or the 'daughter of the grape' (*dukhtar-i angūr*).[44] Wine as the daughter of the vine or grape (*bint al-karm, 'ibnat al-'inab, bint al-'anāqīd*) is similarly a feature of Umayyad and Abbasid poetry,[45] where the wine = female virgin motif is readily prompted by the fact that the Arabic word most commonly used in poetry for wine (the word also used to denote poetic wine description), *khamr*, is grammatically feminine. The daughter of the vine is a beautiful 'bride' (*'arūs*).[46] She is the bride of Kisra,[47] a 'virgin'[48] who should be married to water in the *majlis*.[49] The wine's 'father' is variously the grapevine,[50] the wine casket,[51] the Zoroastrian landowner[52] or a Sasanian king.[53]

Abu Nuwas's wine poems are replete with allusions to Persian kings: to Kisra/Khusraw,[54] Shapur,[55] Anushiravan,[56] Babak[57] and Bahram Gur.[58] These kingly allusions feature chiefly within polemical (mainly Shu'ubi)

discourse or in connection with luxury items, most specifically wine and associated paraphernalia.[59] The apparent conventionality of allusions to pre-Islamic Iranian kings in early Abbasid poetry tells us something about the perceived link between wine and Persian royalty in caliphal Baghdad.[60] This connection perhaps formed in part because of the importance given to wine in all its variety in courtly Middle Persian texts, such as *Husraw i Kawadan ud Redag-e*.[61] Early New Persian poets, seemingly inspired by anacreontic motifs in earlier Arabic poetry, flouted the social and ethical conventions of the pious and incorporated ancient Persian wine tropes into their *taghazzul*s.[62]

The Arabic words *bint* and *ibna*, like *dukhtar* in Persian, require the wine be a 'virgin' (*bikr*, *'adhrā'*). In the Abbasid short lyric, the prized vintage wine is unsealed for the first time in the *majlis*; it is not until the wine party that the hymen of this virgin is torn.[63] Despite her antiquity, the wine is a maiden who has not soured with age – her taste and hue have only improved over time.[64]

Wine continues to be treated as feminine in Persian poetry. Hafiz's daughter of the vine is depicted as entrapped in the wine casket or else 'veiled' by the glass bottle or goblet; H64:6:

جمال دختر رز نور چشم ماست مگر   که در نقاب زجاجی و پردهٔ عنبیست

> The beauty of the daughter of the vine is the light of our eyes,
> Although it bears a glass veil and is behind the grape's curtain.

The *dukhtar-i raz* can also denote the grape itself, born of the vine, the wine being the fruit's 'blood',[65] the association of blood with wine evoking the taking of the girl's virginity on the wedding night. The most celebrated early Persian wine *taghazzul*, that of the Samanid era poet Rudaki, opens with the phrase *mādar-i may-rā bi-kard bāyad qurbān*, 'the mother of the wine must be sacrificed'.[66] This wine discovery or invention myth based around an extended metaphor of the sinful vine and/or grapes that must be sacrificed, the blood of the grapes accidentally fermenting into fine liquor, appears to have been popular with Samanid and Ghaznavid poets.[67]

Hafiz depicts the daughter of the vine as a prostitute or promiscuous female who has 'repented from chaste behaviour' and gained permission from the *muhtasib* to ply her trade.[68] This image can be read as an allusion to the reopening of Shiraz's wine taverns by Shah Shuja' after he ousted his father. It could also be understood, more generically, as a metaphor for the end of the month of fasting and the commencement of the 'Id festivities, which typically involved wine-drinking. The daughter of the vine resides within the non-Muslim space of the tavern; H202:4:

نامهٔ تعزیت دختر رز بنویسید   تا همه مغبچگان زلف دوتا بگشایند

Write a letter of condolence for the daughter of the vine
So that all the Zoroastrian serving boys might loosen their locks.

The 'rose-like face of the daughter of the vine', if unveiled at midnight, will illuminate the convivial nocturnal gathering as though it were the sun.[69] Hafiz depicts wine as a 'bride' and also her 'divorce', presumably an allusion to momentary temperance; H460:12:

عروسی بس خوشی ای دختر رز   ولی گه گه سزاوار طلاقی

O daughter of the vine, you are a most comely bride
However sometimes you deserve to be divorced.

Depictions of wine as *dukhtar* ('virginal daughter', 'young, unmarried girl') emphasize the choiceness of the wine. In his *Saqinama*, Hafiz calls on the wine-server to bring 'that chaste, drunken virgin' (*ān bikr-i mastūr-i mast*) who resides in the tavern.[70]

The rose

The rose is a standard metaphor for the human beloved, symbolizing the beauty of the unveiled cheek.[71] The arrival of the newly bloomed rose in the garden – like the return of a victorious king from battle or a beneficent ruler after a wintry absence – is a cause for celebration, not only for the nightingale (*bulbul, 'andalīb* – a metaphor for the court poet) but also for the royal garden's 'flowers' and 'trees' (the courtiers and those close to power [the *khavāss*]);[72] H239:2:

صفیر مرغ برآمد بط شراب کجاست   فغان فتاد به بلبل نقاب گل که کشید

The bird's warbling has begun; where is the wine flask?
The nightingale is groaning; who removed the rose's face veil?

The fresh rose stands at the centre of the olfactory smellscape that is the royal garden. The rose's scent evokes that of wine[73] and it provides the chief aesthetic trigger or arousing focal point for *tamāshā*; H46:1:

گل در بر و می در کف و معشوق به کام است   سلطان جهانم به چنین روز غلام است

A rose before me, wine cup in my palm, and a beloved to my satisfaction;
On a day such as today, the king of the world is my slave.

The rose stimulates and entices its lovers with its appearance and smell;
H430:3:

چو گل نقاب بر افکند و مرغ زد هوهو   منه ز دست پیاله چه می کنی هی هی

When the rose has cast off its veil and the nightingale has begun to *hū-hū*
Do not let go of the wine cup! What are you doing? Hey!

By virtue of the similarity in colour, feel and scent between the flower's
velvety petals and the boy's downy cheeks,[74] the rose stands as an ephemeral
monument to time spent in intimate communion.[75] The rose is the king of the
flowers and thus the prince of the garden; emblematic of all that is 'noble and
beautiful and all that is transient and fading'.[76] The garden is his court or palace
and he sets up his 'throne' at the central axis of the garden;[77] H13:4:

تخت زمرّد زده است گل به چمن   راح چون لعل آتشین دریاب

The rose has erected an emerald throne on the lawn;
Seize the ruby-like, fiery-red wine!

The rose reigns in 'regal splendour' (*saltanat*),[78] however fleeting his reign may
be. He is the 'rose-king' (*sultān-i gul*),[79] the 'Solomon of roses' (*Sulaymān-i gul*)
and the 'prince of Nawruz' (*mīr-i Nawruzī*).[80] Before the rose-beloved's 'royal
tent' (*sarā-parda*), the nightingale warbles mournfully due to separation.[81]
Other parodies of courtly life include the rose as 'royal parasol' (*chatr*);[82] the
lover travelling with his beloved, wine in hand, to greet the rose in his 'royal
audience' (*salām-i gul*);[83] and the cypress, first acknowledging the superior
beauty of the rose and then becoming its devoted slave attendant (*ghulām*).[84]
    Alongside these masculine depictions of the rose as ruler we also find
feminine depictions of the rose as a virgin bride.[85] The rose awaits her groom
(*dāmād*).[86] She is the 'new bride of the lawn' (*naw-'arūs-i chaman*)[87] who, until
very recently, had been veiled in her bud (*ghuncha*);[88] U49:3:

به صد جمال درآید عروس گل به چمن   صباش دامن گلگون غلاله بردارد

Displaying a multifaceted beauty, the rose-bride appears in the garden
And the messenger breeze lifts the hem of her tight fitting, vermilion robe.

The tulip

Depictions of the tulip (*lāla*) as the focus of adoration are also found, though tulip-
focused metaphors are much less common than those connected to the rose.

The similarity in colour between the two flowers and the comparable brevity of their blooming period may explain why the tulip and rose are paired; H274:1:

به دور لاله قدح گیر و بی ریا می باش   به بوی گل نفسی همدمِ صبا می باش

> In the season of the tulip take up the cup and be free from pretence;
> With the scent of the rose for one moment be a companion to the *sabā* breeze.

Because the tulip is found not only within the garden's confines but also growing wild on the plain beyond, they are in some way evocative of bucolic revelry. The shape of the tulip's flower also evokes that of the wine goblet; H429:1:

ساقی بیا که شد قدح لاله پر ز می   طامات تا به چند و خرافات تا به کی

> Wine-boy, come! For the tulip's cup is brimming with wine.
> For how much longer this boastful vanity? Till when all this superstition?

Like the rose, the tulip's colour recalls the hue of the beloved's cheeks and lips. The rapid rate at which the tulip withers after reaching the height of its beauty stands for the transient allure of the beardless adolescent, but the fact that the tulip lacks the sweet scent of the rose makes it an incomplete metaphor for the human beloved, which perhaps explains why the tulip-as-beloved metaphor is not common in Persian poetry.

Human objects of desire

The female beloved

In the fourteenth-century Persian *ghazal*, the female beloved is the exception, rather than the norm. The poets of the period rarely celebrate an identifiably female beloved, but occasionally the object of desire is referred to as the *ma'shūqa*,[89] the feminine form of the standard word for 'beloved' (*ma'shūq*). But, even in those poems in which we encounter the *ma'shūqa*, a male beloved may still be intended, as the form may only have been used to fit the metre.[90] That said, the *ma'shūqa-bāz* (lit. 'female beloved-player'; the suffix *bāz* carrying a sexual overtone)[91] most likely denotes one who lusts after females, as does *ma'shūqa-parast* (lit. 'female beloved-worshipper');[92] H490:8:

سخن غیر مگو با من معشوقه پرست   کز وی و جام می ام نیست به کس پروایی

> Speak of none other to me, worshipper of the beloved girl
> For I have no care for anyone except her and the wine cup.

And J735:3:

معشوقه به خواب تا دم صبح　　　　بلبل به چمن ز شوق بیدار

> The beloved girl is asleep till the break of dawn;
> The nightingale on the lawn is awake through yearning.

A female beloved is also encountered in a number of Hafiz's mixed Arabic-Persian poems, in which she is given an Arabic female name, such as Su'ad or Salma.[93] In some of these poems, Hafiz mimics the heteroerotic *nasīb* of the pre-Islamic or early Islamic Arabic *qasīda*, hence the heteroerotic tone. In a bawdy *ghazal* that bears the imprint of the brothel, 'Ubayd's erotic focus is a 'whore' (*qahba*); U114:4:

واله دلبر شکردهنیم　　　　عاشق قحبۀ خوش‌آوازیم

> We are enraptured with a sugar-mouthed beloved;
> We are enamoured of a sweet-voiced whore.

Since Persian is essentially a genderless language, it could be argued that the ideal beloved is androgynous or, at any rate, of no definable gender. This is not the case in Persian lyric poetry, where gender markers almost always indicate a male rather than a female beloved. Gender ambiguity, gender blending and/or androgyny feature in many poems by Abu Nuwas, in which the human object of desire is depicted as a young male with stereotypically feminine (or effeminate) behavioural characteristics and/or physical features.[94] In a number of his love poems about females, Abu Nuwas switches from addressing the beloved in the feminine to addressing the beloved in the masculine or appears to be describing a *ghulāmīya*, a female slave purposefully dressed as a boy.[95] Abu Nuwas's beloved is 'gentle',[96] there is 'delicacy in his gentleness'[97] and he is 'tender and delicate'.[98] The boy beloved is 'softly-spoken'[99] and either has a 'lisp'[100] or a nasal voice.[101]

Key markers of the maleness of the beloved of the Persian *ghazal* include: the beloved's newly sprouted beard or moustache (*khatt*); his association with military terms; and his being addressed or referred to as a 'boy' (*pisar*,[102] *bachcha*, *tifl*, *farzand*) or a 'youth' (*javān*, *tāza-javān*).[103] It is age, not gender, that divides the lover from his beloved, and it is the full beard that is the most obvious marker of adult maleness; this is associated with the one who desires, not the one desired.[104]

The male beloved

The boy or youth

The default beloved in Persian lyric poetry is the young male;[105] early in the development of the Persian *ghazal*, the youthful maleness of the beloved became conventional. The social acceptability of the articulation by adult males of passionate attachment for beautiful youths is a prominent feature of premodern Persian literature.[106] This suggests that pederasty was common, largely tolerated and in some contexts normative and highly esteemed.[107] This tolerance is reflected in the homoerotic *taghazzul*s of courtly panegyrics from the early eleventh century.[108] Elite homophilia also left its imprint on much premodern Arabic, Turkish and Urdu literature.[109] Even when the beloved serves a mystic or symbolic function, Lewis reminds us, this is 'founded on a real sub-stratum of physical attraction and the active pederastic attention of older males to younger ones'.[110] Though lover and beloved are technically the same sex, the age disparity and the inability of one to grow a full beard, effectively puts them into two separate male sub-genders. It is this nuanced distinction that allows for the expression of sexual desire by the elder for the younger. The disparity in their social status (high-status lover/subaltern beloved) further reinforces this distinction.

Persian *ghazal*s featuring female beloveds became increasingly uncommon well before the close of the thirteenth century. In the *Gulistan*, *Bustan* and in much of his lyric poetry, Sa'di displays an unabashed acceptance of homoerotic desire and celebrates youthful male beauty.[111] Although some have attempted a heteroerotic reading of a number of Sa'di's *ghazal*s,[112] the depiction of an expressly female beloved is almost totally absent in the *ghazal*s of the fourteenth century: the beloved is an anonymous male youth unless stated otherwise; U34:3:

حلاوت لب جانبخش دلگشای تو نیست   بس اند خوش پسران در جهان ولی کس را

There are many pretty boys in the world, but not one of them
Possesses the sweetness of your life-imparting, heart-soothing lips.

The beloved is the 'darling boy' (*nāzanīn-pisar*),[113] the 'pretty boy' (*khush-pisar*),[114] the 'beautiful boy' (*zībā-pisar*)[115] and the 'sweet boy' (*shīrīn-pisar*);[116] H279:7:

دلا چون شیر مادر کن حلالش   گر آن شیرین پسر خونم بریزد

O heart, if that sweet boy should shed my blood,
Make it as lawful for him as his mother's milk!

The beloved is also called *farzand*,[117] *tifl*[118] and *bachcha*, all of which denote a juvenile male;[119] J1154:6:

ای دوست خطایی تو که گفتت که خطا کن   تو ترک خطایی بچه ای وز تو عجب نیست

> You are a Central Asian Turk, a child; it is not surprising you act so.
> O Central Asian beloved, who told you to sin?

Jahan puns here on the Central Asian Turkic (*Khatā'ī*) origins of the beloved and his predilection for 'sin' and 'transgression' (*khatā*).

As noted already, it is a convention of the Persian *ghazal* (as it is of homoerotic literature of the Islamicate world in general) that the love depicted in the poem be inter-generational. Some have sought to distinguish between passionate infatuation and expressions of same-sex desire and sexual consummation,[120] but what comes across from the poetry and extra-poetical information suggests that this imbalanced, homosocial bonding bears witness to the complex interplay of eroticism, masculinity and power at premodern Muslim courts.[121]

Abu Nuwas's beloved is 'young' and 'just weaned off milk'.[122] Milk-related imagery is also used in the Persian *ghazal* to emphasize the beloved's tender age: his lips smell of the milk that still drips from his sugar-like lips.[123] Jahan builds on the association of the beloved with his mother's milk when she employs the image of the infant craving breast as a metaphor for the lover's desperate desire for the beloved.[124] This lactic imagery prompts the audience to picture a childlike beloved, but there are numerous *ghazals* from this period in which a more mature, post-pubertal beloved – a youth in his prime – is celebrated. Such love objects are referred to as *javān*,[125] which suggests a young male in his late teens. A variant, *tāza-javān* ('fresh youth'), suggests a slightly younger male; H248:4:

ساغر می ز کف تازه جوانی به من آر   در غریبی و فراق و غم دل پیر شدم

> I have grown old through estrangement, separation, and heartache
> Bring me a goblet of wine served by a fresh youth!

The adolescent beloved is evoked through allusions to his being fourteen years old, his age being linked to the fullness of the moon's luminosity at the midpoint of the month; H256:10:

همین بس است مرا صحبت صغیر و کبیر   می دوساله و محبوب چارده ساله

> A two-year-old wine and a fourteen-year-old beloved;
> This is sufficient young and old companionship for me!

And H289:5:

که به جان حلقه به گوش است مه چاردهش   چارده ساله بتی چابک شیرین دارم

I have a nimble, sweet fourteen-year-old idol
Whose slave, I swear, is the moon on the fourteenth night.

The beloved's minimal facial hair (*khatt*; lit. 'line') suggests a youth who is coming out of puberty and into adulthood. The *khatt* is the key indicator of the burgeoning maleness of the beloved[126] and the focus of erotic energy in many *ghazal*s. The boy's *khatt* acts as the erotic boundary for those who engage in *nazar-bāzī* (adult male–juvenile male erotic spectatorship, a kind of 'mystical pederasty').[127] The *khatt* adds to the beauty of the boy's face,[128] enticing the lover to transgress. The appearance of this down signals the imminent end of youth,[129] which is why the first signs of the beard can be a cause of grief.[130] The *khatt* is the red line that divides licit from illicit. The erotic fascination with the beloved's *khatt* as evoked in the poetry suggests that older adolescents were, in fact, more desirable than younger boys because they had facial hair and had demonstrated their potential to grow a full beard. Approaching the *khatt* required bravado as it brought with it the danger of the social stigma associated with adult male–male desire, hence the erotic charge latent within the youth's first dusting of facial hair. The military vocabulary commonly used to describe the beloved also suggests an older, more physically powerful youth.

The non-Muslim

Allusions to the Zoroastrian boy (*mugh-bachcha*)[131] or Christian lad (*tarsā-bachcha*),[132] absent from the *ghazal*s of Jahan, evoke male homoerotic settings such as the wine tavern.[133] These allusions are poetic residue from earlier stages in the development of the Persian *ghazal*[134] and recall the celebration of what can be called 'inter-religious love' (or even 'sexual *jihad*') in early Abbasid poetry.[135] In the Abbasid short lyric, the beloved boy (often as wine-seller and/or wine server) is depicted as non-Muslim: Zoroastrian, Jew or Christian.[136] Christian wine servers also appear when monasteries and convents serve in the poetry as settings for (often debauched) *majālis*.[137] The selling and serving of wine is also associated in Arabic lyric poetry with Zoroastrians and Jews,[138] tropes that transferred into later Persian poetry;[139] H9:3:

خاک روب در میخانه کنم مژگان را   گر چنین جلوه کند مغبچه باده فروش

If the Zoroastrian wine-selling boy should display such coquetry
I shall make my eyelashes into a broom to sweep the tavern's threshold

And U8:4:

$$از رخ زیبای خویش قبله گه عام را \qquad کعبه دیگر نهاد دلبر ترسای ما$$

From his beautiful face – the *qibla* of the masses,
Our Christian beloved has made another Ka'ba.

The *mugh-bachcha* also points to the ever-wise *pīr-i mughān* lauded by Hafiz in particular.[140] Shiraz's Zoroastrian community was numerically small in the fourteenth century, but the importance of non-Muslims as producers and providers of wine should not be underestimated.[141] As already noted, the wine tavern is often evoked in the poetry with the term *kharābāt* (lit. 'ruins') which refers to the rundown area on the outskirts of town populated by non-Muslims to which Muslims who wanted to drink wine would have ventured. The *kharābāt* (whether understood as a tavern, gambling house, brothel or a combination of all three) is a space associated with the purposeful irreligion and 'social anarchism' practised by the *qalandar* or antinomian mystic in his pursuit of 'deliberate and open disregard for social convention in the cause of true religious love'.[142] Symbolically at least, the *kharābāt* stands for the nocturnal and the illicit; it is the site of 'ruination' (*takhrīb*) and the context within which the lover becomes 'ruined' (*kharāb*) through intoxication imparted by the beloved's lips.

Although wine taverns served as settings for less formal, non-elite gatherings at which poetry was performed, the bulk of the *ghazal*s studied here were produced for courtiers and were intended for performance at wine parties held in private gardens and parks or in royal palaces and pavilions. Although individual *ghazal*s might well have migrated in a top-down direction from their primary, elite performance contexts to secondary, non-elite ones, in elite contexts, allusions to the wine tavern would have functioned to evoke the *ghazal*'s bawdier, pre-Ghaznavid, oral origins when the form had stronger ties to music and song and weaker ties to the royal court. In the elite *majlis*, it was no longer the son of the non-Muslim vintner who served the wine to guests, but the host's well-trained wine server; H201:1:

$$شراب بیغش و ساقی خوش دو دام رهند \qquad که زیرکان جهان از کمندشان نرهند$$

Unadulterated wine and the sweet *sāqī* are two snares on the path
From whose noose even the world's most quick-witted cannot escape.

The *sāqī*

Given the centrality of the *sāqī* to the *majlis*,[143] it is unsurprising that he constitutes the focus of amorous attachment within many poems, standing centre stage in the revellers' erotic line of vision.[144] The *sāqī* is likened to an idol (*but*);[145] his narcissus eyes are enchanting;[146] the curve of his eyebrows forms a prayer niche (*mihrāb*);[147] and he has sugary lips.[148] The *sāqī*'s face reflects the silvery sheen of the moon[149] and his full cheeks evoke the ruddy glow of both the wine and the rose.[150] The lover must act fast to take optimum advantage of the *sāqī*'s youthful complexion for all too soon it will be overtaken by manhood;[151] H239:5:

که گردِ عارضِ بستان خطِ بنفشه دمید   ز رویِ ساقیِ مهوش گلی بچین امروز

Pluck a rose from the moonlike *sāqī*'s face today,
For a line of violets has sprouted around the cheeks of his garden.

Some poems contain more provocative descriptions of interactions with *sāqī*s;[152] H206:8:

دستم اندر دامنِ ساقیِ سیمین ساق بود   رشتهٔ تسبیح اگر بگسست معذورم بدار

Forgive me if the prayer bead's thread has snapped;
My hand was inside the silver-legged *sāqī*'s tunic.

Talk of repentance for kissing the *sāqī*'s lips is deemed blasphemous, reproachable speech; H319:4:

می گزم لب که چرا گوش به نادان کردم   توبه کردم که نبوسم لبِ ساقی و کنون

I repented, vowing not to kiss the lips of the *sāqī* and now,
I bite my lips and ask myself why I took the advice of an ignoramus.

Reading panegyrically, the kiss can be understood as a sign of royal favour, one that serves to codify the relationship between poet and patron.[153] Given a more mystical spin, the wine server represents the spiritual guide from pre-existence, an associate of the *pīr-i mughān* and the imparter of heavenly intoxication; H265:7:

جرعهٔ جامی که من مدهوشِ آن جامم هنوز   در ازل داده ست ما را ساقیِ لعلِ لبت

The *sāqī* of your ruby lips gave to us in the eternity that has no beginning,
A gulp from a cup which still astounds me today.

As discussed in Chapter 2, stylized apostrophes to the *sāqī*, phrased as instructions to bring, pass around and/or pour wine, evoke the *majlis* context and are often used to open or close a poem. The hemistich from an early

Arabic wine poem that opens the first poem in Hafiz's *dīvān* provides an earthly frame not only for that particular poem but, arguably, for his collected poems as a whole.[154]

The Turk

The Turk was established as the standard ethnic category for the beloved in Persian lyric poetry by the mid-Samanid period (circa 940–960).[155] But what did encourage the development of this convention? One factor was the profusion of Turkic slaves in the Iranian world from the tenth century; this is reflected in the well-known *qasīda* by Rudaki in which the male and female wine attendants depicted are Turks.[156] We know from early eleventh-century texts that Central Asian Turks were given to the Ghaznavids by neighbouring dynasties and noble houses as part of diplomatic gift exchanges.[157] Turks were prized for their light skin and dark hair and it is on the basis of this Turkic model that the ideal physical beauty of the beloved was developed mimetically in Persian lyric poetry.[158] The whiteness of the Turk is contrasted in the poetry with the dark skin of the Indian.[159] In fourteenth-century Persian poetry, *Turk* denotes a beautiful young male, rather than an ethnic Turk per se,[160] although the Salghurids (themselves of Turkmen stock) are said to have kept a retinue of fine 'slave Turks' (*atrāk-i mamālīk*), whom Vassaf describes as identical to the boy beloveds in lyric poetry: rose-cheeked lads with hair as dark as violets; boys as tall and erect as cypresses who wish their admirers ill.[161]

As slaves, Turks were of the lowest social standing and could, therefore, be traded as commodities and procured to deliver a range of services, including sexual gratification.[162] The Turk's seductive eyes evoke drunkenness[163] and, when under the influence of intoxicating liquor, Turks could be taken advantage of sexually (although, in 'Ubayd's estimation, Turks can play the roles of either 'active' [*fā'il*] or 'passive' [*maf'ūl*] sexual partner).[164] This is where 'Ubayd's prose works and satirical poetry are of especial use. 'Ubayd's depiction of Turks in prose provides context for interpretation of the beloved he depicts in his own *ghazals* and those depicted by his peers. Moreover, 'Ubayd's tales about Turks would not have amused contemporary audiences unless they found them relatable.[165] References to Turks in the poetry work as shorthand for the physical and emotional violence latent in unpredictable love relations: the Turk is a 'lover-killer' ('*āshiq-kush*), he treats his admirer with 'harshness' (*jafā*) and he is always looking for a good 'brawl' ('*arbada*)[166]; H124:7:

ترک ِ مست است مگر میل ِ کبابی دارد   چشم ِ مخمور ِ تو دارد ز دلم قصد ِ جگر

> Your intoxicated eyes wish to make a liver of my heart;
> They are like a drunken Turk – do they desire *kabab*?

When coupled with his beauty, the Turk's drunkenness can lead to 'disturbance' (āshūb, fitna, ghawghā) resulting in an imbalance in the city's social order and, more broadly, an unsettling of the cosmic equilibrium; H346:5:

تا ز اشک و چهره راهت پر زر و گوهر کنم   بازکش یک دم عنان ای ترک شهر آشوب من

Draw back your reins for one moment, O my city-disturbing Turk,
So that I might scatter your path with gold and pearls formed from my tears and cheeks.

Just as the Turk's arresting allure leads to chaos in the world, so evil stems from the unbridled passion caused by intense desire for him; U42:1:

عالمی در شور و شر می گرفت   ترک سرمستم چو ساغر می گرفت

Whenever my inebriated Turk would take the wine cup in hand
He would cast a whole world of people into commotion and tumult.

The threat latent in the Turk also stems from his infidel (kāfir) status or ancestry.[167] The Turk's bow-like eyebrows fire deadly, arrow-like glances at the lover,[168] an image evocative of the military prowess of the 'military Turk' (turk-i lashkarī)[169] or his showmanship on the hunt.[170]

But there is a paradox here: desired slaves are portrayed as all-powerful,[171] whereas in reality they had the lowest social standing and were powerless to resist the advances of their masters. Even when slave soldiers and their descendants (as was the case with the Ghaznavids) came to power or when Turkic dynasties such as the Saljuqs ruled the Iranian world, the most highly prized slaves or ghulāms continued to be sourced from among the Turkic peoples of Central Asia.[172] Given that Turks were the generic overlords of most post-Samanid Persianate societies, it follows that praise for a beautiful Turk can serve as praise for a royal or other politically powerful patron. It also follows that the male beloved eroticized in the ghazal and criticized for being distant, unattainable or cruel should be referred to as a 'Turk', because of the imbalance in the power relationship between the Persian poet-lover and his Turkic patron-beloved.[173]

The overlap between the Turk as beloved and the Turk as patron is most pronounced in relation to those rulers who were of part Turkic descent, such as Shah Shuja'.[174] Due to the partial Turkic origins of leading Muzaffarid princes and their intermarriage with Jalayirids,[175] the depiction of a local, Shirazi Turk in the ghazals of the period carries a strong panegyric subtext. As already noted, it is possible that Hafiz's intention when alluding to his Turk-i Shīrāzī is praise of Shah Shuja''s son, Sultan Zayn al-'Abidin;[176] H3:1:

اگر آن ترک شیرازی به دست آرد دل ما را　　　　به خال هندویش بخشم سمرقند و بخارا را

If that Shirazi Turk were to take my heart in his hand,
For his Hindu mole, I'd give away Samarqand and Bukhara.

Hafiz's readiness to give away Samarqand and Bukhara in H3:1 recalls a poem in praise of Shah Shaykh Abu Ishaq in which a single strand of hair from the patron's head is considered 'better than all of Samarqand and Transoxiana' (*bih az jumla-yi Samarqand u Varā-rūd*).[177] Hafiz's dismissal of the exotic in favour of the local also echoes this line by Sa'di:[178]

دیار هند و اقالیم ترک بسپارند　　　　چو چشم ترک تو بینند و زلف هندو را

They will surrender the lands of India and the Turks' climes
When they see your Turk eyes and Hindu locks!

Elsewhere, Sa'di contrasts local and Central Asian Turks not for their beauty, but for their tyranny:[179]

ز دست ترک ختایی کسی جفا چندان　　　　نمی برد که من از از دست ترک شیرازی

No one experiences as much cruelty from Central Asian Turks
As I do at the hands of the Turk of Shiraz.

Ingenito suggests that Sa'di may be voicing complaint here about the local Salghurid ruler.[180]

Hafiz boasts that the beauties of Kashmir and Turks of Samarqand dance and flirt to his lyrics.[181] Hafiz notes the Samarqandi origins of the beloved and engages in imitation of a well-known poem by Rudaki,[182] perhaps as a subtle allusion to Timur and the heartland of his realm;[183] H470:8:

خیز تا خاطر بدان ترک سمرقندی دهیم　　　　کز نسیمش بوی جوی مولیان آید همی

Arise so that we might gift our heart to that Samarqandi Turk
From whose breeze the scent of the Muliyan stream comes continually.

The soldier

The Turk is synonymous with the soldierly camp: he is a 'military Turk'[184] or 'military idol' (*sanamī lashkarī*).[185] In early Ghaznavid poetry, the beloved is praised for his prowess on the battlefield and his musical talent[186] and the association of the beloved with all things military suggests that the camp and barracks were loci for homoerotic encounters with young males, cementing the correlation between the foot soldier and desire;[187] H294:1:

در وفای عشق تو مشهور ِخوبانم چو شمع   شب‌نشین ِکوی سربازان و رندانم چو شمع

> In fidelity to your love, I am renowned among the fair ones, like a candle;
> I remain awake all night in the lane of the soldiers and libertines, like a candle.

The word 'soldiers' here is *sar-bāzān* which literally translates as 'those who risk their head as a sacrifice for their beloved'. The beloved leads the 'army of love' (*lashkar-i 'ishq*)[188] and is so powerful he can defeat a whole army; H327:5:

گرم صد لشکر از خوبان به قصدِدل کمین سازند   بحمدالله والمنة بتی لشکرشکن دارم

> Even though there might be a hundred armies of beauties waiting to ambush my heart;
> Praise and thanks be to God, that I have an army-defeating idol!

Among his weapons in this 'war' (*jang*) are the 'arrows' (*tīr*)[189] of his wink (*ghamza*)[190] and the 'blade' (*tīgh*),[191] 'dagger' (*khanjar*)[192] and 'sword' (*shamshīr*) of his cruelty;[193] all of which carry rather phallic undertones.[194] It is with these weapons that the beloved inflicts injury on the devoted lover;[195] U92:7:

غمزه‌اش تیری که می‌زد بر عبید   لعل ِاو پیکانش بیرون می‌کشید

> He would strike 'Ubayd with the arrow of his wink,
> Then his ruby lips would remove the tip from the wound.

The lover seeks to make peace, but the beloved is cruel, indifferent and only interested in perpetuating the war between them.[196] Allusions to a 'royal knight' (*shah-savār*, *shāh-i savārān*) in post-Mongol Shirazi *ghazal*s can be read topically as allusions to Shah Shuja', whose epithet was Abu'l-favaris (lit. 'Father of the knights');[197] H109:2:

صد نامه فرستادم و آن شاه ِسواران   پیکی ندوانید و سلامی نفرستاد

> I have sent a hundred letters and that king of knights
> Has neither dispatched a messenger, nor sent greetings.

The 'swift rider' (*chābuk-savār*)[198] or champion polo player[199] suggests a beloved who is manly and endowed with upper body strength.[200] This is a more mature version of the page eroticized in Abu Nuwas's love poems about boys: in which the love interest is a 'military gazelle'[201] who hails from the 'army camp'.[202] His glances are like 'arrows'[203] and he carries his lover's heart on the 'spear of love'.[204] He is 'heavily armed with the weapons of love',[205] injures with the 'sword of his glance',[206] wields the 'sword of desire',[207] has bow-like eyebrows[208] and carries a shield and breast plate.[209] The language of militarized violence permeates the Persian *ghazal* too; H240:9:

تیرِ عاشق‌کش ندانم بر دلِ حافظ که زد   این قدر دانم که از شعرِ ترش خون می‌چکید

> I know not who shot the lover-killing arrow into Hafiz's heart.
> All I know is that blood was dripping from his delicate lyrics.

This mature beloved of the Persian *ghazal* gallops,[210] does 'combat' (*ma'raka*) with the lover[211] and engages in 'pillaging' and 'plundering' (*tārāj, ghārat*).[212] A similarly eroticized threat is imagined by Jahan; J458:5:

ترک چشمت چون به یغما دست برد   در جهان جانِ جهان تاراج کرد

> When the Turk of your eyes pillaged
> He looted the soul of Jahan in this world.

The anti-Turk

Allusions to a non-Turk beloved, however rare, show that, even at this late stage in the development of the Persian *ghazal*, there remained space for deviation from the conventional conceptualization of the ideal. Hafiz sings of his love for a 'playful, intoxicated gypsy' (*lūlī-yi shangūl-i sar-mast*) and a saucy, deceitful 'gypsy-like' (*lūlī-vash*) boy.[213] Gypsies worked as hired musicians and dancers in premodern Iran[214] and allusions to them in poetry carry connotations of sexual liaisons brokered through financial transaction;[215] H51:4:

بندهٔ طالعِ خویشم که در این قحطِ وفا   عشقِ آن لولیِ سرمست خریدار من است

> I am a slave to my stars for in this dearth of fidelity
> Love for that drunken gypsy is what captivates me.

The eroticization of the 'dark-skinned' (*siyāh-charda*) beloved featured in some of 'Ubayd's *ghazal*s violates prevailing poetic and social conventions.[216] 'Ubayd's contrary amorous stance appears to be aimed at provoking a reaction in the audience. The poet's counterhegemonic eroticism is akin to what Greenblatt has observed in Shakespeare's works, where the celebration of dark-skinned beauties is 'always understood to be a paradox, a revelation of desire's ability to unsettle the proper order of things'.[217] The *lūlī* in Persian poetry is a liminal figure who occupies the seedy periphery of society. 'Ubayd praises a beloved who appears to be a Turk, but who is actually a local gypsy boy; U121:2:

لولی ترک شکل ِشیرازی   مست و شنگول و کژ نهاده کلاه

A Turk-like, Shiraz-born gypsy:
Drunk and playful; his cap to one side.

This sexualization of a Shirazi gypsy may have helped 'Ubayd align himself with the indigenous population of the city, rather than with its non-Shirazi Turkic (or Turkicized) elite. We find additional evidence of 'Ubayd's eroto-localism in one of his drinking songs. Understanding 'Ubayd's promotion of the connection between local Shirazi beaus and sordid wine taverns is vital when we interpret his depiction of the beloved; U114:1:

ما که رندان ِکیسه پردازیم   کشتۀ شاهدان ِ شیرازیم

We who are free-spending, generous libertines,
Are murdered by the pretty youths of Shiraz!

'Ubayd's local beloved needs to be read alongside the celebration of the Turks of Shiraz as found in the *ghazal*s of Hafiz, but also in lyric poems by Sa'di and Khvaju.[218] Hafiz's allusion to 'Persian-speaking beauties' (*khūbān-i Pārsī-gū*) in the line quoted below can be read as a preference for the local, non-Turk; *Pārsī-gū* can be interpreted to mean one who speaks the provincial dialect of Fars or perhaps even a Zoroastrian; H5:12:

خوبان پارسی گو بخشندگان عمرند   ساقی بده بشارت رندان پارسا را

Persian-speaking beauties are the ones who impart life.
Sāqī deliver the good news to the libertines of Fars!

In the Sajjadi/Bahramian/Barg-naysi edition, the allusion in this line is to *Turkān-i Pārsī-gū* ('Persian-speaking Turks'),[219] which would perhaps allude to local populations of Turks (whether members of the elite classes or salve-soldiers and attendants) and their characteristic, pleasing pronunciation of Persian.[220] Other allusions to Turks in lyric poetry from fourteenth-century Shiraz invite interpretations that engage the contemporary political reality.[221]

Beloved types

The angelic beloved

The beloved resembles, or is born of, an 'angel' (*firishta*), a 'fairy' (*parī*) or one of the dark-eyed, female inmates of the Qur'anic Paradise (*hūr, hūrī*).[222] The beloved evokes the world to come: he is the 'child of a fairy' (parī-zād)[223] or 'born of a houri' (hūr-zād)[224] and has a 'fairy-like countenance' (parī-chihra,[225] parī-rūy,[226] parī-rukhsār[227]); U38:1:

سر نخوانیم که سودازدهٔ مویی نیست   آدمی نیست که مجنون پریرویی نیست

> There is no head that is not infatuated with a single hair;
> There is no man alive who is not crazy for a fairy-faced beloved.

The beloved is 'fairy-like' (parī-vash),[228] 'angelic in nature' (firishta-khū),[229] 'houri-like' (hūr-vash)[230] and has a 'fairy-like form' (parī-paykar).[231] Firishta, parī and hūr denote female beings, but their offspring are presented in the poetry as young males.[232] These beloveds combine the best of female and male, representing a gender in-between (in the mystical tradition, love itself is beyond gender binaries).[233] The adolescent maleness of the angelic beloved is, however, reasserted when adjectives derived from parī,[234] firishta and hūr are combined with Turk,[235] idol[236] or sāqī; H13:8:

بر رخِ ساقیِ پری پیکر   همچو حافظ بنوش بادهٔ ناب

> Seated across from the fairy-faced sāqī
> Just like Hafiz, drink pure wine.

Abu Nuwas draws a comparison between the earthly beloved and the houris of Paradise,[237] a similar connection being made by Hafiz in his ghazals; H77:8:

چشمِ حافظ زیر بام آن قصر آن حوری سرشت   شیوهٔ جنّات تجری تحتها الانهار داشت

> Hafiz's eyes under the roof of the palace of that houri-like one
> Kept the custom of 'Gardens beneath which rivers flow'.

The incorporation of a Qur'anic phrase here is the focal point as the earthly garden is the envy or rival of the heavenly Paradise.

The beloved as idol

The beloved is to be worshipped and feared.[238] He is a but,[239] a word that originally referred to a Buddhist statue;[240] U10:1:

دارم بتی به چهره چو صد ماه و آفتاب   نازکتر از گل تر و خوشبوتر از گلاب

> I have an idol whose face outdoes a hundred moons and suns;
> He's more delicate than a fresh rose and more fragrant than rose water!

The Arabic loanword *sanam* is also employed to describe the beloved.[241] This is noteworthy, given that *sanam* (pl. *asnām*) is used in a pejorative manner in the Qur'an to denote pre-Islamic Arabian effigies;[242] H127:10:

حافظ اگر سجدهٔ تو کرد مکن عیب   کافر عشق ای صنم گناه ندارد

> If Hafiz has prostrated before you, find not fault with him;
> Love's infidel, O idol, commits no sin.

The equation of the beloved with a pagan idol or effigy is less common in Abbasid poetry.[243] In the Persian *ghazal*, the terms *nigār* and *nigārīn* used to describe the beloved mean 'beautiful image', 'captivating painting', 'idol'[244] and are thought to have their origins in Buddhist, Manichean and Christian iconography; J59:2:

ز نور روی چون خورشید برده   نگار مهوشم از چشمِ ما خواب

> By the light of his sun-like face
> My moon-like idol has stolen sleep from my eyes.

The four terms – *but, sanam, nigār* and *nigārīn* – are essentially interchangeable. In the poetry, worship of the beloved as idol replaces or transforms Islamic ritualistic acts as the beloved becomes the lover's Ka'ba[245] and *qibla*;[246] J1005:6:

روی تو مرا قبله و ابروی تو محراب   اینست همه دینم و آنست همه کیشم

> Your face is my *qibla*; your eyebrow my *mihrāb*
> This one is my whole faith; the other my whole creed.

Given that the equation of the royal patron's threshold and/or his sanctified, inviolable presence with the *qibla* and/or Ka'ba is a feature of the Persian praise *qasīda*, similar imagery in amorous *ghazal*s adds panegyric undertones.[247]

The beloved as witness to divine beauty

Calling the beloved *shāhid*,[248] the perfectly beautiful ephebe who acts as 'witness' to God's beauty, suggests a high degree of passivity and objectification as the focus of *nazar* ('[erotic] gaze'). In the all-beautiful form of the *shāhid*, the singular beauty of God, the supreme beloved, can be observed.[249] Many Sufis believed God was present in beautiful humans; a belief used in defence of gazing on fine-looking boys. The *shāhid* provokes an erotic response in the audience who revel in his human beauty through which they hope to observe the beauty of the Divine.[250] Mystics viewed love of creation as the key to beatific vision and, Ze'evi tells us, in their attempt to relate profane love to heavenly love, 'Sufis developed the idea of gazing at beauty as a path to the true love of God'.[251]

The *shāhid* does not feature prominently in Jahan's *ghazal*s, which is perhaps an indication that the intense homoerotic connotations of the term were considered too risqué for poetry penned by women of her social status. It should be noted that the homoerotic celebration of male beauty and homosociability were in part promoted by Sufis because of the widely held belief in the spiritual and moral inferiority of women.[252] The *shāhid* is a comparative rarity in 'Ubayd's *ghazal*s too, which suggests the *shāhid*'s strong Sufi significance is out of place in his poetry (a notable exception being U114 discussed above). Hafiz deliberately and seamlessly blends the mystical and the erotic in his *ghazal*s. Here we encounter the depiction of a *shāhid* that lends itself readily to a Sufistic interpretation; H15:1:

وی مرغ بهشتی که دهد دانه و آبت   ای شاهد قدسی که کشد بند نقابت

> O holy *shāhid*, who might loosen your face veil?
> O paradisiacal nightingale, who might supply your grain and water?

Elsewhere, Hafiz protests at bawdy depictions of *shāhid*s (such as those included by 'Ubayd in his witty anecdotes, where the *shāhid* is little more than a tantalizing dancing boy);[253] H125:1:

بندهٔ طلعت آن باش که آنی دارد   شاهد آن نیست که مویی و میانی دارد

> The *shāhid* is not the one who has a waist as thin as a strand of hair
> Be a slave to the countenance of he who has that undefinable thing.

As the object of *nazar*, the *shāhid* adorns the wine symposium, augments the beauty of the garden and arouses sensual desire in the ogling onlookers.[254] The lustful feelings thus provoked are intended for transmutation into a yearning for the Divine, a kind of mystico-erotic transposition,[255] although this may have worked better in theory than practice;[256] H239:3:

هر آن که سیب زنخدان شاهدی نگزید   ز میوه های بهشتی چه ذوق دریابد

> What delight can he derive from the fruits of the Paradise garden
> He who has never bitten the apple of a *shāhid*'s chin dimple?

The beardless *shāhid* and the royal patron are complementary loci of the manifestation of God's *jamāl* ('beauty') and *jalāl* ('majesty').[257] The *shāhid* becomes paired or conflated in the poetry with the *sāqī*,[258] and *shāhid-bāzī/ nazar-bāzī* ('[communal] love-play with beardless youths,' 'exchanging flirtatious glances with ephebes') serve as markers of the bawdier, riotous wine bout but were also ritualized activities common to many Sufi groups;[259] H421:6:

شکر شکسته سمن ریخته رباب زده   ز شور و عربدهٔ شاهدان شیرینکار

Through the commotion and brawling of graceful *shāhid*s
Sugar is breaking, jasmine flowers are falling, *rubāb*s are being struck.

The *shāhid* also carries connotations of sexual contact,[260] perhaps even male prostitution. Hafiz speaks of the *shāhid-i bāzārī* ('marketplace beauty', 'commercial *shāhid*'), an appellation that suggests money for sex.[261] Hafiz contrasts the allure of this figure with that of the *parda-nashīn* ('closeted, veiled [female]').[262] The poet also hints at sex for money through the term *har-jā'ī* ('[street] wanderer', 'prostitute').[263]

The passivity of the beloved as *shāhid, but* or *sanam* is contradicted by the simultaneous depiction of him as all-powerful tyrant or hard-hearted, militarized, drunken youth poised to inflict pain and suffering upon the lover. This dichotomy between the beloved's passivity and his active dominance as a menace to the lover is couched in an unresolved, tense ambiguity. The beloved's physical beauty is the true threat and, even though the beloved may not return the *nazar*, this is not a unidirectional erotic encounter: the beloved's seductive allure is predatory and draws the lover to him, as if through magnetism.

The beloved's multiple personae

The beloved simultaneously inhabits a multiplicity of seemingly contradictory personae, through which he exhibits a spectrum of behavioural characteristics. He is at once joker, flirt, predator, disturber, oppressor and breaker of promises. As 'joker' (*shūkh*), the beloved affects his lover in positive ways: he shows favour (albeit infrequently and momentarily) to the lover, thereby reciprocating in part his amorous advances. The beloved's response, however, comes from the distance of ultimate unattainability: as joker or flirt he is no more than a tease. The joker is jolly, jovial, charming, cheerful and playful.[264] This playfulness, however, acts as a film that obscures a more wicked side; U5:1:

فکند سیب زنخدان او به چاه مرا   بکشت غمزه آن شوخ بیگناه مرا

That playful boy's wink killed me though I was innocent;
The apple of his chin dimple cast me into the pit.

The Joseph-beloved wreaks havoc upon the lover, treating him as the jealous brothers did Jacob's favourite son. The joker only thinks of his own needs; J901:7:

چرا کان نازنین شوخیست خودکام   زلعلش کام دل مشکل بیابی

> Only with difficulty will you obtain your heart's desire from his ruby lips
> For that delightful one is a selfish joker.

Shūkh is used to describe the person, behaviour and actions of the beloved. It is also used to describe his eyes,[265] glance,[266] eyebrows[267] and eyelashes;[268] H97:2:

به چین زلف تو ماچین و هند داده خراج   دو چشم شوخ تو بر هم زده ختا و حبش

> Your two playful eyes have upset both Cathay and Ethiopia
> For the twists (*chīn*) of your locks, the Chinese Emperor (*mā chīn*) and all India have paid taxes.

The beloved is 'giddy' (*shang, shangūl*);[269] J281:11:

هیچ شوخی شنگلی چون آن بت عیّار نیست   هست خوبان در جهان بسیار لیکن عقل گفت

> There are many beauties in the world but reason said:
> 'There is no giddy rogue quite like that knavish idol!'

Shangūl is also used to describe the tipsy revellers, whose manner mirrors the object of their desire. The beloved's mischievous, kittenish nature is located in 'flirtation' (*'ishva*), 'coquetry' (*nāz*), 'dalliance' (*ghunj*) and 'inviting glances' (*kirishma*);[270] U122:5:

به راه می‌روی و خلق می‌روند از راه   کرشمه می‌کنی و عقل می‌شود حیران

> You move flirtatiously and my mind is bewildered;
> You walk by and people are diverted from the straight path.

Poets combine these terms with descriptions of the beloved's physical movements to evoke sexually charged *majālis* at which high-status guests would consort with low-status wine servers, dancers and other hired entertainers.

In accordance with the Persian *ghazal's* behavioural code, the beloved must not show favour to the lover; the beloved is programmed to inflict suffering and hardship upon those who fall under his spell, much like an unforgiving, despotic tyrant.[271] What's more, the lover must suffer gladly and pridefully for the sake of love itself, whilst the object of his desire displays complete indifference to him and detachment from him.[272] It is not only the *raqīb* (the beloved's 'guardian'; the lover's 'rival') or the *malāmat-gū* ('blamer') who causes suffering to befall the lover: the beloved also metes out the required punishment to his devotees.

In Arabic lyric poetry, the beloved is likened to a gazelle (*zaby, shādin* or *ghazāl*).[273] In Persian lyric poetry, the gazelle (*ghazāl, āhū*) is predatory;[274] U51:2:

جز دل مجروح ما نشانه ندارد   ناوک جان‌دوز چشم شیرشکارت

The soul-stitching tip of your lion-slaying eye
Has no target save my wounded heart.

The beloved's passivity is suggested by the terms *ma'shūq* and *mahbūb* (the objects of *'ishq* and *hubb* ['love', 'affection'], terms used to denote the Divine, the Prophet, the patron and/or the Sufi master).[275] More often than not, though, the beloved is an active agent in the game of love: he is the 'heart-taker' (*dil-bar*), the 'heart-seizer' (*dil-sitān*), the 'heart-stealer' (*dil-rubā*), the 'heart-desirer' (*dil-khvāh*) and the 'heart-possessor' (*dil-dār*).

As disturber, the beloved unsettles the prevailing order. He causes apocalyptic, eschatological disorder and is the initiator of 'upheaval' (*ashūb*),[276] 'sedition' (*fitna*),[277] 'tumult' (*qiyāmat*),[278] 'commotion' (*shūr*)[279] and 'uproar' (*ghawghā*);[280] J86:6:

می‌کن که از او به شهر غوغاست   ای دل حذر از دو چشم مستش

O heart, be wary of his two intoxicated eyes;
For it is they that cause unrest in the city.

Fattān ('seductive', 'bewitching') is etymologically related to *fitna* and is used to describe the beloved's lethal eyes and glances.[281] Abu Nuwas's boy beloved is a test (*fitna*) to the pious,[282] his seductive whisperings are those of Satan (*waswās*).[283] The beloved's extraordinary beauty is the cause of a disturbance that upsets the lover's state and that of his fellow *nazar-bāzān* as well as that of the entire city[284] and the equilibrium of the marketplace that lies at its heart. As noted in Chapter 1, the beloved is the 'city-disturber' (*shahr-āshūb*) and the 'city-provocateur' (*shahr-angīz*).[285] By cosmic extension, the boy's beauty unsettles the equipoise of the entire world.[286]

The profuse discussion of disturbance of the status quo would have resonated with contemporary audiences, given the dynastic ruptures and resultant social upheavals in fourteenth-century Iran; J897:4:

ترسم که ز جور تو برآید   ناگاه به شهر فتنه عام

I fear that out of your tyranny suddenly
There will rise up mass unrest in the city.

As oppressor, the beloved embodies implacable 'harshness' (*jawr*) and
'cruelty' (*jafā*);[287] U90:6:

ورم به جور براند ز پیش حکم او راست   پسند دوست بود هرچه دوست فرماید

Even if he drives me cruelly from his presence, his command is righteous;
The lover finds pleasing whatsoever the beloved commands.

It is as though he plies cruelty as his trade.[288]

The beloved is a 'tyrant' (*sitam-gar*),[289] who imposes all manner of tyranny
on his victims.[290] He is unkind, uncaring and shows no mercy to those who
would love him. The beloved is 'spiteful' (*kīna-jū*),[291] 'unkind' (*nā-mihrabān*),[292]
'hot-headed' (*tund-khū*)[293] and 'stubborn' (*sar-kish*).[294] He has no shame,[295]
shows no kindness,[296] and has no mercy.[297] The beloved is 'stone-hearted'
(*sang-dil, sangīn-dil*)[298] and his ultimate goal is to murder the lover.[299] As Sa'di
says in the prologue to the *Gulistan*: '[true] lovers are those killed by the
beloved' (*'āshiqān kushtagān-i ma'shūq-and*).[300]

The motif of the murderous beloved is one that remained central to
Islamicate *ghazal* poetry for centuries.[301] If we accept beloved = patron, we
can read this depiction of a violent beloved as a metaphor for the poet's loyalty
as required by a system in which all rewards and punishments derive from
the person of the ruler. The poet's loyalty is considered normative; the ruler
expects it to be offered without regard to the nature of his own behaviour.[302]
The beloved treats the lover worse than any enemy.[303] He overpowers the lover,
who is resigned to this harsh and cruel treatment. Links between sexuality
and violence are found across a wide range of Islamicate poetry.[304] The lover's
yearning for abuse, which he interprets falsely as a sign of reciprocated love,
lends a masochistic layer to their relationship.

As *'ayyār* ('trickster rogue'),[305] the beloved inhabits the character of the
vagabond knave.[306] The *'ayyār* is linked to the circle of the libertine *rind*s and he
shares their flagrant disregard for the conventions of polite society. He hails
from the urban underworld, a world dominated by the *awbāsh* and the *lūtī*s
(louts, ruffians and hired thugs who policed city wards).[307] The *awbāsh* enjoyed
considerable power during the Injuid period and had links to the elite circles of
Shiraz society.[308] The *ghazal*s of Hafiz and several other poets active in Shiraz
in the fourteenth century enjoyed wide and rapid circulation horizontally, from
one elite *majlis* to another inside Shiraz and then to the courts of other major
cities of post-Mongol Iran and Iraq[309] and vertically, downwards from the

court to non-elite contexts. One channel of contact between the sophisticated *majālis* of Shiraz's urbane elite and the world of the *lūtīs* and *awbāsh* was through the hiring of musicians and dancing boys drawn from society's fringes to provide entertainment of various shades.

The resulting overlap between high and low in Shirazi society is most evident in 'Ubayd's anecdotes that would have been readily comprehensible (and therefore amusing) to most. In addition to challenging established norms of exploitation and moral corruption among Shiraz's upper echelons through a comedic medium, 'Ubayd also ridiculed the socially and economically powerless on the edge of society.[310] As trickster rogue, the beloved may also wield 'sorcery' and 'magic' (*jādū, afsūngarī, shu'bida-bāzī*).[311] Indeed, he seduces (and, thereby, misleads) the lover through 'trickery' (*farīb*).[312] These magical qualities provide the beloved with a superhuman advantage over the lover.

The beloved violates covenants: his covenant is 'weak' (*sust*);[313] ultimately he is a 'breaker of promises' (*'ahd-shikan, paymān-shikan, bad-'ahd*).[314] The beloved does not know the meaning of fidelity[315] and fails to fulfil his 'pledges' (*qawl u 'ahd*).[316] The lover knows that his word can in no way be relied upon but, nevertheless, enters into a pact with him;[317] U119:6:

بکن ترک پیمان و یاری مکن   ز جور و جفا هرچه ممکن بود

Do whatsoever is possible in the way of tyranny and cruelty
But do not break our covenant, nor abandon our bond!

Itemization of the beloved's physical charms

Seyed-Gohrab reminds us that description in Persian lyric poetry 'should not be seen as a definition of a concrete subject or an abstract idea: it is usually meant to refer to some quality of the praised person'.[318] A poem admiring the beloved's qualities 'can serve just as well as a panegyric to the patron, especially when the beloved is depicted as haughty and unattainable, acting regally on his/her whim'.[319] In such lyric poems,[320] the ruler is established as the implicit object of affection and desire.[321] In a Sufi context, this homoerotic paradigm allows the spiritual master to play the role of the beloved and his disciple that of the lover.[322]

Many interpret description of the beloved and passionate love for him in Hafiz's *ghazals* in particular as a matrix of mystical signifiers, one that can only be understood through the poet's 'symbolic universe', requiring us to see esoteric meaning in every description of physical beauty.[323] Such interpretations derive from a Sufi tradition of manual writing that dates from as early as the thirteenth century. As Davis has argued, authors of such manuals (such as 'Iraqi [d. 1289] who wrote the *Istilahat-i Sufiya*) posit that when Sufi poets talk about wine, drunkenness and the beloved, they are really talking about Sufi doctrine, spiritual exaltation and God's beauty. Davis believes the fact that 'Iraqi and those who imitated him felt the necessity to write such manuals shows that those who favoured a mystical interpretation of Persian lyric poetry were threatened by and felt compelled, in turn, to counterbalance non-mystical interpretations of it.[324]

If everyone had accepted the mystical interpretation, there would have been no need for 'Iraqi and others to pen such 'corrective' manuals. Moayyad has argued that the ambiguity of the Persian *ghazal* increased following its penetration by Sufi ideology and vocabulary such that, '[a]ny lyrical statement became susceptible to mystical interpretation and eroticism became confused with pure mysticism'.[325]

The present examination focuses on the function of the beloved's description in both evoking and moulding the courtly performance context within a particular patronage framework in a specific time and place. It is not my aim to resolve the debate as to the proportionate measure of mystical and earthly significance embedded within such description. The poet-litterateur, Sharaf al-Din Rami Tabrizi (d. 1393), composed a style manual of stock metaphors used to describe the beloved entitled *Anis al-'ushshaq* ('Companion of the Lovers') dedicated to Shaykh Uvays, in which poetic description of the beloved's beauty is itemized according to body part. Interestingly, Rami shows little interest in the mystical interpretation of *vasf* and divides his work into nineteen short chapters comprising explanatory prose passages interwoven with illustrative poetic quotations from thirteenth- and fourteenth-century Persian poets including Khvaju, Salman, 'Imad, Sa'di and Kamal Isfahani, most of whom made their careers in Shiraz.[326]

His eyes

The beloved's eyes should be 'dark' (*siyāh*; lit. 'black').[327] As noted, the eyes are likened to the narcissus,[328] because of the contrast between its dark centre and light outer portion.[329] Since the narcissus blooms in spring – the season most closely associated with poetic performance – it is a fitting choice for this metaphor. The beloved's eyes are seductively 'languid' (*bīmār*) and manifest an alluring 'illness' (*bīmārī*).[330] His eyes are 'sleepy' (*khvāb-ālūd, pur-khvāb*),[331] 'drunk' (*mast, mastāna*),[332] 'half-drunk' (*nīm-mast, nīma-mast*),[333] 'intoxicated' (*sar-mast*),[334] 'hungover' (*pur-khumār*)[335] and 'inebriated' (*makhmūr*).[336] His eyes display the rowdiness associated with drunkenness being both 'quarrelsome' (*'arbada-jū*)[337] and 'deadly' (*mard-afkan*; lit. 'man-slaying').[338] It is through eye contact that the beloved mesmerizes the onlookers with his bewitching magic,[339] by being playful,[340] 'alluring' (*fattān*)[341] or 'flirtatious' (*ra'nā*).[342] The shape of the beloved's eyes also receives attention: they should be shaped like almonds,[343] 'narrow' (tang)[344] or 'stretched' (kashīda; an adjective that also suggests eyelids outlined with kohl).[345] Rather infrequently, the beloved's eyes are likened to a gazelle's.[346]

His wink

The furtive glance or 'wink' (ghamza) of the beloved can be 'drunken' (mast),[347] 'ill' (bīmār)[348] or playful.[349] In the metaphorical form of the arrow, it can be deadly. The beloved's wink is his response to the lover's erotic gaze and it is via the wink that the boy enraptures the onlooker and takes possession of his heart.

His face

The beloved's 'countenance' (rukh, rukhsār, rūy, chihra; words also used to denote his cheeks) is likened to the rose;[350] the wild rose;[351] and the tulip[352] – because the bright red hue of these flowers evokes the youthful glow of the beloved's cheeks.[353] Abu Nuwas's beloved is a rose.[354] His face is 'rosy'[355] and his cheeks shame the flower.[356] He has a rose in his cheeks[357] that 'whispers' to the 'jasmine' (i.e. whiteness) of his face.[358] In the Persian ghazal, the beloved's beardless face is a 'rose without thorns'[359] and his downy cheeks are like the silky, velvety petals of both the rose and tulip,[360] just as his fragrant scent is associated with that of rosewater.[361]

The beloved's face is a garden[362] or a section thereof: the central portion,[363] the rose bed or a swath of roses.[364] The vegetative metaphors used to depict him in the blush of youth include the 'greenness' (sabza) of his newly sprouted beard and his ruddy, rose-like cheeks. The beloved's physical beauty surpasses that of the garden, thereby embarrassing it, in much the same way that earthly pleasance shames promised Paradise.

Descriptions of the beloved's face veiled by a niqāb or burqa' perhaps demand a more mystical interpretation.[365] That said, Abu Nuwas's boy beloveds also appear veiled in some poems: the boy is 'veiled'[366] or 'concealed' by the light of his forehead[367] and/or by his own beauty.[368] In the Persian ghazal, the lover's desire to see the beloved unveiled has sexual undertones as the word commonly used to mean 'chaste', mastūr, literally means 'covered', 'veiled' or 'concealed'.

The darling's face and body provide adornment: he is 'party-adorning' (majlis-ārā),[369] 'city-adorning' (shahr-ārā),[370] even 'world-adorning' ('ālam-ārā).[371] The boy is a beautifying object and his physical presence at the convivial gathering provides participants with a fittingly alluring subject for their eager gaze.

The beloved's face is luminous and round: he is 'moon-faced' (māh-rū),[372] 'moon-countenanced' (māh-sīmā).[373] His face is 'moon-shaped' (māh-paykar)[374] and of 'moonlike appearance' (māh-manzar, māh-laqā).[375] The moon of his countenance[376] sheds 'moonlight' (mahtāb).[377] The beloved is the new moon,[378] full moon,[379] moon of the fourteenth[380] or two-week moon.[381] As already seen, in addition to māh, the Arabic loanwords qamar, badr and hilāl are also used.[382] The moon face stands as pars pro toto for the whole frame of the sweetheart.[383] The moon's silvery glow is reflected in the youth's hairless, white skin; mention of the moon evokes the nocturnal party (one that the beloved's luminosity sets ablaze).[384]

Comparisons with the 'sun' (khur, khurshīd, āftāb, mihr) are less common.[385] Phrases in which the beloved is likened to the sun arguably have a more panegyric or mystical flavour, given the sun generates heat and nurtures life, in contrast to the moon, whose luminosity is reflective. The beloved is 'the world-illuminating sun' (khurshīd-i jahān-tāb, āftāb-i jahān-tāb),[386] 'the sun of the east' (āftāb-i khāvar)[387] and 'the sun of the realm' (āftāb-i kishvar).[388] The Abbasid beloved is a sun that does not set[389] and his face is brighter than the sun itself.[390] He is the sun on earth[391] and the walking sun[392] who combines the luminescence of both the sun and the moon.[393] In the Persian ghazal the beloved is a 'moon crowned with sun' (mah-i khurshīd-kulāh)[394] or another amalgam of sun and moon.[395]

The beloved's face and cheeks are also likened to the candle[396] and his presence at the night-time majlis emanates light. He is the 'candle of the wine party' (sham'-i majlis),[397] the 'candle of the gathering' (sham'-i jam', sham'-i anjuman)[398] and the 'candle of the night chamber' (sham'-i shabistān).[399] Like the metaphor of the moon, this imagery evokes wine parties held under the cover of darkness. The lover is the 'moth' (parvāna) drawn uncontrollably and in complete rapture to the candle's flame in which he eventually perishes, becoming one with the focus of his desire. This moth-candle metaphor is commonly employed by Persian mystic poets.[400]

His chin

The 'dimple' (zanakh, zanakh-dān) on the beloved's chin resembles a shiny apple ripe for biting.[401] The zanakh-dān is a 'pit' (chāh) [402] into which the lover can fall and become trapped by the inamorato's beauty (the pit being an allusion to Joseph, the epitome of youthful beauty). The boy's face should be chubby – a key element in his attractiveness being his 'double chin' (ghabghab, dhaqan);[403] a sign of health and good fortune.

His eyebrows and eyelashes

The 'curve' or 'bend' (kham) of the beloved's eyebrows resembles the 'prayer niche'[404] in which the devoted lover offers supplication.[405] The boy's eyebrow is the lover's place of devotional prostration[406] and it evokes the curved angle of the archer's bow.[407] The perfect eyebrow resembles an architectural 'arch' (tāq)[408] or the crescent moon.[409] In most instances, the beloved's eyebrows are described as 'joined' (payvasta),[410] but in some poems he is said to have two eyebrows.[411] The beloved's eyelashes are as black as his hair.[412]

His beauty spot

The 'beauty spot' (khāl) is an integral element of the beloved's perfectly beautiful visage.[413] It is black and resembles the colour of musk[414] or the complexion of a dark-skinned infidel (whether an Indian[415] or an East African).[416] The Abbasid beloved's beauty spot is both black and sweet.[417] In Persian, the khāl is 'wicked' and 'mischievous' (siyah-kār; lit. 'black-acting').[418] In shape, the mole is like a perfect dot at the tip of the beloved's forelock, which combine to make the letter jīm.[419] Working in collaboration with the beloved's locks, the beauty spot can entrap: it is the 'seed' (dāna) which entices the lover, the beloved's hair then working as the 'trap' (dām) that ensnares him.[420]

His mouth, lips and saliva

In terms of colour and sheen, the beloved's lips are likened to the ruby[421] and to agate.[422] His lips are the hue of red wine[423] and the lover strives to 'drink wine' (i.e. imbibe saliva) from those lips,[424] which are like a 'wine-selling ruby' (la'l-i bāda-furūsh).[425] As an extension of this metaphor, the beloved's mouth and lips are compared to the bejewelled wine cup.[426] The boy's lips should be 'moist' and 'juicy' (āb-dār, sīr-āb).[427] They should be tight like the letter mīm,[428] a 'rosebud' (ghuncha)[429] or an unripe pistachio.[430] In a more mystical vein, the beloved's saliva is equated with the elixir vitae, the elusive Water of Life[431] and his mouth with the source of eternal life (an allusion to Alexander; see Chapter 4).[432] The beloved's lips – like his sweet breath – are 'soul/life-giving' (rūh-bakhsh, jān-bakhsh)[433] and 'soul/life-increasing' (rūh-afzā, jān-afzā),[434] like the miraculous breath of Jesus (see Chapter 6).

His sweetness

The association of the beloved's physique and behaviour with sweetness is an important motif in the Persian ghazal. The beloved has a sugary or sweet mouth.[435] His lips are 'sweet' (shīrīn),[436] 'sugary' (shikarīn),[437] 'sugar-crunching' (shikar-khā),[438] 'sugar-shedding' (shikar-afshān),[439] 'sugar-dripping' (shikar-bār)[440] and 'sugar-selling' (*shikar-furūsh*).[441] Indeed, the beloved's lips are more syrupy than the sugarcane field (*shikaristān*).[442] This profusion of sugar-related description is possibly indicative of the substantial trading, production and consumption of sugar in thirteenth- and fourteenth-century Iran. Sugar was produced intensively in Khuzistan in this period[443] and it seems also to have been imported from Egypt and India.[444]

Shikar ('sugar'), *nay-shikar* ('cane sugar') and *qand* ('rock candy') denote the sweet words spoken by the beloved and his soul-healing, saccharine kisses.[445] As seen in Chapter 1, *shikar* and *qand* are also metaphors for fine poetry. The beloved's lips are evocative of sweetmeats consumed at the party;[446] his lips and his mouth are both equated with 'honey' (*shahd*,[447] *nūsh*[448] [which can also mean nourishment or wine-drinking]).

The beloved's 'sweetness' (*halāvat*,[449] in contrast to *talkhī*, 'bitterness'[450]) is linked not only to the taste of his mouth or the pleasing timbre of his words but also to his conduct, mannerisms and physical movements. The beloved is both *shīrīn-kār* ('sweet-working', i.e. graceful)[451] and *shīrīn-harakāt* ('sweet-moving').[452] Comparisons between the beloved lauded in the poetry and Shirin (and, by association her royal husband, Khusraw) are used to eroto-panegyric effect (see Chapter 5).

His skin tone

In accordance with aesthetic convention, a light-skinned or 'white' beloved is eroticized,[453] a physical feature of Abbasid beloveds too who are as white as ivory,[454] marble,[455] silver[456] or sweetened milk.[457] In the *ghazal*s of fourteenth-century Shiraz, the shiny whiteness of the beloved's skin, body and limbs recalls 'ivory,'[458] 'crystal'[459] and 'silver'.[460] The beloved has silvery legs,[461] limbs,[462] forearms,[463] cheeks[464] and chest.[465] His *banā-gūsh* (the portion of skin behind or below his ear) is silvery and pearly white.[466] The beloved is 'silver-bodied' (*sīm-tan, sīm-badan*).[467] He is a 'silver-limbed cypress' (*sarv-i sīm-andām*),[468] a 'silvery cypress' (*sarv-i sīmīn*)[469] and a 'silver idol' (*but-i sīmīn*).[470] This emphasis on the beloved's silvery complexion may be connected to silver ornamentation in palaces and the use of silverware at the *majlis*.[471] His white complexion invites comparisons with scented white flowers, in particular jasmine.[472] The comparison with silver, crystal, ivory and jasmine suggests a beloved with very little body hair, a characteristic that Turkic *ghulām*s were prized for.

His facial hair

References to the beloved's downy facial hair underscore the maleness of Abu Nuwas's beloved. The appearance of facial hair does not necessarily detract from the boy's beauty:[473] this 'black cloak' does not signal the 'death' of his allure.[474] The youth's upper lip 'greens'[475] as his beard grows.[476] The beard 'clothes' the boy's face[477] and is likened to the reddish colour around the moon[478] or to a dark frame surrounding the 'white paper' of his face.[479] The down on the boy's upper lip is described as ambergris-scented.[480] It is the rough hair that is less favourable;[481] when the boy's beard grows properly, convention decrees that all his 'sweetness' will be lost.[482] Although he does not have a full beard (rīsh),[483] the shāhid sports the khatt.[484] The khatt is 'musky' because of its dark colour and its powerful aroma[485] and 'rust-coloured' (zangārī).[486] The khatt is 'green',[487] like 'fresh green sprouts' (sabza).

His hair

The beloved's hair carries a 'scent' (bū, nikhat)[488] – a perfume reminiscent of musk,[489] ambergris,[490] camphor[491] and other compound pomades used to perfume the majlis.[492] His hair is mushk-sāy ('musk-spreading')[493] and mushk-bār ('musk-shedding').[494] It bears the fragrance of the musk sack,[495] it is 'anbar-afshān ('ambergris-scattering'),[496] 'anbar-bār ('ambergris-shedding'),[497] 'anbar-shikan ('ambergris-splitting')[498] and 'anbar-sāy ('ambergris-spreading').[499] These descriptions evoke the practices of nadīms who perfumed their bodies and clothes in preparation for the wine party.[500] Turkic warriors are also believed to have perfumed their hair (and worn it long and in plaits).[501] A sweet breeze is said to emanate from the beloved's hair:[502] it is both perfumed and perfuming, like sweet-smelling flowers.[503] The scent of the beloved's hair both incenses the convivial gathering and is evocative of its aroma.

The length of the beloved's hair is celebrated.[504] His hair must be long,[505] hang all the way to his feet[506] and have neither start nor end.[507] It should be black:[508] as black as the night to best frame his moonlike face.[509] The blackness of the beloved's locks (like the blackness of his beauty spot) is compared to the complexion of the 'infidel' (kāfir),[510] most commonly Indians;[511] blackness being a marker of intrinsic wickedness.[512]

As in Abbasid poetry,[513] the beloved's hair is often described as 'dishevelled' (āshufta,[514] parīshān,[515] mushavvash[516]), its messy condition mirroring the lover's inner turmoil and 'unsettled state' (bī-qarārī).[517] This dishevelment also evokes the disturbance of the age in which the poet and audience live.[518] The beloved's hair is like a 'chain of interconnected links' (zanjīr,[519] silsila[520]). His curls resemble rings (sing. halqa),[521] and it is by means of this chainlike hair that he shackles the lover. The boy's locks are also likened to vipers: coiled, deadly and ready to strike.[522] As mentioned already, this curling shape resembles the curve of the letter jīm[523] or the shape of a polo stick.[524] They are like 'knots' (sing. *girih*)[525] and have many 'twists' and 'curls' (*kham*,[526] *tāb*,[527] *pīch*,[528] *chīn*,[529] *shikan*,[530] *shikanj*)[531] which entangle the lover, preventing his escape. The beloved's hair is like a 'lasso' (*kamand*),[532] 'trap' (*dam*)[533] or 'tie' (*band*); it ensnares the lover and his heart.[534] It is as though the boy's hair has a 'hook' (*shast*)[535] with which it grabs hold of the admirer. Descriptions of the hair as curly, twisted and dishevelled do not seem to tally with the images of *sāqī*s and young *ghulām*s in contemporary illustrations in manuscripts and on bowls (in particular *mīnā'ī* bowls dated circa 1200), whose hair is either shown long and straight or bunched and plaited.[536] Some of this imagery suggests a Persian beloved, rather than a Turkic one. Of course, the representation in the poetry is of a composite beloved, one who exhibits all ideal physical attributes. Although based heavily on a Turkic model, the beloved of the Persian *ghazal* combines the best of multiple ethnicities and both sexes.

His stature

The beloved should be tall[537] like the cypress.[538] He is a 'silver-limbed cypress' (*sarv-i sīm-andām*),[539] a 'rose-limbed cypress' (*sarv-i gul-andām*)[540] and a 'jasmine-scented cypress' (*sarv-i saman-būy*).[541] The youth's stature is likened to that of the cypress because of its graceful shape and lush green colour that never fades – characteristics symbolic of youthful good health. The beloved's tall, slender figure is also equated with the pine tree[542] and the *shimshād*[543] (a tall, sturdy box tree).

His gait

The cypress-, box- or pine-beloved is a 'strutting' (*kharām, kharāmān, chamān*) beloved.[544] He is 'gliding' (*ravān*),[545] 'free' (*āzād*),[546] 'erect' (*rāst, sahī*)[547] and full of 'coquetry' (*nāz*).[548] His gait is like that of the partridge[549] and, when in motion, he diverts the pious from the straight path.[550] Abu Nuwas's beloved sways as he walks,[551] he takes small steps,[552] he slips and slides under the weight of his huge buttocks.[553] He appears to 'shake with juicy succulence'.[554]

Description of the beloved's walk is less common in Persian than in Arabic.[555] Making reference to the beloved's buttocks was not considered taboo in Abbasid poetry and many of Abu Nuwas's homoerotic poems celebrate that particular physical feature:[556] his *ākhira* ('end', but also 'afterlife') is as beautiful as his *dunyā* ('nether regions', but also 'this world').[557] His buttocks are domed[558] and shaped like sand dunes.[559] They quiver[560] and are like a *minbar* ('pulpit') for his lover to mount.[561] They are so heavy they weaken his waist,[562] weigh down the 'branch' (*ghusn*) of his torso[563] and cause him to bend.[564] They are so heavy that not even an elephant could carry them![565]

His waist

The beloved's waist should be as thin as a single strand of hair.[566] At the very least it should be 'narrow' (*nāzuk*).[567] The desirability of these unnatural proportions – as tall and as slender as the cypress with a waist as narrow as a strand of hair – may account for the elongated figures of *ghulām*s and *sāqī*s as depicted in medieval Persian miniature paintings.

Conclusion

Persian poetic description is characterized by hyperbolic language employed to transform the ordinary into the sublime. Poets showcased their talents by demonstrating their command of a rich, systemic repertoire of images; they then masterfully introduced novel ways of depicting familiar courtly objects and aspirational ideals:[568] professional survival rested in part upon the poet's ability to achieve originality when constructing metaphors – however nuanced – while avoiding any gross violation of established literary conventions.[569] As can be seen clearly in this chapter, at the heart of *vasf* is the 'attempt to depict the ideal form of an earthly object, idea, or event'. As Seyed-Gohrab argues, the poet was not expected to give a 'real' picture of what he described.[570] Although Seyed-Gohrab is right to emphasize the degree to which Persian poets sought immersion in imagination and, in an attempt to demonstrate originality, turned away from reality to focus on the ideal, the descriptive shorthand employed in the Persian *ghazal* to depict the allure of the beloved was so long-established by the fourteenth century, that this hyperbolic vision of the beloved would in many ways have appeared far more 'real' to a contemporary audience than it would to us. Images that now appear fanciful, far-fetched or contrived to a modern reader would have been anticipated – indeed expected and demanded – by contemporary audiences.

In the next three chapters we study the poets' use of a rhetorical device at the heart of the Persian *ghazal*, namely *talmīh*: an allusion to a historical person or a character from the mythological, literary or religious past used to elucidate a truth in the present. These three *talmīh* case studies are used to explore another form of intertextuality practised by the poets that is not necessarily defined by the imitation of formal features of the poetry of others, but rather their responses (some conscious, some perhaps coincidental) to one another's use of *talmīh*. The poets studied here appear to have consciously built upon the historical, legendary and literary allusions of their colleagues and, because they took from a shared stockpile of such exempla, some of the similarities in their employment of *talmīh* are less an indication of deliberate imitation and more a case of a common language of poetic expression. In these chapters we examine various forms of lyric poetry, not just *ghazals*, as well as the poets' engagement in their lyric poems with canonical masterpieces of narrative poetry. The poets of post-Mongol Iran and Iraq repeatedly re-tweaked standard allusions to fit particular purposes of both a topical and universal nature: to comment on the socio-political status quo, to bemoan the fate of poets and the fraught poet–patron relationship, to hold up a model of behaviour for kings to emulate and to give hope to their listeners and seek spiritual guidance on their behalf.

4

Allusions to Kings and Heroes

Audiences in fourteenth-century Shiraz would have been familiar with stories of kings and heroes of the Iranian past, primarily as retold in Abu'l-Qasim Firdawsi's *Shahnama* (completed 1010), fine copies of which were produced in the city under both the Injuids and the Muzaffarids.[1] The *Shahnama* along with other Persian and Arabic verse and prose texts provided a narrative storehouse that poets tapped into via the concise bursts of kingly *talmīh* that they inserted into their lyric poems. This three-way written, oral and aural intertextuality relied upon the audience's wider knowledge in a way not dissimilar to how medieval Muslims, when reading the Qur'an or listening to it being recited, fleshed out the text's fragmentary prophetic stories with narrative elements they gleaned from other sources.

Listeners were expected to 'amplify' terse allusions in *ghazal*s mentally into full-blown narratives. It is the audience that is the key component to the functioning of *talmīh* since this rhetorical device demands a 'full-knowing listener'.[2] For *talmīh* to work, however, the audience must grasp the allusion. The listener must share a common body of knowledge with the poet to be able to interpret the allusion. In Persian poetry, *talmīh* functions to evoke (and invoke) earlier times and, by doing so, to recreate or re-enact them for the present audience within the context of their own reality. Hafiz and his peers' use of allusion is characterized by dynamism, flexibility and polyvalence. Fourteenth-century *talmīh* is not 'frozen,' nor are its associations set and stereotyped.[3] Through their nuanced use of *talmīh*, post-Mongol Persian poets blurred the boundaries between 'historical' and 'mythological' and succeeded in creating a new order that reinforced the old, while forming something fresh. Instances of *talmīh* in Hafiz's poetry in particular serve to attach the cosmic to the real world; in his vision, history and myth are no longer in opposition, but are viewed as belonging to the same unified cycle. Through topically charged *talmīh*, Shiraz's poets articulated a distinct view of their audience's connection to the past and a sense of their place in the fragmented post-Mongol present.[4]

The lyric poets studied here use *talmīh* to allude to mythico-legendary and historical Iranian shahs, two Jewish prophet-kings and one ancient Greek ruler: all valid *exempla* for understanding their present; all richly endowed with virtues.[5] There was less bifurcation in the premodern context between Iranian and non-Iranian pasts than some have imagined[6] and, by the fourteenth century, non-Iranian figures had become fully integral to Muslim Iranian mythology. The poets' use of *talmīh* does not respect the supposed dividing lines between legendary, mythical and historical since, in their world, the concepts of myth (*ustūra, afsāna*), legend (*dāstān, qissa, hikāyat*) and history (*tārīkh*) often overlapped and/or bled into one another.

Through kingly *talmīh*, pre-Islamic narratives were brought into dialogue with their interlocutors' Islamic reality. In this process, the actual and the historical came to be read through the poetic and the mythico-legendary.[7] The poets of Injuid and Muzaffarid Shiraz found ways to accommodate the past in all its diversity and harnessed this to promote their own narratives about the post-Mongol present.[8] The poets did not simply engage mimetically with their society and the courts they served: they worked to shape their cultural milieu and the history and mythology associated with it. *Talmīh* was central to how they moulded the reality that surrounded them and it was through *talmīh* that they had their say in how that reality should be read.

Although Solomon and David are considered prophets in Islam, allusions to them are discussed here since they concern kingship. Conversely, allusions to Sultan Mahmud (d. 1030) are examined in Chapter 5 alongside those to archetypal lovers, since allusions to the Ghaznavid emperor typically concern his devotion to his favourite slave, Ayaz. Similarly, discussion of most allusions to the Sasanian king Khusraw II (r. 590–628) appears in Chapter 5, since allusions to him primarily concern his love for Shirin and/or the presentation of Khusraw as model royal beloved.

A link between past and present kings

Via royal *talmīh*, the poets of Shiraz warn the court and other elite circles about the transience of life, while linking the contemporary city with its glorious, distant past. Through *talmīh*, mythological and historical personages were made present in ways that only poetry can achieve;[9] through allusions, great kings and heroes of bygone eras were made almost tangible. As Clarke has argued, the premodern distinction between past and present being somewhat blurred, it is possible that many people in such societies believed in the ability of long-dead figures to act upon the here and now.[10]

Poets like Hafiz went beyond merely drawing parallels between royals of the past and their contemporary masters. As Meisami notes, Hafiz's use of *talmīh*, 'reflects the notion that a present event or person recapitulates a significant event or person in the past'. And it is through what Meisami describes as the 'exemplary link between past and present' that the meaningfulness of both is authenticated.[11] This is a two-way relationship of affirmation: the past (as narrated in myths, legends and histories) is reinforced, in turn strengthening the present order that draws on those authoritative sources for validation.

Royal *talmīh* has a long history in Persian poetry. Meisami posits that, approximately two to three centuries before Hafiz was writing, panegyrists focused on celebrating the present rather than glorifying the past and if they likened their patrons to ancient kings, such comparisons were rapidly becoming clichés.[12] But the evidence from early Ghaznavid panegyric poetry suggests that poets did find value in the pre-Islamic past since they likened or compared living rulers to Iranian royals of the distant and primordial pasts.[13] It was through *talmīh* that the greatest Ghaznavid panegyrists created enduring images of their patrons to stand shoulder to shoulder with those of antiquity.[14] In thirteenth- and fourteenth-century praise poems (*qasīda*s or *ghazal*s) we encounter an abundance of allusions to kings of the historical or imaginary past. In the wake of the collapse of Mongol rule, there perhaps existed an even greater imperative for Shiraz's poets to assert a sense of legitimacy rooted not just in a pan-Iranian past, but in the specifics of antique Fars.

Integrating the Iranian within the Islamic

By the ninth century, a symbiosis between the Arabo-Muslim and Iranian pasts had been largely achieved. In Bosworth's estimation, the new Islamic civilization that emerged was 'an amalgam of the two traditions, a coming together on equal terms'.[15] There was an attempt on the part of Muslims writing in Arabic and Persian in the ninth to eleventh centuries to accommodate ancient Iranian history within Islam by promoting an Iranian–Islamic synthesis.[16] Tales of Pishdadian, Kayanid and Sasanian kings were incorporated into Arabic prose works[17] and creative retellings in both languages of pre-Islamic Iranian king and hero stories became popular.[18] Tabari, for one, attempted a coordination of Iran's kingly history with prophetic stories taken from the *Qisas al-anbiyā'*.[19] As Savant has argued, many Muslim scholars were interested in 'comparative chronology' and they synchronized divergent perspectives on the pre-Islamic past, often favouring the Iranian view.[20] In lyric poetry too, novel, hybrid reconstructions of the past were realized, often via *talmīh*.

The *lieux de mémoire* of Fars

Fars abounds in ancient ruins, emotionally charged *lieux de mémoire* ('sites of memory'), a term that, as developed by Nora, denotes sites where memory is embodied and where a sense of historical continuity persists.[21] Nora posits that memory takes root in the concrete in sites, whereas history binds itself strictly to temporal continuities and events.[22] But the physicality of ruins is just one factor in their functioning as *lieux de mémoire*: they are 'sites' in three senses of the word: material, symbolic and functional.[23]

The Injuids and Muzaffarids, like other rulers of Fars before them (most notably the Buyids [934–1055] and the Salghurids [1148–1282]), linked themselves to the kings of pre-Islamic Iran by adopting the title *shāhanshāh* (or its Arabic equivalent, *malik al-mulūk* ['king of kings']) that had been used by Sasanian monarchs until the mid-sixth century CE.[24] Through doing so, these local rulers laid claim to age-old legitimacy and to certain holy aspects of Iranian kingly rule.[25] What sets Shiraz's kings apart in their adoption of this title is the relative proximity of their capital to Iran's most significant Achaemenid and Sasanian ruined sites (Pasargadae, Persepolis, Naqsh-i Rustam, Qasr-i Abu Nasr, Gur and Bishapur).[26] Moreover, the territory of Islamic Fars itself remained defined by its pre-Islamic past, divided as it was into five 'districts' (sing. *kūra, khūrra*): Istakhr, Darabgird, Ardashir, Shapur and Qubad,[27] each associated with one or more mythological or Sasanian king. Writing in the second half of the twelfth century, Tusi says Fars is where Jamshid resided. It is the place of the Sasanian kings and the region from which have hailed 'all world-rulers'.[28]

Savant reminds us that a 'gradual conversion' of ancient Iranian sites into those with Muslim associations took place in premodern Iran.[29] In this transformation, Solomon, the archetypal just king, loomed large. This is unsurprising, given Solomon's strong associations in the Near East with legitimate, monotheistic, righteous sovereignty[30] and with the ruins of majestic, colossal buildings.[31] One reason for the profusion of allusions to Jamshid and Solomon in Shirazi lyric poetry from the first half of the thirteenth century onwards, is that many of the pre-Islamic ruins of Fars had by that time developed strong associations in the vernacular imaginary and among local elites with either or both of these kings.[32] Like Iranian rulers before and after them, those who ruled Shiraz in the thirteenth and fourteenth centuries had an 'intense attachment to the past'.[33] The proximity to Shiraz of ancient sites with intense monarchic associations gave added resonance to kingly *talmīh* as incorporated into poetry. And it was through the poetic that these ruined sites were made part of Shiraz's topography in the present; the poets ever mindful that a sensitivity for and connection to the past is a key element in love of place.[34] As Clarke has argued in relation to Umayyad al-Andalus – a region with its own special connection to Solomon – Solomonic associations provided ambitious local rulers with much prestige and fertile material for legitimizing language.[35] Shiraz's overlords, too, derived much symbolic currency from the deep connection between the land they ruled and this wise prophet-king.

Elite visitation of these sites from the mid-tenth century onwards was endowed with ritualistic significance. These visits helped to reconcile the rulers' Islamic present with their realm's pre-Islamic past. Muslim dialogue with Achaemenid ruins echoes not dissimilar Sasanian practices, the most lasting evidence of which is the monumental Sasanian imperial reliefs carved into the cliff at Naqsh-i Rustam. Another example is the neo-Achaemenid ornamentation found in Ardashir's palace at Gur. For the Sasanians some eight to nine centuries earlier, the past was a place to be approached, crafted and shaped; they did this by constructing 'a wider Persian topography of memory' through the execution of rock reliefs and the construction of grand cities.[36] Through carving inscriptions, constructing Islamic buildings or incorporating Achaemenid spolia into new edifices, successive local Muslim dynasties sought to appropriate the majestic authority associated with Fars's ancient sites. Although now dislodged from their original historical and cultural contexts,[37] it is possible that, as Canepa has argued, these Achaemenid sites served as 'portals' to the past for Muslim dynasties as they had done long before for the Sasanians.[38]

Persepolis

In Iran today, Persepolis is called *Takht-i Jamshid* ('the throne of Jamshid'), a place name alluded to in the *Shahnama*.[39] Shahbazi believes the site became associated with Jamshid in the late Sasanian period.[40] Called *Sad stūn* ('one hundred columns') by the Sasanians,[41] in the premodern period the ruins of Persepolis were most commonly known as *Chihil minār* ('forty minarets').[42] These ruins were variously understood to be those of the city and palace built or developed by Jamshid,[43] or the site of Jamshid's ruined palace that can only have been constructed by demons and fairies.[44] The geographer Zakariya al-Qazwini (d. 1283) repeated the claim that when the Saljuq sultan, Alp-Arslan (d. 1072), conquered Istakhr he discovered a turquoise wine cup inscribed with the name of Jamshid.[45] Other ruins in Fars also enjoy Jamshidian associations: in the vicinity of Hajjiabad there is a 'harem' and also a 'prison' of Jamshid.[46]

When not associated with Jamshid, the ruins of Persepolis were believed to be those of Solomon's 'mosque' (*masjid*),[47] 'hermitage' (*sawma'a*),[48] 'playground' (*mal'ab*),[49] 'seat' (*kursī*),[50] 'throne' (*takht*)[51] or the place where his throne once stood (*takht-gāh-i Sulaymān*;[52] a phrase used in some lyric poems to allude to Shiraz).[53] Persepolis-Istakhr was said to have been Solomon's royal capital or his seat of power where the king pitched his tent to which men, *jinn*s and animals flocked to pay homage and offer tribute.[54] According to al-Qazwini, the local population believed the reliefs at Persepolis to be images of the prophets (*suwar al-anbiyā'*),[55] lending greater weight to the supposed Abrahamic origins of the site.

Mottahedeh believes the association of the Sasanians' cultic centre, Istakhr, with Solomon lies in the site's 'sacred geography.'[56] By the time of Hafiz, the vestiges of Achaemenid Fars had been successfully 'rebaptized' as Solomonic and Jamshidian.[57] As late as 1474 when the Venetian Josafa Barbaro visited Persepolis, he reported that the locals told him that some of the Persepolitan bas-reliefs depict Solomon and that it was Solomon who built the (tenth-century, Buyid) Band-i Amir dam over the Kur River![58]

Melikian-Chirvani has demonstrated convincingly that Persepolis was far from forgotten by medieval Muslims,[59] the most tangible proof of their memorialization of the site being the inscriptions carved onto the ruins by the order of a succession of royal visitors: Buyid (in 955, 1001 and 1046),[60] Injuid (in 1337 and 1347), Muzaffarid (in 1371), Timurid (in 1422) and Aq-Quyunlu (in 1476).[61] Perhaps following the example of the Buyids, these later royal visitors also took more than a passing interest in the ruins of Persepolis.[62] What is most significant to the present study is the fact that several of the Injuid, Timurid and Aq-Quyunlu inscriptions left at Persepolis incorporate Persian poetry heavy in royal *talmīh*.[63] This poetry is lifted (albeit in a somewhat jumbled form) from Sa'di's *Gulistan*, his *Bustan*,[64] and Nizami's *Makhzan al-asrar*.[65]

An inscription carved at Persepolis in 1348 to mark Shah Shaykh Abu Ishaq's visit lists the king's titles in a manner that echoes an inscription left at Pasargadae circa 1223 by the Salghurid Sa'd b. Zangi (see below). Shah Shaykh Abu Ishaq is: *pādishāh-i Islām, shāhanshāh-i Haft Iqlīm, Iskandar-i zamān, vārith-i mulk-i Sulaymān* ('King of Islam, King of kings of the Seven Climes, Alexander of the Age, Inheritor of the Realm of Solomon').[66] Almost identical sets of honorifics in praise of the same king, with the addition of titles such as *sultan-i jahan* ('King of the World'), *Dārā-yi dawrān* ('Dara [or Lord] of the Age'), *mālik-i mulk-i Sulaymān* ('Ruler of the Solomonic Realm'), *malik-i Jam-farmān* ('King of Jamshidian Command'), *shāhanshāh-i Islām* ('King of kings of Islam') and *Iskandar-i thānī* ('Second Alexander'), appear in Zarkub's *Shiraznama*.[67] Zarkub also hails the last Injuid as *shāh-i akāsira-yi jahān* ('King of kings of the world'), using the generic Arabic term for pre-Islamic Persian kings (*akāsira*) to denote all monarchs.[68]

The use of Solomonic epithets extended beyond the person of the shah. Tashi Khatun, Shah Shaykh Abu Ishaq's influential mother, was hailed in an inscription in a copy of the Qur'an she gifted to the shrine of Shah Chiragh thus: *al-khātūn al-a'zam malikat mamlakat al-Sulaymānīya* ('The Mightiest Khatun, Queen of the Solomonic Realm') and *al-khātūn al-mu'azzama sultān al-khavātīn* ('The Mighty Khatun, Sovereign of all [Turkic] Noblewomen').[69] Zarkub builds upon the Solomonic theme by calling Tashi Khatun *Balqīs-i 'ahd u zamān* ('Balqis of the Age'), a fittingly Solomonic allusion to the Queen of Sheba.[70] It should be stressed that royal titles such as these that centred around Solomon were not bound to any one dynasty or individual ruler, but rather were attached to the land of Fars and constituted an important manifestation of its spirit of place.[71]

Pasargadae

By 1200, the pre-Persepolitan Achaemenid ruins at Pasargadae had also developed strong Solomonic associations. Tusi calls Pasargadae *tāj-gāh-i Sulaymān* (i.e. the place where Solomon's crown was kept or where he was crowned). Tusi says anyone who has seen Pasargadae will know that it is the 'work of demons'.[72] Some have suggested that Pasargadae's Solomonic associations were invented by the local Muslim population to protect the ruins from desecration.[73] If these associations originated with the common people who lived in its vicinity (and were only later taken up by local elites),[74] this would suggest that the ruins at Pasargadae were popular with both low- and high-status visitors. The Murghab plain became known as that of Solomon's mother[75] and the tomb of Cyrus the Great was her 'grave' (*gūr, qabr*) or 'martyrium' (*mashhad*).[76] The ruined stone tower half a kilometre north of Cyrus's private palace was Solomon's 'prison' (*zindān*) and the stone terrace on the hill overlooking the plain to the north was *takht-i Sulaymān* or *takht-i mādar-i Sulaymān* – the throne of either Solomon or his mother.[77]

From at least the Salghurid period, Fars as a whole was referred to in verse and prose texts and in inscriptions as *mamlikat* or *mulk-i Sulaymān* (the realm or dominion of Solomon).[78] Fars' ruler was the legitimate heir to Solomon's dominion,[79] just as, in the Qur'an, Solomon rightfully succeeds David.[80] The title *vārith-i mulk-i Sulaymān* carried geopolitical clout as well as mystical impact (the two working in tandem, rather than at odds).[81] At Pasargadae around 1216, more than a millennium and a half after the death of Cyrus, Sa'd b. Zangi constructed a congregational mosque around the ancient king's tomb.[82] Shiraz's Muslim king had an Arabic inscription carved there in which he is hailed as *wārith mulk Sulaymān*, thereby positing continuity in rulership between the prophet-king and himself.[83] In a Persian inscription at

Pasargadae, the same king is hailed not only as the true inheritor of Solomon's realm, but also: *pahlavān-i jahān* ('Hero of the World'), *shariyār-i Īrān* ('King of Iran'), *marzbān-i Tūrān* ('Defender of the Border with Turan') and *khusraw-i āfāq* ('King of the World').[84] Around a century and a half later, Shah Shuja' constructed a building just north of the tomb which may have been used as a *madrasa*.[85]

Qasr-i Abu Nasr

On the eastern edge of modern-day Shiraz lies the intriguing Parthian-Sasanian-Islamic site now known as Qasr (or Takht)-i Abu Nasr. Achaemenid spolia, including several Persepolitan doorways, were taken there and incorporated into what is believed to have served as an Islamic shrine.[86] This site, the current name of which suggests a connection to the Buyid ruler, Baha' al-Dawla Abu Nasr Khusraw-Firuz (r. 998–1012),[87] was known until the early twentieth century as the 'throne' or 'mosque' of Solomon's mother or simply, *mādar-i Sulaymān* ('Solomon's mother').[88] It is perhaps not without significance that the last-known occupation of the site dates to the reign of Shah Shuja'.[89] Qasr-i Abu Nasr is thought by some to be the approximate location of pre-Islamic Shiraz,[90] which makes the strong association of the site with Solomon intriguing in light of the wealth of Solomonic *talmīh* encountered in Shirazi praise poetry and the heavy Solomonic flavour of local regal titulature.

Kingly *talmīh* as legitimizing device

Before examining the function of royal *talmīh* in the fourteenth-century *ghazal*, it is worth pausing to note how such *talmīh* was used in panegyric poetry across the Salghurid, Injuid, Muzaffarid and Jalayirid periods. The profusion of such *talmīh* in Shiraz-centred praise poems makes the examination of panegyric *qasīda*s relevant to our study of similar *talmīh* in contemporaneous *ghazal*s.

The use of the *ghazal* as a vehicle for panegyric (in which the recipient is named or clearly identified via an epithet or pseudonym in the opening, middle, penultimate or final *bayt*) is a salient feature of Hafiz's *ghazal*s,[91] as is the blurring of the line between a long, panegyric *ghazal* and a concise praise *qasīda*.[92] Rastigar Fasa'i believes Hafiz's few *qasīda*s themselves are so influenced by the *ghazal* in form and content that they are essentially *ghazal*s with appended lines of praise.[93] 'Ubayd similarly used the *ghazal* form for encomium,[94] as did a number of fourteenth-century poets.[95]

The panegyrist, a key player at court, would have been privy to its intrigues and would have had a stake in how political tensions played out. Praise poetry played a vital role in the shaping and promotion of a coherent dynastic image and it appears Shiraz's poets saw legitimizing value in presenting their patrons as the rightful inheritors of conjoined Iranian and Abrahamic royal pasts, which they helped tie to the land of Fars.

Panegyric poetry presupposes a patron worthy of praise.[96] Gruendler argues that these poems must be read 'not for their textual properties in isolation, but for their potential to persuade and affect audiences'.[97] The panegyrist not only produces an ideal portrayal of his/her patron (and, by extension, of all patrons), nor is a panegyric a mere record of the patron's noble deeds but, rather, the motivation for them.[98] There is a keen relationship between praise poetry and power, the composition of a praise poem being an opportunity to reaffirm the 'model of ideal monarchy accepted by the community to which the poem is directed';[99] the virtues praised are those regarded as requisite in an authoritative and legitimate ruler.[100]

Although largely lacking in overt praise of identifiable contemporary rulers, Jahan's *ghazals* are characterized by a profusion of generic allusions to royal males (*sultān*,[101] *shāh*,[102] *khusraw*,[103] *pādishāh*)[104] that often appear in the final or penultimate line of a poem where, in a panegyric, one would expect to find direct reference to the patron. This regal vocabulary belies a panegyric subtext in many of Jahan's *ghazals*. Ghani noted a similar profusion of generic royal titles (*shāh, pādishāh, khusraw, shāhanshah, sultān*) in Hafiz's *ghazals* in which the name of the patron is not explicitly stated but which, Ghani believed, evidence a panegyric function.[105] *Ghazals* in which Jahan speaks of her beloved as a royal male of exquisite beauty (specifically *shāh-i khūbān*,[106] *sultān-i khūbān*,[107] *pādishāh-i khūbān*[108] or *khusraw-i khūbān* [all: 'king of the beauties'])[109] may have been composed with Shah Shuja' in mind given the similarity of these eroto-panegyric epithets to those used by Hafiz to allude to the same royal patron.[110] In her ostensibly amorous *ghazals*, Jahan also mimics praise poetry proper by playing with terms such as *madh, thanā* ('[poetic] praise'), *mādih* ('panegyrist'), *mamdūh* ('patron') and *du'ā* ('prayer for the patron's good fortune').[111]

What poets constructed through kingly *talmīh* must not be dismissed as hyperbole,[112] but rather treated as political manifesto and dynastic propaganda that illuminates the official public image propagated by their patrons. As Aigle has noted, the extrapolation of characters culled from the *Shahnama* constitutes a legitimizing literary strategy at the disposal of Muslim rulers.[113] The employment of kingly *talmīh* in Salghurid, Injuid and Muzaffarid *qasīdas* acts as a blueprint against which to read similar allusions deployed in contemporary *ghazals* and it assists us in deciphering the multiple layers of geopolitical signification embedded within them.

Shiraz's Muslims kings as inheritors of pre-Islamic Iran

It was through poetry that royal pasts were rendered tangible. The contemporary king appeared in panegyric *qasīda*s as the return or second coming of one or more royal or heroic figures of the distant past. The nostalgic lament over the vicissitudes of time, *ubi sunt* ('Where are [they]?'), was largely replaced by what I have coined *hic sunt* ('Here [they] are!'): there is no longer any need to lament repeatedly the demise and disappearance of the ancients, for poets have made them manifest before your very eyes in the communally experienced present.

Heirs to the Kayanids

The Salghurid' Abu Bakr b. Sa'd is the 'face of the dominion of the Kayanids' (*rū-yi mulk-i Kayān*).[114] His son, Sa'd, sits upon the Kayanids' ancient throne,[115] possibly embodying the attributes of Alexander.[116] The 'royal seat' (*masnad*) of Turkan Khatun (mother of Muhammad b. Sa'd b. Abu Bakr and *de facto* ruler during his infancy) smashes the feet of Kay-Khusraw's throne.[117] Shah Shaykh Abu Ishaq rules from a Kayanid palace like Kay-Qubad and Afrasiab.[118] He drinks wine in the Kayanid manner,[119] seated upon Kay-Qubad's throne[120] and he both possesses and adds value to the Kayanid crown: he is the splendour of their throne, their true heir, the ruler over their realm and its refuge.[121]

Mubariz al-Din combines the strength of Sam with the wisdom of Kay-Khusraw, whose blade he wields.[122] His son, Shah Shuja', is the 'crown that adorns the Kayanids' heads'.[123] The magical cup of Kay-Khusraw is associated both with Shah Shuja''s *majlis* and with that of Shah Yahya.[124] In Hafiz's estimation, Shah Shuja' is the greatest king to rule Fars since the Kayanids:[125]

این ساز و این خزینه و این لشکر گران   بعد از کیان به ملک سلیمان نداد کس

> After the Kayanids, no one ever gave to the Realm of Solomon
> Such harmony, such a treasury, and such a weighty army!

Heirs to the Sasanians

The justice dispensed by Turkan Khatun outdoes that of Khusraw Anushiravan.[126] Shah Shaykh Abu Ishaq is equal in rank to the same king[127] and is the return of Anushiravan's son, Khusraw Parviz:[128]

گر ندیدی خسرو پرویز را از ملک روم   بار دیگر بر فراز تخت ایران آمده

If you have never seen Khusraw Parviz in person,
He has returned from Byzantium and once again ascended Iran's throne.

Khvaju claims Anushiravan's legendary justice is revived in the equity of Mubariz al-Din[129] and Hafiz also likens Shah Shuja' to the great Kisra.[130]

Kings of the Persians

Abu Bakr b. Sa'd is the 'refuge of the realm of the Persians' (*panāh-i mulk-i 'Ajam*)[131] and his son, Sa'd, is the inheritor of that same dominion.[132] Shah Shaykh Abu Ishaq is the 'king of the Persians' (*shāh-i 'Ajam*),[133] 'king of Iran' (*shāh-i Īrān*),[134] a *shāh* born of a *shāh*[135] and the *shāhanshāh*.[136] Mubariz al-Din is the 'brave warrior' of the Persian realm[137] and its protector:[138]

خسرو غازی محمد حامی ملک عجم   سام کیخسرو حشم دارای افریدون حشر

Muhammad the warrior king, protector of the Persian realm –
A Sam with Kay-Khusraw-like entourage, A Dara of Faridun-like assembly.

Shah Shuja' is the inheritor of the dominion of the Persians[139] and the *shāhanshāh*.[140] Shah Yahya is the 'king of the Persian domains' (*pādishāh-i mulk-i 'Ajam*).[141] His brother, Shah Mansur, is the 'victorious king of kings' (*shāhanshāh-i muzaffar*),[142] a title that puns on the name of the dynasty.

Shiraz's ruler is Jamshid

The Salghurids Abu Bakr b. Sa'd and Sa'd b. Abu Bakr are kings endowed with Jamshid's *farr*.[143] The father is the 'second Jamshid' (*Jam-i duvvum*)[144] and the son possesses Jamshid-like qualities.[145] Jahan's father, Jalal al-Din Mas'ud Shah, bears similarities to Jamshid,[146] as does his younger brother, Shah Shaykh Abu Ishaq:[147]

طرب کردن در این کاخ کیانی   نشستن با نشاط و کامرانی
سلیمان دوم جمشید ثانی   مبارک باد بر شاه جهان بخش
که برخوردار بادا از جوانی   ابو اسحاق سلطان جوان بخت

Sitting taking pleasure, pursuing our desires,
Making merry in this Kayanid palace.
May he be blessed, the world-portioning king,
The second Solomon, the second Jamshid:

Abu Ishaq, the king of youthful good fortune.
May he continually benefit from youthful vigour!

Shah Shaykh Abu Ishaq is the Jamshid of the 'age' (zamān),[148] the 'epoch' ('ahd)[149] and his 'day' (ruzigār).[150] He is the 'crown-bestowing Jamshid' (Jamshīd-i tāj-bakhsh),[151] possesses Jamshid's power and rank,[152] is a Jamshid endowed with Faridun's 'power and ability',[153] a Jamshid of Faridun-like 'customs'[154] and a Khizr of Jamshid-like 'rank'.[155] The same king is the rightful heir and overlord of Jamshid's lands;[156] his royal feast serves as a 'monument' (yādigār) to both Jamshid and Kay-Khusraw.[157]

The first Muzaffarid ruler of Shiraz is 'just like' Jamshid[158] and his royal feast is equated with that of the primeval king.[159] Shah Shuja' is the Jamshid of the Solomonic realm,[160] king of Jamshid-like 'command',[161] the 'gold-scattering Jamshid' (Jamshīd-i zar-afshān)[162] and the king of Jamshidian 'status' (jāh).[163] Hafiz posits that Shah Shuja' challenges the memory of the ancients (although, given the sorry fates of three of the four kings mentioned in this line, some read this as dispraise):[164]

تاج تو غبن افسر دارا و اردوان   تخت تو رشک مسند جمشید و کیقباد

Your throne is the envy of those of Jamshid and Kay-Qubad!
Your crown deceives the diadem of Dara and Ardavan!

Shah Yahya sits victoriously upon Jamshid's 'throne' (awrang), drinking from Jamshid's 'world-seeing cup' (jām-i 'ālam-bīn):[165] he is the Jamshid of his time.[166]

Shiraz's ruler is Faridun and/or Dara

Sa'd b. Zangi is a king of Faridun-esque farr.[167] Shah Shaykh Abu Ishaq is likened to the Iranian hero-king Faridun[168] and the last Kayanid, Dara II (in Iranian lore, Alexander the Great's half-brother).[169] This king is the 'world-possessing Dara',[170] the 'Dara of the age'[171] and the 'Dara of the era'.[172] Mubariz al-Din is a Dara bolstered by a Faridun-esque entourage and a Rustam 'imbued with the majesty of Faridun'.[173] Shah Shuja' is Dara the 'justice-spreader' (dād-gustar), the Dara of the age.[174] Salman depicts Shah Shuja' seated upon an ancient throne:[175]

وگر جم خوانمت شاید جم ملک سلیمانی   اگر کی گویمت زیبد که بر تخت فریدونی

If I name you Kay it is fine for you are seated upon Faridun's throne
If I call you Jam it is befitting: you are the Jamshid of the Solomonic realm.

Shah Yahya is the world-ruling Dara (or world-subduing lord).[176]

Shiraz's ruler is Solomon

Sa'd b. Zangi and his son, Abu Bakr, in turn enjoy the titles 'inheritor of the dominion of Solomon'[177] and 'inheritor of Solomon's throne'.[178] Sa'd is Solomon himself[179] or the 'refuge' of the Solomonic realm.[180] In his *Gulistan*, Sa'di hails Abu Bakr as Solomon's 'deputy' or 'proxy' (*qā'im-maqām*)[181] and his rightful heir.[182] Sa'd b. Abu Bakr has a garden bedecked like the court of Solomon.[183] His grandson, Muhammad, is 'lord of the command of Solomon's dominion'.[184]

Shah Shaykh Abu Ishaq is the 'overlord' (*kārsāz*) of the Solomonic realm.[185] He has received the dominion of Solomon from God and will retain it for all time.[186] He is the 'refuge' of the Solomonic realm;[187] the embodiment of the triumphal Solomon who has regained his lost ring,[188] which he wears on his little finger.[189] He possesses the destiny of Solomon[190] and is seated upon his throne.[191] He is the second Solomon:[192]

چشم بگشا تا ببینی جنت بی اشتباه   گر تفرجگاه جنات نعیمت آرزوست

شاه گیتی دار و جمشید فریدون دستگاه   وندر او تخت سلیمان دوم دارای دهر

سایه حق شیخ ابو اسحاق بن محمود شاه   آفتاب هفت کشور خسرو مالک رقاب

If you desire the delightful meadows of the gardens of Paradise,
Open your eyes and, make no mistake, you will behold the Paradise garden!
And within it the throne of the second Solomon, the Dara of the age –
The world-controlling king, the Jamshid of Faridun-like strength,
The sun of the seven climes, the king who is guarded by the Lord –
The shadow of God, Shaykh Abu Ishaq b. Mahmud Shah.

Shah Shuja' rules over the realm of Solomon in Solomonic style,[193] seated upon a Solomonic throne[194] with the signet ring of Solomon's decree upon his finger.[195] Shah Yahya, seated on the throne of Solomon, possesses a ring that empowers him to rule over Fars.[196]

Shiraz's ruler is Alexander

Mas'ud Shah musters the physical might of both Alexander and Sam.[197] His brother, Abu Ishaq, is the 'second Alexander' (*Sikandar-i thānī*):[198] his pleasure-taking equals that of the Greek warrior-king,[199] he rivals Alexander's record in world-conquest,[200] and he has his 'temperament' (*manish*).[201] Abu Ishaq found the dominion of Alexander and has quaffed the Water of Life.[202] The Injuid's kingly presence is infused with the properties of that revivifying liquor:[203]

سكندرى كه مقيم حريم او چون خضر   ز فيض خاک درش عمر جاودان گيرد

Any Alexander who resides in his sacred, inviolable space can, like Khizr,
attain eternal life through the grave of the dust of its threshold.

Mubariz al-Din is also hailed as the second Alexander.[204] He is a Khizr
endowed with Alexander's glory and an Alexander who leaves Dara-like
traces.[205] In Shah Shuja', we witness the combined qualities of Alexander and
Jamshid.[206]

Kingly *talmīh* in the Shirazi *ghazal*

Shiraz's poets do not draw a clear distinction between legendary and historical
rulers in *talmīh*, and allusions to Pishdadian and Kayanid kings are frequently
combined with those to Sasanians. Unsurprisingly, kingly *talmīh* is frequently
encountered in the *ghazal*s of Hafiz, who made extensive use of the form for
panegryric purposes.

Regnal wine as portal to the past

Allusions to ancient kings are employed to bewail the present and glorify
the past, to rank the present above the past or to dismiss reminiscing about
the past in favour of living in the moment. Wine-drinking in a formal, elite
setting was associated with kingship, the wine cup in royal Persianate
iconography being the princely accoutrement *par excellence*.[207] In medieval
Islamic manuscripts and on ceramics, the ruler is often depicted seated
cross-legged or enthroned, wine cup in hand.[208] The circulation of the royal
wine cup in the *majlis* was a display of kingly favour; being permitted to drink
from the king's cup was considered a great honour. This practice is reflected
in the first hemistich of the opening poem in Hafiz's *dīvān*, a *tazmīn* from
an Arabic wine poem attributed to the Umayyad Caliph Yazid b. Mu'awiya
(d. 683).[209]

Jamshid is by far the Pishdadian king most frequently alluded to by our
poets. Firdawsi tells us that Jamshid enjoyed *farr* and he ruled the world via
'kingship' (*shahriyārī*) and 'priesthood' (*mawbidī*), commanding demons, birds
and fairies,[210] much like Solomon.[211] Jamshid is credited in medieval sources
with the discovery and/or cultivation of the grapevine and wine production
(hence his association with the wine cup [*jām*]).[212] Jamshid is the first king
in the *Shahnama* to be depicted engaging in feasting at court with wine and
music, which he does at Nawruz, a festival he established.[213] After ruling in

splendour for 300 years, Jamshid grew overly proud at his many civilizing achievements, turned away from God, became ungrateful, and lost his divine sanction to rule.[214] These negative elements of Jamshid's story inform the phrases *mulk-i Jam* and *mulkat-i Jam* ('Jamshid's dominion') which are used by poets to denote transitory, ephemeral glory.[215]

There would appear to be a correlation between Jamshidian allusions and the panegyric function of a *ghazal*. This may explain why there are more than thirty separate allusions to Jamshid in Hafiz's *ghazals* and none in 'Ubayd's *ghazals*, whereas 'Ubayd's *qasīdas* contain many.[216] Jahan's allusions to Jamshid are perhaps evidence of her imitation of Hafiz's panegyric deployment of the *ghazal*.

Many Jamshidian allusions in the poetry concern the king's magical world-seeing cup, the *jām-i Jam*. Some invite a mystical interpretation, although many invoke the association of the wine cup with legitimate kingship, one which fuses the Islamic mystical tradition to pre-Islamic themes and patterns. This 'world-displaying cup' (*jām-i gītī-namāy*) is at the disposal of Kay-Khusraw in Firdawsi's *Shahnama*.[217] But, in fourteenth-century Persian lyric poetry, it is most frequently associated with Jamshid;[218] the shift in the cup's myth of origin coming at some point in the twelfth or thirteenth century.[219] Ibn al-Balkhi, writing in the early twelfth century, does not mention Jamshid's magical cup, but notes that the Zoroastrians claim 'prophethood' (*payghambarī*) for Kay-Khusraw.[220]

Allusions to Jamshid and Kayanid kings help construct (and then reinforce) links between Injuid and Muzaffarid royals and their primeval and/or mythical forerunners; H351:4:

کی بود در زمانه وفا جام می بیار   تا من حکایت جم و کاووس کی کنم

When was time ever faithful? Bring the wine cup,
So that I can recount the tales of Jam and Kavus-Kay

Hafiz calls for the 'wine cup' (*jām-i may*) so that he can drink while relating tales of long-dead kings. Relating such stories reminds his audience that fate has repeatedly delivered harsh blows in the past, even to great rulers. In H351:4 Hafiz engages in paronomasia: in the first hemistich *kay* means 'when'; in the second, it is part of the name of king Kay-Kavus (which Hafiz inverted). This *bayt* is similar in content and tone to one from Hafiz's *Saqinama*:[221]

بده تا بگویم به آواز نی   که جمشید کی بود و کاووس کی

Give me [wine] so that, to the melody of the reed flute,
I might tell you who were Jamshid and Kavus-Kay.

Drinking to the memory of those who have passed on is common to cultures where alcohol is consumed. Nasir Bukhara'i dismisses tales of Jamshid and Kay-Kavus in favour of the (true?) *jām-i Jam*; the humble wine cup:[222]

جام جمم بده به سفالین پیاله ای   تا کی حدیث جام جم و کأس لعل کی

Give me the *jam-i Jam* in an earthenware cup.
How long shall we talk of Jamshid's goblet and Kay's ruby chalice?

As noted already, in his *Saqinama*, Hafiz links the magical, royal wine cup to both Jamshid and Kay-Khusraw, evidence that, in Hafiz's day, Kay-Khusraw's association with the cup had yet to be erased from non-epic poetry.[223] Hafiz's dual association of the magical cup demonstrates that the poet saw purpose in associating this wonderous object with both kings as co-representatives of earthly and mystical dominion. This is an example of Hafiz's mythological pluralism which he harnesses to reconcile competing legends both within and across traditions. The recounting of such tales in a *majlis* might have formed an integral but distinct part of the performance repertoire, taking the form of sections within lyric poems, recitation of the *Shahnama* or the recounting of oral, less-polished stories.

There is a complexity in the manner in which Hafiz employs allusions to kings we now consider legendary and his take on the past is nuanced, varied and often reverent; H120:6:

بیفشان جرعه ای بر خاک و حال اهل دل بشنو   که از جمشید و کیخسرو فراوان داستان دارد

Cast a draught on the dust and hear the state of the 'people of the heart'
For it possesses innumerable tales of Jamshid and Kay-Khusraw.

In Khanlari's edition we find *ahl-i shawkat* ('the people of majesty') instead of *ahl-i dil* ('people of the heart'),[224] a variant that evokes kingly glory and suggests a panegyric motive, quite distinct from *ahl-i dil*, that allows for a more mystical interpretation. In H120:6 the chivalrous tradition of sprinkling wine on the ground in memory of the dead before drinking is evoked.[225] Here, too, Hafiz pairs Jamshid with Kay-Khusraw.[226] Zarkub posited that Shiraz was built upon land sanctified by the footsteps of both Kay-Khusraw and Jamshid and that two cups awaited discovery in its soil: one 'brimming with wine' (*may-fazāy*), the other 'displaying the whole world' (*gītī-namāy*).[227] Fars, home to many an ancient site, is the repository of the dead bodies of the majestic kings of the past. Wine symbolizes life and, as it combines with the dust, it brings the dead back to life and they speak forth. Animated by the regenerative force latent in wine, ancient Fars comes alive.

For Hafiz, the glory of the present is in part derived from its link to the past that is itself made present through ritualized wine-drinking and the retelling of epic tales. For Hafiz and his audience, their connection with the past is tangible: history surrounds them. It is through poetry that this past is animated for all to experience.

Elsewhere, Hafiz purports to convey to his audience intimate knowledge of Jamshid's court when he narrates what transpired at the king's wine parties; H179:5:

که جام باده بیاور که جم نخواهد ماند   سرود مجلس جمشید گفته اند این بود

They say that the anthem of Jamshid's *majlis* was this:
Bring the cup of wine, for even Jamshid will not remain!

Hafiz claims to be the best source of reliable information on primeval Iran and suggests that contemporary courtiers should emulate their distant forefathers and, through ritualistic re-enactment, make the ancients present. Elsewhere, Hafiz warns that even if the patron and his entourage consider themselves to be lineal descendants of glorious kings, they must strive to live up to their illustrious memory; H458:6:

ور خود از تخمهٔ جمشید و فریدون باشی   تاج شاهی طلبی گوهر ذاتی بنمای

If you seek the royal crown, you must show innate virtue,
Even if you are born from the seed of Jamshid and Faridun!

The sentiments expressed here share much with what is now called *bāstāngarā'ī*, an ancient revivalism (in particular in art and architecture) with its modern roots in late nineteenth-century Iran that is characterized by neo-Achaemenid and neo-Sasanian motifs.[228] The numerous allusions to kings of the Iranian past in the *ghazals* of Hafiz, coupled with the Injuid and Muzaffarid adoption of the title *shāhanshāh* and the presentation in panegyrics of the living king as the rightful inheritor of the 'dominion of the Kayanids' and the 'realm of the Persians', demonstrate that Shiraz's rulers in the fourteenth century looked far back to legitimize their rule. For Khurramshahi, 'the seed of Jamshid and Faridun' denotes pure, Iranian royal lineage.[229] This is, of course, not true, certainly in terms of the Muzaffarids, although this phrase reflects the fact that many local dynasties, to sanction their rule, claimed descent, often symbolically, from an ancient Iranian ancestor through (usually fabricated) genealogies.[230] As Hanaoka has argued, the audiences for such claims of legitimacy based on prestigious lineages were both local and universal.[231]

Hafiz equates his patron with the glory of Jamshid; H433:9:

باده نوش از جام عالم بین که بر اورنگ جم   شاهد مقصود را از رخ نقاب انداختی

Drink wine from the world-seeing cup, for upon the throne of Jamshid,
You have removed the veil from the face of the desired *shāhid*.

Here, the 'throne of Jamshid' (*awrang-i Jam*) might allude to Fars and the *shāhid* to Shah Yahya. Even though he ruled primarily from Yazd,[232] Shah Yahya was still depicted sitting upon the Solomonic throne, his Balqis-like queen by his side.[233]

Linking the late Muzaffarid period with Jamshidian glory would have flattered Shah Yahya, given how weak he was in the face of Timurid dominance, though perhaps this poem contains veiled criticism of the Muzaffarid prince who was not much more than Timur's puppet. Is this poetic politicking on the poet's part to curry favour with the Timurids? In other poems, Hafiz reminds us that Jamshid ultimately lost his throne, thereby highlighting the negative effects of the poisoned chalice that was the *jām-i Jam*.[234]

The patron as recapitulated hero

In panegyric *qasīda*s, poets promoted the idea of their patrons as heirs to an ancient heroic tradition through favourable comparison to Rustam, Sam and Giv.[235] In his *ghazal*s, Hafiz likens his beloved to the fierce Rustam who stands centre stage in Iran's struggle against its demonic neighbour, Turan. He is so ravishing that he has 'defeated' the beauties of Khallukh (a Turkic people from which prized slaves were sourced) and has struck down their king, Afrasiab. Hafiz encourages his beloved to take up the cup of Kay-Khusraw in celebration; H433:3:

گوی خوبی بردی از خوبان خلّخ شاد باش   جام کیخسرو طلب کافراسیاب انداختی

Rejoice! You have stolen the polo ball of beauty from the beauties of Khallukh.
Ask for the Cup of Kay-Khusraw, for you have toppled Afrasiab!

As noted already, Injuid and Muzaffarid rulers of Shiraz promoted canonical presentations of Iranian mytho-history through patronizing artists and calligraphers to produce illustrated *Shahnama* manuscripts.[236] In a panegyric *ghazal*, Hafiz suggests that he is familiar with variant texts of Firdawsi's *Shahnama* (or perhaps with a number of poems with similar content and form).[237] In the line below, Hafiz makes topical use of the Turk trope to cast his patron as *shāh-i Turkān* ('King of the Turks'), that is, Afrasiab.[238] Hafiz's saviour figure is Rustam, whom he alludes to here via his epithet, Tahamtan ('mighty', 'formidable'); H345:5:

شاهِ ترکان چو پسندید و به چاهم انداخت   دستگیر ار نشود لطفِ تهمتن چه کنم

Since the King of the Turks saw fit to cast me into the pit,
If Tahamtan's kindness does not take my hand, what am I to do?

Hafiz speaks with the voice of the hero Bizhan son of Giv who falls in love with Manizha, a daughter of Afrasiab. After the Turanian king learns of Bizhan and Manizha's clandestine love, he disowns Manizha and shames her publicly.[239] Afrasiab then throws his daughter's lover, Bizhan, into a 'pit' (chāh) as punishment (Bizhan was consigned to a pit by Afrasiab, just as Joseph was thrown into a pit by his envious brothers).

The theme of reprehensible, transgressive Iranian–Turanian love is a recurring theme in the *Shahnama*: Siyavash is unjustly punished by his father-in-law, Afrasiab; Siyavash's half-Iranian, half-Turanian son, Kay-Khusraw, sends Rustam to Turan to avenge his father.[240] Similarly, in the tragic story of Rustam and his half-Turanian son Suhrab, the son must die, in part, to atone for his father's amorous transgression (and also because of his desire to install his father upon Iran's throne).[241] According to Firdawsi, Afrasiab orders a large stone to be placed over the pit into which Bizhan has been cast. Eventually, he is rescued by Rustam, whose superhuman strength is enough to remove the stone.[242]

In H345:5, Hafiz says Afrasiab (the patron) has treated Bizhan (the poet) with indifference and harshness. Elsewhere, the Bizhan-like Hafiz longs to be 'rescued', calling for his patron to show him favour (there is perhaps a link here to what Lescot believes to be Hafiz's 'disgrace poems').[243] By diverting Bizhan's longing gaze away from Manizha and towards Afrasiab, Hafiz introduces a homoerotic undertone to the relationship between the Iranian hero and the Turanian king. Elsewhere, Hafiz praises Rustam as a saviour and hints that he will seek the 'affection' (i.e. employ) of another. Perhaps Hafiz is threatening to leave his patron; H470:4:

شاهِ ترکان فارغ است از حال ما کو رستمی   سوختم در چاهِ صبر از بهر آن شمعِ چگل

I have burnt in the pit of patience for the sake of that candle of Chigil.
The King of the Turks cares nothing for my condition; where is my Rustam?

Hafiz seamlessly marries Qur'anic and Iranian material here:[244] the 'pit of patience' (chāh-i sabr) is an allusion to the *Surat Yusuf* of the Qur'an in which the phrase *sabr jamīl* ('beautiful patience', 'patience is beautiful') is repeated, fusing beauty and patience in the person of Joseph. Jahan also equates her beloved with Iran's finest hero; J112:8:

رخش‌جورش همیشه در زین است　　　مشکل اینست که بی سبب با من

The problem is this: that, for no reason at all,
The Rakhsh of his harshness is always saddled up against me.

In Jahan's poem, Rustam (implied through an allusion to his steed, Rakhsh) is identified with the beloved who is cruel and prone to unprovoked hostility. Rustam is the epitome of masculine prowess; the one who humiliates and emasculates Afrasiab.[245] By equating him with Rustam, Jahan suggests she desires an energetic, mature male. Here Jahan evokes Tahmina's erotic fascination with Rustam's powerful physique as she admires his 'shoulders, arms, and chest'.[246] The erotic identification of the beloved with Rustam suggests a strong-bodied and strong-minded warrior. In another poem, Jahan says that she will tame the wild, marauding beloved and will bring him into the 'arena of fidelity' (maydān-i vafā), even if he be Rustam of Zabulistan himself![247]

Ubi sunt as 'ibrat

Allusions to pre-Islamic Iranian kings are found in Arabic poetry in the form of ubi sunt as far back as the late sixth century, most notably by the Lakhmid poet, 'Adi b. Zayd al-'Ibadi, who was active at Khusraw II's court at Ctesiphon.[248] As already noted, Sasanian kings are alluded to with frequency in early Abbasid poetry,[249] often in connection with luxury items, such as vintage wine and bacchanalian paraphernalia.[250]

It is possible that for fourteenth-century Shirazis, Kayanid shahs were as 'historical' as Sasanians, the Sasanians themselves having initiated and then promoted an Avesta-inspired, mytho-epic reception of the Iranian past that 'historicized' the Kayanids.[251] If this is the case, the differentiation between categories of 'legendary' and 'historical' king becomes a moot point. In the lines below, Hafiz alludes to Jamshid, two Kayanids (Kay-Kavus, son of Kay-Qubad and Bahman, son of Isfandiyar)[252] and one Sasanian monarch (Qubad, father of Anushiravan); H101:4–5:

ز کاسهٔ سر جمشید و بهمن است و قباد　　　قدح به شرط ادب گیر زان که ترکیبش
که واقف است که چون رفت تخت جم بر باد　　　که آگه است که کاووس و کی کجا رفتند

Take up the cup and hold it respectfully, for it is formed
From the skulls of Jamshid, Bahman, and Qubad.
Who knows where Kavus and Kay went?
Who knows how Jamshid's throne was lost?

Hafiz first calls on his audience to be mindful that the clay from which their wine cups have been fashioned was formed from the dust of ancient kings and so they should hold them with respect (the image is strengthened by the use of *kāsa-yi sar* ['bowl of the head'] to denote the skull). In what is possibly a response to a derisory use of similar kingly *talmīḥ* by Sayf Farghani (d. after 1305),[253] Hafiz encourages his audience to enjoy the here and now for, after death, even the memory of great kings fades into oblivion. Hafiz stresses a cyclical understanding of history in which legendary monarchs, who themselves took up the wine cup at court, have long since died; their decayed bodies returning to the dust from which they were formed and which is now mixed by the potter into fine clay to mould wine cups for courtiers.

In such poems, edifyinging tales of the past function as cautionary *'ibrat* (a term that encompasses 'admonition', 'advice' and 'life lessons'). Meisami argues that these historical narratives have a dual exemplary function: they validate the present and, by doing so, 'confirm the universality of history's recurrent patterns'.[254] Drinking cups formed from the skulls of long-dead kings form a macabre image that reminds the audience of the omnipresent spectre of death and the transient nature of worldly power. There is an analogous ominous image in this line; H41:6:

که ریزه اش سر کسری و تاج پرویز است   سپهر بر شده پرویز نیست خون افشان

The sky raised up is a sieve that splatters blood;
It scatters fragments of Kisra's skull, and parts of Parviz's crown

Lescot believes there is allusion here to the public execution in Shiraz in 1357 of Shah Shaykh Abu Ishaq.[255] We know that little was known about the Achaemenids in medieval Iran, as was also the case in the Sasanian period.[256] As Savant has argued, there are compelling questions to ask. How did medieval Muslims choose to remember the pre-Islamic past? What did they judge worthy of being remembered?[257] Ordering the past is a way of governing the future. As Aigle says, the past 'is preserved where it can be made compatible with the present';[258] transformed in line with the needs of the time, the past is given a renewed significance. Just as myths are products of human imagination arising out of a definite situation and intended to do something,[259] so their reworking in the present is both intentional and purposeful.[260]

Links drawn via *talmīḥ* between the patron and the distant past would, in the context of post-Mongol geopolitics, bolster local dynastic claims to a legitimacy grounded in the Iranian past and not framed in narrowly Islamic terms. Ultimately, though, Hafiz's intervention is more of a strategic implementation that forces his audience to turn away from the past and face (up to) their present. Hafiz chastises those who ape the vanity of dead monarchs; H429:2:

چین قبای قیصر و طرف کلاه کی　　　　بگذر ز کبر و ناز که دیده ست روزگار

> Leave all pride and coquetry for Time has seen
> Caesar's robe folded up and Kay's crown tossed aside.

The poet voices disdain for a certain vision of the past and for those who favour nostalgic reminiscence over a fuller engagement with their present reality; H431:4:

که می داند که جم کی بود و کی، کی　　　　بده جام می و از جم مکن یاد

> Give me the wine cup and make no mention of Jamshid
> Who knows who Jamshid was? Who knows who Kay was?

Jamshid and Kay-Kavus have, of course, not been forgotten and Hafiz's assertion here is for rhetorical effect. It has been suggested that instances of *talmīh* in which Hafiz combines allusions to 'mythical' and 'historical' kings demonstrate his incomplete knowledge of Iranian history.[261] This assertion is impossible to substantiate and it ignores the function of such allusions: Hafiz is not concerned with his audience's accurate recollection of the past (in so far as we can speak here of historical accuracy). Rather, he is exhorting his listeners to live in the present, not for (and, therefore, in) the past.

Hafiz also employs allusions to the demise of ancient kings as a mechanism for self-consolation and to commiserate with his interlocutors over their own losses and frustrations; H291:7:

جمشید نیز دور نماندی ز تخت خویش　　　　ای حافظ ار مراد میسّر شدی مدام

> O Hafiz! If that which we desire was always attained,
> Jamshid too would not have been separated from his throne.

However lofty one's station, it is always possible to be brought low as was Jamshid once he became haughty, having perhaps been led astray by a satanic figure.[262] By alluding to Jamshid alongside his *takhallus*, Hafiz suggests that this allusion provides comfort to him personally. He reassures his audience: misfortune and disappointment befall all, even the most powerful of men. Allusions to Jamshid's throne would resonate more deeply for a Shirazi audience because of the proximity of Persepolis. Its strong Jamshidian associations were encouraged by those who believed certain reliefs at the site to be depictions of the king himself.[263] Hafiz uses the example of Jamshid's demise to warn his patron of attachment to this mortal world; H486:4:

زنهار دل مبند بر اسباب دنیوی   جمشید جز حکایتِ جام از جهان نبرد

Jamshid took nothing from this world save the tale of the cup.
Beware! Do not bind your heart to the things of this lowly world.

Perhaps there is a contrast in this line between Jamshid and the poet in which the latter is the possessor of lasting power through the written word (in which he can preserve his patron's name for posterity).[264] In another allusion to Jamshid, Hafiz critiques the prohibition on public drinking and the closure of Shiraz's wine taverns by Mubariz al-Din.[265] Hafiz alludes to the Muzaffarid ruler using the nickname *muhtasib*,[266] the feared inspector of markets who regulated prices and safeguarded public morality; H78:5:

انکار ما مکن که چنین جام جم نداشت   ساقی بیار باده و با محتسب بگو

Sāqī, bring me wine, and tell the *muhtasib*
Do not deny us, for such a cup even Jamshid did not possess!

Elsewhere, Hafiz bewails his personal fate when he contrasts the opulent largesse of Jamshid's court with the miserliness of the companions of his patron, Shah Yahya; H12:6:

گرچه جام ما نشد پر می به دوران شما   عمرتان باد و مراد ای ساقیان بزم جم

Live long and be content, O wine bearers of the feast of Jamshid,
Even though our cup was not filled with wine in your time!

Hafiz bemoans his treatment at the hands of the insufficiently generous courtiers or administrators of Yazd, who have denied him the appropriate financial reward for his art.[267]

In another *ghazal*, Hafiz alludes to both Jamshid's cup and the lasso of Bahram V, the Sasanian king who is remembered in Persian literature and lore as a master hunter of the 'wild ass' (*gūr*; hence his popular name, Bahram Gur); H278:4:

که من پیمودم این صحرا نه بهرام است و نه گورش   کمند صید بهرامی بیفکن جام جم بردار

Cast down Bahram's hunting lasso, take up Jamshid's cup!
For I have traversed this plain; there's neither Bahram nor his wild ass.

Hafiz advises his audience to cease seeking Bahram-like glory, the contrast between Bahram's pleasure seeking and his ignominious end symbolizing the fickleness and unpredictability of fate.[268] Instead, Hafiz urges his audience to take up the cup of Jamshid, a source of earthly as well as other-worldly enlightenment (there is much here that recalls a well-known *rubāʿī* attributed to Khayyam which features allusions to both Jamshid and Bahram).[269] Khanlari's edition has *jām-i may* ('the cup of wine') rather than *jām-i Jam*,[270] which lends the line an even more earthly tone and diminishes the possibility of a mystical reading. Hafiz says that no traces remain of Bahram or of the wild ass he hunted (nor any sign of the king's 'grave' [*gūr*]).[271] Bahram embodies the epitome of royal excess and immature, hot-headed rashness, whereas Jamshid's cup stands for longer-lasting prizes accessed through wine: wisdom and insight. It is not the mature Bahram Gur we encounter at the end of Nizami's *Haft Paykar* that Hafiz presents here, but rather the young Bahram, so aptly depicted by Firdawsi as devoid of self-awareness.

'Ubayd employs allusions to Kay-Qubad and Siyavash to argue that all humans – even royals – are mortal; U44:8:

چرخ همان است که در خاک ریخت   خون سیاووش و سر کی قباد

This wheel of heaven is the very same that flung into the dust
The blood of Siyavash, and the head of Kay-Qubad

Fate's wheel is continually turning, as it was in the past when it caused the most unjust execution of Siyavash and the death of Kay-Qubad. Kay-Qubad's demise bears a local resonance: according to Firdawsi, the king journeyed to Fars and spent his last 100 years at Istakhr seated upon the Kayanid throne.[272] Hafiz combines Kay-Kavus (Kay-Qubad's son who stepped down as king in favour of his grandson and heir, Kay-Khusraw) with Kay-Khusraw (who gave up his throne); H407:4:

تکیه بر اختر شب دزد مکن کاین عیّار   تاج کاووس ببرد و کمر کیخسرو

Do not rely on this night-stealing star for this knave
Stole Kay-Kavus's crown and took Kay-Khusraw's belt too!

Fate, that 'night-stealing star,' had a hand in these kings' demise. Siyavash, having taken refuge in Turan, eventually falls foul of Afrasiab, who executes him. It is eventually Kay-Khusraw, Siyavash's half-Turanian son, who sends Rustam to Turan to avenge Siyavash's murder and take revenge on Afrasiab (his own Turanian grandfather). The killing of Siyavash is an atrocity which leads to much bad blood between Iran and Turan;[273] H105:4:

شرمی از مظلمهٔ خون سیاووشش باد   شاه ترکان سخن مدعیان می شنود

The King of the Turks hears the words of the hypocrites;
May he be ashamed of Siyavash's unjustly spilt blood!

Here 'hypocrites' (*mudda'iyān*) perhaps alludes to Hafiz's rivals. The 'King of the Turks,' within the context of the Persian *ghazal*, given that Turk = beloved can be understood as an allusion to the royal beloved.[274] The depiction of the beloved as the demonized Afrasiab does not jar since the beloved is programmed to inflict suffering upon the lover and to display nothing but indifference to his wretched state.[275] Here, Siyavash stands for Hafiz and *shāh-i Turkān* possibly for the part-Turkic Shah Shuja'.[276] Awhadi has a more light-hearted *ghazal* in which he alludes to a similar cast of characters to describe the beloved: he has a face like Siyavash, hair like Farangis, the build of Fariburz and the custom of Faridun.[277]

Democratizing Jamshid

Allusions to Jamshid also work on a more democratic level as Hafiz promotes the possibility that each and every one of us can become a 'Jamshid' in our own right; H448:1:

جم وقت خودی ار دست به جامی داری   ای که در کوی خرابات مقامی داری

O you who have a station in the tavern's lane!
You are the Jamshid of your age if you have a wine cup in hand.

Here Hafiz de-mythologizes and humanizes Jamshid, bringing him down to the level of his non-elite interlocutor, thereby making the king approachable. Hafiz claims you can become the 'Jamshid of your age', the humble equivalent of assertions in panegyrics that the patron is the 'Second Jamshid'. Hafiz suggests a simple wine cup is greater than Jamshid's all-seeing cup, in a sense presenting himself as the poetic gatekeeper of the memory (and associated potency) of the magical cup. Elsewhere, Hafiz says that whoever holds the wine cup in his day will possess lasting sovereignty; H118:1:

سلطانی جم مدام دارد   آن کس که به دست جام دارد

He who holds a wine cup in his hand
Continually possesses the kingship of Jamshid.

There is a pun here on *mudām*, which means both 'continually' and 'wine'. In Arabic, *mudām* means literally 'made to last' or 'lasting', but almost invariably means 'wine' either because vintage wine is kept for many years in its cask or because one keeps on drinking it.

Hafiz also alludes to ancient kings to argue for the comparative superiority of his beloved. In the following *bayt*, the allusion to the 'messenger breeze' (*sabā*) underlines the amorous nature of the relationship depicted; H121:8:

که صد جمشید و کیخسرو غلام کمترین دارد   صبا از عشق من رمزی بگو با آن شهِ خوبان

Messenger breeze, show a sign of my love to that king of beauties
Who has a hundred Jamshids and Kay-Khusraws as his lowliest slaves

Hafiz's assertion that his beloved commands a host of Jamshids and Kay-Khusraws as his slaves could be considered disrespectful to the ancients. In H121:8, Hafiz echoes instances of *talmīh* in panegyrics by 'Ubayd and Jahan,[278] in which Jamshid, Faridun, Kay-Qubad, Qubad, Dara, Rustam and others are depicted as servants. If not a denigration of the past, such allusions constitute a stand-off with Iranian legend.

Jahan alludes to Jamshid and Kay-Khusraw as a humble pair in a similar manner to Hafiz. But, instead of employing this twin allusion to praise her beloved, Jahan turns the praise towards herself and her exemplary piety; J102:6:

در مقام فقر صد جمشید و کی دربان ماست   من که در کنج قناعت نیم نانی می خورم

I who eat half a piece of bread in the corner of contentment,
In this station of poverty, have a hundred Jamshids and Kay-Khusraws as my gatekeepers.

Prompted by the similarities with H121:8, *kay* is read here as an allusion to Kay-Khusraw, though it could be an allusion to any Kayanid. Jahan presents her poverty as a majestic state, one in which she is waited on by 100 great kings. Jahan may also be stressing her piety because of her gender, as she does in the introduction to her *dīvān*.[279]

Jamshid's magical cup: The enlightened heart?

The 'wine cup' (*jām*, *jām-i may*), the 'Cup of Jamshid' (*jām-i Jam*) and the 'world-seeing' or 'world-displaying cup' (*jām-i jahān-bīn*, *jām-i jahān-namā*) blend into one another as Hafiz cements a connection between the cup's mystico-magical powers and the strong symbolic connection between temporal power and the wine goblet. The innate ability of wine to make merry, intoxicate and create addiction makes it an ideal metaphor for passionate love, whether divine or human. As already noted, the wine symposium was at the centre of court life and ritualistic wine-drinking was a display of kingly wealth and generosity.[280] Only the finest wines would be served at royal *majālis*;[281] it was bad form for guests to bring wine or a server with them to a royal feast.[282] Wine description can dominate Persian praise poetry, and it regularly segues into the praise portion.[283]

Jahan associates the all-seeing cup with Jamshid, either in imitation of Hafiz or because this had become conventional in the Persian *ghazal* by the mid-fourteenth century.[284] Although Jamshid's cup is invoked in some thirteenth-century mystical poetry,[285] Sa'di's *ghazals* are almost devoid of allusions to him. It is possible, given the abundance of allusions to Jamshid in Khvaju's *ghazals*,[286] that the employment of Jamshidian *talmīh* within the short lyric is a particular feature of the fourteenth-century Shirazi *ghazal*.

Jamshid was credited with milestone inventions and civilizational advances.[287] In addition, he was linked to the foundation of great cities and the construction of monumental structures.[288] It is possible that Jamshid's strong connection to Fars made his association with the magical cup a more attractive option than Kay-Khusraw to Shiraz's poets. Tusi says Kay-Khusraw's cup (along with his throne and crown) was tossed into the lake adjacent to the complex now known as Takht-i Sulayman by Zoroastrians, who feared looting by marauding Arabs.[289] Another factor that may have contributed to this transference of ownership is the ever-closer relationship between the Persian *ghazal* and mysticism, leading the magical cup to become associated first and foremost with Jamshid as there was more mystical 'mileage' in this association once he came to be conflated with Solomon (see below).

Some allusions to Jamshid's cup invite a more mystical interpretation than others and draw on the identification of this cup with the inner essence of man.[290] Certain commentators on Hafiz, whilst sketching the mythological hinterland of the *jām-i Jam*, choose to read allusions to the all-seeing cup variously as metaphors for a mirror on the 'secrets of the unseen world' (*asrār-i ghayb*) or as the enlightened heart of the 'true knower' (*'ārif*);[291] H143:1:

وانچه خود داشت ز بیگانه تمنّا می کرد   سالها دل طلب جام جم از ما می کرد

For years my heart sought Jamshid's cup from me,
And that which it possessed, it desired from others.

In H143 (which is in part a response to a poem by the Mongol military man, Tughan Quhistani),[292] Hafiz expounds upon the idea of the enlightened heart as the true cup of Jamshid, since it possesses analogous capabilities. Hafiz claims that he received this cup on the very same day that God created the universe, echoing other statements in which he defiantly provokes the pietistic ascetic with talk of paradisiacal, intoxicating wine, declaring that God gave him wine on *rūz-i alast*,[293] the day of the primordial covenant when God called on men to accept him as their Lord.[294] Jamshid is himself associated with the very origins of human society; H450:7:

گوهر جام جم از کان جهانی دگر است   تو تمنّا ز گلِ کوزه گران می داری

The essence of Jamshid's cup hails from a mine in another world,
And you have expectations from the clay used by wine jug makers?

In the *Saqinama*,[295] Hafiz reiterates the idea that wine can transform him into a modern-day Jamshid:

به من ده که گردم به تأیید جام   چو جم آگه از سرّ عالم تمام

Give me [wine], so that with the help of the cup I may become
Like Jamshid, aware in full of the mysteries of the world

And he expresses much the same sentiments in this line; H488:2:

همچو جم جرعهٔ ما کش که ز سرّ دو جهان   پرتو جام جهان بین دهدت آگاهی

Just like Jamshid, drink the dregs from our cup, so that the light
From the world-seeing cup will inform you of the mysteries of both worlds

Is Hafiz claiming intimate knowledge of God's mysteries and an ability to foresee future events with the aid of the magical cup? I would argue that equating the enlightened human heart with the true cup of Jamshid serves to democratize the king, bypassing the strict hierarchy of Sufi orders. This humanized, relatable Jamshid resonates for all, including the uninitiated, as the king's achievements are brought within the scope of the ordinary human.

Hafiz casts his patron as Jamshid and urges his fellow courtiers to strive for purity of heart; H413:3:

ای جرعه نوشِ مجلسِ جم سینه پاک دار   کآیینه ایست جام جهان بین که آه از او

O wine-bibber at Jamshid's *majlis*, keep your breast sanctified,
For the world-seeing cup is a marvellous mirror!

Here the world-seeing cup functions as a splendid mirror (an allusion to the Alexandrine mirror; see below) and as a metaphor for the true lover's sincere heart. The didactic thrust is aimed primarily at the *khavāss*, but the ruler is also a target; the king must strive for sincerity and surround himself with sincere individuals. Hafiz explains that to fathom the mysteries of Jamshid's magical cup – to gain mystical insight – the seeker must first humble himself in the path trodden by the antinomian mystics;[296] H144:1:

به سرّ جام جم آنگه نظر توانی کرد   که خاک میکده کحلِ بصر توانی کرد

You will only be able to gaze upon the mystery of Jamshid's cup
When you can make the dust of the wine tavern kohl for your eyes.

Here the primary (though not exclusive) meaning of 'tavern' is the meeting place of sincere wayfarers on the mystical path, who are devoid of the hypocrisy that pervades the Sufis and their lodges. These non-conformist mystics are the *sāhib-dilān*: those who possess sound, informed hearts.[297] Hafiz reminds his listeners that to gain insight, they must first practise submission and humility; H452:10:

چو مستعدّ نظر نیستی وصال مجوی   که جام جم نکند سود وقت بی بصری

Since you are not ready to gaze [on the beloved], do not seek reunion,
For the cup of Jamshid is of no use when you do not possess insight.

Elsewhere, Hafiz instructs his audience to associate closely with the world-seeing cup (to become its 'intimate companion'):[298] vital if they wish to be informed, as was Jamshid, of the secrets of the 'unseen realm' (*ghayb*); H274:4:

گرت هواست که چون جم به سرّ غیب رسی   بیا و همدم جام جهان نما می باش

If you desire, like Jamshid, to obtain the secrets of the unseen realm
Come and associate intimately with the world-seeing cup

Hafiz's chief epithet, *Lisān al-ghayb* ('Tongue of the Unseen') suggests that the poet speaks with a primordial voice that stands outside time and space. In some instances of *talmīh*, Jamshid stands for the *pīr-i mughān* who inhabits a space beyond the corrupting hierarchies of organized religion. The cup and the wine can be understood metaphorically here, but one of the attractive features of Hafiz's *ghazal*s is that metaphorical and mystical meanings are bonded with and layered through the worldly. The layered texture of his poetry and the complexity of interpretation required of the reader are accordingly enhanced by intended multivalent meanings.

Jahan also draws a close link between Jamshid's cup and the heart; J1364:1:

جانی و دو دیده جهانی   تو جام جهان نمای جانی

> You are the world-seeing cup of the soul;
> You are the soul, and the two eyes of the world!

For the most part, though, she employs a less-reverent tone when speaking of Jamshid. For Jahan, the king's station is inferior to that of the beloved; J975:6:

به دل یادی ز جام جم ندارم   به دستم گر فتد خاکی ز کویت

> If a handful of dust from your lane should fall into my hand,
> I'd have no memory of Jamshid's cup in my heart

Jamshid is Solomon, Solomon is Jamshid

That both Solomon and Jamshid were perfect temporal rulers – Solomon a prophet-king and Jamshid who, according to Firdawsi, was granted the divine right to rule over a peaceful, disease-free world for centuries – helps to explain in some part why they were linked in medieval Iranian lore. Other facets of their respective stories bear a resemblance beyond mere coincidence: both command magical powers (Jamshid exercising them through his cup, Solomon through his ring); their thrones were carried by demons, transporting them over far distances at rapid speed; both Solomon and Jamshid harnessed the force of the wind; they both orchestrated the building of magnificent cities and structures;[299] and they both grew proud and lost their sovereignty, either temporarily (Solomon) or completely (Jamshid). It may simply be the case, as Omidsalar has argued, that it is precisely these similarities between the legends of the two kings in their respective traditions that led to aspects of their narratives coalescing, rather than there being any genetic relationship between the two.[300] The fact that not all fourteenth-century Shirazi Muslims considered Jamshid and Solomon to be one and the same demonstrates the vibrancy of medieval Muslim negotiations of the Iranian past.

It is the geopolitical context of the topographically informed conflation of Jamshid and Solomon that is most significant to the present study. By combining elements of the individual stories of Jamshid and Solomon, Hafiz created bridges between the Abrahamic and Iranian pasts and his patron's post-Mongol present. Since many medieval Iranian Muslims considered Solomon and Jamshid to be one, Hafiz could work within a Perso-Islamic mytho-historical framework that was already available.[301]

Between circa 1100 and 1400, Muslim Iranians debated the validity or even plausibility of the identification of Jamshid with Solomon.[302] Some believed Kay-Khusraw and Solomon to be one, which is especially interesting given the contested association of the magical cup.[303] That a number of medieval authors protested against the identification of Jamshid with Solomon, is proof that this belief was widely held.[304] Given that this was dismissed by some on the basis that the belief had currency among the 'ignorant masses' ('avāmm),[305] the decision taken by Hafiz and others to reinforce the conflation of these two figures may be evidence of a desire on their part to play to the popular (and not only the elite or scholarly) imagination.[306]

This explains why, in many instances of talmīh, stories associated individually with one or the other are interchanged, giving the impression that the two have been confused.[307] A similar phenomenon can be detected in some earlier, non-Shirazi lyric poetry,[308] but the belief that Jamshid and/ or Solomon had played an intimate role in shaping the landscape of ancient Fars served to intensify the impact of these allusions upon audiences local to southern Iran. That Solomon and Jamshid are held up as exemplars of just kingship reinforces not only the didactic function of allusions to them, but also their relevance to the contemporary ruler and his courtiers, enhancing the panegyric dimensions of this form of kingly talmīh.

Here is a typical example of the conflation of Solomon and Jamshid; H28:4:

زبان مور به آصف دراز گشت و رواست   که خواجه خاتم جم یاوه کرد و باز نجست

The ant's tongue rightly stretched out towards [and chided] Asaf
For he had lost Jamshid's signet ring and did not search for it anew

Of course, it is Solomon's 'signet ring' (khātam), not Jamshid's, which becomes lost and falls into the hands of a demon who then takes on the physical appearance of the king and rules in his place, ushering in a period of cruelty and oppressive rule (not unlike the way in which Jamshid's arrogance and tyranny open the way for the evil foreigner, Zahhak, to seize Iran's throne and rule oppressively). In another poem, Hafiz says it is through the power of the present ruler's that Jamshid's signet ring has been saved from being touched by the satanic Ahriman; H390:3:

خاتم جم را بشارت ده به حسن خاتمت   کاسم اعظم کرد از او کوتاه دست اهرمن

Through the beauty of your signet ring deliver the good news to Jamshid's ring:
The Greatest Name kept Ahriman's hand far from it

There is a possible allusion to Jamshid's ring in the *Shahnama*[309] and it is alluded to in Ghaznavid court poetry.[310] The ring that Solomon lost and the demon then wore, had the *ism-i a'zam-i khudā* ('God's greatest name'; a symbol or phrase of talismanic power) engraved on it, affording protection and might to whomever placed the ring on his/her finger.[311] Most accounts state it was Asaf (Solomon's vizier) who ultimately assisted the court in ousting the demon.

In another poem, Hafiz perhaps praises Jalal al-Din Turanshah when he alludes to a personage who combines characteristics of both Asaf and Jamshid;[312] H272:7:

حافظ که هوس می کندش جام جهان بین   گو در نظر آصف جمشیدمکان باش

To Hafiz, who craves the world-seeing cup, say:
Stay in the sights of the Asaf of Jamshid-like status

Hafiz also asserts that the Muzaffarid vizier, Burhan al-Din Fathullah, combines the qualities of Asaf and the power of Jamshid.[313] The association of kingly attributes with powerful viziers is a prominent feature of Injuid panegyrics: 'Amid al-Mulk is an 'Asaf of Jamshid-like splendour'[314] and an 'Asaf who holds the cup of Jamshid'.[315] The vizier embodies the ways of Dara[316] and recapitulates Alexander such that talk of him makes Khizr's mouth water.[317] Fourteenth-century Shiraz is administered by Asaf-like viziers who serve the Solomonic realm.[318] They are individually hailed as: 'Asaf of the age',[319] the 'second Asaf',[320] the 'Asaf bolstered by the *farr* of Solomon'[321] and 'the Asaf from whose face sparkles divine *farr*'.[322]

It is unclear why in H28 and H390, Hafiz chooses to associate the magical ring with Jamshid (rather than Solomon), although he speaks of the 'signet ring of Jamshid' (*khātam-i Jamshid*) in another poem.[323] One possible explanation is that the shortened version of Jamshid used in both poems, Jam, constitutes just one syllable, rather than the three of Sulayman or the two of Jamshid and is, therefore, somewhat easier to incorporate within a hemistich. Hafiz depicts Shah Shuja' seated on Jamshid's throne and himself as the humble ant who spoke to Solomon; H171:6:

بر تخت جم که تاجش معراج آسمان است   همت نگر که موری با آن حقارت آمد

On the Throne of Jamshid, whose crown is the path of ascent to Heaven,
See the tenacity with which such a lowly ant managed to climb it

Here *takht-i Jam* could stand for Persepolis, Fars, Shiraz or, most specifically, the Muzaffarid throne.[324] In his *qasīda* in praise of the same king, Hafiz declares his patron's throne the envy of those of Jamshid and Kay-Qubad (both associated in Iranian mythology with Istakhr-Persepolis).[325] From his knowledge of the Qur'an, Hafiz would have been fully aware that the ant spoke to Solomon not to Jamshid but, again, the combination of the ant and Jamshid would not have struck the contemporary listener as unusual: the poets of his time reshaped Qur'anic narratives via *talmīh* and thereby contributed to the Iranization and localization of potentially distant figures. It should be noted, however, that in the *ghazals* of this period we do not come across the reverse dynamic: Hafiz does not link Jamshid's magical wine cup with Solomon. The conflation of Jamshid with Solomon is not complete.[326]

The possibility that the Solomonic legends were formed first by Jews residing in the Achaemenid Empire who were strongly influenced by their Iranian environment should not be overlooked.[327] When viewed in this light, it is possible to conjecture that aspects of legends attached to Solomon and Jamshid originated from the same sociocultural milieu. By associating Jamshid with aspects of the Solomon story – the talismanic signet ring engraved with God's Greatest Name or the ant that converses with the prophet-king – Hafiz gives these tales more of an Iranian flavour rather than one that is purely Islamic.

Hafiz ranks Jamshid's cup (here, a metaphor for the pure heart of the sincere mystic)[328] above Solomon's magical ring; H119:1:

دلی که غیب نمای است و جام جم دارد   ز خاتمی که دمی گم شود چه غم دارد

The heart which shows the unseen realm, and has Jamshid's cup
What does it care if it loses its signet ring for a moment?

According to Sudi,[329] this is a subtle allusion to Shah Mansur who, having been driven from Shiraz by the Timurids, subsequently returned to the city triumphant. Hafiz focuses on Solomon as king here and contrasts worldly power (symbolized by the signet ring) with spiritual insight (symbolized by the cup). Although Hafiz is clearly favouring the latter over the former, it would be a mistake to read a chauvinistic bias into this line.

Allusions to Solomon alone

The Qur'anic Solomon, in addition to being a wise and just king, is hailed as a prophet,[330] rendering him innocent of all sin – a distinction that sets him apart from Jamshid. Hafiz contrasts himself, the humble poet, with his majesty Solomonic patron;[331] H31:7:

با سلیمان چون بر انم من که مورم مرکب است   اندر آن ساعت که بر پشت صبا بندند زین

When they fix a saddle to the back of the *sabā* wind,
How can I ride with Solomon when the ant is my mount?

Hafiz is unable to ride alongside Solomon because his steed is the lowly ant, not the messenger wind; an allusion to the prophet-king's harnessing of the wind and directing it at his command.[332] In the popular Islamic imagination, Solomon's throne was transported by or on the wind[333] and allusions to it being carried away (and destroyed) are used to warn of the transience of earthly power.[334] Perhaps the most famous of such allusions is that incorporated by Sa'di into his elegy for the Salghurid Abu Bakr b. Sa'd:[335]

که هرکجا که سریریست میرود بر باد   نه خود سریر سلیمان بباد رفتی و بس

It was not just Solomon's throne that was destroyed by the wind;
Wherever a throne is established, it is eventually laid to waste.

Hafiz uses similar imagery to warn his listeners of the perils of attachment to this world; H100:4:

در معرضی که تخت سلیمان رود به باد   بادت به دست باشد اگر دل نهی به هیچ

There'll be only wind in your grasp if you set your heart on nothingness,
In a place where Solomon's throne goes with the wind

To have nothing but 'wind' in one's hand is tantamount to being empty-handed.[336] Hafiz's message is this: the world is filled with uncertainty and instability and if the members of his audience attach their hearts to it (to 'nothingness', *hīch*), they will ultimately end up with nothing. As noted above, the phrase, *ravad bi bād* ('goes with the wind') can be read in two ways: (a) the throne rides on the wind; (b) it is carried off by it and then destroyed.[337] The relationship between Solomon and the wind is interpreted negatively by Hafiz in this line too; H88:7:

که این سخن به مثل باد با سلیمان گفت   گره به باد مزن گرچه بر مراد رود

Do not tie a knot to the wind, even if it blows as you wish,
This is what the wind said to Solomon in the form of a parable.

In the Qur'an it was of course the ant – not the wind – who warned Solomon of the impending destruction of his throne, and in Khanlari's edition the 'ant' (*mūr*) speaks to the king, not the 'wind' (*bād*).[338] Tying knots to grills in shrines or to trees in holy spots after praying for wishes to be fulfilled is a practice still popular in certain parts of Iran, Afghanistan and Central Asia. Hafiz might also be alluding to a practice mentioned in the Qur'an: sorceresses blowing upon knots to 'tie' them with an incantation. Blowing upon the knot, according to this custom, would make the spell efficacious.[339] Hafiz is highlighting the futility of hoping for things that are not within one's control; even if Solomon could command the wind, we cannot. But as 'Ubayd warns his audience, the very dust of Shiraz is the same that in ancient times worked against Solomon and other great kings; U44:7:

خاک همان است که بر باد داد   تخت سلیمان و سریر قباد

The dust is the very same that delivered to the wind
The throne of Solomon and the seat of Qubad.

'Ubayd localizes his warning by alluding to the throne of Solomon and the seat of Qubad. Hafiz also employs Solomonic *talmīh* to lament his own predicament; H24:7:

حافظ از دولتِ عشقِ تو سلیمانی شد   یعنی از وصل تواش نیست به جز باد به دست

Hafiz became a Solomon through the good fortune of your love,
That is, from union with you he has nothing in his hand but wind.

To become a 'Solomon in love' is to be left disappointed. Alongside these negative portrayals of the wind in Solomon's story, there are others that are positive. It is the 'wind of desire' that has returned the 'Solomon rose' (a metaphor for the royal patron-beloved) to the garden; H174:2:

برکش ای مرغ سحر نغمۀ داوودی باز   که سلیمان گل از باد هوا باز آمد

O dawn bird, take up the song of David once more!
For the Solomon rose has returned with the breeze of desire.

The 'dawn bird' (*murgh-i sahar*, the poet) sings with melodies as sweet as those of Solomon's father, David. 'Ubayd invokes David to create an image contrary to that of Hafiz when he ranks the warbling of the dawn bird (i.e. his poetry) above the songs of the prophet David;[340] U44:3:

زمزمهٔ مرغ سحرخوان شنو   تا نکنی نغمهٔ داود یاد

Listen to the warbling of the bird which sings at dawn
So that you do not call to mind the melodies of David.

Hafiz alludes to the current ownership of Solomon's signet ring to stress the superiority of his royal patron over rival kings or possible usurpers; H57:2:

گرچه شیرین دهنان پادشهانند ولی   او سلیمان زمان است که خاتم با اوست

Even though the sweet-lipped ones are kings,
He who possesses the signet ring is the Solomon of the Age.

In another poem, Hafiz likened the beloved's tight, sweet mouth to Solomon's 'dominion' (*mulk*); a sign that his patron is Solomon's rightful heir.[341] The beloved's lips are as potent as Solomon's ring itself with which they command man and *jinn* alike. Hafiz asks his patron to provide him with protection, whether in the form of a 'protection ring' or a kiss (a sign of royal favour); H161:2:

از لعل تو گر یابم انگشتریِ زنهار   صد ملک سلیمانم در زیر نگین باشد

If from your ruby [lips] I obtain a protection ring
I will have a hundred realms of Solomon under my ring.

When Hafiz receives favour from his patron, he is protected from all woe, just as Solomon was by God's *ism-i a'zam* engraved on his ring;[342] H327:6:

سزد کز خاتم لعلش زنم لاف سلیمانی   چو اسم اعظمم باشد چه باک از اهرمن دارم

It is fit that I claim to be Solomon when I have his ruby signet,
When I have the Greatest Name, what fear have I of the Devil?

Hafiz likens the beloved's lips to the ruby because of their deep red hue and lustre and to allude to the ring's gemstone. Jahan, like Hafiz, identifies with the ant that spoke to Solomon; J521:2:

موری ضعیفم و شده ام پایمال هجر   حالم مگر به گوش سلیمان نمی رسد

I am a weak ant and have been trampled by separation
Will news of my state ever reach the ear of Solomon?

The poet laments her separation from her indifferent, royal patron and expresses the hope that he will notice her suffering and take pity on her. In the Qur'an, Solomon is impressed by the prudence of the ant and takes him into his service;[343] a fitting parallel for the imbalanced relationship between an all-powerful patron and an aspiring poet. In a series of *ghazal*s, Jahan speaks as the weak, downtrodden ant whose groaning and story of sorrow and pain have not reached the ears of her Solomon.[344] In the *bayt* below, Jahan uses the word *ghamm* ('grief,' 'woe'), a shorthand term for sorrow borne out of unrequited love, as she harnesses the language of passionate desire to describe the force of emotion present in the patronage bond; J985:7:

تو به شاهیّ ما سلیمانی   من به پای غم تو چون مورم

In your role as our king, you are a Solomon;
I am like an ant at the foot of my grief for you.

Appealing to the munificence and grace of his patron, Hafiz depicts a similarly uneven relationship.[345] 'Ubayd suggests that securing such royal favour is not easy for all those who petition it; U16:6:

در حریم وصل هر موری چه داند راه برُد   این سخن کاری است کز دست سلیمان بر نخاست

How can every ant know how to enter the sanctuary of reunion?
These words were never uttered by Solomon.

Allusions to Solomon are also coupled with those to the land of Sheba, the homeland of his beloved queen, Balqis.[346] In a *ghazal* that Lescot believes Hafiz sent to Sultan Ahmad b. Shaykh Uvays to curry favour with the new Jalayirid ruler, Baghdad is transformed into the Land of Sheba (and Sultan Ahmad, in effect, into Balqis);[347] H90:1:

ای هدهدِ صبا به سبا می فرستمت   بنگر که از کجا به کجا می فرستمت

O hoopoe of the *saba* wind! I am sending you to Sheba
See how I send you from one place to another!

In a similar vein, Salman draws parallels between Dilshad Khatun (Shaykh Uvays's powerful mother) and the Queen of Sheba. 'Dilshad Shah', as Salman addresses her,[348] is the 'Balqis of the Age'.[349] She is a 'Balqis of Jamshidian force' and a 'Mary with Jesus-like breath'.[350] Two Salghruid women are also likened to the Queen of Sheba: Abish Khatun and her daughter Kurdujin, both of whom are dubbed the 'Balqis of the Age'.[351] Mourning the death of Abish Khatun (d. 1286), Vassaf wrote a poem that contains this line:[352]

وارث ملک سلیمان رفت در خاک ای دریغ   کو سلیمان تا بدان بلقیس خوش بگریستی

Alas, the rightful heir to Solomon's realm has gone to her grave!
Where is Solomon to weep profusely for this Balqis?

In Persian, *sabā* ('messenger wind') and Saba ('Sheba') form a homonymous pair: they are pronounced identically, even though they differ orthographically.[353] The news received by Solomon from the land of Sheba parallels the joy felt by Hafiz at the coming of spring and the arrival of the rose – standard metaphors for the return of the royal patron. The beloved alluded to in the line below might be Shah Mansur, the royal identity of the beloved being hinted at through the twinned allusion to David and Solomon: "that appears in the second line of the same poem (as already discussed)"[354] H174:1:

هدهد خوش خبر از طرف سبا باز آمد   مژده ای دل که دگر باد صبا باز آمد

Glad tidings, O heart, the *sabā* breeze has returned!
The hoopoe of good news has come back from Sheba

It is the hoopoe (*hudhud*), Solomon's messenger bird, which carries messages to Balqis. In the following *bayt*, 'Ubayd alludes to Solomon to express the lover's frustration at not receiving word from his beloved; U132:1:

تشنه را کی رسد از چشمهٔ حیوان خبری   کی رساند ز صبا مرغ سلیمان خبری

When will Solomon's hoopoe deliver news from the *sabā* breeze?
When will the thirsty one receive news of the source of eternal life?

'Ubayd combines the allusion to Solomon and his longing for correspondence with his beloved with an allusion to Alexander and his futile search for the Water of Life. The tone is a hopeless one: When (ever) will the messenger bring news from the beloved? When (ever) will the ardent seeker reach his ultimate goal?

Alexander and Khizr

Fabulous accounts of Alexander (d. 323 BCE) abound in Iranian and Islamic folklore, where as Iskandar, Sikandar and Dhu'l-qarnayn,[355] he is celebrated as both a king-conqueror and a sage-prophet.[356] Allusions to Alexander in the poetry of Injuid and Muzaffarid Shiraz reflect this positivist, Muslim image of the conqueror. In the Islamic tradition, Alexander is an instrument of the Abrahamic God and the knowledge he possesses is a divine gift that came to him through lived experience.[357] In his *Shahnama*, Firdawsi presents Alexander in an extremely favourable light.[358] Firdawsi's Alexander is Iranized and appears as the son (and legitimate successor) of Darab and his Greek wife, Nahid, the daughter of Filqus of Macedon.[359] Alexander's half-Iranian heritage was asserted by al-Dinawari in the late ninth century who, interestingly, attributed the genealogical claim to the people of Fars.[360] In Firdawsi's epic, after defeating his half-brother, Dara,[361] Alexander marries Dara's daughter, Rawshanak.[362] Ibn al-Balkhi depicts Alexander as 'most shrewd' and 'wise'; a king who followed the path of justice.[363]

Other important early Persian recensions of the Alexander romance include Tarsusi's twelfth-century *Darabnama* and the anonymous *Iskandarnama* (written at some point between the twelfth to fourteenth centuries).[364] As Rubanovich has noted, the premodern Persian Alexander tradition emerged from the merging of a group of 'variegated sources',[365] including: Greek, Zoroastrian, Qur'anic-Islamic and Arabic written material, in addition to oral folk traditions. Nizami's retelling of the Alexander legend (the most relevant to the present study) was completed in the 1190s in two parts: the *Sharafnama* which is an account of Alexander as king-conqueror and the *Iqbalnama*, in which he is depicted as sage-prophet.[366] Askari believes Nizami's *Iskandarnama* was 'primarily understood as a book of wisdom on kingship' in which Alexander is presented as a model king by Nizami to his patron.[367] The Alexander of the *Sharafnama* is a composite character: he destroys fire temples,[368] makes a pilgrimage to the Ka'ba,[369] sits on Kay-Khusraw's throne[370] and drinks from the all-seeing cup.[371] Alexander's sage-prophet status in the premodern Persianate world is in part facilitated by the king's equation in Islamicate literature with Solomon, something that allows for the legitimization of Alexander's prophetic profile.[372] Piemontese, while underlining the connections between Alexandrine and Solomonic lore, suggests that these characters are sometimes joined, because they 'represent the sovereign of the universal and monotheistic kind'.[373]

Khizr (derived from the Arabic for 'green', 'greenery', 'verdure') is a mysterious figure whose origins are obscure.[374] Sometimes conflated or paired with the prophet Elijah,[375] Khizr is not mentioned by name in the Qur'an but is linked to both Moses and Dhu'l-qarnayn:[376] Khizr acts as spiritual guide to Moses, Alexander and any Sufi adept along the journey of initiation. Khizr rules over nature and everything turns verdant under his step. His immortality is derived from the Water of Life and he possesses extreme old age and knowledge of the past and future.[377] In the *ghazals* of post-Mongol Shiraz, Khizr is most regularly associated with Alexander whom he guided in the 'Land of Darkness' (*zulmat, zulamāt*) on his quest to find the source of the water of eternal life. Khizr drank from the source and became immortal, but Alexander failed to do so.[378]

By the fourteenth century, Alexander had been fully integrated into the Iranian mythological and narrative traditions. Local resonances of allusions to

Khizr were mediated through sites in Fars infused with mystical potency such as Dasht (or Dast)-i Khizr on the outskirts of Shiraz and other cultic shrines associated with him, including one at Bishapur.[379] At these spots, pilgrims hoped to encounter their supernatural helper[380] and the existence of local shrines to this mysterious figure calls for a reading of *talmīh* that acknowledges the mythological topography of Shiraz and its environs.

Although the present ruler can be lauded as the 'Alexander of the Age', ultimately, the poets declare their patrons greater than the king; H410:7:

جرعه ای بود از زلال جام جان افزای تو　　　آنچه اسکندر طلب کرد و ندادش روزگار

That which Alexander sought and Fate denied him
Were the dregs from the crystal liquid of your soul-reviving cup.

Allusions to Khizr's Water of Life are used to solicit favour from the patron; H93:7:

چو می دهند زلال خضر ز جام جمت　　　روان تشنۀ ما را به جرعه ای دریاب

Comprehend my thirsty soul with just a single sip
For they serve you Khizr's crystal clear water from Jamshid's cup

Here 'Khizr's crystal clear water' stands for the wine served in the king's royal cup and is emblematic of the bestowal of kingly favour. The Water of Life stands first and foremost in this *bayt* for the material sustenance that the poet seeks from his patron and, on a secondary level, for mystical enlightenment. In a panegyric *ghazal* for Shah Shuja', Hafiz combines allusions to both Khizr and Alexander; H167:5:

به جرعه نوشی سلطان ابوالفوارس شد　　　خیال آب خضر بست و جام اسکندر

He desired the water of Khizr and the cup of Alexander,
He came to drink the dregs from the cup of Sultan Abu l-Favaris.

By associating the Water of Life with the dregs of the wine drunk at Shah Shuja''s court, Hafiz flatters his patron: the only true life-perpetuating liquor that can be obtained in this realm of human existence is found in the nurturing patronage of his generous king. Khanlari's edition has Kay-Khusraw instead of Alexander, which arguably works better, since Alexander *failed* in his quest to imbibe the water of eternal life, whereas Kay-Khusraw was not failed by his cup.[381] The poets also employ allusions to Khizr's vivifying aqua in praise of their fourteenth-century present. As noted in Chapter 1, Injuid and Muzaffarid poets manifest acute Shirazophilia, and loci such as the Ruknabad canal, the

Musalla and Ja'farabad pleasure gardens and the audience hall of the patron all emit a life-giving force equal or superior to that associated with Khizr.[382] Shiraz's cultural flourishing is sustained by this life-giving force, a metaphor for liberal patronage.

Khizr's elixir is also associated with the wine tavern. Such allusions invite a this-worldly, hedonistic interpretation: the search for the source of eternal earthly life is a vain one, so it is best to seek out the intoxicating 'water of the tavern' and, through consuming it, enjoy the transient present. Exhortations to search for the *āb-i hayāt* in the tavern can also be interpreted as instructions to the audience to seek out the wise counsel of the *pīr-i mughān* who resides there;[383] H118:2:

در میکده جو که جام دارد   آبی که خضر حیات از او یافت

The water from which Khizr derived eternal life
Search for it in the wine tavern, for the cup has it.

The lips, mouth and saliva of the beloved evoke Khizr and/or the Water of Life itself.[384] The beloved's rejuvenating, Khizr-like saliva, works in tandem with his restorative, Jesus-like breath:[385] his lips are Khizr and his mouth is the Water of Life; what Khizr succeeded in quaffing was no more than a 'mirage'.[386] The lover searches, Khizr-like, for the beloved's 'life-bestowing' lips.[387] And, just as the haughty boy can withhold his vivifying Jesus-like breath from his frustrated admirer, so too can he stubbornly refuse to impart his rejuvenating spittle.[388]

Alexander failed in his quest which was both futile and flawed. Through his failure, as Rubanovich has argued, Alexander becomes 'both an emblem of condemnable vanity and a symbol of man's vulnerability in the face of Destiny and God's decree'.[389] Alluding to Alexander's frustrated quest, Hafiz advocates an acceptance of the fundamental mortality of man and discourages the pursuit of any quest in search of terrestrial immortality; H290:7:

نزاع بر سر دنیای دون مکن درویش   نه عمر خضر بماند نه ملک اسکندر

Neither Khizr's life nor Alexander's dominion lasted forever
O true mystic, do not argue over this lowly world!

The 'true mystic' (*darvīsh*) – a uniformly positive character in Hafiz's poetry in contrast to the vilified Sufi – should strive to attain a station that lies morally beyond the examples set by both Alexander and Khizr. Hafiz's suggestion in H290 that Khizr did not enjoy eternal life goes against convention. It is unclear where Hafiz took this idea from, though perhaps the poet is simply using the reference to Khizr's extraordinary longevity in a hyperbolic manner to draw attention to the necessity to live a life free from hypocrisy.

Jahan's allusions to Khizr are more conventional. She urges her addressees to follow the example set by him and contrasts the vain trials of Alexander with the ease of Khizr's success; J768:10:

خضر چون خواهد چشیدن آب حیوان غم مخور   چون سکندر چند گردی در طلب گرد جهان

How long will you traverse the earth searching like Alexander?
Since Khizr will surely taste of the Water of Life, grieve not.

The *radīf* here, *ghamm makhur*, is not only in dialogue with H255 (see Chapter 6), it also echoes words spoken by Khizr in the *Sharafnama*: *makhur ghamm* ('do not grieve').[390] Despite his immense worldly power and glory, Alexander was denied the one thing he truly desired; H245:7:

به زور و زر میسّر نیست این کار   سکندر را نمی بخشند آبی

They will not bestow the Water of Life upon Alexander
Such a thing cannot be obtained by force and gold.

It is those allusions to Khizr as guide which are the most overtly mystical in tone.[391] Khizr (like the *pīr-i mughān*) guides those who truly seek union with God, severed from worldly attachment and devoid of hypocrisy; H195:7:

پیاده می روم و همراهان سوارانند   تو دستگیر شو ای خضر خجسته پی که من

Take my hand, O Khizr of auspicious step!
For I travel on foot, whereas my companions ride.

Embarking on the spiritual journey without Khizr (i.e. without a reliable and informed guide) is unwise, as it is likely one will lose one's way.[392] Khizr will come to the aid of the wayfarer in times of difficulty. He is *khujasta-pay, pay-khujasta* and *farrukh-pay* ('auspicious of step', 'blessed of step')[393] and is therefore able to lead the seeker confidently along his spiritual path.

Hafiz also alludes to Khizr to discuss the sorry state of the age in which he lives and to highlight the need for a saviour figure to turn its fortunes around; H169:2:

خون چکید از شاخ گل باد بهاران را چه شد   آب حیوان تیره گون شد خضر فرخ پی کجاست

The Water of Life has turned dark, where is the auspicious-step Khizr?
Blood has dripped from the rose's stem, what has happened to the spring breeze?

The *radīf* here, *rā chi shud* ('What has happened to ... ?') underscores the poem's mournful tone.

While Khizr, who succeeded in his search, stands for the true mystic who realizes reunion with God (thereby attaining eternal life), Alexander epitomizes those who, because of their attachment to the material world, are denied this bounty and perish. Jahan posits that Alexander's effort amounted to nothing, suggesting all must emulate the example set by Khizr; J716:6:

بی توقف به لب چشمۀ حیوان برسید   نکند جهد سکندر پس از این سود که خضر

The efforts of Alexander have no benefit hereafter
For Khizr, without pausing, reached the edge of the spring of eternal life

For 'Ubayd, suffering and toil is necessary in this quest and, if one endures trials equal to those of Khizr, one will reach the life-giving source; U129:2:

رنج ظلمت گر کشیدی آب حیوان یافتی   زندۀ جاوید خواهی بود زین پس همچو خضر

You would have eternal life from now on if, just like Khizr,
You had endured the suffering of the darkness and found the Water of Life.

Alexander's motivation for seeking out the elixir of eternal life stemmed from arrogance and a greedy desire for more temporal power. Khizr's motivation was nobler: spiritual enlightenment. The fate of Khizr is contrasted with that of Alexander by Hafiz to instruct the audience as to how to tread the path towards God; H439:5:

آب خضر نصیبۀ اسکندر آمدی   فیض ازل به زور و زر ار آمدی به دست

If eternal bounty could be obtained through force and wealth,
Alexander too would have received a portion of the water of Khizr.

The variety with which Alexandrine legends are incorporated into the *ghazals* studied here shows the diversity of Shiraz's poets' individual re-fashionings of these tried and tested tales. Any one narrative element can lend itself to multiple (and sometimes contradictory) readings. The poets' approach in turn produces a spectrum of possible interpretations. Since mythological narratives are continually retold and recast, they are always in flux, never fixed.

Jahan identifies her lover persona with the desperate character of Alexander and his fruitless search;[394] J730:5:

در ظلمت گیسوی تو جوییم دگربار   مانند سکندر منم و چشمۀ حیوان

I am just like Alexander, and once more I seek
In the darkness of your locks the source of eternal life

By casting herself as Alexander, Jahan suggests that her quest for the
'Water of Life' (here the beloved's mouth concealed by his dark forelocks)
is doomed from the outset. Elsewhere, Jahan inhabits Zulaykha's frustrated
desire for Joseph and likens it to Alexander's frantic, fruitless quest; J745:7:

چون سکندر گشته ام از آب حیوان شرمسار   من به جستجوی آن چاه زنخدان در جهان

In search of that pit of his chin dimple throughout the world
I have become like Alexander, shamed by the Water of Life

Other allusions to Alexander concern his magical mirror, a source of
supernatural guidance not unlike Jamshid's world-seeing cup.[395] This mirror,
supposedly fashioned by Aristotle for Alexander, allowed the king to view
future events. This subset of Alexandrine allusions is similar in tone to those
in which Jamshid is linked with the invention of wine-making: just as before
Jamshid there was no wine, before Alexander there were no mirrors. Not
every maker of mirrors knows the art of *Sikandarī* (the performance of kingly
duties with Alexandrine wisdom);[396] H177:1:

نه هر که آینه سازد سکندری داند   نه هر که چهره برافروخت دلبری داند

Not everyone who paints their face knows how to ravish hearts
Not everyone who makes mirrors knows how to act like Alexander

Mirrors were made of burnished metal and required regular polishing to
keep from tarnishing, so the analogy with the heart of the believer which
must undergo continual cleansing through the sustained and repeated
performance of good deeds and the endurance of pain and suffering on the
path towards reunion with God is an obvious one. Hafiz vows to take hold of
the beloved's heart one day, just as Alexander took hold of the magic mirror;
H149:12:

اگر می گیرد این آتش زمانی ور نمی گیرد   من آن آیینه را روزی به دست آرم سکندروار

One day I will take that mirror into my hand, Alexander-like,
Whether this fire takes hold one day, or not

By 'this fire' (*īn ātash*), Hafiz could mean the fiery language with which he
plans to thaw the beloved's icy heart: a rich example of metapragmatics on
the part of Hafiz who is not only aware of his poetry as verbal practice, but
also theorizes its potential effect on the listener. In this line, Hafiz draws a
direct parallel between Jamshid's cup and Alexander's mirror;[397] H5:11:

تا بر تو عرضه دارد احوال ملک دارا   آیینهٔ سکندر جام می است بنگر

Alexander's mirror is the wine cup; look into it
So that it might display to you the state of Dara's realm.

The poet alludes here to the defeat of Darius III in 332 BCE at the hands of Alexander (Hafiz refers to the king according to the Kayanid tradition: Dara, son of Darab).[398] In some versions of this story, Alexander's mirror helps him to gain the upper hand in the battle. Alexander's army later set fire to and destroyed Persepolis, but here *mulk-i Dārā* ('Dara's realm') refers to Iran as a whole,[399] so Hafiz may be sending a warning of impending doom to his patron on the eve of the Timurid capture of southern Iran.[400]

Conclusion

There is a direct correlation between the use of kingly allusions and the panegyric function of a poem in all forms of Persian lyric poetry. It is therefore unsurprising that both Jahan and 'Ubayd employ few allusions to legendary and/or historical kings in their *ghazal*s since they only irregularly used the form for overtly panegyric purposes: 'Ubayd because he composed many panegyric *qasīda*s and Jahan because, as a woman of high social status, she would have had limited access to the semi-public performance space of the royal *majlis-i sharāb*. Hafiz, who composed so few *qasīda*s and expressed almost all praise of the patron through the short lyric, made frequent use of kingly *talmīh* in his *ghazal*s. The abundance of royal allusions is a distinguishing feature of Hafiz's *ghazal*s.[401]

It is clear that Hafiz and his contemporaries saw not only relevance but also significance in drawing comparisons between their patrons and a select repertoire of past royal figures (in particular Jamshid and Solomon) and that the comparisons they drew transcended cliché and bore a direct relation to the contemporary geopolitical reality the poets and their patrons inhabited. Shiraz's rulers were the living Jamshids, Daras, Solomons and Alexanders of their age and they remanifested the glory of the past, serving as bridges that spanned time and space. There is a strong loco-descriptive dimension to the use of kingly *talmīh* in the *ghazal*s of this period especially because the mytho-legendary and historical figures most frequently alluded to by the poets enjoy an intimate connection to Fars, its land and its ruins. As used by the poets of post-Mongol Shiraz, kingly *talmīh* is topographically rooted in the physical environment inhabited by the patron and the audience: the remains of the ancients are attached to that specific locus, making the poets' use of kingly *talmīh* particularly effective.

From *talmīh* as used by the poets to explore questions of model kingship and notions of divine authority to rule as rooted in the physical environment of Fars, we move to allusion used amorously to explore the universal qualities of the ideal lover and beloved and the intimacy of the poet-patron relationship.

5

Allusions to Lovers

This chapter examines allusions to celebrated amorous couples who manifest desire that is more often than not reciprocal, whether from the beginning of their romance or at its conclusion. These lovers are presented more evenly in terms of desiring and being desired than the conventional lover and beloved of the *ghazal*. Bar one important exception, each pair of archetypal lovers discussed here is made up of one male and one female who belong to the same social class and epitomize opposite-sex desire (although, as we shall see, strong homoerotic subtexts are detectable). In the functionally homoerotic Persian *ghazal*, allusions to archetypal heteroerotic lovers inject complementary erotic vistas. When the Persian *ghazal* is used for panegyric purposes, the love bond depicted is to be understood as a means through which the poet elucidates his/her relationship with their patron.

In many Persian narrative poems, female and male protagonists simultaneously play the roles of lover and beloved; neither is merely a passive object and almost all these characters are active agents of desire. This is less the case with Layli, who remains somewhat two-dimensional. Layli is a beloved who exists primarily through the love of the ever-eager Majnun. But the same cannot be said for other heroines: Shirin, for one, displays forceful personality both in her relationship with Khusraw and her dealings with Farhad. This variation in the directionality and the intensity of the erotic dynamics at play requires a nuanced approach when we analyse allusions to exemplary or prototypical lovers. The pairs of lovers most frequently alluded to in Injuid and Muzaffarid *ghazal*s are: Layli and Majnun, Khusraw and Shirin, Farhad and Shirin, and Mahmud and Ayaz. Vamiq and 'Adhra, Vis and Ramin, Varqah and Gulshah, and Awrang and Gulchihr are alluded to with less frequency.[1]

In the *ghazal*s of fourteenth-century Shiraz, it is Nizami's late twelfth-century *Layli u Majnun* and *Khusraw va Shirin* whose influence is most keenly felt. We know of at least four manuscript copies of Nizami's *Khamsa* (quintet of *mathnavī*s) produced in Muzaffarid Shiraz in the 1360s: three in the time of Shah Shuja' (in 1362, 1363 and 1366) and one during the brief rule of his rival brother, Shah Mahmud (in 1365).[2] Wright believes this vogue for copying romance poetry was encouraged by the flourishing of the *ghazal*.[3] The parallel and symbiotic thriving of *mathnavī* and *ghazal* was facilitated, I would argue, by their point of intersection: romantic *talmīh*.

Layli and Majnun

As Gabbay has noted, Nizami's poems 'set the standard for Persian romantic epics for centuries to come'.[4] Pairs of lovers were used by mystics to explicate and demonstrate aspects of devotion. Nizami's *Layli u Majnun* came to be the most commonly employed for metaphorical and mystical purposes.[5] Allusions to Majnun and Layli, however infrequent, appear in pre-Nizamian poetry;[6] their tenor belies the fact that, initially, the love of Majnun for Layli did not have a direct relationship with mysticism. Some poets even found the subject matter of the romance reprehensible and frivolous because they believed its focus to be mortal love.[7]

The story of Layli and Majnun, which originated in seventh-century Arabia, is of non-Iranian origin and has a semi-historical basis.[8] The legend circulated in Arabic as anecdotes that were mostly short, loosely connected and generally lacking in plot development.[9] Nizami immortalized the story in his *Layli u Majnun* which he completed in 1188. From the thirteenth century, anecdotes drawn from or based upon episodes from the story of Majnun's love for Layli began to appear in Persian belles-lettres.[10]

It was through Nizami's *mathnavī* that the story of Layli and Majnun was brought firmly within the Persian literary repertoire: until Nizami's poem, no major poetic version of the tale existed in either Persian or Arabic. Nizami moulded a distinct Majnun[11] and it is to this Nizamian Majnun that the poets of Shiraz allude. Majnun epitomizes the pained longing of unrequited love and the true lover's tireless, selfless devotion to a distant, unattainable beloved. Majnun's love for Layli is never consummated and remains unfulfilled, unlike that of Khusraw and Shirin or Vis and Ramin, which involves sexual union. Physical contact is absent from their narrative:[12] ultimately, Majnun's love for Layli is a quest of love for love's sake to the exclusion of all else.[13]

Majnun's crazed devotion

The literary character Majnun (Arabic lit. 'madman', 'crazed') is based on an historical person, Qays ibn al-Mulawwah, who died in the last quarter of the seventh century. Early doubts about the person of the poet and the authenticity of the poetry attributed to him were voiced by Ibn Qutayba (d. 890) and Abu'l-Faraj al-Isfahani (d. 967). Although, initially, the romance was not specifically related to mysticism, Sufis used it as an *exemplum* from the ninth century.[14] Narrative elements from the story are used to illustrate the trials of passionate love in mystical Persian texts such as the *Savanih* of Ahmad Ghazali (d. 1123 or 1126),[15] but it was Nizami who contributed greatly to the 'spiritualization' of the Majnun-Layli story.[16] To post-Nizami lyric poets, they were arguably just another pair of romantic archetypes from a stockpile of lovers to which allusions could be made.[17] As Anvar notes, the mere allusion to Majnun and/or Layli, 'immediately evokes radical and maddening desire'.[18] Majnun epitomizes the persistent, desperate lover who seeks union with his beloved and whose frustrated quest eventually leads him to madness (though some poets assert that Majnun's reaction to Layli's beauty is a sign of his sanity).[19]

Majnun, denied physical union with his beloved, must content himself with union of the heart; the fusion of his spirit with that of Layli is sufficient. Majnun's sole function is to suffer patiently, often at the hands of an indifferent Layli.[20] Hafiz takes pity on Majnun and asks God to intercede and bring Layli closer in order, paradoxically, to calm him through the disturbance that proximity to her will cause (a scenario Hafiz may have borrowed from Nizami's *Khusraw va Shirin*);[21] H115:4:

عماری دار لیلی را که که مهدِ ماه در حکم است   خدایا در دل اندازش که بر مجنون گذار آرد

Layli's litter bearer, who controls the cradle of the moon,
O God, bear on his heart so that he might pass by Majnun!

In Nizami's reworking of the story for a courtly audience, he portrayed Majnun and Layli as aristocrats who meet at school, not in the desert. Despite the poet's addition of this urbane film, the Bedouin origins of the romance manifest themselves via allusions to Arab tribes[22] and Layli's 'stopping-place' (*manzil*); H141:4:

برقی از منزل لیلی بدرخشید سحر   وه که با خرمن مجنونِ دل افگار چه کرد

At dawn a bolt of lightning shone from Layli's stopping-place.
Alas, what it did to the harvest of the heartbroken Majnun!

Layli's *manzil* is depicted far off on the horizon, beyond the reach of Majnun. The image of the bolt of lightning at dawn is a vivid one; the bolt (a sign of hope, a glimmer of possible reunion?) has scorched the 'harvest' of Majnun's heart.[23] Hafiz, having inhabited the character of Majnun, seeks to rid himself of the torment of separation; H349:1 and 5:

گفت کو زنجیر تا تدبیر این مجنون کنم   دوش سودای رخش گفتم ز سر بیرون کنم

...

ربع را بر هم زنم اطلال را جیحون کنم   ای نسیم منزل لیلی خدا را تا به کی

Last night, I resolved to remove my infatuation for her face from my mind
He said: 'Where is the chain, so that I can deal with this madman?'
...
O soft breeze blowing from Layli's encampment, by God, until when
Should I demolish these dwellings; shed an Oxus of tears upon these traces?

Hafiz is unable to cure himself of his Majnun-like state and asks the breeze how much longer he should weep bitter tears over the 'abandoned traces' (*atlāl*) of Layli's encampment.[24] Weeping over the *atlāl* is a nostalgic motif in the pre-Islamic and early Islamic Arabic *qasīda*,[25] one that is imitated, evoked and parodied in some early Persian lyric poems.[26] Hafiz's poem contains a direct quotation (*atlāl-rā Jayhūn kunam*) from the opening lines of a well-known *qasīda* by the eleventh-century poet, Amir Mu'izzi:[27]

تا یک زمان زاری کنم بر ربع و اطلال و دمن   ای ساربان منزل مکن جز در دیار یار من

اطلال را جیحون کنم از آب چشم خویشتن   ربع از دلم پر خون کنم خاک دمن گلگون کنم

O camel-driver! Do not alight except in the abode of my beloved
So that I might weep a while over that spot, its abandoned traces, and ruins
I will fill that spot with my heart's blood and paint its ruins rose-red;
I will turn its abandoned traces into an Oxus with my own tears.

Jahan has four *ghazals* with the same *qāfiya* and *radīf* as H349. There is considerable overlap between all five *ghazals*, with seven of the eight words or particles that carry the rhyme in Hafiz's *ghazal* performing the same function across Jahan's poems.[28] In one of her four poems, Jahan addresses her 'Layli-like' (*Laylī-sifat*) beloved from a Majnunian perspective. Jahan embodies at once Majnun the absolute lover and the archetypal poet of love;[29] J1047:2:

این دل پر درد را هر ساعتی مجنون کنم   تا کی ای لیلی صفت در آرزوی روی تو

How much longer should I, O Layli-like one, in longing for your face
Turn my pain-filled heart at every moment into a Majnun?

Speaking as Majnun, Jahan voices an ostensibly male yearning for a female beloved and engages in gendered poetic role-playing. The complex gendering of Jahan's poetic voice compels us to read the question of homoeroticism in the Persian *ghazal* somewhat differently. Women poets worked within the dominant homoerotic aesthetic of the tradition, the Saljuq poet Mahsati

Ganjavi being perhaps the best example of a female poet who adopted a male homoerotic voice and eroticized young adult males.[30] In the case of Mahsati, genre trumps gender. Female poets did not state their gender openly in the framework of the Persian *ghazal*, but they also did not hide it (their chosen pen name often being a giveaway). There is no female poetic transvestism in Persian as there is in some western literary traditions where women wrote using male pseudonyms. As noted in the Introduction, in the preface to her *dīvān*, Jahan channelled the boldness of monarchic women poets of the past,[31] thereby framing her collected poems in light of her gender.

The path of true love

As Seyed-Gohrab has noted, in *Layli u Majnun*, Nizami 'operates at the boundary of the profane and the mystic, although he leans more towards mystical concepts'.[32] This poem, more so than Nizami's other romances, lends itself to a mystical interpretation.[33] The story of Majnun's endless quest for reunion with Layli is a rich metaphor for the ardour of a 'true lover' ('*āshiq-i sādiq*) or the fervour a 'seeker' (*tālib*) or 'wayfarer' (*sālik*) must harness if s/he is to successfully traverse the path to God. A brief allusion to the story of Majnun and Layli functions as an efficient didactic device through which poets convey their philosophy on the divine love journey; H458:3:

شرطِ اوّل قدم آن است که مجنون باشی   در رہ منزل لیلی که خطرہاست در آن

On the path to Layli's stopping-place, wherein lie many dangers,
The condition of the first step is that you be 'love-crazed'.

And similarly; J1103:1:

مجنون صفت همیشه به کوہ و کمر رویم   در راہ عشق روی تو ما بی خبر رویم

Ill-informed, we walk the path of love for your face,
Majnun-like, we always head for the mountains and foothills.

Here, Jahan uses the adverb *Majnūn-sifat* ('in a Majnun-like manner') to describe the attitude with which she and her fellow travellers tread this path. There is no need for her to mention Layli directly because, by alluding to Majnun, the audience is signalled to equate the beloved with her. By not naming the beloved, Jahan broadens the interpretational scope to include not only the mystical love of the Prophet or God, but also constancy in devotion to the patron. Just as for Jahan, the path of love is one she does not tread alone, so too for 'Ubayd, love is a universal phenomenon: all humans are 'crazed' by their desire for their own 'fairy-faced' beauty.[34] 'Ubayd plays down the mystical significance of the lovers' tale, choosing to amplify the human dimension.

Not all allusions to Layli and Majnun are reverent. Sa'di says there is no need to recount Layli's 'story' (qissa) or speak of Majnun's 'sorrow' (ghussa), for his beloved has wiped out all mention of those who came before.[35] Sa'di claims you will forget the 'night time tales' (samar) of Layli and Majnun if you catch a glimpse of his moon-faced beloved;[36] he boasts that the 'tale' (hadīth) of his beloved's beauty and the 'story' (dāstān) of his passionate love surpasses that of Layli and Majnun.[37] In the Gulistan,[38] Sa'di claims that if Majnun were to come back to life in his day, he would write the 'story of love' (hadīth-i 'ishq) based on Sa'di's 'notebook [of poetry]' (daftar). In a similar vein, 'Attar Shirazi asserts the story of Majnun is but 'half a letter' (nīm harf) of his own suffering.[39] Kamal Khujandi goes one step further: Layli's beauty no longer has i'tibār ('credibility', 'importance') because the beloved has entrapped a thousand crazed lovers in the twists of his locks.[40] Despite the story's mystical reworking by Nizami, a century-and-a-half later, Majnun's constancy and commitment to Layli was used by Jalal to express the force of the poet's devotion to his patron.[41]

Combined allusions to pairs of lovers

There often appears to be no logic behind the configuration of the combinations of pairs of lovers alluded to in a poem, which suggests that they were considered largely interchangeable. The technique of fusing compacted allusions to multiple pairs of lovers in a single bayt is employed with frequency by Khvaju:[42]

حدیث مستی وامق ز چشم عذرا پرس   دل شکسته مجنون ز زلف لیلی جوی

Search for Majnun's broken heart in Layli's forelocks;
Ask 'Adhra's eyes for the story of Vamiq's intoxication.

In such doubled allusions to exemplary lovers, Khvaju often pairs amorous couples whose stories are used primarily for edifying or mystical purposes (Khusraw and Shirin; Layli and Majnun) with Vis and Ramin or Vamiq and 'Adhra,[43] whose stories address carnal desire 'as a matter of intrinsic interest needing neither allegory nor a spiritual context to justify it'.[44] The fusion in the ghazal through talmīh of lovers that represent distinct poles in the Persian romance tradition serves to disrupt dichotomous interpretations of premodern Persian poetry into either mystico-allegorical or eroto-sensual.

Possibly responding to Sa'di,[45] Hafiz combines allusions to two pairs of archetypal lovers in the following manner;[46] H40:5–6:

کوته نتوان کرد که این قصّه دراز است
رخسارهٔ محمود و کف پای ایاز است

شرح ِ شکن ِ زلف خم اندر خم جانان
بار دل مجنون و خم طرّهٔ لیلی

The description of the twists of the beloved's curls
Cannot be cut short, for it is a long story.
It's the burden on Majnun's heart, and the curls of Layli's locks;
It's Mahmud's cheeks, and the soles of Ayaz's feet.

In line 5, Hafiz plays with the concept of length, slipping from the length of the curls of the beloved's hair (be they Layli's locks or those of Ayaz), to the length of the poetic description of those locks. For Majnun, separation from Layli is like 'one long night' (layli tavil).[47] Here, Hafiz parallels Majnun's devotion to Layli with that of Mahmud to Ayaz: the first a heteroerotic tale dating from seventh-century Arabia, the second a story of male homoerotic desire from eleventh-century Ghazna (the historicity of the latter being arguably greater than the former). What unites these love stories is the reputedly chaste nature of the amorous relationships they narrate.

It would seem that the heteroerotic or homoerotic dynamics of each story are not of paramount relevance,[48] even though the dominant erotic paradigm in romance mathnavi is male–female. That said, one must remain mindful that the target audience of both Nizami's mathnavis and the later ghazals in which exemplary lovers are alluded to was male, as were most poets. The amorous descriptions of male protagonists (including Khusraw and Ramin) carry homoerotic undertones channelled through the ogling gaze of the poet and responded to by the audience. Poets of both sexes present erotically stimulating depictions of male heroes primarily to appeal to male listeners. We shall see in Chapter 6 how a male homoerotic reading of Zulaykha's desire for Joseph is possible, where Zulaykha is read as the erotic enabler who channels male–male desire and longing. By analogy, a homoerotic reading of Shirin's desire for Khusraw (or that of Vis for Ramin) is also possible.

Hafiz also combines the story of Majnun's love for Layli with that of Farhad for Shirin, thereby underscoring the complementarity of these two tales of impossible, unrequited love; H54:4:

شکنج طرّهٔ لیلی مقام مجنون است
حکایت لب شیرین کلام فرهاد است

The story of Shirin's lips constitutes Farhad's speech;
The twists of Layli's hair make up Majnun's station.

The term translated here as 'station' is maqām which bears mystical significance and can denote a station on a spiritual path or the shrine of a venerated saint-sage. In this ghazal (attributed by some to Haydar),[49] Farhad is a more fitting parallel to Majnun than Mahmud: both embody the attributes and virtues of the selfless, self-sacrificial lover; both are perfect – if tragic – models for emulation.

Role-playing through the story of Layli and Majnun

Jahan identifies directly with Majnun, a strategy also employed, though rarely, by some male poets;[50] J494:8:

خبرت هست که در حسرت لیلی رخت   دلِ مجنون صفتم رو به بیابان آورد

Are you aware that in longing for the Layli of your face
My Majnun-like heart headed for the wilderness?

Jahan's heart acts the part of Majnun, while the role of Layli is played by her beloved's face. When Jahan speaks through an allusion to a male protagonist she can be read as addressing a beloved who is playing the role of the female beloved. The fact that Jahan was a woman who was conscious of the perils of composing poetry and committing it to writing as a woman (but who did not shy away ultimately from revealing her gender on paper), perhaps meant that she had a broader range of gender roles at her disposal than did her male contemporaries. In her poetry, we witness the conflation of an assertively female poetic voice with the conscious desire to emulate a style of *ghazal* shared by Sa'di in particular, in which direct association of the poetic voice with exemplary or legendary lovers is tolerated. Jahan, although expected to speak for the most part with a masculine voice – the conventional voice of the Persian *ghazal* – was able, as a woman, to play with the gender of her poetic voice in a way male poets were not, layering (and, thereby, complicating and contesting) the standard masculine poetic voice with the insertion of feminine touches, albeit faint and cautious.

Adjectival and adverbial compounds formed from the names of legendary lovers, such as *Majnūn-sifat* or *Laylī-sifat*[51] indicate that such mythopoetic figures are types or archetypes rather than real entities. Their reality is poetry and through the use of adjectives or adverbs formed from their names, qualities that are associated in the collective consciousness with legendary figures are appropriated by and linked to the lover and/or the beloved within the world of the poem. This same cast of characters is given tangible, historical dimensions when coupled with living patrons in panegyric poetry. The mytho-poetic is made present (both temporally and in body) and thus realized or actualized through the processes of poetic evocation.

Jahan plays the role of one turned *majnūn* by desire for the beloved; J1114:7:

که عشقت می برد آب لبیبان   اگر مجنون شوم از غم عجب نیست

If I become crazed by your grief, it is not strange
For your love saps the majesty of the wise.

Majnūn functions here as the adjective 'crazed'; Layli is unnamed but implied via the allusion to her devoted lover.[52] Praising a male beloved, it perhaps made sense not to address the beloved as Layli, but rather to opt for indirect comparisons, afforded via adjectives or adverbs that incorporate her name or through other indirect means such as speaking of the 'Layli' of the beloved's face (i.e. his bewitching, compelling beauty). With a female poet writing in a male mode, there is the added potential of a heterosexual dimension to the love dynamic through the eroticization of a male figure from a feminine perspective. Interestingly, male poets rarely speak through female protagonists.

In an intriguing *ghazal* (J1117) discussed in full below, Jahan engages in male role-playing within a heteroerotic framework and inhabits a series of male lovers perhaps to laud a female beloved. There is little evidence of female homoeroticism in Persian poetry and it is possible that in this poem Jahan is eulogizing a female patron, a contemporary woman of economic and political power. There is a similar gendered dynamic at play in this *bayt* by Jahan;[53] J1185:4:

سرگشته به کوه و دشت مجنون   لیلی صفتا منم ز شوقت

O Layli-like one, out of longing for you
I am wondering love-crazed over mountain and plain!

In another poem, Jahan hails her beloved as the 'Layli of the Age' (*Laylī-yi 'ahd*), a phrase with panegyric resonances; J1371:3:

در غم عشق خودم مجنون کنی   تا کی از هجر خود ای لیلی عهد

How long with your separation, O Layli of the Age,
Will you make love-crazed through grief from love for you?

Jahan's beloved is the living reincarnation of Majnun's beloved; a Layli for her time. The phrase *Layli-yi 'ahd* echoes royal epithets used to praise patrons in fourteenth-century Persian poetry and prose (see Chapter 4). Fourteenth-century Shiraz is a city inhabited by a host of reincarnations of archetypal lovers: second Laylis, Majnuns, Shirins, Farhads and Khusraws.

Perhaps, in an attempt to integrate herself into the literary scene of her day, with the aspiration to be taken seriously alongside male peers, Jahan identified her lover persona directly with legendary male lovers to stress that she was speaking with a male voice; the voice of poetic authority. Within this context of male-dominated poetic production, it is conceivable that Jahan might have felt pressure to conform to the homoerotic or male-led heteroerotic style in her *ghazal*s, whilst clearly mindful of her gender difference. If the reports of misogynistic attacks on Jahan in poetry have any foundation, Jahan's insistence on speaking through male archetypes would seem only prudent.

Khusraw, Shirin and Farhad

The story of Khusraw and Shirin is of Iranian origin, based as it is on tales surrounding the last great Sasanian, Khusraw II ('Parviz'; r. 590–628) and the most cherished of his many wives, Shirin, a Christian woman who was most likely from Khuzistan.[54] Tales about Khusraw and Shirin were retold and embellished by Firdawsi, who drew on oral (and, possibly, written) versions with Pahlavi roots. In the late twelfth century, Nizami mined Firdawsi's *Shahnama* when he composed *Khusraw va Shirin* but, unlike Firdawsi, Nizami focused squarely on the couple's love relationship,[55] possibly deriving thematic and stylistic inspiration from Gurgani's *Vis u Ramin*.[56]

Meisami sees in Nizami's *Khusraw va Shirin* evidence of how the poet recuperated Firdawsi's treatment of the Iranian past.[57] In Firdawsi's *Shahnama*, the reign of Khusraw Parviz is the second-longest section of the Sasanian section (more than 4,000 verses), but his love affair with Shirin is covered in a brief 150 verses.[58] Their love affair is of little importance to Firdawsi and his treatment of it pales in comparison to, say, the story of Bizhan and Manizha which reads like a romance embedded within the framework of the epic poem.[59]

Nizami's much-amplified retelling of the romance totals more than 6,000 couplets. The poet refocuses the tale on *'ishq-bāzī* ('the game of passionate love') and, though he expands the narrative greatly, he devotes minimal attention to the historical–political backdrop, instead adding depth and complexity, not only to the relationship between the main protagonists, but also to the characterization of Shirin in particular.[60] Nizami claims Shirin is more beautiful than Layli[61] and he depicts Khusraw's queen as affectionate and straightforward.[62]

Allusions to Farhad's love for Shirin are found in tenth- and eleventh-century Persian poetry.[63] Farhad only plays a minor role in Firdawsi's *Shahnama*, but in the late eleventh century, Nizam al-Mulk mentions the 'story' (*hadīth*) or 'night time tale' (*samar*) of Khusraw, Shirin and Farhad (and Shirin's eventual receptivity to Farhad's advances) in his *Siyasatnama*.[64] Farhad is also mentioned in the anonymous twelfth-century *Mujmal al-tavarikh wa'l-qisas* as the 'general' (*sipahbud*) who fell in love with Shirin and left his mark on Bisutun through the artistry of a Byzantine master craftsman whose work he supervised.[65]

In his Persian adaptation of Tabari's history, Bal'ami names Shirin as Khusraw's maidservant-turned-wife, the woman with whom Farhad fell passionately in love.[66] Writing in the mid-twelfth century, Tusi is full of praise for Shirin. He claims that she was both a descendant of the Byzantine kings and a woman of high birth.[67] Tusi describes Shirin as *kāmil* ('perfect'), *muhtarama* ('a respected/respectable woman') and in possession of *'aql-i tamām* ('sound/ complete intellect', unlike, in his view, the generality of womankind).[68] Tusi also places great emphasis on what he says was Shirin's impeccable chastity.[69] He echoes Nizami's portrayal of a strong-minded Shirin when he asserts that Khusraw was 'subject to her command' (*bi hukm-i vay būd*).[70]

The popularity of the story of Khusraw and Shirin informed the aesthetics of the post-Mongol built environment: mural paintings depicting Khusraw and Shirin and other amorous images adorned the walls of a garden pavilion in Yazd that served in the Muzaffarid period as a pleasure ground for the great and good.[71] Extracts from Nizami's *Khamsa* were also inscribed on a Muzaffarid-period kiosk in another garden in the same city.[72] These pictorial and calligraphic representations of Nizami's poems demonstrate the importance of his *Khamsa* in the fourteenth and early fifteenth centuries and the deep connection between romances and the contexts and settings of poetic appreciation.

A number of significant ruined sites in western Iran that date to the Sasanian period were linked in local lore variously with Khusraw, Shirin and/or Farhad:[73] 'Imarat-i Khusraw, the large ruined palace near Qasr-i Shirin; Utaq-i Farhad; Suffa-yi Shabdiz; Dukkan-i Khusraw; Khum-i Khusraw; Taq-i Shirin (or Taq-i Gara) near Sarpul-i Zahab; the carved grottoes at Taq-i Bustan; the large engraved rampart known as Farhad-tarash or Takht-i Farhad at Bisutun; and Farhad-tash, a site twenty-five kilometres south of Bisutun. Khvaju alludes to Sasanian rock reliefs associated with the tragic love of Farhad for Shirin in this manner:[74]

حديث غصۀ فرهاد و قصۀ شيرين   بخون لعل ببايد نوشت بر كهسار

The story of Farhad's grief and Shirin's tale
Must be written in ruby-red blood on the mountainside

In the words of Le Strange, the legends of these figures became 'localized' in these places.[75] In a lengthy strophic poem in praise of Dilshad Khatun, Khvaju imagines the breeze carrying his message of devotion to his Shirin beloved in Baghdad thus:[76]

چون گذارت بر حدود قصر شيرين اوفتد   وصف سيلاب سرشک ديدۀ فرهاد کن

When you pass within the vicinity of Shirin's palace
Describe the flood of tears that flows from Farhad's eyes!

In Firdawsi's *Shahnama*, Khusraw marries the Byzantine princess Maryam and then Gurdiya, the sister of Bahram Chubin, making these two noblewomen Shirin's chief rivals.[77] Nizami adds into the mix the seductive Shikar, a courtesan whom Khusraw meets in Isfahan and subsequently marries.[78] Firdawsi's Shirin is a non-Zoroastrian of low birth.[79] Medieval Christian sources suggest that the historical Shirin was an Aramaic-speaking Christian from Khuzistan.[80] The historical Khusraw and Shirin are believed to have done much to promote and protect Christians in the Sasanian realm.[81] Nizami transforms Shirin into an Armenian princess, thereby opening up royal panegyric dimensions to the depiction of the protagonist.[82] Orsatti notes that Nizami follows a tradition that is in favour of Shirin and remakes her into a chaste and passionate woman who is not easily seduced by Khusraw.[83] It is possible that Nizami may have transferred some of Firdawsi's negativity vis-à-vis Shirin onto Shikar.

Essentially a celebration of non-mystical love, Nizami's *Khusraw va Shirin* is eminently suitable as a basis for allusions in courtly panegyrics, as the chief protagonists are royals.[84] When employed to panegyric ends, allusions to Khusraw and/or Shirin in *ghazal*s articulate the ideal attributes of the ruler-patron. Meisami argues that this love story 'provides a vehicle for treating broader issues of kingship and justice'.[85] Drawing on a *havasnāma* ('romance', 'book of lustful desire') when panegyrizing, the poets express their devotion to the patron through the language of erotic desire. 'Ubayd puns on both royal lovers to panegyric effect; U96:7:

عبید از دولت خسرو در این فصل   بنای عیش شیرین می کند باز

'Ubayd from the good fortune of the king (*khusraw*) in this season
Will once again construct sweet (*shīrīn*) merriment.

Nizami's *Khusraw va Shirin* is set in Sasanian Iran and Byzantium, Gurgani's *Vis u Ramin* in Parthian times, and the story of Vamiq and 'Adhra is a Persian retelling of a romance drawn from the Hellenistic tradition.[86] By setting their romances in the pre-Islamic period, poets carved out a space in which to approach topics that contravened conventional morality, with a freedom that would otherwise have been unthinkable, especially in relation to female characters.

In the *ghazal*s studied here, Khusraw II is depicted as being devoted to Shirin, who is equally devoted to him, the two longing for one another in times of separation. In *talmīh*, the pair are often treated as inseparable: Kamal Khujandi says it is 'not pleasant' for there to be Khusraw without Shirin.[87] Farhad's love for Shirin, as depicted in Nizami's romance and as alluded to in the post-Nizamian *ghazal*, is more sincere than that of Khusraw and far more tragic. Farhad's love remains unrequited, culminating in his suicide prompted by the false news of Shirin's death fed to Farhad via a messenger sent by a malicious Khusraw.[88] The impossible nature of Farhad's love for Shirin readily facilitates his equation with Majnun.

Khusraw as royal beloved

In a *qasīda* in praise of Abish Khatun,[89] Sa'di says his patron embodies the best attributes of royalty, female and male: she simultaneously outdoes Khusraw in kingship and Shirin in beauty:[90]

چنین خسرو کجا باشد در آفاق وگر باشد چنین شیرین نباشد

Where in the world is there such a king (*khusraw*)?
And if there is, he cannot be as sweet (*shīrīn*)!

In her *qasīda* in praise of Sultan Ahmad b. Shaykh Uvays, Jahan casts the cruel beloved as Shirin and the benevolent sultan as Khusraw:[91]

ور نه ز دست جور تو شیرین روزگار داد آورم به بارگه خسرو زمن

And if not, because of your harshness, Shirin of the Age,
I will seek justice at the court of the Khusraw of the Time.

More often than not, though, the beloved in the fourteenth-century *ghazal* fuses key traits of the shah and his bride.[92] He is the *khusraw-i shīrīn* ('sweet king') and, although the beloved unites masculine and feminine in one, in the label *khusraw-i shīrīn* there is more than an echo of the *shīrīn-pisar* which invites a strong homoerotic reading.[93] Hafiz claims a status for his beloved that is higher than that of the historical Khusraw; H52:8:

حافظ از حشمت پرویز دگر قصّه مخوان که لبش جرعه کش خسرو شیرین من است

Hafiz, tell no more tales of the majesty of Parviz,
For his lips sip wine from those of my sweet king.

Hafiz calls his beloved *khusraw-i shīrīn-i man* ('my sweet king'). It has been argued that Hafiz's *ghazal*s in which the phrases *khusraw-i shīrīn*, *shāh-i khūbān* ('king of beauties'), *pādishāh-i husn* ('king of beauty') and *pādishāh-i khūbān* ('king of beauties') appear were composed during the reign of Shah Shuja', who was praised by contemporary poets and prose writers for his physical beauty.[94] Hafiz celebrates the return of his royal beloved whom he alludes to as *khusraw-i shīrīn*; H176:1:

گفت برخیز که آن خسرو شیرین آمد   سحرم دولت بیدار به بالین آمد

At dawn, waking fortune came to my pillow and said,
Arise, for that sweet king has arrived!

This is perhaps an allusion to Shah Shuja''s triumphal return from
Isfahan to Shiraz following the brief period (1364–1366) during which his
rival brother, Shah Mahmud, ruled Fars.[95] Elsewhere, Hafiz employs the
same descriptive phrase and also identifies himself with the tragic Farhad;
H190:4:

که به رحمت گذری بر سر فرهاد کند   یا رب اندر دل آن خسرو شیرین انداز

O Lord, influence the heart of that sweet king,
So that he might pass Farhad's way and show him mercy.

Inhabiting the person of the dejected Farhad, Hafiz calls on God to
soften the heart of his patron so that he might show him 'mercy' (rahmat).
Alluding to the harshness with which Khusraw treats Farhad in Nizami's
poem, Hafiz asks his patron for a favour, so far denied to him, be that
renewed financial reward or readmission to the court circle. The poem
ends with a somewhat tongue-in-cheek threat on the part of Hafiz to
leave Muzaffarid Shiraz for Jalayirid Baghdad. By presenting the patron as
Khusraw (one who simultaneously embodies Shirin's qualities) and himself
as Farhad, Hafiz inserts a homoerotic element into Farhad's relationship
with Khusraw, an element that is in keeping with the conventional erotic
framework of Persian panegyrics and court histories in which the beauty
of the ruler is admired. Here Hafiz presents the male–male bond between
Khusraw and Farhad as pivotal to what could be called the Khusraw–Shirin–
Farhad 'erotic triangle'.[96] In another poem, Hafiz uses a love relationship
between *khusraw-i shīrīn-dahanān* ('king of the sweet-mouthed ones')[97]
and Farhad as a metaphor for the often-fraught dynamics of the patron–
poet bond; H481:5:

گر نگاهی سوی فرهادِ دل افتاده کنی   اجرها باشدت ای خسرو شیرین دهنان

You will reap many rewards, O king of the sweet-mouthed ones
If you cast a gaze upon the crestfallen Farhad.

Here it is the submissive, forlorn Farhad, rather than the stoic Shirin, who
patiently awaits a sign of favour from the dominant, indifferent Khusraw. It
is as though Shirin has been converted into a catalyst for the love between
Farhad (the poet) and Khusraw (his patron). The blending of gendered

attributes in the person of the patron is also suggested elsewhere by Hafiz; H475:2:

ای خسرو خوبان تو شیرین زمانی   شیرینتر از آنی به شکرخنده که گویم

With your sugary smile you are sweeter than I can say;
O king of the beauties, you are the Shirin of the Age!

Not only is Hafiz's beloved the 'king of the beauties' (khusraw-i khūbān),[98] he is also the living embodiment of Shirin: the 'Shirin of the Age'. This is the second line of H475 which opens with the statement that the beloved is more alluring than the contemporary incarnation of Joseph. The mimicry of royal titulature in the allusion to Shirin invites a panegyric reading. Sa'di employs Shīrīn-i zaman in the following manner:[99]

که به دیوانگی از عشق تو فرهاد زمانم   گر تو شیرین زمانی نظری نیز بمن کن

If you are the Shirin of the Age, cast your gaze upon me
For, out of madness caused by my love for you, I am the Farhad of the Age.

In a lengthy, seventeen-line eroto-panegyric ghazal with the same rhyming scheme (perhaps composed in praise of Abish Khatun),[100] Sa'di addresses his Shirin-beloved in a similar manner: he is the humble servant (Farhad) of the Khusraw of his day:

من بندهٔ خسرو زمانم   شیرین زمان تویی بتحقیق

You, for certain, are the Shirin of the Age;
I am the humble servant of the Khusraw of the Age.

The coalescence of feminine and masculine in the beloved is a feature of the Persian ghazal. What we witness here is something beyond androgyny; the beloved is at once everyone and everything. In the line below, Jahan identifies herself with the queen and her beloved with Khusraw; J249:6:

عمر شیرین شد به بادم چاره نیست   در غم هجران خسرو در جهان

In the grief of separation from my king (khusraw) in this world (jahān),
My sweet life ('umr-i shīrīn) has vanished, and there is no recourse.

As noted above, Jahan exercised greater freedom than most male poets when engaging in heteroerotic role-playing. Interestingly, neither Hafiz nor 'Ubayd cast themselves in the role of Shirin.

The poet as Farhad

The selfless lover is more commonly equated in the poetry with Farhad than with Khusraw.[101] The king's desire for Shirin is dismissed as being fixated on physical contact: Khusraw sought cuddling and cavorting with Shirin in contrast to Farhad's 'sincere affection' (*mahabbat*), the manifestation of which was the carving of Bisutun.[102] 'Ubayd depicts Farhad as the exemplary lover focused wholeheartedly on his beloved, who is devoid of lustful distraction; U29:3:

رغبت به نوش دارو و حاجت به قند نیست   فرهاد را که با لب شیرین تعلق است

Farhad, who has an attachment to Shirin's lips,
Has no desire for the panacea and no need of candy.

The 'panacea' here is the *nūsh-dārū*, the magical elixir that can cure all ills. In the *Shahnama*, Iran's greatest hero, Rustam, famously implores Kay-Kavus to heal his wounded son Suhrab who lies dying on the battlefield.[103] In 'Ubayd's poem, the Shirin-beloved's lips are his *nūsh-dārū* as they are fortified with the same transformative powers.[104] Shirin's kisses and saliva act as a cure-all for the soul, in contrast to *qand* ('rock candy'), an allusion to Shirin's inferior rival, Shikar.

Hafiz fears becoming a Farhad – a crazed lover who is unable to control his emotions, is mocked for them and who suffers as a consequence. Junayd tells us that every true lover suffers the same fate as Farhad;[105] and Haydar is 'killed' by the 'sweet sugar' (*shikar-i shīrīn*) of his beloved, just like Farhad.[106] Hafiz's beloved displays Shirin's alluring charm; H316:7:

شور شیرین منما تا نکنی فرهادم   شهرۀ شهر مشو تا ننهم سر در کوه

Don't become the talk of the town so that I won't run for the hills,
Don't display Shirin's passion, so that you won't make of me a Farhad.

The poet asks his beloved to refrain from becoming 'infamous in the city' (*shuhra-yi shahr*) through displays of passion, as this will force him to flee out of love-intoxicated madness, in an attempt to conceal his love from those who might reproach him for it. Elsewhere, Hafiz revels in his own *shuhra-yi shahr* status.[107] In the second hemistich of H316:7, Hafiz asks his beloved not to display the same 'passion' (*shūr*) as Shirin. There is a pun on the word *shūr*, which means both 'saltiness' (which contrasts with Shirin's 'sweetness') and 'intense passion', as in the phrase *shūr-i 'ishq*, 'all-consuming passion of love'.[108] In a similar vein, Haydar juxtaposes the *shūr-i Farhad* with the beloved's sweet, sugar-crunching, pistachio-like lips.[109] In Persian, salt is related to physical beauty, hence *namakīn* and *bā-namak* (lit. 'salty') mean 'pretty', 'cute'. In Arabic *malāha* ('saltiness') also means 'beauty', 'elegance'.

In H316:7 the dynamic of the gender role-playing is heteroerotic: the poet plays the male role of Farhad and his beloved that of Shirin. And yet, although the gender balance may well be drawn along heteroerotic lines, the power imbalance remains: Shirin is a royal and she controls the devoted commoner Farhad, partly through her superior wealth and status and partly by virtue of his unrelenting desire and devotion. The dynamic depicted here is not dissimilar to that found in J1117, although Hafiz is much less emphatic about the identification of his beloved with Shirin and himself with Farhad. Jahan bemoans the fate of her soul and the indifference of her beloved through a similar use of romantic *talmīh*; J396:3:

وز حسرت روی تو جان داد چنین فرهاد   شیرین لب تو هرگز کی داد شبی کامم

When did your sweet (*shīrīn*) lips grant my desire for even one night?
And out of longing for your face, they gave me this Farhad-like soul.

Although the poets on occasion liken their tribulations in the game of love to those of Khusraw,[110] self-identification with Farhad is far more common.[111] Hafiz says he has suffered more in love than Farhad, the 'mountain-carver' (*kūh-kan*);[112] H138:4:

ناله ها کرد در این کوه که فرهاد نکرد   دل به امید صدایی که مگر در تو رسد

My heart, hoping that its voice might somehow reach you,
Let out such cries in these mountains as even Farhad did not.

Given Farhad's suicide, Hafiz's hyperbolic claim that his own heart has suffered more, serves to highlight his own sorry plight. 'Imad hails Farhad as a martyr to love[113] and Kamal presents us with a Saint Sebastian-like image when he says that every stray arrow shot by Shirin while out hunting was later found lodged in Farhad's liver.[114] Kamal depicts the Shirin-beloved drinking Farhad's blood tears from the pool he constructed for her;[115] the channel he carved flows with tears shed by the mountain for the woeful Farhad.[116] Kamal says the day will come when Shirin's (now remorseful) lips will beg forgiveness for branding Farhad's chest.[117] Jahan's love-crazed heart roams mountains and foothills, longing for the beloved's sweet lips: J106:3:

فرهادصفت گشته به کوه و به کمرهاست   از حسرت شیرین لبت ای کام دل من

My heart's desire, in longing for your sweet lips,
is wondering Farhad-like in the mountains and foothills.

Awhadi says all the inhabitants of his city have been transformed into Farhads by the Shirin-beloved.[118] Hafiz states he is just one of the many Farhads who have been betrayed by this world; H354:3:

كه كرد افسون و نيرنگش ملول از جان شيرينم   جهان پيراست و بيبنياد از اين فرهاد كش فرياد

The world is old and unstable; save me from this Farhad-slayer
Whose deceit and deception have caused me to tire of my sweet soul.

Farhad exemplifies unwavering fidelity in the face of indifference and cruelty: the poet-lover will not forsake his beloved just as Farhad never sought to avoid association with Shirin.[119] Farhad's love for Shirin was so strong that it left an eternal mark on the earth, one which is renewed every spring; H101:6:

كه لاله مى دمد از خون ديدهٔ فرهاد   ز حسرت لب شيرين هنوز مى بينم

From his longing for Shirin's lips, I still see tulips,
Sprouting from the blood which flowed from Farhad's eyes.

Hafiz declares he will die with a heart turned bitter by disappointment in love (like Farhad) and he alludes to Shirin, saying that there will be 'sweet tales' (*hikāyat-hā-yi shīrīn*) told about him after he is gone; H401:5:

بس حكايتهاى شيرين باز ماند ز من   گر چو فرهاد به تلخى جان بر آيد باک نيست

If, like Farhad, my soul should exit my body bitterly, there's nothing to fear
For many sweet tales of me will still remain.

These *hikāyat-hā-yi shīrīn* are tangentially linked to the idea of the poet as *shīrīn-zabān* ('sweet-tongued') or *shīrīn-sukhan* ('one of sweet speech')[120] and of the poet's verses as sugar/y (a common motif, especially in Hafiz's *takhallus* lines where his boasting about his poetic skill is framed in saccharine metaphors);[121] H106:7:

كه حاجتت به علاج گلاب و قند مباد   شفا ز گفتهٔ شكرفشان حافظ جوى

Seek your healing from the sugar-scattering words of Hafiz,
So that you may have no need of the treatment of rosewater and candy.

In both *ghazal* and *qasīda*, Salman employs Khusraw-Shirin *talmīh* to depict the relationship between his patron and his poetry: the patron is Salman's *khusraw-i khūbān* whom he implores to recognize how 'sweet-tongued' (*shīrīn-sukhan*) he is;[122] and it is for the kingly rose (*khusraw-i gul*) that Salman as 'sweet-voiced nightingale' (*bulbul-i shīrīn-guftār*) performs the songs of Barbad and Nakisa, the legendary Sasanian musicians of Khusraw's court.[123]

Returning to Farhad, it should be noted that not all of Hafiz's allusions to him bear a sympathetic tone. In one poem, Hafiz criticizes Farhad for the extreme nature of his emotion and his excessive devotion to Shirin; H112:3:

من همان روز ز فرهاد طمع ببريدم   كه عنان ِ دل ِ شيدا به لب شيرين داد

I gave up my hope in Farhad that very same day
He gave over the reins of his infatuated heart to Shirin's lips.

Hafiz's negative portrayal of Farhad's desperation following separation from his beloved shows that, even in instances of *talmīh* involving one legendary figure in the *ghazal*s of a single poet, there is no uniformity: in some poems Hafiz praises Farhad for his selfless devotion to Shirin; in others he criticizes him for his unwavering fidelity. This demonstrates that even though poets adhered to the standard, Nizamian version of the Khusraw–Shirin–Farhad romance, there was room for a poet to remould and recast this popular narrative to fit his or her individual message.

Khusraw's relationship with Farhad

Khusraw and Farhad's bond is male–male, characterized by an acute power imbalance, two key features that tally with the standard lover–beloved relationship portrayed in the Persian *ghazal*; the strong homoerotic convention enabling the poet–patron relationship to be treated within that same framework.[124] And so we find the portrayal of Khusraw's relationship with Farhad bears a homoerotic subtext:[125]

خسرو خوبان به شيرينى تويى   اى من شوريده دل فرهاد تو

You are the king of beauties in your sweetness
And I, with my love-crazed heart, am your Farhad!

Here Farhad is wholly dependent on Khusraw's generosity of spirit; he is subject to Khusraw's will; it is to Khusraw (not Shirin) that he looks for favour. The panegyric mileage in the relationship between Khusraw and Farhad is exploited by Hamgar in a *qasīda* for a Salghurid ruler of Shiraz in which the poet casts himself as the 'Farhad of the Epoch' (*Farhād-i dahr*) and his royal patron as the sweetest of Khusraws.[126]

'Imad reminds us that Khusraw attained his heart's desire through Shirin's lips, indifferent to what befell his rival.[127] And Jahan implies that Khusraw's selfishness (and his disregard for Farhad's suffering) was his downfall: the king failed to consider the plight of Farhad (who epitomizes sincerity) and thought selfishly of his own happiness; J441:5:

آری خبر از سوزش فرهاد ندارد   خسرو به وصال رخ شیرین شد خرّم

> Khusraw became refreshed through union with Shirin's face.
> Yes, he knows nothing of the burning in Farhad's heart!

Here Jahan forges distance between her voice and the Khusraw–Shirin–Farhad narrative by referring to the protagonists in the third person. Yet the poet displays her sympathy for Farhad's plight and appears to equate it with her own: she claims to have been rejected in love (perhaps a metaphor for the patron–poet dynamic) and her needs and tribulations have been ignored by Khusraw. In what could be construed as a mildly misogynistic take on the story and a defence of Khusraw's actions, Jahan argues that it was merely the king's desire for Shirin that caused him to treat Farhad so poorly, implying that Shirin's unparalleled beauty was really to blame; J639:7:

خسرو ببین چه ظلم به فرهاد می کند   بلبل ز بهر گل بکشد جور بر هزار

> It is because of the rose that the songbird mistreats the nightingale;
> Look what injustice Khusraw inflicts upon Farhad!

Just as the attributes of Shirin and Khusraw are combined in the *khusraw-i shīrīn*, so Jahan combines Khusraw with Farhad when she says that 'kings' (*khusruvān*) can adopt Farhad-like qualities (infatuation, devotion) when they hear words from the beloved's 'sweet lips' (*lab-i shīrīn*; perhaps her own); J601:2:

تا یک حدیث از آن لب شیرین شنیده اند   فرهادوار عاشق و زارند خسروان

> Farhad-like, the kings are enamoured and wailing bitterly,
> Having heard just one utterance from those sweet lips.

Shikar, Shirin's chief rival

A character from Nizami's *Khusraw va Shirin* who is mentioned with much greater frequency in the poetry of Jahan than in that of her male contemporaries is Shikar, the Isfahani slave-girl/courtesan.[128] Khusraw's desire for Shikar represents the king's lustful, earthly self, whereas his love for Shirin displays his nobler side. Zarrinkub has suggested that Nizami created Shikar from the negative traits ascribed to Shirin in Firdawsi's epic poem and other sources.[129] Consequently, in Jahan's poetry, Shikar is portrayed as secondary in importance to Shirin; J255:2:

خسرو ببین در او که چه شیرین شمایلیست   نسبت نمی کنم به شکر لعل دلکشش

I will not liken her heart-tugging ruby lips to sugar
Khusraw, see what a sweet-faced girl she is!

Jahan asks Khusraw (a prospective Muzaffarid or Jalayirid patron?) to recognize the beauty of a girl who is 'sweet-faced' (shīrīn-shamāyil),[130] perhaps an allusion to herself. Jahan seeks the attention of a patron who has already been courted by a rival poet with whom she is engaged in competition for his/ her 'affection' (where patronage is understood as a relationship based in part on intimacy).[131] Jahan asks this Khusraw to see how similar she is to the Shirin of the past and, in recognizing that similarity, to acknowledge how worthy she is of his beneficence in the present. A princess of the Injuid house, the comparison Jahan draws between herself and Nizami's royal Shirin is apt. In another ghazal, Jahan addresses her patron and urges him, if he truly is the 'king of passionate love' (khusraw-i 'ishq), to seek only Shirin's sweet lips (i.e. her own) and to 'give up sugar' (tark-i shikar kun), that is, disregard the advances of her rival; J1162:7:

مجوی جز لب شیرین و ترک شکر کن   اگر تو خسرو عشقی به دور دلبر ما

If you are the king of love in the age of our beloved
Seek nothing but sweet lips, and give up sugar.

Elsewhere, Jahan explains that Khusraw, having been refused by Shirin, sought the affections of Shikar.[132] If it were Shirin's chastity that drove Khusraw into Shikar's arms, does Jahan mean to criticize Shirin for her modesty or rebuke Khusraw for his fickleness? In this sexually charged couplet, Jahan speaks as a jilted lover, assuming the role of Khusraw whose 'sweet-lipped' (shīrīn-lab) beloved has denied him physical pleasures and who is now forced to seek comfort in the euphemistic 'sugar bowl' (tung-i shikar); J1094:5:

بیا تا خسروآسا جان به تنگ شکر اندازیم   اگر شیرین لب یارم نمی افتد به دست ای دل

If my sweet-lipped beloved does not fall within my reach
Come, O heart, and, like Khusraw, let's cast our soul into the sugar bowl!

Elsewhere, Jahan depicts Khusraw as repentant following his affair with Shikar and sincere in his love for Shirin, whose sweet lips are the only ones he recalls.[133] Jahan warns her Khusraw of turning once again to Shikar having been rejected by Shirin.[134] In the line quoted below, Jahan alludes to these four protagonists of Nizami's poem, either directly or indirectly, as well as to herself; J1286:5:

شور فرهاد چه دانی تو که شکر داری   ای به شیرین سخنی خسرو خوبان در جهان

> O you with your sweet talk (*shīrīn-sukhanī*), king of the beauties (*khusraw-i khūbān*) in the world (*jahān*)!
> What do you know of Farhad's passion, you who have Shikar?

Jahan's beloved has risen to the rank of 'king of the beauties' in this world through his 'sweet talk' or 'sweet way with words', possibly an allusion to the addressee's poetic talent. Jahan identifies her plight with that of Farhad, but she also works as Shirin and competes with her Shikar-like rival (via imitation or poetic response?) for her beloved's attention.

The poet-lover: Khusraw or Shirin?

A feature we find in a number of Jahan's allusions to Khusraw and Shirin, but not in the *ghazals* of Hafiz and 'Ubayd, is the poet's direct identification of her poetic persona with either Shirin or Khusraw.[135] In the following *bayt*, Jahan speaks as Shirin; J134:2:

ور نه ز گفت و گوی نظامی حکایتست   خسرو تویی حقیقت و شیرین منم یقین

> In truth you are Khusraw, and certainly I am Shirin
> If not, then this is a story from Nizami's tale.

This is a significant statement on Jahan's part, not only because it is an expression of heteroerotic desire, but because the direction of the desire expressed is female to male, with the male as the object of feminine desire. Like Jahan, Shirin is both female and royal. Shirin, who falls in love with Khusraw independently after viewing his portrait and before meeting him,[136] is the object of the affections of two males who pursue her at different stages in the narrative. Setting Shirin's allure to one side, Jahan stresses the heroine's agency as a lover persona when she casts Khusraw as the beloved.

As a woman poet, it would appear that Jahan was able to identify herself more readily with female characters than were male poets. If we understand the role of Shirin in this poem to be that of the beloved (now with Khusraw as the lover), Jahan is going against convention by casting herself in the role of the desired, rather than the desirer. The allusions to Nizami's *mathnavī* are employed by Jahan in a number of ways here: firstly, the poet suggests that the 'real' love story of her and the beloved (the 'realness' of their love story emphasized by the use of the terms *haqīqat* ['truth'] and *yaqīn* ['certainty']) is on a parallel with Nizami's romance. By labelling Nizami's poem a *hikāyat* ('story', 'illustrative tale'),[137] Jahan further stresses the gap between the reality of her love adventure and the fictitious nature of Nizami's retelling. Here, literature mirrors life and in evoking the memory of an authoritative poetic giant like Nizami, Jahan plants the seed in the minds of her listeners that she is a wordsmith of comparable status and talent.

It was, of course, the norm for poets not to reference their contemporaries by name and only to reference past masters sparingly. Kamal quotes a half-line from Nizami's *Layli u Majnun* to close a *ghazal*;[138] elsewhere he boastfully compares a five-line *ghazal* he has composed to Nizami's five *mathnavī*s.[139] Hafiz similarly asserts that, at times, the eloquence of his poetry surpasses that of Nizami.[140] Jahan claims that the love that binds her to her beloved has surpassed that spoken of by him; J1181:7:

از آن زنند به هر کوچه داستان از ما   گذشت عشق من و تو ز خسرو و شیرین

My and your love has surpassed that of Khusraw and Shirin
That's why they tell tales of us in every lane.

Here 'tales' renders *dāstān* ('fictive story'). Nizami himself uses the term *dāstān* when introducing the tale of Khusraw and Shirin.[141] In J1181:7, Jahan appears to respond to the following boastful line by Sa'di:[142]

چون داستان شیرین فردا سمر باشد   امروز قول سعدی شیرین مینماید

Today Sa'di's words appear sweet (*shīrīn*)
Tomorrow, like Shirin's tale (*dāstān*), they will be stories.

In J1181:7 it is due to the exceptional intensity of their love that the lovers are talked about throughout the city. Is this an oblique reference to contemporary criticism of Jahan for alleged moral laxity? Or, is Jahan alluding to the popularity of her poems in Shiraz during her lifetime? Both Hafiz and Jahan equate their own love trials with those of characters from Nizami's *Khusraw va Shirin*. Hafiz opens a *qit'a* with the following statement:[143]

این حکایتها که از فرهاد و شیرین کرده اند   شمه ای از داستان عشق شورانگیز ماست

These tales that they have related about Farhad and Shirin
Are snippets from the story of our arousing love affair.

Jahan similarly equates her romantic adventures with those told by Nizami; J1258:

عشقی که با رخ تو مرا هست در جهان   باشد حدیث خسرو و شیرین فسانه ای

The love for your face that I experience in this world
Is a fairy tale from the story of Khusraw and Shirin.

It is as though Jahan has brought the stories told by Nizami to life. This kind of heteroerotic role-play is rare in the *ghazals* of her male contemporaries.[144]

Sultan Mahmud and his beloved slave, Ayaz

It is chiefly through the incorporation of allusions to pairs of pseudo-historical lovers culled from earlier poetry and prose texts who are themselves quasi-legendary (in part because of their exposure to literary embellishment), that heteroerotic desire is injected into the Persian *ghazal*. The only homoerotic pair of lovers to which allusions are made with any frequency in the *ghazals* of our period are the Ghaznavid sultan, Mahmud (d. 1030) and his favourite slave-boy, Ayaz (Abu'l-Najm b. Uymaq, d. 1057). This love story has an arguably solid historical basis as there are accounts of Sultan Mahmud's special affection for Ayaz (his chief royal cupbearer) in sources written a few years after the king's lifetime.[145] Although initially perhaps a case of intense *shāhid-bāzī*, their relationship morphed into something transgressive as Ayaz began to mature.[146]

Both Mahmud and Ayaz were of Turkic origin, although Mahmud's mother was a Persian speaker from Zabulistan. Farrukhi panegyrized Ayaz in a *qasīda* in which he stressed both his physical beauty and his bravery in battle.[147] In later Sufi works Ayaz is presented as a paragon of purity and sincerity, with some drawing mystic inferences from Mahmud's (supposedly chaste) desire for him.[148] In *ghazal* poetry, allusions to Mahmud and Ayaz are employed in much the same fashion as those to heteroerotic lovers: Mahmud's attachment to Ayaz became a 'literary commonplace for devoted love'.[149]

Given that Mahmud died only three centuries or so before Hafiz began his career in Shiraz, 'Ubayd migrated to the city Shiraz from Qazvin, and Jahan married her uncle's *nadīm*, one might expect to find less clichéd, somewhat more historical portrayals of this love story in the *ghazals* of these poets than of other love stories with Sasanian or Parthian settings. But the story of Mahmud's love for Ayaz, of the king who became his slave's slave,[150] although temporally and culturally closer to post-Mongol Iran, is treated as an illustrative literary narrative in the same manner as stories from more distant (and fictitious) times and places.

Well before the fourteenth century, Mahmud's love for Ayaz had become the stuff of the literary imagination (both mystical and profane)[151] and the king and his serving boy had mutated into proverbial figures.[152] For the Persian mystics, Mahmud came to symbolize the 'bondage' (*asīrī*) inherent in 'loverhood' (*'āshiqī*) and Ayaz personified the 'sovereignty' (*amīrī*) at the core of 'belovedhood' (*ma'shūqī*).[153] In Persian *ghazal*s, allusions to Mahmud and Ayaz are often combined with those to more fictionalized pairs of lovers. In H40:5–6 discussed above, Hafiz draws a parallel between Mahmud's subservient, chaste devotion to Ayaz and Majnun's unconsummated love for Layli. Hafiz invokes the image of Mahmud's head being trampled under Ayaz's feet, which is also found in the *ghazal*s of Kamal Khujandi.[154] But in 'Attar's *Ilahinama*, it is Ayaz who kisses Mahmud's feet as a sign of intimacy and it is Ayaz's reciprocation of Mahmud's amorous advances that constitutes a violation of the principles of *shāhid-bāzī*.[155] Nasir states that Ayaz's only function is to serve Mahmud;[156] Jalal promotes an image of slavish devotion in the Mahmud/Ayaz dynamic, rather than subjugation per se:[157]

سر محمود و آستان ایاز   گوش مجنون و حلقهٔ لیلی

[It's] Majnun's ear and Layli's earring;
[It's] Mahmud's head and Ayaz's threshold.

Here rendered as 'earring', the *halqa* is the ring placed in the ear of the slave by his owner. A secondary meaning of *halqa* implied here is a loop of hair, evoking Sultan Mahmud's desire for Ayaz that was centred on the slave's alluring forelocks.[158] Although Mahmud is conventionally depicted as wholly devoted to Ayaz, Hafiz suggests that Ayaz is superfluous to Mahmud: 'the beauty of Mahmud's good fortune (*dawlat*) has no need for Ayaz's forelocks' (possibly an allusion to the reign of Shah Mahmud).[159] Perhaps, Hafiz intends the Mahmud–Ayaz love dynamic to be read as a metaphor for the precariousness of the career of the court poet, who could be ejected at any moment from the court circle. As with allusions to Majnun, Hafiz uses the story of Mahmud to symbolize the devotion required from the true lover who seeks to follow the path of love, whether earthly or mystical; H334:8:

گر سر برود در سر سودای ایازم   محمود بود عاقبت کار در این راه

Praiseworthy would be the outcome of my actions on this path
Even if I lose my head over passionate love for my Ayaz.

Hafiz alludes to the king through the adjective *mahmūd* ('praiseworthy', 'praised') and here there is an oblique allusion to *maqām mahmūd* ('praised station') as mentioned in the Qur'an.[160] On the path of love, a lover's achievements will be deemed worthy of praise if he loses his mind in contemplation of the beloved. According to Ghazali, all manifestations of love derive ultimately from one eternal, primordial love.[161] Hafiz's sentiment is echoed by Jahan; J784:7:

که هست عاقبت کار عاشقان محمود　　　　به عشق روی تو جان دادنم روا باشد

It is permitted for me to lose my soul in love for your face
For the outcome of the actions of true lovers is praiseworthy.

In their respective *bayt*s, both Jahan and Hafiz use the phrase '*āqibat-i kār* ('the outcome of actions') and the adjective *mahmūd* to allude to the Ghaznavid sultan. This could be seen as an instance of imitation between Hafiz and Jahan, but Khvaju too plays with '*āqibat* and *mahmūd*:[162]

همچو محمود شو غلام ایاز　　　　تا ترا عاقبت شود محمود

So that your outcome might be praiseworthy,
Just like Mahmud, become a slave to Ayaz.

But the web of *istiqbāl* does not stop with Khvaju. There is a transregional dimension to this intertextual dialoguing, since the second hemistich in the line by Jahan is also found in a *ghazal* by the Tabriz-based Kamal:[163]

که هست عاقبت کار عاشقان محمود　　　　تو چاکر در سلطان عشق شو چو ایاز

Become the servant of the threshold of the sultan of love, like Ayaz
For the outcome of the actions of true lovers is praiseworthy.

Jahan uses the story of Mahmud and Ayaz to illustrate her own predicament by reminding her audience of the power imbalance between the two: the all-powerful sultan and the 'humble servant' (*banda*); J442:8:

این بنده ایازیست که محمود ندارد　　　　گر بندهٔ محمود ایازست حقیقت

If, in truth, Ayaz is Mahmud's humble servant,
This humble servant is an Ayaz who has no Mahmud.

Jahan refers to herself in the polite manner still current in Iran by using the phrase *īn banda* ('this humble servant'): she is an Ayaz (i.e. a desirable, younger individual at court worthy of [and actively seeking?] royal favour and protection). She has no Mahmud – no royal protector; no patron.

The standard word for patron in Persian, *mamdūh*, carries a meaning almost identical to that of *mahmūd*: it means one who is the object of *madh* (i.e. praise expressed through poetry). It is possible that the Arabic trilateral roots *H-M-D* and *M-D-H*, from which *mahmūd* and *mamdūh* are respectively derived, are etymologically related.[164] If we understand *mahmūd* to mean patron in J442:8, the line can be read as Jahan's plea for financial or other support. Mahmud–Ayaz allusions in the poetry of 'Imad, Jalal and Khvaju also lend themselves to such readings.[165] In this line by Jahan, the phrase *tu mahmūdī* can be read as 'you are Mahmud', 'you are a Mahmud' or 'you are a praised one/one worthy of praise/a patron'; J600:6:

تو محمودی و جان در بندگیت   تو خود دانی ایازی نیک داند

You are a Mahmud and my soul is in your service;
You know yourself how well it plays the role of Ayaz!

By equating herself with Ayaz, Jahan engages in homoerotic role-playing in which she plays the young, seductively beautiful youth of whom others at court are jealous, just as Ayaz's rivals were envious of him. Kamal plays with this panegyric use of the Mahmud–Ayaz romance to different effect when he says his beloved (whom he declares a sultan) is a Mahmud whereas all the other (beggarly) kings of the age are mere avatars of Ayaz.[166] Another ostensibly panegyric riff on these lovers is found in a *ghazal* by 'Imad in which the beloved *khusraw-i khūbān* combines the 'rank' (*mansab*) of Mahmud with the 'beauty' (*husn*) of Ayaz.[167] In contemporary *qasīdas*, the patron is likened to Mahmud of Ghazna in terms of religious fervour, Sultan Mahmud having been instrumental in firmly establishing Islam in western India.[168]

I am all the lovers; You are all the beloveds

The rareness of allusions to Vamiq and 'Adhra, Varqah and Gulshah, and Vis and Ramin in the *ghazal*s of Hafiz, 'Ubayd and Jahan might suggest that the tales associated with these lovers had declined in popularity by the mid-fourteenth century.[169] That said, Vis and Ramin and Vamiq and 'Adhra, alluded to more regularly in the poetry of Khvaju,[170] are not absent from the poetry of Salman, Jalal and Haydar[171] and there is the suggestion that fragments of Gurgani's romance may have been reworked by Hafiz in his lyric poetry.[172] It is possible that the eleventh-century *mathnavī*s, which tell the stories of these lovers ('Unsuri's *Vamiq u 'Adhra* ['The Ardent Lover and the Virgin', an intensely Persian reworking of a Greek novel],[173] 'Ayyuqi's *Varqah va Gulshah* [based on the Arab legend of 'Urwa ibn Hizam],[174] and Gurgani's erotically charged, Parthian-inspired *Vis u Ramin* [completed circa 1055]) had fallen out of favour in Hafiz's day because of their relatively simple style and the fact that the relationships they narrate do not lend themselves so readily to multi-layered interpretation.[175] As Davis has argued, the rhetoric of these three early Persian romances 'contains no hint of the mystical ... they avoid both tragedy and transcendence'.[176]

Nizami's romances are imbued with a moral, even spiritual tone, which invites allegorical interpretation and suggests an underlying edifying or mystical meaning, but this is absent from *Vis u Ramin*, *Vamiq u 'Adhra* and *Varqah va Gulshah*.[177] Schimmel blames the diminished importance of these tales on the fact that they were not incorporated into the *Khamsa*, 'to which all later writers referred openly or obliquely'.[178] In terms of Gurgani's *Vis u Ramin*, the negative moral example of Vis may have been a contributing factor.[179] That said, it should be acknowledged that Nizami modelled certain characters and scenes in *Khusraw va Shirin* on Gurgani's *Vis u Ramin* and, according to Meisami, Nizami makes both explicit and veiled allusions to Gurgani's romance on the levels of language and imagery, thereby creating an inter-textual dimension to the relationship between the two poems.[180] It has been argued that Nizami built upon the psychological depth of Gurgani's characterization.[181] However, allusions to these lovers are relatively one-dimensional when compared to, say, Layli and Majnun or Khusraw and Shirin.[182]

'Ubayd suggests that reading Gurgani's *Vis u Ramin* can provoke women to commit adultery[183] and in his *ghazal*s he does not mention the lovers, although he does allude to Vamiq and 'Adhra; U74:4:

لطف عذرا سبب مرحمت وامق شد   بوی یوسف به سوی غم کش کنعان آمد

The kindness of 'Adhra was the source of her compassion for Vamiq
Joseph's scent reached the nostrils of the grief-stricken one of Canaan.

Jahan mentions all three pairs of lovers, but only in one poem, J1117. J1117 is reminiscent of a *ghazal* by Sa'di in which four pairs of lovers are listed in the form of a 'catalogue of exempla';[184] albeit in a more detached manner than in Jahan's poem:[185]

دودش بسر در آمد و از پای در فتاد   فرهاد را چو بر رخ شیرین نظر فتاد
فارغ ز مادر و پدر و سیم و زر فتاد   مجنون ز جام طلعت لیلی چو مست شد
یکبارگی جدا ز کلاه و کمر فتاد   رامین چو اختیار غم عشق ویس کرد
کارش مدام با غم و آه سحر فتاد   وامق چو کارش از غم عذرا بجان رسید

When Farhad's gaze fell upon Shirin's face
The smoke of his enflamed heart rose and he collapsed.
When Majnun became drunk on the cup of Layli's countenance
He lost all attachment to mother and father, silver and gold.
When Ramin chose the grief of love for Vis
At once he became detached from crown and royal sash.

When Vamiq was at the point of death through pining for 'Adhra
He was continually occupied in grieving and dawn supplications.

   In the fifth *bayt* of this poem, Sa'di links the suffering of Farhad, Majnun,
Ramin and Vamiq to his own and that of 'a hundred thousand others, both
old and young'. The idea that legendary suffering in love is manifested in the
tribulations of the living poet is also found in the works of others.[186]
   Since Vis, Ramin, Vamiq and 'Adhra are more frequently encountered in the
ghazals of earlier poets,[187] it is possible that here Jahan is emulating their use
of romantic *talmīh*. In 'Ubayd's *'Ushshaqnama* ('book of lovers', completed in
September 1350 and dedicated to Shah Shaykh Abu Ishaq)[188] – a *mathnavī*
with embedded *ghazals* on profane love modelled after the far more mystical
homonymous work attributed to 'Iraqi[189]– there is a five-line section in which
exemplary amorous pairs are catalogued in a style not dissimilar to that found
in Sa'di's *ghazal*.[190] 'Ubayd's chosen amorous couples include: Majnun and
Layli, Shirin and Farhad, Joseph and Jacob, Vis and Ramin, Vamiq and 'Adhra
and Gulchihr and Awrang. (In his *'Ushshaqnama* 'Iraqi brings Vamiq and 'Adhra,
Shirin and Khusraw, Layli and Majnun, Vis and Ramin, and Farhad and Shirin as
exempla.)[191] In J1117, Jahan alludes to a not dissimilar array of characters; J1117:

تویی لیلی تویی لیلی تویی درد مرا درمان
منم مجنون منم مجنون منم مجنون سرگردان
تویی شیرین به عهد خسرو و پرویز بنشسته
منم فرهاد کوه افکن به بادم رفته شیرین جان
تویی شیرین تویی شیرین تویی شیرین چو جان در تن
منم خسرو منم خسرو گرفتار شب هجران
تویی عذرا تویی عذرا گرفتارم به درد تو
منم وامق منم وامق بکن درد مرا درمان
تویی گلشه تویی گلشه تویی گلبوی همچون مه
منم ورقه منم غرقه به بحر هجر بی پایان
تویی ویس گل اندامم ز جانت بسته در دامم
منم رامین که می سوزد دلم در غم ترا دامان
ز جان گویم ثنای آن جهانداری که او باقیست
که دادستم به لطف خود همم جان و همم ایمان

You are Layli! You are Layli! You are the cure for my pain!
I am Majnun! I am Majnun! I am the wandering madman!
You are Shirin, seated in the time of Khusraw Parviz
I am Farhad, the mountain-hacker. My sweet soul has expired.
You are Shirin! You are Shirin! You are as sweet as the soul in my body.
I am Khusraw! I am Khusraw! Preoccupied with the night of separation
You are 'Adhra! You are 'Adhra! I am preoccupied with the pain of your love
I am Vamiq! I am Vamiq! Provide a cure for my pain!

You are Gulshah! You are Gulshah! You are rose-scented, just like the moon
I am Varqah, I am drowning in the endless ocean of separation.
You are the rose-limbed Vis, because of your soul I am snared in the trap
I am Ramin, the hem of whose heart burns in grieving for you.
From my soul I sing the praise of that eternal world ruler
Who, from his kindness, has given me cares of the soul and of faith.

Jahan assumes the identity of a succession of exemplary male lovers (Majnun, Farhad, Khusraw, Vamiq, Varqah and Ramin), while casting her beloved in the corresponding female roles (those of Layli, Shirin, 'Adhra, Gulshah and Vis). Jahan's *ghazal* ends with a flourish of panegyric sentiment. In a Nawruz-themed *ghazal*, Haydar complicates the gendered framing of the beloved in a manner that recalls some of what is accomplished by Jahan in J1117 and which problematizes the dichotomy offered by strictly homo- and/or heteroerotic readings of Persian *ghazal*s:[192]

تویی خسرو که چون شیرین هزاران کوهکن داری   تویی لیلی که چون مجنون هزاران خسته دل کشی

You are a Layli who slays many thousands just like Majnun
You are a Khusraw who has thousands of mountain-carvers like Shirin

In J1117, Jahan incorporates the repeated phrases: *tu'ī tu'ī tu'ī/man-am man-am man-am* ('you are, you are, you are'/'I am, I am, I am'), giving the poem a songlike, rhythmic structure.[193] An almost identical sentiment and form can be found in this *bayt* by Sa'di:[194]

منم امروز و تویی وامق و عذرای دگر   وامقی بود که دیوانهٔ عذرایی بود

There was once a Vamiq madly in love with an 'Adhra
Today, you and I are another 'Adhra and Vamiq.

But it is Sa'di's elder contemporary, Hamgar, who encapsulates with concision the style of heteroerotic role-playing Jahan channels so masterfully in J1117:[195]

عذرا و ویس و لیلی و شیرین من تویی   فرهاد و رام و وامق و مجنون تو منم

I am your Farhad, Ramin, Vamiq and Majnun;
You are my 'Adhra, Vis, Layli and Shirin!

Elsewhere, Hamgar compares his devotion to the Shirin-lipped beloved to that of both Khusraw and Farhad, the ultimate conclusion of this devotion being death.[196] In two odes for Baghdad, Hamgar expresses the intensity of his longing for the city through the analogy of Farhad's love for Shirin.[197] As already noted, Unsuri's *Vamiq u 'Adhra*, Gurgani's *Vis u Ramin* and 'Ayyuqi's *Gulshah u Varqah* are all pre-Nizamian romance *mathnavi*s. As such, they do not readily lend themselves to mystical interpretation. It is, therefore, possible that by including allusions to these lovers in her poetry, Jahan signalled she favoured a more human, less divine, focus for her love poems. In this aspect, Jahan's *ghazal* style can be said to be closer to that of Sa'di, Hamgar and her older contemporaries, 'Ubayd and Khvaju.

Conclusion

In this chapter we have witnessed the variety of the strategies used by the poets in order to weave heteroerotic romance narratives into their conventionally homoerotic *ghazal*s. We have also seen how and why some poets (Jahan being one of them) chose to align their poetic persona very closely with one or more of the protagonists of widely read romance *mathnavi*s and how *talmih* involving archetypal lovers can be harnessed to expound upon the intimacy that lies at the heart of the poet–patron relationship.

Given the contemporary popularity of Nizami's *Khamsa*, it would have been unnecessary for poets composing *ghazal*s to discuss in any detail the stories of Layli and Majnun or Khusraw and Shirin in their own poems. The shorthand allusions they delivered through concise injections of *talmih* conjured up for their listeners the salient features of those lengthy narratives and prompted associations with a myriad of unspoken plot details. Over time and via intertextual processes through which poets responded to a contemporary or earlier poet's use of *talmih*, such allusions evolved in meaning and took on a life of their own. The number and breadth of their referents increased to include not only other *ghazal*s from various periods and places, but also the romance *mathnavi*s of Nizami, imitations of those poems penned by others in the thirteenth and fourteenth centuries, sections of Firdawsi's *Shahnama*, and chapters from Sa'di's *Gulistan* (as well as prose texts in which the stories associated with exemplary lovers are retold). The interplay of distinct poetic forms and genres within the framework of the Persian *ghazal* via the medium of *talmih* is one that deserves additional scrutiny.

From the relationship between poet–patron, we widen our vision to view the court as a whole. In the last chapter we explore how poets use prophet stories adapted from canonical and non-canonical texts to foster purpose, hope and reassurance in their listeners. But even here, given that the textual focus is the *ghazal*, the amorous looms large.

6

Allusions to Prophets

Allusions to Abrahamic prophets woven into the *ghazal*s of fourteenth-century Shiraz are mediated either through the lens of the Qur'an or through non-canonical Islamic texts collectively known as *Qisas al-anbiyā'* ('stories of the prophets'). Like myths, prophet stories are textually variable, not fixed and, although the prophets discussed here appear in the Bible and the Qur'an, not all of their stories as alluded to in the poetry studied here correspond exactly with biblical or Qur'anic narratives. Some allusions in the poetry tally more closely with popular retellings of such stories found in Arabic and Persian texts produced in the eleventh to thirteenth centuries. As Brinner notes, the Muslim authors of *Qisas al-anbiyā'* works sought to expand the brief and enigmatic aspects of those stories.[1] Mediated through this folk-religious, imaginative Islamic material (more akin to popular entertainment than religious preaching)[2] Jewish sources also play a role (as do the narrative possibilities and variation opened up by orality).[3]

Not every narrative element found in Islamic texts is traceable to earlier traditions and care must be exerted before declaring any individual element to be 'derivative'. The mutuality of the dynamic in the relationship of extra-biblical Jewish legends and early Islamic patterns must also be acknowledged.[4] As Lowin notes, Judaism and Islam have a complex, intertwined connection.[5] In the particular case of Jewish and Iranian legends, Zoroastrian influence on Judaism may indeed have facilitated the (re)moulding of certain Jewish prophet stories. Iran witnessed 3,000 years of Jewish-Iranian and Judaeo-Islamic interactions that are, in the words of Yeroushalmi, 'still shrouded in obscurity'.[6] Accepting that Judaism and Zoroastrianism are both Sasanian religions, we acknowledge that Late Antique Iran was a religiously heterogeneous world where contact between diverse communities was commonplace.[7]

Multiple versions of these shared scriptural stories featuring the 'same cast of characters'[8] co-existed within and across religions. Those (including poets) who recounted prophet stories often did so in a free fashion encouraged by their individual authorial license. As Kugel has noted, exegetes, who regarded the Bible as an elliptical text in which extreme economy in written expression was applied, added extras implied but not explicitly stated in the holy text into their retellings of prophet stories, resulting in 'narrative expansion'.[9] Adjustments in prophetic narratives were not caused by the 'vagaries of time and the whim of storytellers', but rather resulted from 'intentional adaptations of material' aimed at conveying specific messages within particular contexts.[10] Lowin draws our attention to what she calls Islam's 'creative appropriation' of earlier Jewish and Christian cultural artefacts which it 'consciously remoulded and refashioned ... in its own image and according to its own values'.[11] As Gregg has argued, interpreters retold the prophets' stories 'using story expansions and noticeable twists in order to advance their own communal interests'.[12]

Persian court poets embedded somewhat simple allusions to prophets and the miraculous stories associated with them into their lyric poetry from at least the late ninth to early tenth centuries,[13] the oldest period for which written evidence of New Persian poetry survives.[14] In Islam, many came to view prophetic figures as prototypes of the mystical experience.[15] Persian poets used allusions to the lives of prophets and emblematic elements of their stories to bolster praise of a patron through analogy[16] either as moral or heroic exempla[17] or as pedagogical topoi (as we find abundantly in Rumi's poetry, for example).[18]

The prophets alluded to with some frequency in the *ghazals* of post-Mongol Shiraz are: Adam (Adam), Noah (Nuh), Abraham (Ibrahim or Khalil ['the Friend [of God]']), Jacob (Ya'qub), Joseph (Yusuf), Moses (Musa) and Jesus ('Isa or Masih/Masiha ['the Messiah', 'Christ']).[19] The Kirmani poets, Khvaju and 'Imad, also allude to Job (Ayyub) and identify their sorry plight in their home town with his implacable patience.[20] In contemporary panegyric *qasīdas*, patrons are said to embody the emblematic qualities of prophets. Salman, for one, praised various Jalayirid royals using combined allusions to Muhammad, Jesus, Joseph, Moses and other holy figures.[21]

Most instances of prophetological *talmīh* in the *ghazals* studied here are allusions to Joseph, his father Jacob and Joseph's would-be lover, Zulaykha. The Judaic kings David (Davud) and Solomon (Sulayman) are considered prophets in Islam but, since allusions to them concern legitimate monarchy,[22] they are discussed in Chapter 4. In addition to prophets, there is Khizr, the mysterious guide linked to Moses, who is associated more frequently in lyric poetry with Alexander (allusions to him are also discussed in Chapter 4).

The Prophet Muhammad is not mentioned specifically in the *ghazals* of Hafiz, Jahan or 'Ubayd, perhaps because many of their short lyric poems contain evocations of illicit or otherwise frowned-upon activities: musical performance, song and bacchanalian pursuits. Allusions to the prophet Muhammad (by name or via the epithets Mustafa and Ahmad) are relatively common in the *ghazal*s of Rumi who composed with Sufi performance contexts in mind.[23]

It should be noted that fourteenth-century Shiraz was not a homogeneously Muslim city. Writing in the mid-tenth century, Istakhri says Zoroastrians make up the largest non-Muslim community (followed by Christians and then Jews).[24] It is believed that in the Buyid period, Shiraz's non-Muslims freely practised their respective religions.[25] While post-Mongol Shiraz perhaps did not boast a large Zoroastrian population, the city was home to significant Christian and Jewish communities. Two centuries earlier, Shiraz's Jewish population possibly stood at around 10,000, equating to perhaps as much as 15 per cent of the total population.[26] The celebrated Jewish poet of Shiraz, Shahin, who was active in the early Injuid period, composed Torah-inspired *mathnavī*s and panegyrics for powerful notables in Judaeo-Persian.[27]

Adam and Eve

Adam embodies legitimacy and was central to caliphal self-representation as far back as the Umayyad period.[28] In Arabic wine poetry, allusions to Adam are used to stress the ancient vintage of wine.[29] A connection between Adam and the bacchanal is maintained in Persian: Hafiz says Adam's clay was kneaded by the angels in the tavern and then cast into the wine-measuring cup.[30] It is also via an Adamic allusion that Hafiz claims primordial pedigree for his poetry which, he says, adorned the jonquils and roses in the Paradise garden at the time of the prophet.[31] Jahan alludes to Adam (Adam) and Eve (Havva) together and she presents their 'sin' (*gunāh*) as that of passionate love, rather than disobedience towards God per se; J947:9:

گناه اوّل ز حوّا بود و آدم   نه من کردم به عالم عشق بازی

It was not I who created lovemaking in the world
The first sin came from Eve and Adam.

The second hemistich of Jahan's *bayt* is a *tazmīn* from a *ghazal* by Sa'di.[32] Jahan says that *'ishq-bāzī* ('lovemaking', 'the game of love') has existed since time immemorial and that she is not the first to fall victim to it. This defensive tone echoes retorts by the lover to the harsh words of the 'blamer' (*lā'im, 'ādhil*) in the Arabic short lyric. The blamer emerges in Persian poetry as the *malāmat-gū/malāmat-gar* who chides lovers for falling madly in love. Jahan's suggestion is that the foundation of Adam and Eve's transgression was their intense love for one another. Elsewhere, Jahan denies any responsibility for this sin through a pun on *havā* ('desire') and Havva (Eve) – pronounced almost identically in Persian.[33]

Their sin, as alluded to by Hafiz, is forbidden, reprehensible passion; H348:2:

کآتش اندر گنه آدم و حوا فکنم   از دل تنگ گنهکار بر آرم آهی

From my weary, sinful heart I raise up a sigh
To set ablaze the sin of Adam and Eve.

Hafiz's sin is all-consuming love and it is punishable by his being separated from his beloved. This could be interpreted as the expression of desire on the part of Hafiz to use his love to kindle a fire that will obliterate all previous (inherited?) sin.[34]

Noah

In light of the mystification of Noah as encountered in much Persian lyric poetry, it is interesting to note that in Abbasid wine poetry, allusions to Noah carry vinous associations. Noah is the first vintner and, because of his longevity, he is associated with antique wine.[35] The prophet has some Iranian connections: some believed him to be Faridun[36] and he is credited with the foundation of Nahavand (or *Nūh-āvand*) in western Iran.[37] Noah is also said to have stayed in a place he then named Qum.[38]

Allusions to Noah in the *ghazals* studied here concern the Flood (*tūfān, sayl*). Noah and his Ark (*kashtī*; 'ship') are symbols of divine salvation and, by extension, the protection provided by the patron. Noah delivered a warning to mankind and, by those who boarded the Ark, was recognized as a saviour sent by God. Given the tenor of the allusions to Noah found in Persian *ghazals*, it is unsurprising that these instances of *talmīh* are frequently subjected to mystical interpretation. That said, as with allusions to Joseph, allusions to Noah can also be read topically.[39] Hafiz calls on his interlocutor to befriend the 'men of God' (*mardān-i khudā*), possibly an allusion to sincere mystics;[40] H9:6:

هست خاکی که به آبی نخرد طوفان را   یار مردان خدا باش که در کشتی نوح

Be a friend to the men of God, for in Noah's Ark
There is dust that considers the Flood a mere trickle.

There is a saying of the Prophet (known as *Hadith al-safina* ['Tradition of the Ark']) in which the Prophet's family is likened to Noah's Ark. Rumi uses taking refuge in Noah's ark as a metaphor for seeking the tutelage of a Sufi *shaykh*,[41] but allusions to Noah in the poetry studied here can be read as illustrative of the reliance of the poet upon the beneficence of the patron;[42] H18:7:

ورنه طوفان حوادث ببرد بنیادت   حافظ از دست مده دولت این کشتی نوح

Hafiz, do not lose hold of the good fortune of this Noah's Ark
For if you do, the storm of events will sweep away your foundation

In place of *dawlat* ('good fortune'), Khanlari's edition has *suhbat* ('intimate association'; a term, as already noted, that has convivial, erotic connotations).[43] *Kashtī* can also denote a ship-shaped drinking vessel, so the *kashtī-yi Nūh* Hafiz alludes to here might actually be wine and the escapist intoxication it proffers.[44] The 'storm of events' (*tūfān-i havādith*) is perhaps an allusion to the turbulence of the current political climate in Shiraz.

Punning on her pen name and responding to a line by Sa'di,[45] Jahan writes about the reassurance the prophet Noah provides to those who beseech him; J392:5:

کسی که دست امیدش رسد به دامن نوح   اگر جهان همه طوفان بگیرد او چه غمش

If the world is engulfed in the flood, what should she fear
Whose hopeful hand reaches to the hem of Noah's robe?

Elsewhere, Jahan speaks of the 'flood of separation from the beloved' (*tūfān-i firāq-i dūst*) and the prophet's 'people' or 'community' (*ummat-i Nūh*).[46] Noah, as captain of the Ark, is the wayfarer's guarantor; whatever tribulations one encounters, if one holds fast to the hem of Noah's cloak (the embodiment of God's guidance and mercy and/or the patron's benevolence), one will be safe from life's torments; H255:6:

چون تو را نوح است کشتیبان ز طوفان غم مخور   ای دل ار سیل فنا بنیاد هستی بر کند

O heart, if the flood of annihilation should uproot the foundation of existence,
Since Noah is your captain, because of the storm, grieve not!

The second hemistich of this *bayt* echoes one found in the introduction to the *Gulistan*: 'What fear of the sea's waves has he whose captain is Noah?'[47] Elsewhere, Hafiz presents Noah as the epitome of forbearance. He withstood the opposition of his people and, when the flood came, he waited patiently until the waters subsided. Noah's patient obedience was rewarded by God, who made him the second father of the human race; H234:6:

گرت چو نوح نبی صبر هست در غم طوفان   بلا بگردد و کام هزارساله برآید

If you have the same patience as the prophet Noah in the grief of the flood,
The calamity will pass, and a thousand-year-old desire will come to fruition.

Patience in times of adversity – as exemplified here by Noah – ultimately leads to lasting rewards. Alluding to Noah, Jahan identifies her own plight directly with his; J605:7:

غرق طوفان بلا گشته دل و جان و چو نوح   دست امید برآورده و درمان طلبند

My heart and soul have drowned in the flood of calamity and, like Noah,
They have stretched out their hands in hope, seeking a cure.

Allusions to the Flood are also metaphors for the intensity and volume of the lover's tears shed in separation from the beloved; H28:2:

سرشک من که ز طوفان نوح دست برد   ز لوح سینه نیارست نقش مهر تو شست

My tears, which surpassed even the flood of Noah,
Could not wash the imprint of your love from the tablet of my breast!

Here Hafiz claims that his tears are greater than the Flood but that, despite their intensity, they are unable to erase his love for his patron. The poet employs almost identical imagery elsewhere to say that no amount of tears could ever erase his beloved's 'imprint' (*naqsh*) from the 'tablet of [his] heart'.[48] Jahan similarly boasts that her torrent of tears outdoes tales of the legendary Flood itself; J313:4:

اگرچه هست ز طوفان نوح هم شرحی   ولی چو دیده من اشکبار باران نیست

Even though there is a description of the flood of Noah
There is no downpour like the tears which flow from *my* eyes.

Abraham

Jews consider Abraham to be the first patriarch, while for Muslims, he is *Khalīlullāh* ('the Friend of God')[49] and the builder of the Ka'ba. In a story adapted from the Midrashim and elaborated in the *Qisas al-anbiya'*, Abraham, the monotheistic idol-smasher, is saved from a fire he is cast into by Nimrod.[50] Abraham is said to have remained in the fire for a full seven days, whereupon God caused a spring of fresh water to appear in the fire and roses to sprout beneath him (hence the prophet's association in Persian poetry with the rose garden).

According to Tha'labi, Abraham was born in Shush in southwest Iran.[51] Around the tenth century, a theory emerged that the Persians were descended from Abraham through his son Isaac.[52] Some medieval Muslims also came to identify Abraham as Zoroaster or a son of Zoroaster.[53] Shahin is the first Judaeo-Persian poet to make extensive use of Abraham-related material, most notably in his *Bereshitnama* completed around 1358 in Muzaffarid Shiraz.[54]

In one poem, Hafiz alludes to the miracle involving Nimrod's great fire;[55] H308:4:

سرد کن ز ان سان که کردی بر خلیل   یا رب این آتش که در جان من است

O Lord, this fire which is in my soul
Cool it, just as you did for Abraham.

Hafiz calls on God to save him from being consumed by this fire of love. By utilizing a well-known story from the Islamic tradition, Hafiz invites the formation of a graphic image in the mind of his listeners. Drawing a parallel between one's own plight and that of a prophet who came before Muhammad was acceptable in a way that drawing a similar parallel with the prophet of Islam was not.

Jahan alludes to Abraham as destroyer of polytheistic idols,[56] and allusions to Abraham as the enemy of the idols worshipped by his ancestors were used by panegyrists to stress their patron's pious credentials.[57] Jahan says her devotion to the beloved has obliterated thoughts of all other false beloveds in her mind, just as Abraham destroyed all effigies of false gods;[58] J140:3:

جز صورت خیال تو در یکدگر شکست   باری خلیل خاطر ما هر صور که دید

The Abraham of my mind smashed together
All the images it saw, except for the image of you.

Jahan also alludes to the energy and determination with which Abraham destroyed idols when describing how she will combat her rivals (sing. *raqib*). In Arabic, *raqib* denotes a 'guardian' or 'chaperone' whereas in Persian, it normally stands for a 'rival' or 'competitor'. Jahan's rivals are those who wish her ill and would prevent her from reuniting with her beloved, perhaps adversaries (poets included) who seek to interfere between her and her patron; J467:6:

بر بتان آزری خواهیم کرد   بر رقیبان حمله ای همچون خلیل

Against the rivals we will launch an attack,
Just as did Abraham against the idols of Azar!

Jacob and Joseph

The prophets alluded to with the greatest frequency in the *ghazal*s studied here are Joseph and his father Jacob.

Joseph

Variations of the Joseph story are found in Genesis, the Qur'an and various non-canonical Jewish and Islamic texts. In the Qur'an, Joseph's story is *Ahsanu'l-qisas*, the 'best of all stories'[59] and is the Qur'an's longest sustained narrative of one character's life.[60] Though the story opens with Joseph's betrayal at the hands of his jealous brothers, it has a positive conclusion; Joseph comes to symbolize how right conduct can triumph over treachery and envy.

Joseph is the 'prototype for beauty which is sufficient unto itself and which disdains love offered to it'.[61] He is the paragon of beauty, something that is stressed in the *qisas* literature[62] as well as in Persian poetry and prose.[63] According to Renard, Rumi sees Joseph's striking beauty as the reason for his favoured position among Jacob's sons and the cause of disarray in the marketplace when he is sold in Egypt.[64] In Persian lyric poetry, Joseph is synonymous with the *shāhid*. Joseph's father, Jacob, is the epitome of patient longing when he is separated from his favourite son. Jacob grows old and blind waiting for Joseph to return to Canaan and, like a true lover, never gives up hope that he will be reunited with him. When Jacob hears the news that Joseph has been found, he regains his sight.

Although allusions to Jacob and Joseph are discussed in this chapter, the intense bond between the two and the intense suffering of the father in separation from the son share much with motifs that reoccur in romance *mathnavī*s: involuntary, unavoidable, often forced separation; the distraught lover's unceasing loyalty; the ultimate consolation of reunion. Indeed, the intensity of this father–son relationship is frequently evoked in the Persian *ghazal* as a metaphor for longing endured in passionate, human love.

Sufis presented the Jacob–Joseph bond as a model for the relationship between the manifestation of divine beauty (Joseph) and the loving soul of the mystic (Jacob). As de Bruijn has argued, to *ghazal* poets, the Joseph story 'offered a very rich store of motifs … which were not exclusively used in a religious context'.[65] Here I explore the panegyric and performative aspects of these motifs, rather than their mystical potential.

Jacob embodies the core characteristics of the perfect lover: he bears the pain of loss, the anguish of separation and the heightened ecstasy of reunion.[66] Though motivated by paternal affection and filial devotion, the love between Jacob and Joseph shares many parallels with amorous homoerotic relations as depicted in Persian poetry: Joseph is young, beautiful, longed for by an older male and, for most of the narrative, unattainable. Joseph's desire for reunion diverges from convention: the beloved should maintain an implacable, disdainful aloofness at all times. In this respect, his desire for reunion recalls the love dynamic in many romance *mathnavīs* and comparison of the beloved to Joseph is common in fourteenth-century lyric poems.[67] In terms of the pre-Hafizian *ghazal*, Rumi is perhaps the most semiotically charged employer of Joseph-beloved topoi.[68]

Jacob's longing for Joseph

The poet relates to the character of Jacob, with whom he or she finds a natural affinity in their common experience of suffering caused by separation from the beloved:[69]

كاندوه دل سوختگان سوخته داند   سوز دل يعقوب ستمديده ز من پرس

Ask *me* about the burning of Jacob's oppressed heart –
For only one who has burned knows the grief of the burnt!

Longing for a sign from the long-lost object of her desire, Jahan casts herself even more directly as Jacob:[70]

نزدم آور بويى از پيراهنش   اى صبا گر سوى كنعان بگذرى

O zephyr! If you pass by Canaan
Bring me a whiff from his shirt!

In the Qur'an, when Joseph's true identity is disclosed to his brothers, he sends his shirt back with them as a gift to his father.[71] Once thrown over Jacob's face, Joseph's shirt miraculously restores Jacob's sight.[72] The motif of Joseph's shirt and its sight-restoring properties is popular in the Persian *ghazal*.[73] The 'shirt' (*pīrāhan*) symbolizes Joseph's purity and chastity, reminding the reader of his betrayal at the hands of his envious brothers. The garment's smell as sensory signal conveys the message to Joseph's grief-stricken father that his son still lives. On the olfactory level, it reunites father and son; H196:9:

پیراهنی که آید از او بوی یوسفم   ترسم برادران غیورش قبا کنند

The shirt from which comes the scent of my Joseph,
I fear his jealous brothers may tear it to shreds.

Just as comparisons to Joseph are used to flatter the patron in the panegyric
qasīda[74] and allusions to the prophet can be read panegyrically,[75] so the jealous
brothers can be read as allusions to those who would do harm to the patron.
The poetry contains clues to the contemporary socio-political situation, which
come to light when we examine the poets' topical, not merely tropological,
use of talmīh and when we resist the pressure to read such allusions as being
exclusively abstract or mystical. In the particular case of Shah Shuja', Joseph's
jealous brothers would stand for the king's chief familial rival, his younger
brother, Shah Mahmud or perhaps his recalcitrant nephew, Shah Yahya.[76] This
use of Joseph topoi by Hafiz mirrors the psychological employment of the
same by Rumi to depict the jealousy of his family and close associates that
his bond with his spiritual mentor, Shams-i Tabrizi, aroused.[77]

Shah Shuja' was ousted from Shiraz by Shah Mahmud, but returned
triumphantly some years later. Lescot believes H147, H176 and H312 to have
been written either to entreat Shah Shuja' to return to Shiraz or to celebrate
his homecoming.[78] The historical fact of the intense rivalry among members
of the Muzaffarid clan helps to explain why Hafiz drew parallels between his
patron's plight and that of Joseph.

The poets say the Joseph-beloved's healing and revivifying scent is carried
by the messenger breeze.[79] The bād-i sabā transports memories and scents
of the beloved to the lover; its fusion with the Joseph narrative in the poetry
further facilitates the reading of the Jacob–Joseph bond as an amorous one;
J109:7:

صبا سوی من رنجور هجران   ز مصر آمد مگر بوی بشیر است

The sabā breeze came from Egypt to me, one tortured by separation
Is it the scent of the bearer of good news?

Here Jahan uses bashīr (lit. 'bearer of good news') to allude to Joseph,
whereas in the Qur'an,[80] al-bashīr (identified in the commentaries as a brother
of Joseph) is the one who casts Joseph's shirt over Jacob's face.[81] It is also
al-bashīr who brings false news of Joseph's death in the form of a shirt stained
with animal blood.[82] In another poem, Jahan says the unannounced arrival
of the bashīr has the potential to transform Jacob's abode of sorrow into a
'paradisiacal flower-garden',[83] just as Joseph's triumphal return, Hafiz assures
us, will make his father's sorry shack a 'rose-garden'.[84] Jahan depicts the

bashīr as the go-between who transports messages from the beloved to his lover in the form of a sweet scent; J726:4:

حالت دیدهٔ مهجور ستم دیده ببین   ای بشیر دل من بویی از آن پیرهن آر

See the state of my forsaken, oppressed eyes
O harbinger of my heart! Bring me a scent of that shirt!

Elsewhere, Jahan combines the 'sweet breeze of [Joseph's] shirt' (*nasīm-i pīrāhan*) and the 'breath of the messenger' (*nafas-i bashīr*) to suggest Joseph and the *bashīr* are one.[85] Given the centrality of the sweet scent to the beloved's attractiveness, the fact that the senses play a pivotal role in the reconnection of Jacob with Joseph facilitates further the use of their story as a metaphor for the relationship between the lover and beloved; J1179:2:

نسیم زلف تو گر بشنوم ز باد صبا   چنان بود که به یعقوب بوی پیراهن

If I smell the sweet breeze of your locks from the messenger breeze,
It will be just like the scent of Joseph's shirt for Jacob.

Jahan recognizes Joseph's original scent in the scent of her own beloved; J1235:5:

نکهت پیرهن یوسف جان می شنوم   چشم یعقوب حزین بوی تو بینا کرده

I can smell the perfume of the shirt of the Joseph of the soul;
It was your scent that restored sight to the eyes of the sorrowful Jacob.

These permutations in the narrative details of the story as alluded to via *talmīh* suggest that the story of Joseph was repeatedly and deliberately recreated through successive historical and contemporaneous poetic re-imaginings.

Jacob is the epitome of patience, but his long wait is ultimately rewarded; H319:8:

این که پیرانه سرم صحبت یوسف بنواخت   اجر صبریست که در کلبهٔ احزان کردم

The fact that I enjoy Joseph's company in my old age
Is the reward of the patience endured in the hut of sorrows.

Hafiz here is an aged, Jacob-like lover who has spent a lifetime in anticipation of the return of his youthful beloved, an apt metaphor for an elderly poet committed to his far younger patron. Hafiz's career as a court poet spanned well over four decades. At the end of his life, he was in the employ of relatively young

Muzaffarid princes,[86] Shah Shuja''s nephew-successors, Shah Yahya[87] and Shah Mansur.[88] There was a considerable age gap between the poet and his royal supporters at the end of his life, so allusions to a Jacob–Joseph bond can be read as evocative of Hafiz's experience of patronage at this late stage in his career.

'Ubayd draws a direct parallel between the affection he feels for his beloved (and the resultant grief he suffers in separation from him) and the mutual love of Jacob and Joseph (which he calls a 'story' [hadīth]); U19:8:

بیان شوق عبید و غم جدایی تو   حدیث یوسف مصری و پیر کنعان است

The expression of 'Ubayd's desire and his grief at separation from you
Constitutes the story of Joseph of Egypt and the old man of Canaan.

In paralleling passionate, human desire with the story of Jacob and Joseph, 'Ubayd too highlights a homoerotic subtext buried in the narrative. 'Ubayd, by equating himself with Jacob, suggests a significant age gap between himself as lover and the object of his affections.[89] This fits the standard parameters of the depiction of older, male homoerotic fascination with a younger male, in accordance with the mono-gender, inter-generational erotic dynamic of the Persian ghazal. As noted above, Jahan also identifies herself with Jacob and her beloved with Joseph making it necessary to look beyond Jahan's gender and to focus instead on her engagement in the dominant male modes of poetic production; J1342:4:

گر نه بوی یوسف مصرم وزیدی گاه گاه   همچو یعقوب از غمت صد پیرهن بدریدمی

If the scent of the Egyptian Joseph did not waft towards me from time to time
Just like Jacob I would tear a hundred shirts to shreds out of grief for you.

Tearing one's shirt is commonly associated in Iranian culture with intense grieving. There is, of course, an implied play here on the shirt torn from Joseph's back by the lustful Zulaykha.[90] Here, Jahan fuses the would-be seductress and the grieving father.

Zulaykha and Joseph

In an early poetic version of the romance of Joseph and Zulaykha (the prophet's would-be seducer turned selfless lover), de Bruijn detects an emphasis on the religious rather than mystical significance of the subject.[91] Early narrative versions of this romance may have inspired lyric poets to incorporate allusions to the love of Zulaykha for Joseph into their poetry as early as the late eleventh/early twelfth century.[92] Sufi authors, however, came to use the Joseph-Zulaykha story to elucidate key concepts of their discourse.[93] The emphasis placed by *ghazal* poets of the 'Iraqi school on Zulaykha's desire for Joseph underscores the erotic element of this tale, thereby blurring the line between prophet story and romance.

In the Qur'an, the wife of al-'Aziz, Joseph's wealthy Egyptian master,[94] lusts after her husband's new male slave. In vain, al-'Aziz's wife (known in later sources as Zulaykha) tries to seduce Joseph who sees the 'proof of his Lord' and escapes her advances.[95] The elite women of her city gossiped about Zulaykha's desire for her slave-boy, so she invited these women to her home to view him for themselves.[96] According to the Qur'an,[97] Zulaykha commanded Joseph to enter the room in which the women were gathered. Joseph's beauty astounded the guests to such a degree that they cut their hands with the knives they were using to slice fruit.

Zulaykha is depicted most negatively in the Qur'an and many texts beyond.[98] Writing in the mid-twelfth century, Tusi dubs Zulaykha Joseph's *mihnat* ('ordeal', 'severe trial'). Tusi, who associates women in general with *fitna* ('test', 'sedition') and *shūm* ('misfortune', 'ill-luck'), concludes that good women are few in number.[99] The tale of Joseph and Zulaykha is an exemplary moral tale warning of the danger posed by uncontrolled female sexuality. In effect, Joseph is the object of the hopeful, erotic gaze of a group of women who represent their gender as a whole. For Spellberg, Zulaykha embodies the 'nexus between female sexuality and danger',[100] arguing that she is prevented from seducing Joseph because 'the triumph of feminine force over male prophets would have produced moral and political disaster'.[101]

Female seductiveness and cunning are central to the interactions between Zulaykha, her women guests and Joseph.[102] Some scholars have gone so far as to argue that the literary roots of misogyny in Islam are to be found in the *Surat Yusuf*. Malti-Douglas argues that the phrase 'your guile' (*kayda-kunna*),[103] since it appears in the feminine plural, 'transposes the seductive act of a single woman and exploits it to pass judgement on the totality of womankind'.[104] Merguerian and Najmabadi, noting the strong association of female heterosexual desire with threat and guile, argue that Zulaykha and the other women of her town are presented as though attempting a 'collective seduction' of Joseph.[105] Mahmood has recently offered a somewhat measured reading of *kayd* which allows for a positive interpretation and complicates the readings offered in some earlier scholarship.[106]

The guile and other negative qualities associated with Zulaykha and her sister-accomplices are absent from the depiction of Zulaykha found in the *ghazals* studied here. The negativity surrounding the expression (or manifestation) of female sexuality has been dimmed in Persian lyric poetry. Merguerian and Najmabadi have noted that in Persian romances, Zulaykha is not only rehabilitated, she is actually recreated: first punished for her dangerous sexuality, she is then redeemed and finally controlled (in part through her marriage to Joseph which legitimizes her earlier expression of sexual desire).[107]

In Jami's *Yusuf va Zulaykha* (completed 1483), Zulaykha's love for Joseph occupies centre stage so that their roles become balanced in the narrative: Joseph personifies the epiphany of eternal beauty and Zulaykha the response to that perfect beauty on the part of the human soul.[108] Zulaykha, now the embodiment of selfless love and devotion, regains her sight (like Jacob, she had also gone blind through weeping), her youth and her beauty.[109] She comes to manifest a 'worthy form of desire'.[110]

In the Persian *ghazal*, we witness the salvation of Zulaykha:[111] what Malti-Douglas terms the 'problematic of the female as a negative force'[112] is missing in this poetry. In the Persian *ghazal*, Zulaykha is depicted not only sympathetically, but also positively. In this poetry, we witness Zulaykha's absolution as her devotion is viewed as being no less sincere than that of any other archetypal lover.[113] Zulaykha has a love-filled breast (*sīna-yi pur-mihr*)[114] and she is an inseparable partner for Joseph:[115]

عاشقی سوخته خرمن چو زلیخا برخاست   هر کجا سروقدی چهره چو یوسف بنمود

Wherever a cypress-tall beloved showed his face like Joseph
A forlorn lover like Zulaykha rose up.

This positive image of Zulaykha foreshadows her Timurid redemption and is found in Persian lyric poetry from at least the thirteenth century. Awhadi goes so far as to parallel Zulaykha's physical beauty with that of Joseph:[116]

چو غنج و ناز کنی بهتر از زلیخایی   چو روی باز کنی نیستی کم از یوسف

When you unveil your face, you are no less than Joseph;
When you flirt and play the coquette, you outdo Zulaykha!

In an eleventh-century version of the tale, Zulaykha takes on distinctly Jacob-like qualities as she weeps for seventeen years out of love for Joseph, only to then turn blind.[117] In lyric poetry too, Zulaykha's trajectory comes to mirror Jacob's sorry plight:[118]

عزیز من برو از دیدهٔ زلیخا پرس   بهای یوسف کنعان اگر نمی‌دانی

If, my dear ('*azīz*), you know not Joseph's price
Go ask it from the eyes of Zulaykha!

'Imad strikes a misogynistic tone when he warns that a man who does not lose his life like Zulaykha almost did in passionate yearning for the beloved is less worthy than a woman.[119] But 'Imad also expresses respect for the 'melancholic passion' (sawdā) Zulaykha experiences.[120] For Salman, Zulaykha maintains her association with the initiation of desire.[121] Kamal says, since Zulaykha's female companions 'stole' furtive glimpses of Joseph's beauty, they cut the palms of their hands, because the hands of thieves are always cut off.[122]

In Timurid retellings of the story, Joseph, upon his marriage to Zulaykha, finds his bride's virginity to be intact, which suggests that she had not been desired by her first husband.[123] This echoes the depiction of Potiphar in Midrashic texts, where he is portrayed either as a eunuch or as himself harbouring sexual desire for Joseph.[124] Potiphar's desire for Joseph is a homoerotic element in the story that long pre-dates its incorporation within Persian lyric poetry. The homoerotic dynamic between Potiphar and Joseph is amplified when Joseph's youthful, male beauty (rather than Zulaykha's feminine allure) forms the focus of the male audience's erotic attention. The listener's gaze inhabits Zulaykha's as she observes Joseph with lustful eyes and eager hands. Although on the surface heteroerotic, the force that propels Zulaykha's desire for Joseph can thus be read homoerotically. This reading can be extended to other ostensibly heteroerotic encounters in romance and epic mathnavīs in which the physical beauty of male protagonists is celebrated, such as the depiction of Ramin's physical charms in Vis u Ramin.[125]

Merguerian and Najmabadi posit that female seduction is presented in the story of Joseph as a threat to two key male homosocial bonds: the bond between Joseph and God and the bond between Joseph and his (potentially lecherous) male master.[126] Other elements of the story (such as the laments of the merchants who retrieve Joseph from the pit) also lend themselves to homoerotic readings.

Joseph as the embodiment of perfect beauty

One of Hafiz's celebrated allusions to Joseph is found in his Shirazi Turk ghazal, which resonates with the courtly performance context[127] and whose varied renderings into English have themselves attracted scholarly attention.[128] In this poem, Hafiz stresses Joseph's matchless, irresistible beauty, the intensity of which grows continually; H3:5:

من از آن حسن روزافزون که یوسف داشت دانستم
که عشق از پردهٔ عصمت برون آرد زلیخا را

I knew that daily-increasing beauty that Joseph possessed
Would draw Zulaykha, through love, out from behind chastity's veil

'Ubayd uses the identical phrase, *husn-i rūz-afzūn* ('daily increasing beauty') when describing his beloved; U79:6:

حسن روزافزون تو در دلبری   هر زمان نیکی دگرسان می کند

Your daily-increasing beauty in heart-stealing
At every moment performs another beauty

If Hafiz's poem was composed after 'Ubayd's, then the younger poet's use of the phrase *husn-i rūz-afzūn* can be read not only as a verbatim quotation, but also as an interpretative gloss on his colleague's poem: since 'Ubayd's beloved has daily increasing beauty, it follows that he be the Joseph of the Age. 'Ubayd was older than Hafiz and established at the Injuid court before him, so the suggestion that Hafiz imitated 'Ubayd in this poem is plausible.

In the final line of another *ghazal* with panegyric overtones, Hafiz uses the phrase *husn-i rūz-afzūn* when addressing his beloved with an elite title normally reserved for kings: *sāhib-qirān* ('Lord of the Happy Conjunction') promising to offer a 'prayer for his good-fortune'.[129] 'Attar Shirazi uses the words *husn, afzūn* and *gum-gasht* when speaking of the infidelity of the Josephine friend.[130]

As Joseph firmly resists Zulaykha's lustful advances, so his desirability grows. Zulaykha becomes increasingly sexually aroused until she can resist the temptation no longer and moves to initiate physical intimacy. The emphasis on Zulaykha's chastity in H3 is perhaps an allusion to her virginity being intact even after her marriage to al-'Aziz. The *parda-yi 'ismat* ('curtain of chastity') evokes the *parda-yi bikārat* ('curtain of virginity'), which is a euphemism for the hymen. Hafiz does not speak as Zulaykha but draws a comparison between his experience of desire and hers: he claims intimate familiarity with a beauty comparable to Joseph's ravishing good looks which caused Zulaykha to transgress the boundaries of morality. Here, Zulaykha is absolved from sin: it is Joseph's allure that causes her to behave immorally. Zulaykha is often depicted as helpless in the face of Joseph's irresistibility.[131]

As already discussed, H3 may have been composed in praise of a Muzaffarid prince.[132] Praise of the patron's physical beauty is a standard feature of the Persian panegyric,[133] his physical appearance being compared favourably to that of Joseph.[134] Praise for the patron's beauty is often mediated through the arousing description of a youth in the *taghazzul*, foundational examples of which can be found in the *dīvan* of Farrukhi (d. 1037).[135] 'Ubayd has a number of *qasīda*s that open with amorous preludes, including one for Shaykh Uvays which begins with a description of a capricious, beloved Turk.[136] Laudatory descriptions of the ruler's physical charms are also found in contemporary works of *adab* and court histories; just one example of the ways in which prose texts are in step with trends current in contemporaneous lyric poetry.[137]

Meisami argues that Hafiz employs allusions to Joseph and his brothers to comment on the political situation in southern Iran at the time of writing, asserting that his courtly audience 'would have demanded not only mastery of the *ghazal*'s form and its conventions, but relevance to contemporary circumstances'.[138] Dadbeh argues a king or a vizier can be likened to Joseph to highlight the hardship he endured before coming to power.[139] Interestingly, Shah Shuja' employs Josephine *talmīh* in a self-referential manner in his own poetry. In an Arabic poem which contains subtle Qur'anic allusions,[140] the king says he was sold by his brothers in Istakhr because he was more beautiful than them. In a Persian *ghazal*, Shah Shuja' consoles himself thus:[141]

بوی قمیص از گذر کاروان مجوی   در چاه وحشت است تو را یوسف ای عزیز

O 'Aziz, your Joseph is captive in the pit of terror;
Do not seek out the scent of his shirt as the caravan passes!

Shah Shuja''s use of Joseph *talmīh* in his own poetry adds complexity and depth to the local panegyric dimensions to such allusions found in the poetry of Muzaffarid court poets in particular. Hafiz asserts that his beloved's beauty is superior to that of Joseph (rather than merely comparable to it). It is his beloved, not the prophet himself, who is the true paragon of youthful male beauty; H23:2:

هزار یوسف مصری فتاده در چه ماست   ببین که سیب زنخدان تو چه می گوید

See what the apple of your chin dimple is saying:
'A thousand Egyptian Josephs have fallen into our pit.'

Here the apple stands for the beloved's plump chin. The indentation of the 'chin dimple' (*zanakhdān*) is an allusion to the pit into which Joseph was thrown by his jealous brothers.[142] To fall into the beloved's pit means to fall in love; Hafiz's sweetheart is so beautiful that 'a thousand Josephs' (i.e. a host of exceptional beauties) have themselves fallen for him.[143]

Jahan's beloved is her 'darling' (*'azīz*); her very own Joseph. Her heart resembles that of Zulaykha and it has fallen into her Joseph's pit.[144] Jahan employs the metaphor of the chin dimple as a trap for her love-struck heart; J654:6:

به سان یوسف مصری اسیر خواهد بود   عزیز من دل من در چهِ زنخدانت

O my darling, my heart in the pit of your chin dimple
Will be held captive, just like Joseph of Egypt!

Through her use of the word *'azīz*, Jahan alludes to Joseph's Qur'anic master. The title al-'Aziz means 'the mighty one', but in Persian, *'azīz* is commonly used as a term of endearment. The phrase *'azīz-i Misr*, although on one level an allusion to Joseph's master, is first and foremost an allusion to the prophet himself as the 'darling of Egypt'. Ultimately, Joseph achieves a superior rank in Egypt and, in a sense, he replaces al-'Aziz, both as a husband to Zulaykha and as a wielder of temporal power.[145] 'Imad casts himself as the lovesick Jacob when he laments the absence of his 'dear beloved' (*yār-i 'azīz*), an absence that transforms Kirman, which otherwise resembles a blossoming Egypt, into an abode of sorrows.[146] Khvaju uses *'azīz* in the sense of 'held dear', 'treasured', to boast of how his poetry is valued in Egypt just as was Joseph.[147] Hafiz combines the name of the prophet and his Egyptian master in the following manner; H473:8:

کز غمش عجب بینم حال پیر کنعانی   یوسف عزیزم رفت ای برادران رحمی

My dear Joseph has gone. O brothers, show some mercy!
For, in grieving for him, I see the sorry state of the old man of Canaan.

For Sa'di, the beauty of his Joseph-like beloved defies description;[148] for Jahan, this extraordinary beauty is a 'sign' – one that, on occasion, is manifested in the night-black locks of her beloved.[149] Jahan draws on the concept of a cyclical saviour figure when she says; J135:6:

چه چیز ارزد اگر ناید او به عهد درست   اگر به حسن بود یوسف زمانه کسی

If there were someone as beautiful as the Joseph of the Age
What use would it be if he were not to appear in the right era?

In most instances, the beauty of the contemporary beloved is rated above that of the historical Joseph; H475:1:

چون نیک بدیدم به حقیقت به از آنی   گفتند خلایق که تویی یوسف ثانی

People have said that you are the 'Second Joseph';
When I looked closely, in truth you are far better than that!

Hafiz's beloved outdoes the 'Second Joseph' (*Yūsuf-i thānī*), Joseph's 'return', his fourteenth-century Shirazi doppelgänger.[150] The phrase *Yūsuf-i thānī* could be translated as 'another Joseph', however, Hafiz is adamant that his beloved is not merely an archetypal reincarnation of Joseph;[151] for Haydar, his beloved is superior to the prophet himself.[152] In H475, Hafiz moves on to say the beloved's 'sugary smile' (*shikar-khanda*) makes him the 'king of beauties' (*khusraw-i khūbān*) and, concomitantly, the 'Shirin of the Age'.[153] The beloved embodies the best of both male (Joseph and Khusraw) and female (Shirin and Shikar) and, in this sense, transcends gendered categories.

Zulaykha's desire for Joseph

On the surface, Zulaykha represents female-driven sexual desire, an impulse celebrated infrequently in Persian lyric poetry. That Zulaykha seeks to initiate a sexual liaison with her love object recalls Vis's desire for Ramin and Shirin's for Khusraw, examples of erotic initiation or openness to intimacy on the part of the female protagonist, albeit of a less-aggressive nature.[154]

As already discussed, though ostensibly a demonstration of heteroerotic desire, Zulaykha's lust can be read as homoerotic when male listeners join her in her yearning for Joseph.[155] Najmabadi explores the socio-literary implications of Zulaykha's channelling of the male homoerotic gaze:

> When the location of desiring subject in the text is shifted onto the woman, male homoeroticism can masquerade as the desire of a woman for a young man. That is, the occurrence of heterosexual desire in the text could be generative of homoeroticism for (presumed male) writers, readers and listeners of these stories.[156]

Zulaykha, an older woman, finds the young Joseph attractive for the same reasons older men find themselves aroused by him. The beloved's allure does not acknowledge gender boundaries and his beauty can arouse (and through that arousal, disturb) both men and women alike.[157]

'Ubayd alludes to Zulaykha in a single poem, in which he portrays her as a tragic, Jacob-like figure; U132:2:

گو نسیم سحری بار دگر رنجه شود   به زلیخا برد از یوسف کنعان خبری

Suppose the morning breeze will once again turn sorrowful
And deliver to Zulaykha news from the Joseph of Canaan.

Although Zulaykha is remembered as the one responsible for Joseph's imprisonment,[158] her suffering when separated from him is also a motif in the Persian *ghazal*.

Jahan alludes to Zulaykha more frequently than do her male contemporaries, presumably because of her gender. Here, she draws on versions of the story in which Zulaykha becomes the object of Joseph's desire; J917:6:

تا رخ زیبای تو گشت زلیخای حسن   یوسف جان در پیت جامه دران کرده ام

When your exquisite face became the Zulaykha of beauty
I caused the Joseph of my soul to tear his robes in pursuit of you.

Here, in a reversal of the Qur'anic narrative, it is Joseph, not Zulaykha, who tears his own shirt, in exasperation over his frustrated desire. In the Qur'an, Zulaykha tears Joseph's shirt from behind as he snubs her advances and attempts to retreat from her salon. Through this image, Jahan makes Zulaykha the object of Joseph's desire, transforming the tearing of Joseph's shirt into a marker of the pain of his longing for her, rather than proof of her wilful lust. The roles of lover and beloved, desirer and desired, have been disrupted. This is a significant shift in the erotic dynamic of the story, one which allows Jahan to identify her voice with that of the male protagonist in pursuit of his female beloved. This shift in the direction of the desire from that depicted in the standard narrative complicates homoerotic readings of the story and demonstrates the malleability of this narrative and others like it. Numerous versions of tales such as that of Joseph and Zulaykha exist both within and outside of the *ghazal*; each subtly remade by every successive poet.

Khvaju tells us not to engage in 'denial' (*inkār*) of the veracity of Zulaykha's longing for Joseph;[159] rather we should ask Jacob's heart about the pain of separation and should listen to the description of Joseph's beauty from the lips of Zulaykha.[160] In a more mystical vein, Khvaju claims that the light that emanated from Joseph's sun-like countenance is that which first manifested within Zulaykha.[161] A sufficiently positive image of Zulaykha is presented in lyric poetry that Khvaju and Jalal deem it appropriate to draw favourable comparisons between Zulaykha and Dilshad Khatun in their panegyrics.[162]

In addition to identifying with Zulaykha, Jahan compares her poetic persona to the wolf falsely accused of having mauled Joseph.[163] The treacherous brothers lie to their father about Joseph's fate and present him with a shirt upon which they have splattered 'false blood';[164] J912:9:

از دهان یوسفم حاصل نشد کامی چو گرگ   لب به خون آلوده و خالی دهان افتاده ام

From the mouth of my Joseph I have received no satisfaction
Like the wolf, my lips are tainted with blood, but my mouth is empty.

Here Jahan likens herself both to the wolf denied the satisfaction of devouring Joseph and to Zulaykha, who saw no 'sexual satisfaction' (*kām*) from the perfectly chaste prophet. The imagery here echoes an earlier use of similar *talmīh* by Sa'di:[165]

در کوی تو معروفم و از روی تو محروم   گرگ دهن آلودهٔ یوسف ندریده

I am notorious in your lane, and deprived of your face
I am the wolf whose mouth is tainted with the untorn Joseph.

Note the sexual connotations of *na-darīda* ('untorn'; an alternative reading of which would be *na-durīda* ['un-reaped']) and *ma'rūf* ('notorious'). A similarly sympathetic tone is struck by Sa'di who absolves Zulaykha of her adulterous desires when extolling the irresistible charms of a male youth whose beauty should be veiled:[166]

گرش ببینی و دست از ترنج بشناسی   روا بود که ملامت کنی زلیخا را

If you see him and are able to discern hand from citrus,
Only then can you heap blame upon Zulaykha!

A minority of male poets (including Rumi) identify themselves with Zulaykha and/or the women she invites into her home to gaze upon Joseph.[167] The eleventh-century poet Qatran of Tabriz (d. 1072) equates his desired transformation with that of both Zulaykha and Jacob in this paralleled manner:[168]

چون زلیخا باز برنا گردم از دیدار دوست   باز چون یعقوب بینا گردم از پیوند یار

Like Zulaykha, I will be rejuvenated through seeing the beloved;
Like Jacob, I will regain my sight through union with the friend!

In a *ghazal* in which *'azīz* forms the *radīf*, Khvaju identifies himself directly with Zulaykha and her female companions when he states there is no 'fault' (*'ayb*) if he, like the band of ogling Egyptian dames, cannot discern citrus from hand, for there is none as dear to him in all 'Egypt' (here meaning Kirman or Shiraz) as Joseph of Canaan (i.e. his patron).[169] Sa'di argues that full disclosure of Joseph's beauty would redeem Zulaykha:[170]

تا عذر زلیخا بنهد منکر عشاق   یوسف صفت از چهره برانداز نقابی

In order for the denier of the lovers to forgive Zulaykha
Cast off the veil from your face, just like Joseph!

Hamgar aligns his suffering with that of Potiphar's wife when he says that a Joseph has occupied the throne of the Egypt of his heart who has no understanding of his 'Zulaykha-like pain' (*dard-i Zulaykhā'ī*).[171]

The story of Joseph: A story of hope

Allusions to Joseph have been employed by Persian poets from at least the eleventh century to inspire hope in their addressees by providing reassurance that their present situation will ultimately change for the better.[172] The best-known example of an allusion to Joseph employed in this manner is in the *matla'* of a celebrated *ghazal* by Hafiz;[173] H255:1:

كلبهٔ احزان شود روزی گلستان غم مخور   یوسف گمگشته باز آید به کنعان غم مخور

> The long-lost Joseph will return one day to Canaan; grieve not!
> The hut of sorrows will one day become a rose garden; grieve not!

The reunion of Jacob and his 'long-lost Joseph' (*Yūsuf-i gumgashta*)[174] after a prolonged, anguish-laden separation, is an emotive, hopeful image also found in other *ghazal*s.[175] The second hemistich of H255:1 is a *tazmīn* from the opening line of a *ghazal* attributed to Shams al-Din Muhammad Juvayni (d. 1284), the *sāhib-dīvān* (chief of the secretariat) and an influential Ilkhanid statesman who was responsible for the civil administration of Mongol Iran (a post he held from 1263 for approximately two decades).[176] Shams al-Din Juvayni, the younger brother of the historian 'Ata-Malik Juvayni, lavished a good portion of his sizeable annual salary on those who crafted effective written propaganda in his praise.[177] Shams al-Din is known to have provided patronage to Sa'di, Hamgar and Humam Tabrizi (d. 1314).[178] The *ghazal* attributed to Juvayni opens thus:[179]

بشکفد گلهای وصل از خار هجران غم مخور   کلبهٔ احزان شود روزی گلستان غم مخور

> The hut of sorrows will one day become a rose garden; grieve not!
> The roses of reunion will bloom from the thorn of separation; grieve not!

Juvayni's poem may have been composed in response to a six-line *ghazal* attributed (perhaps falsely) to the mystic Baba Kuhi who died in Shiraz in 1037.[180] The tone of Hafiz's poem echoes that of Juvayni in its optimism: however unpromising and negative the current situation may seem, the ultimate outcome will be a positive one. The phrase *ghamm makhur* ('grieve not'), repeated as the *radīf* at the end of each line, infuses the poem with a sense of reassuring calm (in contrast to poems in which the lost Joseph will never again be found in this world).[181]

Reading comparatively, we note that Jahan penned two *ghazal*s with the exact same rhyme, refrain and metre as H255. The poems of Hafiz and Jahan that share these technical and semantic similarities can be classed either as instances of *javāb* or *nazīra* ('parallel poem'). The intertextual dynamics of poetic imitation, the penning of poetic responses and the composition of parallel poems within and across periods are complex negotiations in terms of literary hierarchy.[182] A half-line that might be *tazmīn* from H255 is found in one of the *ghazal*s by Jahan; J769:3:

یوسف گمگشته باز آید به کنعان غم مخور   گرچه چون یعقوب گشتی ساکن بیت الحزن

Even though, like Jacob, you have come to inhabit the abode of sorrows,
The long-lost Joseph will return one day to Canaan; grieve not!

Given the greater fame of Hafiz, this might seem to be a clear-cut case of *javāb* by Jahan; her response being emboldened via the incorporation of Hafiz's half-line in her own poem. However, it is by no means clear (nor will it ever be possible to verify with certainty) who is quoting whom in this intertextual play. It is impossible to know which poet first penned a poem in imitation of Juvayni's and whether the hemistich, *Yūsuf-i gumgashta bāz āyad bi-Kan'ān ghamm makhur*, was originally penned by Hafiz or Jahan. But if Jahan did borrow from Hafiz, why would she place the verbatim quotation in as insignificant a section of her poem as the second hemistich of the third line? It seems more likely that Hafiz lifted this half-line from Jahan's *ghazal* and combined it with the opening hemistich from Juvayni's to form the *matla'* for his own. By combining two borrowed half-lines from one long-dead poet and one less well-known contemporary, perhaps Hafiz intended, by imitating them both, to demonstrate both his knowledge of and superiority over earlier and current poetry.

From reading their *dīvāns* closely, it seems clear that Jahan and Hafiz were aware of one another's poetic output. A number of their *ghazals* overlap in form (*qāfiya* and *radīf*) as well as semantically and in terms of content.[183] Perhaps Jahan cited Hafiz, because he was a professional, remunerated, commercial poet whose *ghazals* enjoyed wide dissemination in and beyond Shiraz during his lifetime, whereas she was an amateur poet who did not produce poetry for the court on a commercial basis with the same degree of regularity.

What is the relationship between Jahan's two poems and the *ghazal* by Juvayni? The rhyme and refrain of Jahan's poems appear to have been inspired by Juvayni's poem, making J768, J769 and H255 instances of *istiqbāl*, though Jahan may have imitated Juvayni indirectly by responding to Hafiz. Most interestingly, Salman also composed a *ghazal* with the same formal features.[184] It is also noteworthy that Jahan is the only one of the four poets to have more than one poem with this rhyme scheme and refrain, although this could signal that Jahan intended – but did not complete – an amalgamation of her two lyrics. Dialogue across these five *ghazals* is facilitated through the use of a shared lexicon of phrases and words, some of which (with some minor tweaks) carry across as many as four of the poems:

Table 1. Lexical overlap between the *ghazals* of Juvayni, Hafiz, Jahan, and Salman

Juvayni	Hafiz	Jahan (J768)	Jahan (J769)	Salman
gulistān (l.1)	gulistān (l.1)			gulistān (l.3)
khār-i hijrān (l.1)	khār-i mughilān (l.7)	khār-i hijrān (l.6, l.7)	khār-i mughilān (l.5)	
gardūn (l.2)	gardūn (l.4)			
sar-gashta'i (l.2)		sar-gashta (l.2)	sar-gashta'i (l.1)	sar-gashta (l.2)
rūzi bi-pāyān (l.2)	pāyān (l.8)			rāzi bi pāyān (l.1)
hāl-gardān (l.3)	hāl-gardān (l.9)			
darmān (l.4)		darmān (l.1)	darmān (l.6)	
	ay dil (l.2)	ay dil (l.1, l.2)	ay dil (l.1)	ay dil (l.2)
	bi sāmān (l.2)	sāmān (l.2)	bi sāmān (l.9)	
	dawrān (l.4)	dawrān (l.4)	dawrān (l.1)	
	vāqif na'i (l.5)	na'i vāqif (l.4)		
	pinhān (l.5)	pinhān (l.8)		pinhān (l.7)
	Ka'ba (l.7)		Ka'ba (l.5)	
	jānān (l.9)	jānān (l.1)		

There is a good deal of overlap between the *ghazal* of Juvayni and H255, between Juvayni's J768, between Juvayni's and Salman's and between H255 and both poems by Jahan. In addition to the verbatim quotation of a single hemistich from Juvayni's poem in that of Hafiz and the shared hemistich in H255 and J769 (the directionality of the *tazmīn* in these twin poems being undiscernible) and the evidence of imitation across the five *ghazals* evidenced in shared items of vocabulary and phraseology, there is also a great deal that semantically binds this group of poems and even others beyond.[185]

Detailed analysis of the relationship between these poems that span more than a century (circa 1260–1390) proves the existence of a community of poets that existed across, as well as within, specific periods (Ilkhanid to Injuid/Muzaffarid/Jalayirid) and two locales (Shiraz and Baghdad). These poems are evidence of an intertextual literary system in fourteenth-century Iran and Iraq along the lines mapped out by Lowin in a different context, in which, as a matter of course, each new text 'receives the imprint of those texts that preceded it'.[186] Erudite audiences would have been able to both recognize and appreciate the intertextual features of contemporary poems and would have detected engagements with the literary past in these new compositions.[187] The *nazīra*s of Juvayni's poem show us how Persian poets in the thirteenth and fourteenth centuries could be colleagues in person and in pen; Jahan – who was as bold an imitator and responder as any of her male counterparts – was an equal player in this poetic matrix.

In addition to the semantic and formal similarities between the five poems in this group, there is also overlap in terms of prophetological *talmīh*. Juvayni's allusion to Jacob's abode of sorrows transforming into a 'rose garden' can be read as an oblique reference to Abraham's trial in Nimrod's fire. In J769, Jahan alludes to Jacob and Joseph and in J768, to Alexander and Khizr (interestingly, there is no coherence across her two poems in terms of *talmīh*). Salman neither alludes to Joseph nor to Jacob, but in line three of his poem we encounter the image of fire becoming a rose garden which, as noted above, carries strong Abrahamic resonances.

A story of triumph

Royal sibling rivalry lends itself to Joseph-centred *talmīh* and Hafiz uses the story of Joseph's triumph over his treacherous brothers to celebrate the ousting of Shah Yahya (then a puppet of Timur) in 1391 from Shiraz by his brother, Shah Mansur;[188] H242:5:

عزیز مصر به رغم برادران غیور   ز قعر چاه برآمد به اوج ماه رسید

The darling of Egypt, despite his jealous brothers,
Rose up from the depths of the pit and reached the moon's zenith.

Despite having been betrayed by his brothers and sold into slavery, Joseph, *'azīz-i Misr* ('darling of Egypt') triumphed over them, ultimately gaining a station far above theirs. Other allusions by Hafiz to Joseph which invite political interpretation include one in a poem for the Muzaffarid vizier, Khvaja Jalal al-Din Turanshah, who, on release from incarceration, took up the coveted position of chief minister once more;[189] H9:9:

ماه کنعانی من مسند مصر آنِ تو شد   وقت آن است که بدرود کنی زندان را

My Canaanite moon, the Throne of Egypt is now yours;
It is now time for you to bid farewell to the prison!

The appellation 'Throne of Egypt' (*masnad-i Misr*) is akin to mythologically charged epithets used to allude to Shiraz, Fars and/or the ancient ruined sites of Pasargadae and Persepolis (as discussed in Chapter 4). If we read particular instances of Josephine *talmīh* as allusions to the contemporary ruler, then interpreting 'Throne of Egypt' as Shiraz fits. An allusion to Joseph from another poem by Hafiz can be interpreted as an admonition to a young prince who has succeeded his father on the throne, but is not showing sufficient favour to the long-established court poet; H440:4:

پدر را باز پرس آخر کجا شد مهر فرزندی   الا ای یوسف مصری که کردت سلطنت مغرور

O Egyptian Joseph whom kingship has made proud!
Ask the father once more: Where is the kindness of the son?

Jahan casts herself as Jacob in the guise of a humble dervish (i.e. a sincere ascetic) who, despite the attacks of her jealous rivals, has endured great suffering and ultimately been rewarded for it through reunion with her beloved. The poet might be referring to her survival of the puritanical rule of Mubariz al-Din and her newfound favour within the court circle of Shah Shuja'; J716:3:

یوسف مصر نکویی سوی کنعان برسید   رنج درویش علی رغم رقیبان بگذشت

The suffering of the dervish, despite the rivals, passed;
The Joseph of the Egypt of beauty finally reached Canaan.

Here, we are encouraged to equate Canaan with Shiraz.

Joseph's story as a didactic tool

Allusions to the story of Joseph are also used to instruct listeners in how best to conduct themselves with the beloved, be he earthly or Divine. Poets allude to the traders who sold Joseph for a 'paltry sum' (the Qur'anic phrase is *thaman bakhs*);[190] H211:7:

آنکه یوسف به زر ناسره بفروخته بود   یار مفروش به دنیا که بسی سود نکرد

Do not barter the beloved for this mortal world
He who sold Joseph for impure gold made a measly profit.

'Trading' the beloved by betraying him for anticipated increased material gain is as heinous as the crimes committed against the prophet Joseph.[191] Here, Hafiz's ethical message is that material wealth will not bring lasting benefit, a statement that could be seen to contradict his position as a successful commercial poet. An allusion to Joseph being sold into slavery provides a source of 'monition' or 'cautionary instruction' ('*ibrat*). Elsewhere, Hafiz alludes to the paltry sum paid for the captive Joseph and appears to speak in favour of the virtues of an ascetic lifestyle; H477:3:

فروخت یوسف مصری به کمترین ثمنی   هر که کنج قناعت به گنج دنیا داد

Whosoever trades the corner of contentment for worldly treasure,
Has sold the Joseph of Egypt for the most trifling of sums.

Just as Hafiz uses such instances of *talmīh* to bolster didactic injunctions to entreat his listeners to strive for integrity in love relationships of all kinds, so the poet also speaks with the voice of Jacob about the nature of true love itself; H88:1:

فراق یار نه آن می کند که بتوان گفت   شنیده ام سخنی خوش که پیر کنعان گفت

I heard something fitting that the old man of Canaan once said:
'Separation from the beloved does something that cannot be told.'

Hafiz adds weight to his words by claiming to have heard them uttered first hand by Jacob. By speaking on behalf of the prophet in this manner, Hafiz demands added respect from his listeners for his amatory pronouncements.

The poet-lover as Joseph

In a number of her allusions to Joseph, Jahan (not unlike Salman[192] and Hamgar)[193] identifies directly with the prophet. Addressing her beloved, she says; J739:8:

گشتیم بر تو در جهان خوار   بودیم عزیز مصر دلها

I once was the darling of the Egypt of hearts
Before you, I have become abased in this world.

Here Jahan styles herself as '*azīz-i Misr-i dil-hā* ('the darling of the Egypt of hearts'). By so doing, she claims that, just like her legendary model, she was once young, beautiful and universally desired. Jahan enacts the role of Joseph as the object of Zulaykha's desire more directly than do Hafiz and 'Ubayd who do not embody Joseph, but merely observe him. In the second hemistich of J739:8, Jahan puns on her *takhallus* and so lends the line an autobiographical tone. Elsewhere, Jahan casts herself as Joseph when addressing her patron, the embodiment of al-'Aziz; J955:6:

بودم عزیز دلها جانا مدار خوارم   گرچه عزیز مصری بنگر به حال یوسف

Even though you are the Mighty One of Egypt, look at the state of Joseph –
I was once the darling of the hearts, O beloved, do not abase me!

Here the word *'azīz* is used simultaneously to refer to both Joseph and Joseph's master. The line reads as a plea to the patron for favour. Elsewhere, Jahan alludes to Joseph's master in a third way; J1079:2:

چون یوسفی به درهم قلبی فروختیم   از جور روزگار و عزیزان بی وفا

By fate's cruelty and a host of unfaithful beloveds (*'azīzān-i bī-vafā*)
You have sold me like a Joseph for counterfeit coins

As discussed earlier, in some poems, Jahan calls Joseph the *bashīr*. By calling herself *tifl-i bashīr-i ghamm* ('child of the harbinger of grief'), Jahan suggests she is Joseph's spiritual heir and the inheritor of his trials; J1166:5:

خداوندا به فضل خود نظر بر بی گناهی کن   منم طفل بشیر غم ز کنعان گشته سرگردان

I am the child of the harbinger of grief, wandering aimlessly from Canaan
O God, out of your bounty look upon this innocent one!

Given what we know of the bloody struggle between the Injuids and Muzaffarids for control of Fars, the eventual execution in 1357 of her uncle and the reputedly intolerant reign of Mubariz al-Din, Jahan's identification with Joseph in his pre-triumphal period is apt.

Moses

Hafiz strikes a doctrinal tone when he says that the fire of Moses has 'blossomed' (*namūd gul*) so that the audience might learn the lesson of 'divine unity' (*tawhīd*) from the burning bush.[194] Hafiz also alludes to Moses' encounter with God on Mount Sinai; H19:2:

آتش طور کجا موعد دیدار کجاست   شب تار است و ره وادی ایمن در پیش

The night is dark, and the path to the blessed valley lies ahead;
Where is the Sinai fire? Where is the appointed meeting spot?

The prophet is not mentioned explicitly here, but the reference to the 'fire of Sinai' (*ātash-i Tūr*) and the 'appointed meeting spot' (*maw'id-i dīdār*) make it clear these are Mosaic allusions. Hafiz identifies his own plight as a desperate lover with that of the hopeful Moses who, the Qur'an tells us,[195] sought face-to-face communion with God (we find similar allusions in Khvaju's *ghazals*, where the poet's identification with Moses is even more direct).[196] Hafiz calls out in the manner of Moses, searching for the heat of the fire of his divine beloved. The 'blessed valley' (the *vādī-yi ayman*, a Persian poetic reworking of the Qur'anic *min shāti'i l-wādī l-ayman* ['towards the right bank of the valley'])[197] is where Moses beseeched God and received the response, *lan tarā-nī* ('you shall not see Me').[198] Perhaps it would have been considered too blasphemous in Hafiz's day to make the same analogy with a similarly pivotal event in the life of Muhammad, such as the *Mi'rāj* (his night journey and ascent to heaven).

In another poem, Hafiz stresses his affinity with Moses through the insertion of *hamchu* ('just like'); H373:4:

همچو موسی آرنی گوی به میقات بریم   با تو آن عهد که در وادی ایمن بستیم

Let us take that covenant I made with you in the *Vādī-yi ayman*
To the meeting spot and, just like Moses, call out: 'Show yourself to me!'

Hafiz's allusions to Moses invoke the Qur'anic narrative but the contemporary Jewish poet, Shahin, in his *Musanama* (completed 1327) turns Moses into an epic hero modelled after Firdawsi's *Shahnama*.[199] Some medieval Muslims conflated Moses with figures from the legendary Iranian past: Tusi says some believe Kay-Khusraw is Moses and Afrasiab Pharaoh.[200]

Jesus

Allusions to Jesus focus on his miraculous ability to bring the dead to life.[201] Khvaju draws the analogy between Jesus's miracle-making and his own poetic mastery,[202] but almost all instances of Jesus *talmīh* in fourteenth-century Persian *ghazals* broadcast the belief in the resuscitating powers of the beloved's breath, kisses and saliva. Just as the stories in John's Gospel could be interpreted to argue that Jesus bestowed new physical as well as spiritual life on the dead, so the beloved's Jesus-like 'breath' (*dam, nafas*) demands interpretation on both a mystical and earthly level. It is the beloved's breath that revives the weary; H36:7:

عکس روحیست که بر عظم رمیم افتادست سایه قد تو بر قالبم ای عیسی دم

The shade of your stature on my form, O Jesus-breath beloved
Is the image of the spirit, which has fallen on decaying bones.

The phrase, *'azm-i ramīm* ('mouldering bones') is adapted from the Qur'an.[203] Elsewhere, Hafiz claims that if the beloved were to pass by his grave even a century after his death, his 'mouldering bones' would rise up dancing.[204] Hafiz's use of the word *rūh* ('spirit') in the line quoted above is a subtle nod to Jesus's Islamic epithet, *Rūhullāh*, the 'Spirit of God'. Hafiz – whose soul has burned in love – calls on his Jesus-beloved to revive him.[205] The qualities of Jesus's breath recount the 'anecdote' (*latīfa*) of the beloved's ruby lips.[206]

The reviving breeze can also take on Christ's qualities,[207] therefore it is able to bring the garden back to life in springtime.[208] Hafiz also likens the messenger breeze to Jesus: it resuscitates the lover by bringing him the beloved's scent.[209] Hafiz contrasts the joyous atmosphere of the moment spent in the company of his Jesus-beloved with the cautionary tales of the destruction of heedless Arabian peoples who rejected the prophets Hud and Salih;[210] H219:5:

شراب نوش و رها کن حدیث عاد و ثمود ز دست شاهد نازک عذار عیسی دم

From the hand of the delicate, Jesus-breath beauty,
Drink wine, and leave tales of 'Ad and Thamud!

It is possible that, in the fourteenth century, Shiraz's wine taverns were in the hands of Christians; allusions to Jesus that are combined with depictions of an eroticized non-Muslim *sāqī* speak to this contemporary reality. Jesus and his followers are associated with wine in the Persian *ghazal*,[211] reflecting the association of Christians with the production, sale and serving of wine established in the earliest New Persian poetry and even earlier Arabic lyric poetry.[212] The equation of the earthly beloved with Jesus (depicted in both the Islamic and Christian traditions as a young man) and the emphasis on the beloved's power to impart new life by mouth, lends an erotic undertone to these allusions. Jahan, too, likens her beloved's life-giving breath to that of Jesus; J1236:1:

وز دم عیسویت جان جهان زنده شده ای سلاطین جهان پیش رخت بنده شده

O you, before whose face the kings of the world (*jahān*) have become servants!
And from whose Jesus-like breath the soul of Jahan has been revived!

Note the pun on the poet's pen name. To Jahan, her beloved is the 'Messiah of the Age' (*Masīhā-yi zamān*) whom she entreats to breathe into her soul;[213]

the appellation 'Messiah of the Age' echoing mythologically charged royal epithets. The poets on occasion go so far as to claim superiority for the beloved's breath over that of Jesus;[214] H70:6:

زان که در روح فزایی چو لبت ماهر نیست   از روانبخشی عیسی نزنم دم هرگز

I will never speak of the life-giving power of Jesus
For he is not as skilled in reviving the soul as are your lips

Here the beloved is ranked above Jesus, something that would not be possible if the comparison were made to Muhammad. The miracles performed by Jesus were perhaps seen to be within the reach of ordinary mortals; with divine assistance, men could perform similarly fabulous feats; H143:9:

دیگران هم بکنند آنچه مسیحا می کرد   فیض روح القدس ار باز مدد فرماید

If the bounty of the Holy Spirit were to assist once more
Others might do that which Jesus Christ did.

Elsewhere, Hafiz says God sent to him a beloved with Jesus's breath, a saviour to bear the 'burden of grief' (*bār-i ghamm*) which had caused his mind to grow weary.[215]

In a departure from the magnanimous example of Jesus, the beloved, despite being in possession of life-sustaining breath, does not always choose to impart new life to his weary lover. This beloved is a cruel reworking of the compassionate Jesus, one who withholds favour and thereby feeds the lover's complaint; H57:6:

کشت ما را و دم عیسی مریم با اوست   با که این نکته توان گفت که آن سنگین دل

To whom can I explain that that stone-hearted one killed me
Even though he possesses the breath of Jesus, son of Mary?

There is a paradoxical contrast between the beloved's ability to give life and his cruel and murderous tendencies (which prevent him from acting benevolently). This is the dichotomy of passionate love as portrayed in the Persian *ghazal*; H204:2:

معجز عیسوی ات در لب شکرخا بود   یاد باد آنکه چو چشمت به عتابم می کشت

May it be remembered that as your eyes slew me with reproof,
Your sugar-crunching lips possessed the miracle of Jesus.

Some allusions to Jesus in the *ghazal*s of Hafiz have a more overtly mystical tone. Hafiz argues that the 'physician of love' (*tabīb-i 'ishq*; God, the Prophet or the spiritual elder) cannot 'cure' the seeker unless they provide evidence of having endured true torment in the path of love; H187:4:

طبیب عشق مسیحادم است و مشفق لیک   چو درد در تو نبیند که را دوا کند

The physician of love is endowed with Jesus's breath, and is merciful, but
As long as he sees no pain in you, whom can he cure?

The idea of lovesickness and the beloved as a physician who provides the cure is a well-established trope in Arabic and Persian poetry. 'Ubayd says of his beloved; U68:2:

گویبا دارد از انفاس مسیحا بهره ای   کز دم او دردمندان را دوایی می رسد

They say that he has a portion of the breath of Christ
From whose breath those in pain receive a remedy.

Iranian prophets

There are very few allusions to pre-Islamic Iranian religious figures in the *ghazal*s of this period. In a panegyric *ghazal* in which a range of allusions to Islamic-Biblical and Iranian prophetological persons is blended seamlessly, Hafiz points to Zoroaster. In this poem, written in praise of Shaykh Abu Ishaq's long-serving and influential vizier 'Imad al-Din Mahmud,[216] Hafiz lauds his patron in a kingly manner, tacitly suggesting that the true power lies with him, not the monarch. 'Imad al-Din Mahmud is the newly bloomed rose – a metaphor normally reserved for young princes or new sovereigns. Hafiz is the ever-devoted nightingale; H219:7–9:

سحر که مرغ در آید به نغمۀ داود   چو گل سوار شود بر هوا سلیمان وار
کنون که لاله برافروخت آتش نمرود   به باغ تازه کن آیین دین زردشتی
وزیر ملک سلیمان عمادِ دین محمود   بخواه جام صبوحی و به یاد آصف عهد

When the rose mounts the breeze, in Solomonic style,
And when at dawn the bird appears singing the song of David
Renew the rites of the Zoroastrian religion in the garden
Now that the tulip has kindled the fire of Nimrod!
Ask for the morning draft, in memory of the Asaf of the age,
The vizier of the Realm of Solomon, 'Imad-i Din Mahmud

Here, the garden is depicted in its full, early-spring glory. The poem ends with a call for wine to be brought to toast the vizier who, presumably, rewarded Hafiz for the poem. In this example of extended, polysemic, multi-voice *talmīh*,[217] the poet fuses allusions to Solomon,[218] David, Nimrod, Abraham and also Zoroaster, via *ā'īn-i dīn-i Zardushtī* ('rites of the Zoroastrian religion'); a euphemism for wine-drinking.[219] As noted in Chapter 2, Zoroastrians are often associated with the production and serving of wine in Persian poetry. Hafiz, in his *Saqinama*, demands he be given that 'glittering fire' (*ātash-i tābnāk*; a euphemism for wine) that Zoroaster seeks in the earth,[220] and Khvaju makes an oblique reference to the '*qibla* of Zoroaster', which may also carry bacchanalian connotations.[221] In H219, Hafiz illustrates well the variety of sources, traditions and histories that he draws upon, combines and reworks through *talmīh* in his *ghazals*. Given that this poem contains praise for 'Imad al-Din Mahmud, it must have been composed before the Muzaffarid conquest of Shiraz in 1353.

Most medieval Iranian Muslims would not have considered Zoroaster a prophet in the Islamic sense, although many may have held him in high regard, given that Zoroastrians were generally included within the category of 'protected people'.[222] It would be a mistake, however, to read this allusion to Zoroaster as a promotion of pre-Islamic Iranian religion. In H219, Hafiz conflates Zoroaster with Abraham, combining *ā'īn-i dīn-i Zardushtī* with an allusion to the miraculous transformation of Nimrod's punitive fire into a lush rose garden. Such an amalgam of Zoroastrian and Jewish legends does not jar. Given the antiquity of the Jewish communities of Iran and the sacred associations of Iran found in Jewish text and practice, many of the biblical prophets' stories have elements that bind them closer to Iran than one might first think. There are a number of sacred Jewish sites in Iran (chiefly the tombs of Esther and Mordechai at Hamadan, that of Daniel in Shush and the shrine of Serah Bat Asher [a granddaughter of Jacob] to the south of Isfahan).[223] As Soroudi has noted, 'the absence of [historical] evidence did not diminish the people's belief in the sanctity of these places'.[224]

In addition to the oblique allusion to Zoroaster in H291, there are a handful of allusions in the *ghazals* of this period to Mani, the revolutionary religious figure of the third century CE and founder of what became Manichaeism. As far back as the early Ghaznavid period, Mani is lauded in Persian poetry as a master painter.[225] Jahan employs allusions to Mani and his artistic skill to stress the inimitable beauty of her beloved; J630:6:

مانی ار صورت روی تو ببیند در خواب   به جهان دعوی صورت گری چین نکند

If Mani were to see the image of your face in a dream,
To Jahan he would not claim to be the best painter in China.

In characteristically self-conceited, boastful style, Hafiz employs an allusion to Mani to laud the artistic mastery of his own pen. The inclusion in the line quoted below of the word *nuskha* (a manuscript copy or a single leaf of poetry) strengthens the association between Hafiz's bewitching pen and the master illustrator; H356:7:

اگر باور نمی داری رو از صورتگر چین پرس
که مانی نسخه می خواهد ز نوک کلک مشکینم

> If you do not believe me, go ask the painter of China
> For Mani wants a copy from the tip of my musk-scented pen.

Conclusions

This chapter has shown how prophetological allusions in the *ghazal*s of post-Mongol Shiraz deserve to be read topically and panegyrically, not merely tropologically. Such *talmīh* also works on a complementary moral or didactic level: allusions to some of the most significant figures of the Islamic tradition (in particular Abraham, Noah, Jacob and Joseph) are employed by poets to illustrate the need for patience in testing times – whether those tests pertain to this earthly existence or to the spiritual path. Among the most common allusions are those to Noah's perseverance when faced with the deluge; Abraham's triumph over Nimrod's fire; Jacob's reunion with his long-lost son; and Joseph's triumph over his spiteful brothers. Allusions employed in a more mystical manner include those to Moses's attempt to see God face-to-face. Two undercurrents exist beneath the surface of many prophetic allusions studied here: (1) devotion to the earthly beloved (the Jesus-breathed wine-boy who rejuvenates the soul of the weary lover) and, via that erotic construct, (2) devotion to the patron. This is particularly true in Hafiz's *ghazal*s, many of which welcome (if they do not always require) a panegyric reading.

In this period, allusions to Jacob, Joseph and Zulaykha dominate. The case of this father, son and his would-be lover best illustrates the overlap between allusions to prophets and those to exemplary lovers. The popularity of Josephine allusions, given their connection to the political reality of post-Mongol Shiraz, strengthens the validity of a reading that recognizes the relationship between *ghazal* poetry and the socio-political landscape of Injuid/Muzaffarid Fars. Indeed, few of the allusions to prophets found in the poetry studied here demand a primarily mystical interpretation.

The absence of any obvious allusions to the Prophet Muhammad (coupled with Hafiz's attacks on the hypocritical leaders of Sufi orders and on the false piety of other religious leaders, such as the *faqīh* [jurisprudent] and the *vā'iz* [public preacher]) speaks to the poet's aversion to organized religion and its corrupt hierarchies. Although not discussed here, Hafiz's profuse references to the Magian 'convent' (*dayr*) or 'tavern' (*kharābāt, may-kada*) – the abode of the *pīr-i mughān* – suggest a religiosity beyond that of popular or Sufistic Islam. It would be a mistake, however, to interpret such references as a promotion of a return to pre-Islamic religion. The almost total lack of references to Zoroaster in the poetry, along with Hafiz's praise of Mani as a master painter rather than as a religious reformer, are two factors that seem to counter any such hypothesis.

By Way of Conclusion

The word 'conclusion' suggests the end of a text, the finishing point in a process. I see this study rather as a starting point: an opening, not a closing. What I hope to have done with this book, in some small way, is point to a potentially more productive way of reading Hafiz which is to contextualize his poetry not only socio-politically and historically, but also culturally and with keen attention to the intensely competitive literary culture that he was part of and did much to shape. Fourteenth-century Shiraz was at the heart of a post-Mongol poetic network that spanned a vast area, but as a city it was a relatively compact space that teemed with poets and other litterateurs all vying for the attention of patrons and would-be sponsors. The reality of this artistic environment manifests itself intertextually in the poetry and it is my firm belief that, to understand the poetry of canonical figures such as Hafiz, their poetry must be read alongside the poetry of their contemporaries who, for one reason or another, have not been as valorized in Persian literary history.

My primary focus has been on textual interactions between contemporaries, rather than an examination of the veneration and memorialization of past masters or nascent canon-formation, although these too are valid paths of inquiry. But this study proposes that one way for the field to move forward in the study of giants of Persian court poetry is not by looking at their reception or attempting to piece together the sources they used, but rather to examine how they worked alongside their peers within the institution of the specific court or series of courts to which they were attached.

In this study, Hafiz has been 're-contextualized' and by that I mean his poetry has been read in a manner that approximates the way in which it most likely would have been consumed and read by audiences in the fourteenth and early fifteenth centuries who engaged with him either aurally, via the intertextual performance space of the *majlis-i sharāb*, or by reading his *ghazal*s as collected in anthologies or manuscripts produced within a generation or so after his death in which Hafiz's poetry sits side-by-side with that of his contemporaries, often in the margins. It is my firm belief that Hafiz intended his poetry to be enjoyed within a multi-author framework and not in the isolation imposed by the structure of the single-author *dīvān*.

In addition to bringing Hafiz into meaningful and textually informed dialogue with his contemporaries, this study has rather unconventionally opted for one liminal poet and one marginalized poet as his core intertextual interlocutors, a move aimed, in part, at combatting the facile and unhelpful categorization of poets into first, second and third tier. This core corpus of poems has been complemented by the comparative reading of lyric poetry produced by a constellation of poets active across post-Mongol Iran and Iraq. As a result, this book is not a study of a small band of poets attached to one court, but rather an examination of Shiraz's poets which recognizes their privileged position within a broad network of poets to whom they responded and who competed with them in return. By locating the poetry in its socio-political, historical and cultural contexts, an attempt has been made to correct what can be seen as a bias in favour of the mystical interpretation of the Persian *ghazal* at the height of its development; this can, at times, be rather unhelpful in its dogmatism. That said, this book is fundamentally an exercise in disrupting the anachronistic polarities and rigid binaries (such as mystical/non-mystical; serious/humorous) that have hindered our understanding of Hafiz and his place in Persian literary history.

Perhaps the single most significant contribution made here to the study of premodern Persian poetry is my engagement with the *dīvān* of premodern Iran's most prolific woman poet, Jahan-Malik Khatun. I have brought Jahan for the first time into meaningful and in-depth intertextual dialogue, bar perhaps one or two exceptions, with the full spectrum of her male peers. When not treated as a poet to be consigned to a separate category, Jahan is no longer seen as a marginal figure, but as integral to the literary community she acted within. It is through reading the *ghazals* of Jahan – an elite woman writer who sought patronage but who was not a professional poet – that the literary texture of Hafiz's courtly environment truly comes to life. Holding up Jahan's *dīvān* in all its eloquence as Exhibit A, it becomes increasingly difficult to argue for Hafiz's exceptionality.

By examining other forms of lyric poetry (in particular the praise *qasīda*) and not restricting my discussion to the *ghazal*, I have paid homage to Hafiz and those around him who famously blended the amorous with the panegyric, themselves disrupting generic expectations. Through focusing the second part of my book on *talmīh*, I have been able to show how poets, who chiefly worked within the lyric, brought other genres to bear in their *ghazals*. This study has also demonstrated that, even at what is generally accepted as the pinnacle in the development and refinement of the Persian *ghazal*, a good measure of dynamism and diversity is discernible in the ways poets employ tone, structure, imagery and intent in their *ghazals*.

Notes

Introduction

1   See Dawlatshah Samarqandi 1901: 302; Nava'i 1944: 355; Jami 1988: 105; Jami 1991: 611; Khvand Mir 2001: 315–316.
2   Hafiz Shirazi 1999: 58.
3   See Browne 1920: 159.
4   See Spiegel 1997: 27.
5   See Schimmel 1986.
6   See Squires 2014: 425–426.
7   Culler 2015: 35.
8   Ibid: 15, 125–130.
9   Feeney 2016: 179.
10 Culler 2015: 3.
11 See Galvez 2012: 217.
12 Bashir 2011: 17.
13 See Barletta 2005: 2.
14 Spiegel 1990: 77–78.
15 Wickens 1971: 55.
16 See Davis 2012: xxxvii.
17 See Soucek 2003: 147.
18 de Bruijn 2003: 473. See also Avery and Heath-Stubbs 1952: 2.
19 See Ahur 1984: 517.
20 Wickens 1971: 56.
21 See Shafi'i-Kadkani 1989: 425.
22 de Bruijn 2009.
23 Shafi'i-Kadkani 1989: 421–422. See also Ahur 1984: lx.
24 See Moayyad 1988: 141; Meisami 2003: 386.
25 See Glassen 1991: 42.
26 Firdawsi 2008: 11.
27 Ibid: 25.
28 Ibid: 27.
29 Ibid: 25, 32–48.

30 See Glassen 1991: 46.

31 Ibid: 49.

32 Dawlatshah Samarqandi 1901: 302.

33 Ibid.

34 Jami 1988: 105.

35 Dawlatshah Samarqandi 1901: 303.

36 Nava'i 1944: 355.

37 Jami 1991: 612.

38 'Ubayd Zakani 1999: 201–344. See also Sprachman 1988: 226–234; Zipoli 1994; Sprachman 1995: 44–75; Halabi 1998: 9–14, 186–211; Brookshaw 2009; Meneghini 2010; Brookshaw 2012; Sprachman 2012: 71–127.

39 See Browne 1920: 230.

40 Hamdullah Mustawfi 1960: 805. See also Mahjub 1999.

41 'Ubayd Zakani 1999: 9, 11–14, 17–24, 27–30, 32–35, 37–42, 45–47, 49–52, 53–54.

42 See Sprachman 2012: 32–34.

43 See Dawlatshah Samarqandi 1901: 289–290; Browne 1920: 233; Ingenito 2018: 197–198, 202.

44 Dawlatshah Samarqandi 1901: 290–292; Wing 2016: 15, 136–142.

45 See 'Ubayd Zakani 1999: 10–11, 26–27, 30–32, 35–37, 59–60; Jackson 2008a: 415.

46 `Ubayd Zakani 1999: 9–10, 16–17, 24–25, 47–49.

47 See Nafisi 1968; Nafisi 1971; Dawlatabadi 1988; Brookshaw 2005; Brookshaw 2008; Ingenito 2018.

48 See Dawlatabadi 1988: 41–80.

49 See Havlioğlu 2017: 18.

50 J303:2, 306:3, 421:5, 693:3, 947:3. See also Brookshaw 2005: 177.

51 See Davis 2012: I.

52 Ingenito 2018: 178. See also Hammond 2010: 148–150.

53 See Havlioğlu 2017: 75.

54 See Natanzi 1957: 170–172.

55 See Ghani 2001: 87, 102.

56 See Jahan-Malik Khatun 1995: iii–x.

57 See Dawlatshah Samarqandi 1901: 289–290; Fakhri Hiravi 1968: 122–124.

58 See Blochet 1928: 222; Massé 1972: 4–5; Szuppe 1998; Blair 2014: 196–198.

59 Jahan-Malik Khatun 1995: 1–4.

60 Sharma 2009: 150.

61 See De Nicola 2017: 137, 157.

62 See Vassaf al-Hazrat 1959: 291–292; Munshi Kirmani 1983: 70–71, 77–79; Mernissi 1993: 99–102; De Nicola 2017: 108–110, 219–221.

63 Vassaf al-Hazrat 1959: 292; Fakhri Hiravi 1968: 121–122; Shabankara'i 1984: 202; Quade-Reutter 2003: 192–199; Pfeiffer 2014: 26–28.

64 Kutubi 1985: 37, 70.

65 See Blochet 1928: 222–223.

66 See Karatay 1961: 215.

67 See Browne 1932: 237–238.

68 See Bashari 2009: 746–760.

69 See Junayd Shirazi 1949: 281–282; Vassaf al-Hazrat 1959: 222, 291, 623–624; Shabankara'i 1984: 187, 198–203; Lambton 1988: 272–280; Lane 2003: 96–106, 109–110, 116–118, 121–131, 144, 149; Quade-Reutter 2003: 417–418; Aigle 2005: 131–136, 157–158; Sa'di Shirazi 2007: 713, 744–745, 747; De Nicola 2014: 149–150; Hope 2016: 137, 141; De Nicola 2017: 110–113.

70 See Junayd Shirazi 1949: 289–292; Arberry 1960: 50; Mustafavi 1964: 59, 63–64, 347; Ibn Battuta 1975: 218–222; Junayd Shirazi 1985: 336.

71 See Wright 2012: 251, 254–256, 265–266.

72 Fakhri Hiravi 1968: 122–123.

73 See Dawlatshah Samarqandi 1901: 289–290; Fakhri Hiravi 1968: 122–123.

74 Blair 2014: 203–207.

75 Jahan-Malik Khatun 1995: 3.

76 Fakhri Hiravi 1968: 124, 129–130.

77 See Blachère 1965: 1031–1032.

78 Lewis 2012: 570.

79 See Meisami 1987: 248; Moayyad 1988: 135; de Bruijn 2000; Meisami 2003: 45; Lewis 2012: 570.

80 de Bruijn 2000: 356.

81 Bürgel 2005: 301.

82 Meisami 2003: 46.

83 H3:9, 4:8, 25:9, 34:9, 39:10, 41:7, 105:8, 199:8, 206:10, 214:8, 258:9, 281:9, 328:7, 333:9, 367:11; U1:7, 3:7, 23:4, 33:7, 117:7; J254:5, 264:4, 314:8, 469:3, 536:9, 1050:7, 1133:9.

84 See Ritter 2003: 450.

85 Meisami 1987: 245.

86 Yarshater 2003: 462.

87 Meisami 2003: 46.

88 Ibid: 47.

89 Meisami 2005: 333.

90 See Yarshater 2006; Zipoli 2009: 175.

91 Bausani 1965: 1036.

92 Avery and Heath-Stubbs 1952: 10.

93 Hillmann 1976: 147–148.

94 Bausani 1965: 1034.

95 de Bruijn 2000: 356.
96 See Schimmel 1988.
97 Dashti 2011: 40–44.
98 Lewisohn 2010: 10.
99 Shamisa 2000: 216.
100 Meisami 1987: 279.
101 See Shamisa 2000: 217, 240–242, 256. See also Lewis 2006: 136.
102 See Yarshater 2006; de Bruijn 2009.
103 See Lewisohn 2010: 31–73.
104 de Bruijn 2000: 355–356.
105 See Yarshater 2003: 462.
106 H20:4, 133:9, 355:2, 367:2, 492:7.
107 Lewis 2003a: 485–486.
108 H35:1, 83:7, 88:2, 131:8, 199:1, 227:1, 257:10, 347:7, 352:3, 356:9, 372:5.
109 H7:2, 26:5, 31:6, 69:11, 71:1, 80:1, 84:6, 118:4, 142:4, 150:4, 158:3, 170:1, 196:4, 197:1, 202:2, 205:4, 254:5, 264:8, 271:4, 332:3, 355:7, 362:2, 373:7, 400:9, 417:4, 419:6, 466:4, 467:5, 480:6.
110 Lewis 2003a: 484.
111 H69:11, 111:11, 220:7, 242:6, 296:8, 373:1, 375:1, 473:6, 474:3.
112 de Bruijn 2003: 472.
113 H7:2, 25:1, 48:1, 105:1, 170:2, 260:5, 275:1, 483:2, 485:2.
114 Yarshater 2003: 462.
115 U24:3, 37:6, 61:6, 71:1, 73:4–5, 77:1, 91:4, 117:1–4.
116 U2:6, 6:5–6, 7:3, 61:7, 91:2.
117 See Junayd Shirazi 1941: 2, 8, 16, 17, 19; 'Attar Shirazi 1990: 10, 55.
118 Shamisa 2000: 243.
119 Moayyad 1988: 136.
120 Shamisa 2000: 220.
121 See Ahur 1984: lxxxvi; Meisami 2003: 46.
122 Ahur 1984: 514.
123 de Bruijn 2000: 357.
124 Meisami 1987: 281.
125 Meisami 2003: 184.
126 See Mu'in 1991: 68–69.
127 See Browne 1920: 266; Shamisa 1983: 116.
128 See Lewis 2006: 127.
129 Wickens 1971: 55.
130 Moayyad 1988: 141.
131 See Bürgel 1991: 10, 32.
132 Lewis 2012: 571.

133 See Dawlatshah Samarqandi 1901: 326–330; Jami 1988: 106–107; Jami 1991: 609; Losensky 2011: 412–413.

134 See Jami 1991: 612.

135 See Bürgel 1991: 27.

136 See Yarshater 1986: 970; Davis 2012: xxvii.

137 Yarshater 2003: 465.

138 See Avery and Heath-Stubbs 1952: 9. See also Sharma 2017: 54.

139 See Arberry 1960: 49; Roemer 1986a: 1, 4; Melville 2016: 324.

140 Limbert 2004b: 143.

141 See Jackson 2008b; Wing 2014.

142 Jackson 2008a: 415.

143 See Roemer 1986a: 6; Wing 2014.

144 Roemer 1986a: 11.

145 See Quade-Reutter 2003: 399–401.

146 See Natanzi 1957: 175, 182, 190.

147 See Roemer 1986a: 12–13; Aigle 2005: 217–218.

148 H207:8; see Hafiz Shirazi 1999: 384.

149 See Kutubi 1985: 37; Khurramshahi 2003: 467; Limbert 2004a: 116–119.

150 See Browne 1920: 161.

151 See Wing 2014.

152 See Zarrinkub 1975: 22; Roemer 1986a: 16; Roemer 1986b: 63; Wing 2014.

153 See Dawlatshah Samarqandi 1901: 300–302; Bayani 1966: 397–402; Halat 1967.

154 H48:9, 245:11, 304:9, 329:14.

155 Arberry 1960: 157–158.

156 Wing 2014.

157 See Britland 2012: 1011.

158 H48:9, 219:10; Dawlatshah Samarqandi 1901: 292, 295; Jalal 1987: 209, 224; Jami 1988: 102.

159 H11:10, 304:3, 343:9, 356:5.

160 See Gruendler 2003: 9, 15.

161 Stetkevych 2002: 183. See also Meisami 2001c.

162 See Lefèvre 2014: 89.

163 See Busch 2011: 19.

164 See Yarshater 1986: 968.

165 H153:10, 284:8.

166 See Toorawa 2010: 598.

167 Gruendler and Marlow 2004: v.

168 See Meisami 1987: 10–11, 45; Stetkevych 2002: 34, 204.

169 Sharlet 2011: 22–23.

170 Ibid: 58–59.

171 H126:9, 292:5, 329:1, 381:1, 469:9.

172 Hafiz Shirazi 1999: 391–392.

173 Khvaju Kirmani 1957: 15–17, 91–92, 117–119, 574–575.

174 Nasir Bukhara'i 1974: 127.

175 Khvaju Kirmani 1957: 155–157.

176 H207; Hafiz Shirazi 1999: 80–85, 384, 388.

177 U87; see 'Ubayd Zakani 1999: 7–9, 11–12, 12–13, 13–14, 17–18, 18–19, 19–20, 20–21, 21–23, 23–24, 27–28, 28–29, 32–33, 33–34, 34–35, 37–38, 38–40, 40–41, 41–42, 45, 45–46, 46–47, 49, 50–51, 51–52, 52, 53–54, 57–58, 131–132, 135.

178 Khvaju Kirmani 1957: 78–79, 86–88, 95–96, 114–116, 581–582, 594–595, 603–605, 619–622.

179 Salman Savaji 1957: 529–531.

180 'Imad Kirmani 1969: 238, 256–257, 287, 345–346.

181 Jalal Yazdi 1987: 136–137, 202–203, 210–212, 212–214, 220–222, 223–226, 226–230, 248–249.

182 'Ubayd Zakani 1999: 14–15, 42–43, 43–45, 49–50, 52–53, 55–57, 127–128, 128–129, 129–130.

183 Khvaju Kirmani 1957: 27–30, 79–81, 122–123.

184 H11, 327; Hafiz Shirazi 1999: 384, 388–389.

185 H219.

186 Hafiz Shirazi 1999: 387.

187 Khvaju Kirmani 1957: 2–4, 13–15, 23–25, 36–38, 59–61, 105–107, 109–110, 590–593, 595–597.

188 'Imad Kirmani 1969: 329–335, 344–345.

189 Jalal Yazi 1987: 217–220.

190 H167, 283, 284, 292; Hafiz Shirazi 1999: 71–75.

191 'Ubayd Zakani 1999: 9–10, 16–17, 24–25, 29–30, 30–32.

192 Jahan-Malik Khatun 1995: 7–8.

193 'Imad Kirmani 1969: 10–11, 32–33, 179–180, 199, 316–319, 339–342.

194 Salman Savaji 1957: 475–477, 610–612.

195 Ibid: 612–614.

196 'Imad Kirmani 1969: 312–314.

197 H212:7, 304:1, 392:7, 421:11, 433:13.

198 Haydar Shirazi 2004: 56, 57–59, 60–62.

199 H147:7, 153:10, 242:1, 329:9, 381:7, 402:8.

200 J156, 288.

201 H362.

202 Khvaju Kirmani 1957: 67–69.

203 'Imad Kirmani 1969: 311–312, 323–326.

204 H112, 319; Hafiz Shirazi 1999: 76–79, 386, 391.

205 'Imad Kirmani 1969: 322–323.

206 'Attar Shirazi 1990: 98–100.

207 H48:9, 343:9, 356:8, 361:9, 454:13, 473:11, 481:8, 484:12, 488:8; Hafiz Shirazi 1999: 383.

208 Salman Savaji 1957: 358, 426–428, 437–44, 447–479, 488–490, 508–511, 532–533, 546–547, 564–570, 585–587, 596–598, 605–606.

209 Khvaju Kirmani 1957: 610–613.

210 Jalal Yazdi 1987: 231–233.

211 Salman Savaji 1957: 361–363, 502–503, 514–517, 527–529, 533–535, 537–540, 552–554, 585, 594–595, 598, 607–610.

212 U95; see 'Ubayd Zakani 1999: 10–11, 26–27, 35–37, 47–49, 59–60.

213 Salman Savaji 1957: 344–348, 349, 353–360, 369–374, 376, 383–385, 394–399, 402–420, 430–437, 440–442, 444–475, 479–488, 492–508, 511–514, 517–519, 521–524, 526–527, 561–562, 562–564, 571–584, 590–596, 598–602, 614–623.

214 Nasir Bukhara'i 1974: 45–47, 102–104, 221–222.

215 Salman Savaji 1957: 360–366, 379–382, 386–391, 490–492.

216 Khvaju Kirmani 1957: 38–40.

217 Nasir Bukhara'i 1974: 107–109.

218 H162, 225, 472.

219 Jahan-Malik Khatun 1995: 6–7.

220 Stetkevych 2002: 82.

221 See Purnamdarian 2003: 142.

222 See Bednarz 2001: 2, 15.

223 Ingenito 2014: 81.

224 See Losensky 1998: 100–114.

225 See Browne 1920: 298–299; Zipoli 1993: 6; Gruendler 2003: 6.

226 Losensky 1994: 229.

227 See Zipoli 1993: 5.

228 Lewis 1994: 199–200.

229 See Browne 1920: 298–299.

230 Zipoli 1993: 13.

231 Lewis 1995: 108. See also Lewisohn 2010: 11–12.

232 Lewis 1995: 107.

233 Zipoli 1993: 13.

234 de Bruijn 2003: 469. See also Dashti 2011: 35–39.

235 Ahur 1984: 363–364, 539; Dawlatabadi 1988; Mu'in 1991: 309–314, 319–322, 324–326, 341–342; Haydar Shirazi 2004: 64, 81, 86, 98; Tajdini 2012: 203–205.

236 Awhadi Maragha'i 1961: xxvi-xxviii; Ahur 1984: 869; Mu'in 1991: 329–339; Lewisohn 2010: 8; Tajdini 2012: 213–236.

237 See Rypka 1968: 611; Mu'in 1991: 331; Haydar Shirazi 2004: 75; Bushaq Shirazi 2014: 61–62, 81, 82, 85–86.

238 Lewisohn 2010: 12.

239 Shamisa 1983: 123.

240 H470:8.

241 H349:4–5.

242 See Ghani 1987: 71.

243 Ibid.

244 Kamal Isfahani 1969: lxxix–lxxx.

245 See Riyahi 1989: 215.

246 Nizari Quhistani 1992: 347–374.

247 See Ghani 1987: 72; Rastigar Fasa'i 2006: 210; Dashti 2011: 184–199.

248 J230:5–6; see Kamal Khujandi 1958: 211; 'Imad Kirmani 1969: 238; Haydar Shirazi 2004: 96, 97.

249 See 'Imad Kirmani 1969: 136.

250 H469:10; Kamal Khujandi 1958: 118–119, 204, 263, 295, 370, 377, 390; 'Imad Kirmani 1969: 164; Nasir Bukhara'i 1974: 115; Jalal Yazdi 1987: 213.

251 Lewis 1994: 211.

252 See Lewisohn 2010: 9.

253 Kamal Khujandi 1958: 394, 395.

254 Dawlatshah Samarqandi 1901: 290.

255 Haydar Shirazi 2004: 95.

256 Ibid: 96. See Fitzherbert 1991: 140.

257 See Kamal Khujandi 1958: 384.

258 See Jalal Yazdi 1987: 214.

259 'Attar Shirazi 1990: 114–115.

260 Browne 1920: 260.

261 See Rehder 1974: 149.

262 Ibid: 150.

263 Ibid: 151.

264 Ibid: 153.

265 Moayyad 1989.

266 H3, 64, 77, 80, 111, 112, 117, 127, 161, 179, 196, 199, 203, 205, 214, 226, 271, 298, 407, 419, 473.

267 Valavi 2016: 195.

268 See Mu'in 1991: 314.

269 See von Grunebaum 1944b: 245–246; Shamisa 1987: 5–7; Purnamdarian 1990: 5–6; Kilito 2001: 17–19; Lowin 2014: 10.

270 Wetzsteon 2012. See also Nwiya 1970: 177–178.

271 See Meisami 1990a: 141–142, 153; Zakeri 2015: 299–300.

272 See Shams-i Qays 2009: 383–384.

Chapter 1

1 See Rollason 2016: 1–2.

2 See Martines 1988: 72–80; Hansen 2006: 1–12.

3 Ingenito 2014: 98.

4 See Sharma 2004: 73.

5 Sharma 2011: 244.

6 See Sa'di Shirazi 2007: 726.

7 Arberry 1960: 112.

8 See Mahallati 1962: 10–20, 33–35; 'Attar Shirazi 1990: 112; Manoukian 2012: 4–5.

9 See Ingenito 2014: 98.

10 See Aubin 1970: 68; Hourani 1970: 16; Aigle 2005: 72. See also Vassaf al-Hazrat 1959: 149; Kutubi 1985: 70; Redford 2000: 316.

11 Tusi 1996: 467.

12 al-Qazwini 1984: 210–211.

13 Ibn Battuta 1975: 223.

14 Hamdullah Mustawfi 1957: 137.

15 Ibid: 137–138. See also Zarrinkub 1975: 10.

16 See Suvorova 2011: xi.

17 H279.

18 See Johnston 1984: 22.

19 See Ahur 1984: 395–396; Shahbazi 2004.

20 See 'Isa b. Junayd 1985: 393–478; Islami Nudushan 2003: 65.

21 See Ahur 1984: 217; Alemi 2008: 537.

22 Snir 2013: 3.

23 See Zarkub Shirazi 1931: 5, 22.

24 See Tuan 1974: 113. See also Sharma 2017: 2.

25 Sa'di Shirazi 2007: 726.

26 See Lewis 1995: 107.

27 See Melikian-Chirvani 1971: 11–12.

28 See Shams-i Fakhri 1887: 43, 45, 64. See also Sperl 1977: 23.

29 See Shams-i Fakhri 1887: 10; Jalal Yazdi 1987: 211; 'Ubayd Zakani 1999: 28, 39, 41, 45, 50–51, 149; Sa'di Shirazi 2007: 733. See also Nizam al-Mulk 1955: 129; Bayhaqi 1971: 230, 407; Durand-Guédy 2013: 166.

30   See Hanaoka 2016: 168.

31   See Alemi 2008: 554.

32   See Hanaoka 2016: 180–181.

33   See Hämeen-Anttila 2008: 34.

34   See Arberry 1960: 61–111; 'Isa b. Junayd 1985: 477.

35   See Hamdullah Mustawfi 1957: 138–139; Limbert 2004a: 102.

36   Rollason 2016: 2, 273.

37   See al-Qazwini 1984: 313.

38   Sa'di Shirazi 2007: 30–31.

39   Hamgar 1996: 585.

40   Zarkub Shirazi 1931: 83.

41   Jalal Yazdi 1987: 202.

42   See Meisami 2003: 273.

43   'Ubayd Zakani 1999: 41.

44   See Browne 1920: 237–238.

45   Haydar Shirazi 2004: 73.

46   Hamgar 1996: 584. See also Shafi'i-Kadkani 2006: 192, 356.

47   See Q5:65, 10:9, 22:56, 31:8, 37:43, 56:12, 68:34. See also Nizari Quhistani 1992: 1237.

48   Sa'di Shirazi 2007: 704.

49   'Ubayd Zakani 1999: 45.

50   Haydar Shirazi 2004: 91.

51   Awhadi Maragha'i 1961: 420.

52   See H436:5.

53   Vassaf al-Hazrat 1959: 147.

54   Zarkub Shirazi 1931: 3–4, 14, 22–23.

55   Ibid: 10–11.

56   See Vassaf al-Hazrat 1959: 147.

57   Zarkub Shirazi 1931: 22.

58   Ibid: 22.

59   Ibid.

60   Ibid: 23.

61   Jalal Yazdi 1987: 244.

62   Sa'di Shirazi 2007: 733.

63   Hamgar 1996: 345.

64   Shams-i Fakhri 1887: 45; Hamgar 1996: 350.

65   Hamgar 1996: 390.

66   Ibid: 349.

67   'Ubayd Zakani 1999: 41.

68 Ibid: 32.

69 Ibid: 50.

70 See H81:5; Jahan-Malik Khatun 1995: 542.

71 See Aryanpur 1986: 307–318.

72 Hamgar 1996: 385–386.

73 Haydar Shirazi 2004: 91.

74 'Ubayd Zakani 1999: 38–40, 45.

75 Shams-i Fakhri 1887: 29.

76 Kamens 1997: 28, 30.

77 Ibid: 28.

78 Ibid: 30.

79 Alemi 2008: 525.

80 Zarkub Shirazi 1931: 3–4.

81 Ibid: 4–5.

82 See Zarkub Shirazi 1931: 22; Vassaf al-Hazrat 1959: 147–148.

83 See Ghani 1987: 303; Shahbazi 2002; Shafi'i-Kadkani 2006: 375.

84 'Ubayd Zakani 1999: 21, 22, 37, 45, 48.

85 See Ghani 1987: 74.

86 Sa'di Shirazi 2007: 468.

87 Ibid: 714.

88 Ibid: 789.

89 Tuan 1974: 100.

90 See Salman Savaji 1957: 125; Nasir Bukhara'i 1974: 165, 174.

91 'Ubayd Zakani 1999: 50.

92 Ingenito 2014: 96–98.

93 'Imad Kirmani 1969: 104.

94 Haydar Shirazi 2004: 86.

95 Salman Savaji 1957: 89.

96 See Meisami 1987: 285–289.

97 Salman Savaji 1957: 475–476, 610–612.

98 'Attar Shirazi 1990: 114–115.

99 Jahan-Malik Khatun 1995: 534.

100 Sa'di Shirazi 2007: 531.

101 H39:7.

102 See Sharma 2000: 63–65.

103 See Keen 2003: 119.

104 See Khvaju Kirmani 1957: 581; 'Imad Kirmani 1969: 32, 237; Jalal Yazdi 1987: 212, 243; Hamgar 1996: 322.

105 Sa'di Shirazi 2007: 588.

106 Ibid: 475.

107 See Lescot 1944: 72.

108 Haydar Shirazi 2004: 75.

109 See 'Attar Shirazi 1990: 122.

110 Sa'di Shirazi 2007: 429.

111 See Meisami 2003: 195.

112 See Khvaju Kirmani 1957: 201.

113 See Jalal Yazdi 1987: 211; 'Ubayd Zakani 1999: 41.

114 See Sharma 2000: 47–48.

115 Ibn Battuta 1975: 223.

116 Khvaju Kirmani 1957: 759.

117 See Haydar Shirazi 2004: 91.

118 Sa'di Shirazi 2007: 503.

119 See Aubin 1970: 73.

120 See Junayd Shirazi 1941: 4, 7–8, 9, 10, 12, 14–15, 16, 17, 18, 19, 21, 37, 38; Shafi'i-Kadkani 2002: 173.

121 Limbert 2004a: 121.

122 See Johnston 1984: 4.

123 See Yazdi 1947: 11; Kutubi 1985: 81–83; Salman Savaji 1957: 475; 'Isa b. Junayd 1985: 474; Jahan-Malik Khatun 1995: 7–8; Hafiz Shirazi 1999: 71.

124 Junayd Shirazi 1949.

125 J534:1, 1213:4.

126 See Sharma 2000: 107–116.

127 Haydar Shirazi 2004: 74.

128 Sa'di Shirazi 2007: 415. See ibid. 463.

129 Haydar Shirazi 2004: 89.

130 Jalal Yazdi 1987: 29. See also Awhadi Maragha'i 1961: 334.

131 Sa'di Shirazi 2007: 601.

132 Ibid: 419.

133 See Limbert 2004a: 121–123.

134 See Lescot 1944: 70–72; Valavi 2016: 177–179.

135 Sa'di Shirazi 2007: 552.

136 See Halabi 1998: 121–137; Sprachman 2012: 27–40.

137 See Ingenito 2014: 77, 80–81, 96.

138 Ibid: 98.

139 Sa'di Shirazi 2007: 626.

140 Awhadi Maragha'i 1961: 214.

141 'Imad Kirmani 1969: 136.

142 Ibid: 238.

143 Sa'di Shirazi 2007: 744.

144 'Imad Kirmani 1969: 164.

145 Ibid: 345.

146 Kamal Khujandi 1958: 119.

147 Ibid: 204.

148 Ibid: 295.

149 Ibid: 263.

150 Ibid: 390.

151 Ibid: 211.

152 Ibid: 207.

153 See Green 1980: 197–198.

154 Shafi'i-Kadkani 2002: 165.

155 Hafiz Shirazi 1999: 59–60. See also Glassen 1991: 42; Lewis 2003b: 493.

156 Hafiz Shirazi 1999: 387.

157 Kamal Khujandi 1958: 162, 384.

158 Ibid: 99.

159 Ibid: 161.

160 Ibid: 283.

161 See Glassen 1991: 43, 46–47.

162 Bushaq Shirazi 2014: 57–58, 59, 60–61, 61–62, 69–70, 70, 71–72, 74–75, 76, 77–78, 78–79, 81, 83, 85, 85–86, 93, 93–94, 96. See also Moayyad 1989.

163 See Jami 1962: 144, 147, 293, 349, 362, 593. See also Losensky 1998: 171–175.

164 See Losensky 2008.

165 Lewis 2010: 255–265.

166 Khvaju Kirmani 1957: 340. See ibid. 247, 287.

167 See Schimmel 1973: 21; Ahur 1984: 118–119.

168 See Melikian-Chirvani 1971: 16–18; Hope 2016: 11.

169 See Ghani 2001: 64.

170 Sa'di Shirazi 2007: 525.

171 See Tsugitaka 2004.

172 Khvaju Kirmani 1957: 666.

173 Kamal Khujandi 1958: 211.

174 Sa'di Shirazi 2007: 637.

175 Lewis 2001: 82–83.

176 Sa'di Shirazi 2007: 595.

177 Schimmel 1992: 151.

178 al-Qazwini 1984: 313–314. See also von Grunebaum 1944a: 61–62.

179 Vassaf al-Hazrat 1959: 524.

180 Ibid: 25–26.

181 See Kutubi 1985: 156.

182 Hamgar 1996: 434, 561.

183 Ibid: 609.

184 Salman Savaji 1957: 355.

185 Ibid: 532.

186 'Attar Shirazi 1990: 43. See also Haydar Shirazi 2004: 71.

187 Zarkub Shirazi 1931: 3–8.

188 See Ahur 1984: 109; Sudi Busnavi 1995: 1109.

189 See Sudi Busnavi 1995: 2528–2533.

190 Sa'di Shirazi 2007: 548.

191 See also H133:4.

192 J762, 763.

193 Jahan-Malik Khatun 1995: 6–7.

194 See Hafiz Shirazi 1999: 391; Valavi 2016: 180.

195 See Ahur 1984: 428–429; Ghani 1987: 162.

196 Khvaju Kirmani 1957: 312. See Ahur 1984: 429–430.

197 See Valavi 2016: 180.

198 Ibid: 182–183.

199 See al-Mafarrukhi 1933: 21, 54, 59–68.

200 See Ahur 1984: 96–97; Zaryab 1989: 216–217.

201 al-Mafarrukhi 1933: 55.

202 See Khvaju Kirmani 1957: 657.

203 See 'Ubayd Zakani 1999: 9.

204 See Kutubi 1985: 71; Ghani 1987: 54.

205 See Ahur 1984: 430.

206 Junayd Shirazi 1941: 13.

207 See Mallah 1984: 48–49.

208 See Zarrinkub 1975: 2.

209 Hafiz Shirazi 1999: 82. See also Nasir Bukhara'i 1974: 46, 316.

210 Kamal Khujandi 1958: 236.

211 Ibid: 382.

212 Ibid: 388.

213 Jalal Yazdi 1987: 213.

214 See Suvorova 2011: 21.

215 See al-Mafarrukhi 1933: 21, 77.

216 al-Qazwini 1984: 299.

217 See Swietochowski and Carboni 1994: 15–17; Bagci 1995; Wright 2012: 19–20, 25, 30, 44, 288; Adamova and Bayani 2016: 64–67.

218 'Ubayd Zakani 1999: 142.

219 Ibid: 214.

220 See Brookshaw 2012: 55–57.

221 See Brookshaw 2012: 65–66.

222 See Jamalzada 2005: 145–147, 151–152.

223 Sudi Busnavi 1995: 1109.

224 Sa'di Shirazi 2007: 548.

225 Arberry 1960: 144–146.

226 Ghani 2001: 213–223.

227 Arberry 1960: 147–148.

228 Lescot 1944: 68.

229 Sudi Busnavi 1995: 1010–1011.

230 See Islami Nudushan 2003: 206.

231 Jahan-Malik Khatun 1995: 533.

232 'Ubayd Zakani 1999: 144.

233 See also U32:5.

234 U101:1.

235 Brookshaw 2012: 54–68.

236 Sharma 2000: 47–48. See also Awhadi Maragha'i 1961: 319, 405.

237 'Ubayd Zakani 1999: 41. See also Awhadi Maragha'i 1961: 231.

Chapter 2

1 See Bauman and Briggs 1990: 69.

2 See Gruendler 2003: 5–9, 29, 48–49.

3 See Bauman 1975: 290.

4 Lewis 2001: 82.

5 de Bruijn 1983: 158.

6 Bauman 1975: 298.

7 Bauman and Briggs 1990: 68.

8 Lewis 1995: 111.

9 Ibid: 109.

10 Duranti 1986: 240.

11 Ibid: 243.

12 Ibid: 244.

13 See Caton 1990: 250.

14 Bauman 1975: 305.

15 See Gruendler 2003: 6.

16   Gruendler 2008: 329.

17   Losensky 1998: 257.

18   See Clinton 1972.

19   von Grunebaum 1969: 293.

20   H208:7, 350:3; Khvaju Kirmani 1957: 266; Jalal Yazdi 1987: 226; 'Attar Shirazi
     1990: 100.

21   von Grunebaum 1969: 292.

22   H375:4; Shafi'i-Kadkani 2002: 175.

23   Subtelny 1984: 144.

24   See Zarkub Shirazi 1931: 111, 126, 155; Yazdi 1947: 50, 77.

25   See Kraemer 1986: 58, 140; Stroumsa 1999.

26   H164:4, 393:7, 467:4; U61:7.

27   H46:2, 90:10, 121:5, 142:2, 149:9, 153:3, 167:1, 171:5, 179:5, 206:6, 208:7,
     219:10, 225:8, 257:10, 258:7, 397:1, 415:11, 432:1, 452:5 and 488:8. See
     also Zarkub Shirazi 1931: 24, 28; Kutubi 1985: 35; Yazdi 1947: 15, 18,
     105–106; Bayhaqi 1971: 86, 152, 192, 310–312, 329, 460, 570–571; Nizami
     Aruzi 1920: 29–30, 35, 44, 47; Kay-Ka'us b. Iskandar 1951: 110, 118–119,
     135; Nizam al-Mulk 1955: 95–97; Farrukhi Sistani 1999: 37–38, 53–55;
     Manuchihri Damghani 1996: 101–105, 179–181.

28   See Meisami 1987: 3–39; Lewis 1995: 69–92, 108–109; Brookshaw 2003;
     Ali 2010: 15–19, 26–32.

29   See Elias 1983: 78.

30   See Green 1980: 178, 183.

31   See *Kitab al-taj* 1914: 153.

32   See Chejne 1965; von Grunebaum 1969: 292–293; Kushajim 1999: 59–60,
     66–68, 70–77, 111–118; Bayhaqi 1971: 4, 84, 148, 158, 373, 459, 786; Nizam
     al-Mulk 1955: 95–97, 129; Meisami 1987: 6–7; Gruendler 2003: 48.

33   U93:4. See also Bayhaqi 1971: 407; Gurgani 1959: 29; *Tarikh-i Sistan* 1994:
     178.

34   See *Tarikh-i Sistan* 1994: 178–179; Bayhaqi 1971: 235.

35   J114:7, 137:5, 141:4, 147:8, 470:4, 570:9, 612:4, 699:2, 741:6, 743:3, 773:1,
     774:1, 828:1, 839:6, 863:5, 898:2, 921:6, 957:2, 971:6, 975:2, 976:4, 987:4,
     1010:7, 1045:2, 1212:2, 1268:1.

36   J853:5, 1021:1, 1175:4.

37   J986:4.

38   J662:6, 1175:9, 1237:3.

39   Sharlet 2011: 17.

40   See Sperl 1977: 34; Gruendler 2003: 49.

41   Toorawa 2010: 598.

42   See Bayhaqi 1971: 359–360, 572, 697.

43 See Kutubi 1985: 81–82, 156–158; Ghani 2001: 214–215, 352–355, 358–360; Bayani 1966: 380, 397–402; Mu'in 1991: 65–67; Valavi 2016: 74, 98, 100, 143–144.

44 See Khvand Mir 2001: 315–317.

45 Toorawa 2010: 598.

46 H309:7, 392:7; J1269:1.

47 H54:9, 86:8, 123:9, 145:9, 149:14, 151:7, 171:8, 247:7, 328:7, 367:11, 387:3, 390:11, 398:9.

48 H112:4, 121:9, 123:5, 167:10, 196:12, 206:7, 243:2, 306:3, 349:6, 366:4, 411:4, 413:9, 415:7, 468:1, 472:5; U11:7, 34:8, 59:5, 66:7, 70:4, 72:4, 74:2, 110:1, 111:2, 130:5, 139:5.

49 See Bayhaqi 1971: 157; Kay-Ka'us b. Iskandar 1951: 135.

50 Nizami 'Aruzi 1920: 47.

51 H149:14.

52 H328:7. See Nizami 'Aruzi 1920: 35, 44.

53 See de Bruijn 1987: 15.

54 H79:2, 204:5, 256:12, 302:7, 309:4, 413:8.

55 U22:2.

56 See Bayhaqi 1971: 659, 689.

57 See *Tarikh-i Sistan* 1994: 178; Bayhaqi 1971: 460; Gurgani 1959: 324.

58 H491:3; J340:5.

59 U22:3. See also Farrukhi Sistani 1999: 131; Gurgani 1959: 30–31, 503.

60 See Bayhaqi 1971: 435.

61 H374:1, 495:1; U75:6, 93:4, 96:4.

62 See Gurgani 1959: 51.

63 H12:5, 46:5, 50:5, 84:8, 257:4, 260:3, 374:3; U42:3–4, 116:5, 126:2, 126:4. See King 2017: 277.

64 King 2017: 336–339.

65 Meisami 2001b: 23, 27.

66 Blair 1993: 241.

67 See 'Ubayd Zakani 1999: 38–40, 45, 50–51, 52.

68 Kushajim 1999: 114.

69 H437:4; U21:9. See also Kushajim 1999: 67–68; Gurgani 1959: 79, 101.

70 See Ghazi 1959.

71 J314:7, 1326:5, 1393:1; H164:8, 175:7, 204:3, 218:8, 309:1.

72 J562:4.

73 H43:1, 403:5.

74 H65:1.

75 H115:3, 206:2, 288:5.

76 H21:2.

77 U109:3.

78 U111:5.

79 H160:1, 244:2, 415:2; U22:3, 27:2; see Khvaju Kirmani 1957: 478. See also Sa'di Shirazi 2007: 136; Bayhaqi 1971: 350.

80 H7:4, 21:2, 69:6, 257:10, 304:6, 329:6; J47:2; see Jalal Yazdi 1987: 248.

81 Khvaju Kirmani 1957: 114.

82 Schimmel 1992: 284.

83 H7:4. See also Zaryab 1989: 99–100.

84 J1278:1; H189:7, 350:4.

85 Shehadi 1995: 91, 122; Klein 2014: 215.

86 J1093:2.

87 H1:6, 207:4, 217:7; 'Attar Shirazi 1990: 100.

88 Khvaju Kirmani 1957: 476, 477.

89 H139:7, 160:1, 233:6, 273:7, 327:3, 390:5, 477:2; U138:5.

90 H5:4, 206:2, 210:1, 230:4, 272:3, 275:3; J687:9.

91 H20:2, 101:10, 203:7, 257:8, 377:4, 473:7; U31:9, 74:1, 93:3, 95:2.

92 H454:11.

93 H134:5, 293:3.

94 H189:7; see Nasir Bukhara'i 1974: 148.

95 J754:3, 944:5.

96 J1115:7. See also Kamal Isfahani 1969: 735.

97 H175:1, 376:2; J1281:2; see Haydar Shirazi 2004: 72.

98 H329:16; U74:2.

99 H1:3, 41:5, 48:4, 65:1, 152:5, 154:10, 182:3, 191:6, 197:8, 315:4, 358:3, 382:7, 386:3, 396:3, 397:12, 417:1, 448:4, 451:4, 471:8, 473:2, 474:7, 481:3, 486:6; U10:9, 35:2, 45:8, 61:9, 88:8, 89:5, 95:2, 96:7, 100:1, 115:7, 126:11, 129:3.

100 U74:1.

101 H175:1, 254:4.

102 H295:7, 483:6. See also Kamal Isfahani 1969: 771.

103 See Mu'in 1991: 67; Shafi'i-Kadkani 2006: 356.

104 H5:9, 25:5; U24:6, 67:1.

105 H65:1, 356:1, 414:1.

106 U18:1.

107 J169:7; H175:1; U1:1, 44:4; see Junayd Shirazi 1941: 4; Jalal Yazdi 1987: 124.

108 J653:7, 669:4, 1055:6.

109 Junayd Shirazi 1941: 23.

110 H121:5, 126:5, 164:5, 175:4, 231:8, 248:6, 267:5, 288:2, 348:7, 373:5, 376:1, 421:5.

111 H295:7, 483:6; J405:2; Jalal 1987: 127. See also Haydar Shirazi 2004: 72; Bayhaqi 1971: 19, 152, 343, 659; Nizam al-Mulk 1955: 128.

112 H164:7, 295:7, 298:4; U44:4, 45:8.

113 H182:3, 392:6; U45:8, 129:3.

114 See Kamal Isfahani 1969: 735.

115 See Ghani 1987: 74.

116 U94:1; J260:1, 316:1, 340:6.

117 'Attar Shirazi 1990: 75.

118 U88:8. See Shabankara'i 1984: 199, 315.

119 See U55:5; H163:1, 298:1.

120 See Ghani 1987: 129–130; Shafi'i-Kadkani 2006: 212–213.

121 H165:6, 298:1, 298:4.

122 See H218:8; J491:8, 536:1.

123 See Nazari 2007: 112–116; Ilahi Ghomshei 2010: 83–84, 96–99.

124 Lewis 1995: 547.

125 See Yazdi 1947: 105–106, 174.

126 See Jamalzada 2005: 133, 144; Hasuri 2016: 168–169.

127 Matthee 2005: 40.

128 See J239:6, 1358:3.

129 H396:6.

130 H479:3.

131 See Brookshaw 2014: 11–43.

132 Q2:219, 5:90–91.

133 See Ghani 2001: 302.

134 H230:1, 243:3, 263:4, 325:6. See also Kamal Isfahani 1969: 770.

135 H30:4–5, 262:1, 263:4, 403:1; U10:3.

136 H132:2, 162:4, 264:1, 275:8, 218:5, 256:8, 269:5. See also Haydar Shirazi 2004: 82; Bayhaqi 1971: 290, 460; Nazari 2007: 110–114.

137 H323:4, 397:11.

138 H356:2, 431:1.

139 J236:7–8, 598:3–7; H162:3, 430:1.

140 H79:1; U42:1.

141 H13:8.

142 See Azarnouche 2013: 135–137; Daryaee 2017.

143 H1:1, 46:4, 276:7.

144 H1:1, 11:2, 18:1, 30:4, 81:7, 84:1, 86:1, 99:5, 133:3, 141:5, 166:7, 176:6, 212:4, 215:1, 225:1, 246:1, 256:7, 265:3, 275:3, 275:8, 276:7, 285:5, 286:9, 305:2, 313:1, 329:16, 406:5, 429:1, 432:1, 451:4, 470:2, 485:1.

145 Shafi'i-Kadkani 2006: 354.

146 See Kamal Isfahani 1969: 770; Junayd Shirazi 1941: 4; Haydar Shirazi 2004: 82.

147 See Purnamdarian 2003: 344.

148 H329:16.

149 H264:1.

150 U39:4. Zipoli 2009: 210.

151 H275:8.

152 H323:5, 332:6, 428:3, 468:1; U91:2.

153 J453:8.

154 J240:1.

155 See Kennedy 2005: 68–70.

156 H47:1, 118:2, 198:5, 202:1, 203:1, 252:2, 423:1; U73:3, 106:1, 115:1.

157 H10:1, 17:5, 47:3, 53:1, 71:8, 170:1, 175:8, 184:1, 199:7, 202:6, 252:1, 334:6, 371:1; U6:1, 24:2, 78:2.

158 H22:6, 254:5; U89:3; J1150:6.

159 H17:5, 20:1, 29:1, 162:5.

160 H10:3, 17:5, 63:3, 76:3, 111:5, 127:6, 131:3, 201:8, 335:1, 448:1; U8:5, 58:6, 95:3.

161 See Dashti 2011: 56.

162 Bürgel 2005: 296.

163 Melikian-Chirvani 1992: 106–107, 114–127.

164 H215:3, 351:3, 365:2.

165 H35:1, 83:7, 131:8, 199:1, 227:1, 257:10, 347:7, 352:3, 356:9.

166 H64:5, 83:7, 127:6, 175:8.

167 H285:3, 292:2. See also Ghani 1987: 66.

168 H10:2, 178:3, 459:4.

169 H119:4, 283:1, 285:6; U78:6, 114:1, 115:1.

170 H202:1 and 6.

171 H292:2; U27:4.

172 U13:8, 44:5.

173 H43:1; U33:4. See also Kamal Isfahani 1969: 735, 740.

174 Nasir Bukhara'i 1974: 325.

175 H88:6, 477:1; U49:7. See Natiq 2004: 248–251.

176 H214:2, 256:10.

177 H483:2.

178 H201:1, 298:1, 338:1. See Natiq 2004: 237–239.

179 H265:3; U78:1. See Natiq 2004: 239–241; Shafi'i-Kadkani 2006: 272–273.

180 U8:7.

181 U49:7.

182 H478:1.

183 H245:6, 264:5, 300:5.

184 U136:5.

185 See Bayhaqi 1971: 311–312.

186 Babaie 2008: 225.

187 See J47:2–3, 55:1–3; H297:10; U25:7.

188 H326:5.

189 J528:5, 798:4, 860:3, 1177:6, 1225:8.

190 J115:6, 668:8, 929:5, 1063:5, 1066:9, 1111:1, 1143:8, 1172:3, 1263:7.

191 J668:8, 786:8.

192 J671:7, 786:8.

193 J668:8, 786:8, 1063:5.

194 J115:6, 786:8.

195 J668:8, 1063:5, 1066:9, 1143:8, 1263:7.

196 See also Schimmel 1992: 287–289.

197 U59:4.

198 H71:3.

199 Sa'di Shirazi 2007: 168, 475, 590, 594, 802. See also Nasir Bukhara'i 1974: 45, 302–303.

200 H108:1, 169:6, 267:6, 271:7, 334:1, 375:7, 379:3, 390:6, 482:2; U129:3; J344:5, 575:7, 724:6.

201 See Bayhaqi 1971: 152, 343, 659, 689; Nizam al-Mulk 1955: 134. See also Seyed-Gohrab 2007: 186–188.

202 Schimmel 1992: 284–286; Seyed-Gohrab 2007: 196–202.

203 See Stetkevych 2016: 1.

204 H475:5; U56:6.

205 J1143:3; H362:2, 459:8

206 See Kennedy 1997: 61–65.

207 See Brookshaw 2009: 737–744.

208 J67:5, 373:7, 491:10, 552:2, 653:7; H163:4, 165:5, 362:1; U25:5, 28:7, 30:4, 36:5, 42:5, 55:7, 63:6, 84:5, 88:3, 120:7, 126:7, 127:7, 130:3, 135:4; Haydar Shirazi 2004: 72, 82.

209 H168:5, 182:4, 198:7, 212:1, 301:4, 314:7, 392:5, 457:8, 495:2; U61:5, 93:9–10.

210 H219:2.

211 H270:5, 319:4.

212 H105:6, 282:6.

213 H165:5, 282:4; J468:5, 835:1, 986:7, 1004:2, 1186:6.

214 H42:3, 336:6; U48:3.

215 H206:8, 210:6, 224:7, 348:4.

216 H224:7, 240:2, 257:6, 450:9.

217 H353:6. See Bayhaqi 1971: 192, 329; Kutubi 1985: 35.

218 H212:3. See Shamisa 2002: 14–16; El-Rouayheb 2005: 111–117.

219 H273:1. See Andrews and Kalpakli 2005: 72, 100–102; El-Rouayheb 2005: 42–43; van Gelder 2008.

220 H393. See also 'Attar Shirazi 1990: 80.

221 See Gruendler 2003: 8.

222 Lewis 2003b: 495.

223 See Nizami 'Aruzi 1920: 56.

224 H391:7.

225 Lewis 2003b: 492–493, 496. See also Purnamdarian 2003: 94–96.

226 Wright 2010: 555.

227 See Meisami 2003: 120.

228 Khvaju Kirmani 1957: 410; 'Attar Shirazi 1990: 91.

229 J878:4.

230 See Shafi'i-Kadkani 2002: 170–171.

231 H11:1, 479:4; Khvaju Kirmani 1957: 477, 500.

232 J1146:4; Khvaju Kirmani 1957: 477; 'Attar Shirazi 1990: 72, 83. See Meisami 2003: 109–110.

233 H34:9.

234 H277:4. See Lewis 2003b: 492.

235 H90:10, 241:2–3.

236 H479:6; Nasir Bukhara'i 1974: 272.

237 Hafiz Shirazi 1999: 378–379.

238 H25:9, 39:10, 214:8, 238:9, 404:7, 419:11, 469:10.

239 Losensky 1998: 258–259.

240 H377:7.

241 Mallah 1984: 10–11.

242 H3:9, 460:14. See also H352: 8; Ahur 1984: vi-vii; Shafi'i-Kadkani 2002: 170; Purnamdarian 2003: 96; Hasuri 2016: 171.

243 See Mallah 1984: 6–9; Shafi'i-Kadkani 1989: 437–463; Lewis 2003b.

244 H258:9, 333:9. See also Shafi'i-Kadkani 2002: 170.

245 H283:3, 320:7.

246 See Bayhaqi 1971: 4; Shabankara'i 1984: 199; Shafi'i-Kadkani 2006: 107–109; Lewis 2014: 57–58.

247 Khvaju Kirmani 1957: 36, 89.

248 See de Bruijn 1987; Boyce 1957.

249 H146:5.

250 H30:6, 90:8, 133:4, 203:6, 351:2; U27:2, 78:3, 88:9.

251 H3:8, 16:8, 144:2, 178:9, 181:2, 193:5, 240:1, 332:7, 376:6.

252 H193:5, 332:7.

253 H154:1.

254 See H8, 13, 20, 29, 82, 92, 99, 103, 148, 163, 282, 396, 417, 432, 478, 479; U10, 27, 58, 78, 114, 121. See also Salman Savaji 1957: 59; 'Attar Shirazi 1990: 54; Nasir Bukhara'i 1974: 271, 302–303.

255　See Manuchihri Damghani 1996: 7, 8, 11, 12, 16, 21, 73, 78, 104; Brookshaw 2014.

256　See Lewis 2003b: 491–492.

257　See Husaynian 1995: 83–84; Klein 2014: 215.

258　See Husaynian 1995: 108; Gruendler 2003: 8–9.

259　Klein 2014: 217.

260　See Shehadi 1995: 119–122; Klein 2014: 215.

261　See Fallahzadeh 2005: 118–205.

262　Ibid: 128, 133–137.

263　H276:8, 428:1.

264　U91:1, 126:8.

265　See Bayhaqi 1971: 310–312; Mallah 1984: 63–67.

266　J244:3, 1094:3; H163:3, 440:8.

267　Khvaju Kirmani 1957: 410. See also Ridgeon 2012: 12–13.

268　H184:5, 474:3; 'Attar Shirazi 1990: 72.

269　H245:5, 440:8; Khvaju Kirmani 1957: 477.

270　H153:3. See Lewis 2003b: 495.

271　See During 1988; Ridgeon 2012: 4–5, 30. See also H2:3, 30:6, 136:5, 197:6, 257:5, 292:4, 340:9, 460:6.

272　Ritter 2003: 508, 513; Fallahzadeh 2005: 52, 120–123, 134–137.

273　Klein 2014: 224; Fallahzadeh 2005: 123, 127.

274　Hafiz Shirazi 1999: 60. See also Shafi'i-Kadkani 2002: 175.

275　See Ahur 1984: viii; Lewis 2003b: 494–495; Natiq 2004: 166–180.

276　See Shehadi 1995: 156–158; Klein 2014: 218–219, 224.

277　H29:8, 46:4, 101:10, 158:5, 200:1, 202:5, 219:2, 236:7, 238:4, 241:2, 244:3, 283:3, 286:4, 292:4, 296:6, 320:5, 335:7, 348:6, 351:2, 391:7, 428:1, 431:5, 460:6, 466:4, 479:5; U27:2, 61:6, 69:1, 89:4, 114:5; J348:2, 430:4, 491:9, 528:6, 535:6, 832:6, 874:9, 1114:4, 1249:9, 1319:8, 1372:5, 1383:8. See also Haydar Shirazi 2004: 88; 'Attar Shirazi 1990: 75.

278　H158:5, 165:4, 215:2, 219:2, 296:6, 391:7, 490:9; U126:8; J491:9, 874:9, 1319:8.

279　J289:9, 491:9, 832:6, 874:9, 1017:5, 1249:9, 1372:5, 1383:8; H46:4, 165:4, 191:2, 215:2, 219:2, 335:7, 350:9, 351:2, 431:9; U91:1, 126:8.

280　J289:9, 348:2, 655:5, 832:6, 1372:5, 1383:8; H200:1, 219:2, 238:4, 256:4, 374:4; U114:5.

281　H2:3, 29:8, 238:4, 244:3; U27:2 69:1; J1383:8; Khvaju Kirmani 1957: 500.

282　H137:5, 350:9, 351:2, 360:3, 386:6. See also Mallah 1984: 57.

283　H334:6.

284　U61:6, 89:4; Khvaju Kirmani 1957: 490. See also Mallah 1990.

285　See Azarnouche 2013: 140–145.

286　H29:8, 466:4; U27:2.

287 H46:4.

288 J289:9, 832:6, 1372:5.

289 J348:2; H200:1; U114:5.

290 H296:6, 391:7.

291 J491:9; see 'Attar Shirazi 1990: 54.

292 H219:2.

293 Khvaju Kirmani 1957: 410.

294 'Attar Shirazi 1990: 91.

295 U126:8; H215:2, 490:9.

296 H428:1; U61:6, 89:4.

297 H351:2.

298 H350:9.

299 See Lewis 2003b: 493.

300 H22:4, 186:6, 245:5, 324:3, 431:5. See also Mallah 1984: 67.

301 J348:2; H2:3, 46:4, 219:2, 241:2; U69:1, 115:3.

302 J528:6, 832:6; U69:1.

303 J535:6; H350:9. See also Mallah 1984: 57.

304 J430:4, 782:1; H22:9; U115:3.

305 J348:2; H333:9, 351:2.

306 H495:3.

307 H241:2, 283:3, 374:7, 460:11. See also Bayhaqi 1971: 86.

308 H46:4, 320:5. See Shafi'i-Kadkani 2006: 315.

309 See also J430:4, 655:5, 1017:5, 1249:9, 1319:8, 1372:5.

310 See Beelaert 2000: 181–198.

311 Rumi 1998: 5.

312 Haydar Shirazi 2004: 99.

313 H218:8.

314 See Nasir Bukhara'i 1974: 316. See also Shafi'i-Kadkani 2002: 169–171.

315 See Lewis 2001: 71–74.

316 Ibid: 82.

317 See Schlumberger 1952: 259–260; Schlumberger 1978: 38–41; Bombaci 1966: 6, 32; Fehévári and Shokoohy 1980: 81, 91; Bier 1986: 57–58; Golombek and Wilber 1988; Blair 1993: 239–240; Meisami 2001b; and Brookshaw 2003: 201–203.

318 H15:9.

319 H24:5, 47:9, 144:2, 206:3, 348:6, 454:5.

320 See 'Ubayd Zakani 1999: 39, 45, 52, 135.

321 J78:6, 339:5, 865:7; H154:5, 411:6.

322 J131:3; Khvaju Kirmani 1957: 476, 477.

323 H313:8.

324 H232:8.

325 J762:1. See also Vassaf al-Hazrat 1959: 161; Kutubi 1985: 70, 111.

326 H37:1, 146:3, 181:6, 397:4; U102:4.

327 J354:6, 791:3–4; H226:9, 372:8.

328 Blair 1993: 239. See also Yoch 1978: 403.

329 H49:3, 268:3.

330 H353:2.

331 H254:5, 353:2, 354:8.

332 Robinson 1997: 145, 153.

333 H167:6.

334 H402:3.

335 J1278:2; H23:5; U99:4.

336 J354:6, 823:2, 1162:4; U75:5 82:1; H397:1.

337 J864:2, 865:7; U99:4; H12:13, 294:10.

338 H411:7.

339 H397:3.

340 H430:7.

341 Ja'far b. Muhammad 1959: 33–34, 140–141; Ahmad b. Husayn 1966: 100, 203–204.

342 See O'Kane 2006: 348–349.

343 Simpson 2013: 74–76.

344 Blair 1993: 243–244.

345 Shafi'i-Kadkani 2002: 190–191.

346 Ja'far b. Muhammad 1959: 33–34, 68–69.

347 Losensky 2004: 214.

348 See Zarkub Shirazi 1931: 28; Hafiz Abru 1999: 147–148.

349 See Durand-Guédy 2013: 174–175, 177.

350 J536:3; U69:4.

351 See Moynihan 1980.

352 See Ahmad b. Husayn 1966: 75, 98, 178, 180, 206, 209.

353 See Redford 2000: 319.

354 H79:2, 150:6; U67:5, 93:2; Kamal Isfahani 1969: 735; Khvaju Kirmani 1957: 229, 266; Nasir Bukhara'i 1974: 91, 147. See also Bayhaqi 1971: 570; Durand-Guédy 2013: 159–160.

355 See Bayhaqi 1971: 152, 570–571.

356 See Ahmad b. Husayn 1966: 205; Wilber 1979; Gronke 1992.

357 See Brookshaw 2003: 202–204.

358 J832:3–6.

359 Meisami 1995: 257.

360 See Subtelny 2002: 103–110.

361 H163, 479; U126; J851.

362 See Rollason 2016: 2.

363 Meisami 1985: 245.

364 Ibid: 248–249, 253.

365 See Zarkub Shirazi 1931: 28, 72–73, 93, 132, 151; Yazdi 1947: 18, 105–106; Aryanpur 1986: 140, 141, 154, 168, 264.

366 See Arberry 1960: 10–11.

367 See Ahmad b. Husayn 1966: 75, 180, 198; Miller 1989: 76.

368 Miller 1990: 120.

369 Ibid: 268.

370 Redford 2000: 313.

371 Meisami 1995: 250.

372 Meisami 1985: 229.

373 H39:1, 48:8, 115:7, 228:1, 321:3, 356:1, 393:4, 436:5; J366:5, 924:4.

374 H356:1; J242:9, 669:4.

375 H393:4; J71:7, 428:6, 429:1, 724:7.

376 H12:5, 43:1; J416:1, 554:5, 913:6.

377 J416:3, 784:1, 864:1.

378 U23:6, 85:4.

379 J101:1, 256:1, 592:3, 695:3, 851:1; H11:5.

380 H225:7.

381 U18:3.

382 H85:5; J1281:1.

383 H65:4, 269:1.

384 J256:4, 366:5, 428:2, 972:7; U44:1, 45:3; H16:4, 85:5, 106:4, 107:3, 219:1, 234:2, 255:3, 268:1, 275:3, 456:4, 457:5, 467:6.

385 U22:2, 61:9.

386 H9:2.

387 H173:3.

388 J40:10, 78:3, 102:4, 290:2, 322:3, 350:3, 358:3, 643:6, 719:1, 851:2, 865:6, 922:4, 1087:10, 1192:1, 1196:2, 1240:9, 1251:6, 1350:2.

389 Clavijo 1928: 242–245, 258, 260–261.

390 Marefat 1993: 29.

391 Ahmad b. Husayn 1966: 212.

392 See Hillenbrand 2003; Manz 2003.

393 See Ibn Battuta 1975: 221–222; Zarkub Shirazi 1931: 52, 132; 'Isa b. Junayd 1985: 335–337; Natanzi 1957: 175, 182, 190. See also Brookshaw 2005: 173–178.

394 Zarkub Shirazi 1931: 5–6, 22.

395 J227:2.

396 Q52:23, 56:17–19.

397 See Jalal Yazdi 1987: 104.

398 J67:6, 535:6; H115:7, 268:4; 'Attar Shirazi 1990: 83.

399 J1358:2; U100:2.

400 J528:6; H288:1; U10:2, 69:4.

401 J491:8, 794:9.

402 J176:1; H216:8, 484:1.

403 H65:4.

404 U93:1.

405 J348:2.

406 Q20:76.

407 J470:6, 1063:3; H163:2.

408 J463:1. See also Vassaf al-Hazrat 1959: 524.

409 J1143:2, 1145:2.

410 H429:11.

411 H234:1, 239:5.

412 See Yazdi 1947: 11; Kutubi 1985: 81.

413 See Zarkub Shirazi 1931: 5–6, 20, 22–24.

414 See Ahmad b. Husayn 1966: 198.

415 J592:6; H33:1; U138:2; Kamal Isfahani 1969: 735; Khvaju Kirmani 1957: 229, 266; Haydar Shirazi 2004: 72.

416 Aryanpur 1986: 109.

417 Sa'di Shirazi 2007: 521.

418 U93:2.

419 H29:7.

420 H195:4.

421 H253:1, 288:5; U100:3; J463:2; Khvaju Kirmani 1957: 314.

422 H163:1.

423 Jalal Yazdi 1987: 61.

424 Manuchihri Damghani 1996: 1, 3, 17, 22, 29, 31, 43; Farrukhi Sistani 1999: 13, 53, 60, 82.

425 U44:1–6, 93:1–3, 96:1–6, 126:1–6.

426 H239:8.

427 J253:3, 398:8, 734:3, 1070:9, 1146:1, 1234:6, 1323:1; H240:1, 454:1.

428 H21:4, 175:2–3, 414:1; U44:2, 49:5, 96:3, 105:4.

429 H102:5.

430 H325:6.

431 J336:7; H79:3, 112:6.

432 J397:1.

433 U44:6, 61:3.

434 H18:5, 166:2.

435 H235:6, 429:4.

436 H174:2.

437 H414:1, 423:7.

438 H350:1; Haydar Shirazi 2004: 99.

439 H274:2.

440 H173:3.

441 H230:6.

442 U94:1, 100:1; H33:1, 176:2; J536:3, 851:4–5.

443 See Meisami 1995: 250.

444 H117:4, 219:1, 255:3.

445 H113:1, 219:1.

446 H262:4, 346:4, 429:1, 444:6; U49:1, 96:4.

447 U22:2.

448 U96:4; H58:6.

449 J592:3, 1358:1.

450 Junayd Shirazi 1941: 4.

451 Ibid: 11; Haydar Shirazi 2004: 82.

452 Junayd Shirazi 1941: 15.

453 H246:2, 376:1.

454 H276:1.

455 H117:4.

456 U44:2, 49:1, 94:3.

457 H219:3.

458 H43:1.

459 H418:4.

460 H164:6.

461 See 'Iraqi 1998: 88, 93–95, 105, 132–133, 137–138, 141, 152–153, 159–160, 162–163, 239.

462 'Attar Shirazi 1990: 10, 54.

463 H272:2, 467:1.

464 See H31:1, 206:9; U18:1.

465 Nasir Bukhara'i 1974: 175.

466 'Attar Shirazi 1990: 101–103.

467 H18:1.

468 Haydar Shirazi 2004: 99.

469 H20:1, 132:2.

470 H84:1. See also H246:10; U91:1.

471 See Kamal Isfahani 1969: 735. See also Hanaway 1988: 76.

472 Junayd Shirazi 1941: 23.

473 Salman Savaji 1957: 20.

474 J65, 66.

475 Lewis 2010: 260.

476 Ibid: 261–264.

477 See Melikian-Chirvani 1992: 102; Melikian-Chirvani 1996: 95.

478 J821:6.

479 H130:6, 153:5, 275:8.

480 J332:3, 398:3, 535:10, 1162:4, 1326:5, 1327:3.

481 H158:5.

482 H150:6.

483 H206:2, 288:5.

484 U67:3, 129:1.

485 U133:2.

486 H396:1, 479:1; U44:5, 49:1, 69:3, 89:1, 104:4, 117:6; J463:1, 535:6, 767:1, 986:7, 1142:6.

487 H13:1, 147:2, 202:3, 204:3, 219:2, 236:7, 253:4, 275:8, 452:3, 479:1; see Salman Savaji 1957: 532; Haydar Shirazi 2004: 72, 88.

488 See Shafi'i-Kadkani 2002: 165–167; Lewis 2014: 53–54, 57–60, 66–67.

Chapter 3

1   See Ritter 2003: 457.

2   Ghazali 1942: 30–31.

3   Lumbard 2016: 163, 175.

4   Ghazali 1942: 29.

5   Lumbard 2016: 178.

6   Bürgel 2005: 290.

7   Meisami 1996: 140–142.

8   de Bruijn 2006: 20.

9   See Shamisa 2002: 46–47.

10 See Kamal Isfahani 1969: 716; 'Attar Shirazi 1990: 69.

11 See Brookshaw 2009: 739–743.

12 See Bauer 1998: 504–511; Hameen-Anttila 2000: 137.

13 'Ubayd Zakani 1999: 257–258.

14 See Southgate 1984; Zipoli 2001; Zipoli 2006.

15 ♂50:3, 51:11, 63:11, 76:3, 91:1, 294:7, 346:2.

16 ♂8:7, 27:3, 27:6, 32:3, 51:7, 90:1, 151:1, 169:4, 187:2, 223:2, 234:7, 236:1, 237:2, 294:12, 303:8, 309:4, 384:3.

17 Meisami 2003: 45. See also Zipoli 2009: 172.

18 See Danner 1975; Clinton 1988: 77–78.

19 Schoeler 1990: 275–276.

20 Minuvi 1954; Kennedy 2005: 2–3.

21 van den Berg 1998: 29.

22 ♂19:1, 20:8, 44:1, 246:2, 285:1, 349:3, 398:3.

23 ♂45:7, 50:2, 76:2, 95:6, 147:1, 268:2, 345:3, 375:5.

24 van Ruymbeke 2007: 57–62.

25 Kamal Khujandi 1958: 359; Haydar Shirazi 2004: 65, 66.

26 H339, 412; J1001.

27 Moayyad 1988: 131.

28 See Avery and Heath-Stubbs 1952: 7; Zipoli 2009: 172.

29 J263:9; H46:3.

30 J836:3; 'Attar Shirazi 1990: 8.

31 J1064:3.

32 J1147:2.

33 Haydar Shirazi 2004: 78. See also Meisami 1985: 245.

34 J805:1, 938:1, 1172:1, 1174:1, 1175:1, 1176:1.

35 Ansari 1987: 47, 53, 56, 58, 131.

36 Hameen-Anttila 2000: 137; Kennedy 2005: 59–61.

37 ♂59:1.

38 ♂64:3.

39 ♂92:1.

40 ♂93:1.

41 H111:1, 114:2.

42 H111:1.

43 H448:5.

44 H18:3, 299:6; Khvaju Kirmani 1957: 207, 479; Nasir Bukhara'i 1974: 90, 309. See also Melikian-Chirvani 1996: 105–108; Natiq 2004: 199–201.

45 See Zaryab 1989: 103–105; ♂62:5, 63:7; K30:1, 33:1, 67:5, 129:14, 150:2, 167:1, 214:5, 216:4, 220:5, 231:2, 239:1, 240:1, 281:3, 305:7.

46 K109:18, 160:5, 211:8, 263:3, 286:6, 403:7 and 418:2.

47 K111:5.

48 K406:3.

49 K137:2, 191:7.

50 ♂27:8.

51 K106:1.

52 K8:4, 111:4, 281:3.

53 K8:14, 43:5, 126:8.

54 K8:14, 25:17, 43:5, 45:1, 52:6, 111:5, 124:2, 126:4, 129:8, 150:8–10, 242:3, 276:3, 278:14, 296:4, 310:2, 398:13.

55 K126:4.

56 K122:5, 150:8–10.

57 K191:8–9.

58 K404:6.

59 Meisami 1998: 65, 69–70.

60 Kennedy 1997: 37.

61 See Azarnouche 2013: 135–139; Gignoux 1999: 42–49.

62 Zipoli 2009: 173–174. See also Brookshaw 2014: 7–8; Manuchihri Damghani 1996: 11, 120–121, 125–127.

63 ♂41:10; K8:6, 23:3, 58:3, 75:1, 137:3, 160:4, 170:6, 182:4, 209:5, 253:4, 339:14, 381:17.

64 K33:3, 67:6, 74:6.

65 H132:4. See Melikian-Chirvani 1992: 109.

66 *Tarikh-i Sistan* 1994: 178–179.

67 See Manuchihri Damghani 1996: 13–14, 47, 101, 154–156, 174–176, 195–198, 203–206; Farrukhi Sistani 1999: 219, 312–313. See also Brookshaw 2014.

68 H142:1.

69 H263:6.

70 Hafiz 1999: 378. See Natiq 2004: 194–195.

71 H130:7.

72 H9:1, 25:1, 240:5; U104:1.

73 Melikian-Chirvani 1996: 123.

74 H120:1.

75 H56:7.

76 Meisami 1985: 249.

77 H431:6.

78 H429:8.

79 H390:1.

80 H454:7.

81 H164:3.

82 H255:3.

83 U104:4.

84 U104:2.

85 Junayd Shirazi 1941: 4.

86 H173:5.

87 H225:2, 492:5.

88   H388:5.

89   H205:7, 228:6, 277:5, 310:2. See also Kamal Isfahani 1969: 740; Junayd Shirazi 1941: 19; Jalal Yazdi 1987: 178; Haydar Shirazi 2004: 63, 67, 81, 99.

90   See Ghani 1987: 280–281; Hafiz Shirazi 1996: 1228–1229.

91   H400:2.

92   H490:8.

93   H190:2, 267:2, 281:3, 438:1, 461:2, 469:2.

94   ♀47:14, 145:1, 303:8, 308:3.

95   ♀1, 66, 84, 89, 117, 139, 144, 171.

96   ♂13:6

97   ♂167:2.

98   ♂186:3.

99   ♂374:3.

100   ♂57:2.

101   ♂172:3, 227:1, 234:2, 341:1, 356:2 and 359:9.

102   H398:5, 450:8, 455:1, 486:8; U13:5; J677:5, 686:6, 762:1, 763:1, 881:4, 1264:5. See also Awhadi Maragha'i 1961: 223–224.

103   See Southgate 1984: 429; Zipoli 2009: 204.

104   See El-Rouayheb 2005: 26–27.

105   Shamisa 1983: 34.

106   See Southgate 1984: 433; Shamisa 2002.

107   Meisami 1987: 246. See also Zeikowitz 2003: 2–3.

108   Shamisa 1983: 38.

109   See Bauer 1998: 334–335, 462–463, 466–467, 495; Wright 1997; El-Rouayheb 2005: 12; Andrews and Kalpaklı 2005: 32–43, 137–138; Naim 1979.

110   Lewis 1995: 507.

111   Sa'di Shirazi 2007: 128–129, 131–132, 134–135, 142–146, 283–284, 323–325, 340–341, 357–359. See also Southgate 1984: 431–433; Yohannan 1987: 77–80; Keshavarz 2015: 144–146.

112   See Katouzian 2006: 43–44.

113   H39:2.

114   Junayd Shirazi 1941: 19.

115   'Attar Shirazi 1990: 68.

116   Kamal Isfahani 1969: 751.

117   J409:8.

118   H289:2, 333:5.

119   J336:6, 699:7; H185:5.

120   See El-Rouayheb 2005: 14.

121   See Toorawa 1997: 251; Andrews and Kalpaklı 2005: 59–84, 143.

122 ♂348:1.

123 See H68:3; Sa'di Shirazi 2007: 492; 'Attar Shirazi 1990: 27.

124 J109:3, 774:2, 775:8 and 776:9.

125 H197:3, 295:7, 338:3, 460:3.

126 van den Berg 1998: 22.

127 See Ritter 2003: 477.

128 El-Rouayheb 2005: 6.

129 Meisami 1987: 251.

130 van den Berg 1998: 22.

131 H16:8, 170:4, 193:11, 202:4, 296:6, 421:3, 423:2. See also Khvaju Kirmani 1957: 232, 301, 313, 401.

132 H123:8, 490:9. See also Khvaju Kirmani 1957: 278, 334, 338; Salman Savaji 1957: 237; 'Attar Shirazi 1990: 69.

133 See Khvaju Kirmani 1957: 651; Salman Savaji 1957: 14, 36. See also Nazari 2007: 65–66, 75–76.

134 Lewis 2009: 712–723.

135 See Bauer 1998: 478–479, 482; Wright 1997: 9, 13.

136 ♂40:12, 56:1, 63:10, 69:2, 171:3, 185:1–2, 308:4. See also Montgomery 1996; van Gelder 2001; Kennedy 2005: 54–56; Bauer 1998: 473.

137 ♀176:1; K74:4, 81:8, 107:8, 255:10, 277:4, 280:12. See also Wright 1997: 15.

138 K28:10, 80:4, 102:2, 191:5, 237:8, 272:1, 312:2, 360:1, 413:1.

139 Melikian-Chirvani 1997: 68–69.

140 Khurramshahi 1987: 97–99.

141 Limbert 2004a: 52; Melikian-Chirvani 1997: 69.

142 Karamustafa 1994: 33.

143 Natiq 2004: 289–291.

144 H493:7; Nasir Bukhara'i 1974: 272. See also Yarshater 1960; Nazari 2007: 132–135; Zipoli 2009: 210.

145 H92:3.

146 H170:7.

147 H89:7.

148 H109:5.

149 H312:7.

150 H149:3.

151 H159:4.

152 H192:8.

153 Lewis 1995: 449.

154 Meisami 2007: 166–167.

155 Schimmel 1975; Schimmel 1992: 138–142; Brookshaw 2009: 726–729.

156 *Ta'rikh-i Sistan* 1994: 179.

157 Bayhaqi 1971: 20, 41, 235, 293, 689, 891.

158 See Esin 1970; Esin 1979.

159 H3:1; U17:4, 131:5.

160 H47:6, 82:1, 131:1, 180:8, 199:4, 302:9, 412:2, 454:6; U93:1. See also Kamal Isfahani 1969: 709; Nasir Bukhara'i 1974: 390; Khvaju Kirmani 1957: 283, 408, 473, 480, 695; Salman Savaji 1957: 48, 305; Haydar Shirazi 2004: 63.

161 Vassaf al-Hazrat 1959: 182.

162 See 'Attar Shirazi 1990: 33.

163 U1:4, 40:3, 48:1, 131:5; J115:3, 144:3, 406:5.

164 Brookshaw 2009: 736–743.

165 Ibid: 732. See also Andrews and Kalpaklı 2005: 131.

166 H205:5; J23:1, 115:3.

167 Khvaju Kirmani 1957: 408.

168 J153:3, 1224:3.

169 H145:8.

170 H185:5. See also Shafi'i-Kadkani 2014: 304–316.

171 See Bürgel 2005: 283.

172 See Tetley 2009: 21–23.

173 See Schimmel 1988: 224.

174 See Kutubi 1985: 37, 70.

175 See Miller 1990: 245.

176 See Ghani 2001: 375.

177 Shams-i Fakhri 1887: 33.

178 Sa'di Shirazi 2007: 418.

179 Ibid: 627.

180 Ingenito 2014: 97–99.

181 H440:8.

182 Rudaki Samarqandi 2014: 113.

183 See Ahur 1984: 501.

184 H145:8.

185 H314:8. See Lewis 1995: 509–510; Shamisa 2002: 44–46.

186 van den Berg 1998: 26.

187 See Moayyad 1988: 132.

188 J242:2, 397:2, 607:5, 620:1, 864:3, 1019:4, 1079:5, 1139:5, 1162:8.

189 H125:6, 137:8.

190 H322:5, 352:6, 412:8; U14:2, 63:5, 79:7.

191 J25:1, 81:6.

192 H91:7.

193 H89:6, 111:9, 209:1, 419:2.

194 See Kennedy 2005: 51.

195 U38:6, 129:5; H165:7, 476:5 and 491:7.

196 J23:6, 83:12, 434:3, 461:6, 870:2, 878:3, 1289:3.

197 H390:6; J502:6, 1232:3.

198 J150:9, 592:6, 687:8, 697:6. See also Junayd Shirazi 1941: 17.

199 H390:6; J344:5, 379:1, 761:7, 865:9, 943:4, 1209:3.

200 J60:4, J477:1.

201 ♂303:1.

202 ♂98:14, 392:4.

203 ♂17:4, 56:5, 59:6, 144:4, 243:4, 294:10.

204 ♂58:1.

205 ♂59:3.

206 ♂59:4.

207 ♂164:1.

208 ♂59:5.

209 ♂111:7.

210 H420:1.

211 J687:8.

212 H314:8; U53:3, 79:1, 84:1.

213 H279:6, 266:1. See also Zakavati 1991: 225.

214 See Ahur 1984: 770; Zakavati 1991: 217–219, 222; Digard 2002: 413.

215 Brookshaw 2009: 740–742.

216 See Awhadi Maragha'i 1961: 248.

217 Greenblatt 2010: 41.

218 Sa'di Shirazi 2007: 627; Khvaju Kirmani 1957: 557.

219 Hafiz 2000: 36.

220 See Zaryab 1989: 120–121.

221 See Islami Nudushan 2003: 63–64.

222 H188:3, 335:4, 412:6; J563:4, 770:8, 1312:1.

223 J728:4, 943:5.

224 J1237:2.

225 H187:2, 491:2.

226 H194:1; U52:6.

227 J859:4.

228 H59:2.

229 H59:2.

230 J52:1.

231 H13:8; J312:8, 670:7

232 H375:3.

233 Lumbard 2016: 158.

234   H125:2, 326:2, 412:6, 421:5, 433:8.

235   H82:1.

236   J943:5.

237   ♂76:2, 99:2, 124:5, 134:5, 184:1, 227:1, 328:1, 341:1, 374:3, 377:1.

238   Khvaju Kirmani 1957: 266.

239   H52:1, 92:3, 104:5, 110:8, 120:1, 123:8, 143:10, 148:1, 269:5, 282:1, 296:5, 336:5; U35:7, 38:3, 39:1, 69:2, 98:1, 106:4, 125:6, 126:6, 130:4; J6:7, 21:2, 27:1, 49:4, 84:3, 101:2, 109:9, 126:6, 159:1, 164:4, 223:7, 281:11, 284:5, 424:7, 437:1, 459:3, 582:2, 649:7, 704:1, 723:9, 774:1, 776:1, 779:1, 900:5, 960:4, 964:2, 1272:5, 1332:2, 1341:2, 1393:9, 1399:2, 1402:1, 1403:1. See also 'Attar Shirazi 1990: 7.

240   Melikian-Chirvani 1974: 35–46.

241   H198:4, 314:8, 326:1, 333:5, 347:1, 471:7, 490:3; U3:4; J4:6, 16:6, 25:7, 28:1, 52:1, 123:6, 138:2, 139:4, 252:4, 272:3, 299:3, 360:1, 424:4, 468:5, 479:2, 508:6, 535:10, 621:1, 647:2, 672:9, 1060:7, 1182:2, 1187:4, 1360:8.

242   Q6:74, 7:138, 14:35, 21:57, 26:71.

243   ♂33:2, 358:3, 401:2; ♀27:1, 142:4.

244   H153:3, 235:7, 282:2, 444:1, 457:5, 473:13; U19:6, 100:1, 119:5; J5:1, 9:1, 11:1, 25:3, 28:1, 29:4, 32:3, 35:4, 42:2, 43:2, 45:1, 67:4, 70:1, 77:3, 90:7, 164:6, 168:7, 274:1, 298:1, 351:3, 361:5, 424:8, 553:3, 587:7, 803:1, 843:1, 965:2, 1042:1, 1329:7, 1360:3, 1410:5.

245   J116:4, 304:6, 564:6, 769:5, 825:3, 859:6, 1055:7, 1182:2. See Beelaert 2000: 145–159.

246   J528:4, 780:6, 784:6, 983:8, 1067:2.

247   See 'Ubayd Zakani 1999: 149.

248   H11:7, 105:2, 113:5, 133:2, 170:3, 197:1, 212:2, 240:2, 289:2, 375:4, 433:9, 456:7, 480:6; U45:4, 114:1.

249   Bashir 2011: 146. See also Ridgeon 2012: 7–11.

250   See Ritter 2003: 377; Lumbard 2016: 172.

251   Ze'evi 2006: 82.

252   Ibid: 141.

253   'Ubayd Zakani 1999: 292, 304.

254   See Ze'evi 2006: 83; Jalal Yazdi 1987: 82.

255   H293:6.

256   See Yaghoobi 2017: 72–76.

257   See Schimmel 1988: 222.

258   H215:1, H219:3, 275:3, 305:2.

259   See Ridgeon 2012: 3–5, 12. See also Khvaju Kirmani 1957: 427; Junayd Shirazi 1941: 10.

260   Ze'evi 2006: 86.

261   See Ahur 1984: 502.

262   H161:6.

263 H493:6. See also Ahur 1984: 502.

264 H34:6, 126:8, 307:5, 444:8; U140:1; J40:4, 46:1, 77:5, 123:3, 281:11, 284:5, 290:2, 346:5, 378:9, 462:1, 472:1, 558:2, 626:5, 642:1, 704:1, 720:5, 723:9, 753:2, 823:6, 1061:3, 1153:5, 1177:5, 1232:7, 1319:7, 1339:4, 1398:1, 1410:5.

265 H139:4, 171:7; U48:1, 81:2, 98:2, 121:1; J357:4.

266 H124:5, 252:6.

267 H16:1; J119:5.

268 H290:4.

269 H279:6, 282:2, 288:7; U137:4, 140:1; J432:5, 871:1.

270 H16:3, 85:4, 215:4, 239:6, 287:1–3, 322:4, 365:6, 400:1, 402:2, 403:4, 409:2; U4:1, 9:1, 10:2, 13:2, 14:4, 48:3, 53:1, 59:2, 93:1, 114:2, 123:5, 126:6. See also Jalal Yazdi 1987: 190; Haydar Shirazi 2004: 88.

271 See Bürgel 2005: 291.

272 Ritter 2003: 413–414.

273 ♂1, 3, 5, 6, 8, 9, 10, 12, 17, 23, 25, 41, 47, 51, 54 55, 62, 63, 64, 66, 75, 80, 84, 95, 98, 99, 100, 122, 125, 128, 129, 131, 144, 145, 169, 171, 182, 184, 193, 204, 223, 234, 236, 245, 247, 256, 268, 276, 280, 286, 289, 294, 301, 303, 324, 332, 339, 341, 345, 349, 352, 354, 358, 369, 374, 378, 390, 395, 398, 409.

274 H4:1, 110:3, 402:2. See ♂63:5, 67:3, 84:2.

275 See Moayyad 1988: 133.

276 H21:5, 45:4, 132:5, 221:4, 429:4, 443:2; U16:1, 138:3; J48:7, 100:2, 103:7, 107:5, 154:7, 324:6, 344:3, 410:3, 505:5, 762:5, 874:2, 925:3, 1259:4.

277 J77:5, 81:8, 107:5, 123:7, 433:4, 507:1, 587:10, 632:1, 797:1, 874:2, 910:5, 912:11, 1176:13, 1232:8; H16:3, 107:4, 155:1, 210:4, 221:4, 258:6, 321:8, 412:1, 435:6, 484:1; U13:1, 21:2, 115:1, 128:3. See also Kamal Isfahani 1969: 737; Nasir Bukhara'i 1974: 398.

278 J131:1.

279 J433:4, 491:1, 626:8, 1232:8.

280 J85:7, 93:1, 125:1, 126:3, 268:1, 341:9, 363:5, 620:1, 626:9, 627:6, 634:3, 637:4, 762:1, 1247:1; U23:1, 46:1, 84:1, 128:3, 138:3; H332:8.

281 H75:1, 271:6; U15:4, 63:5, 69:2; J154:7.

282 ♂170:7, 315:5, 349:2.

283 ♂125:1, 129:6, 134:6, 295:1.

284 Jalal Yazdi 1987: 190.

285 H120:12, 211:2, 346:5; J81:2, 652:14, 1212:7. See Glünz 1986: 133–137.

286 J502:4, 1083:7.

287 H96:2, 192:9, 273:9, 361:2, 445:6–7; J1:3, 4:9, 5:3, 9:3, 23:1, 26:1, J75:6, 101:11, 113:6, 121:2, 248:2, 250:3, 284:5, 302:1, 345:2, 427:5, 479:7, 573:3, 617:3, 640:8, 709:2, 1030:5, 1160:3, 1413:1; U9:3, 34:4–6, 36:1–3, 45:7, 50:2, 59:1, 90:6, 93:12, 98:2, 103:2, 119:6, 120:5, 125:2.

288 J108:7, 257:2, 263:2, 447:5, 629:3, 1329:7.

289 H177:5, 399:3; J28:4, 30:4, 177:3, 226:10, 434:6, 461:2, 723:3, 953:2, 1057:5, 1185:5, 1279:4.

290 U15:7, 93:12; J130:6, 245:1, 302:1, 368:3, 610:3, 628:6, 1141:3, 1174:1.

291 J906:7.

292 H88:4; U137:4; J245:1, 614:3, 753:2, 776:1, 1265:2, 1341:2, 1351:4.

293 H291:4, 483:9; U94:6; J372:6, 640:8, 1381:6, 1412:2.

294 H435:6; U31:7, 59:2, 98:1, 105:1, 120:5; J252:2, 459:3.

295 J258:4, 440:6, 1380:1.

296 U81:5.

297 U59:3, 98:3; J2:8, 3:1.

298 H10:6, 57:6, 97:6, 139:6, 211:5, 282:1, 296:5, 400:8, 439:9, 473:13, 492:6; J36:2, 46:1, 88:3, 122:7, 135:1, 245:7, 272:6, 284:5, 501:3, 573:5, 672:2, 844:7, 878:2, 1217:4, 1265:2, 1286:3, 1341:2, 1347:5, 1366:3, 1389:2, 1402:1, 1410:5.

299 H19:1, 205:5, 211:2, 480:1; U50:2, 81:2, 85:1, 98:5.

300 Sa'di Shirazi 2007: 29.

301 Bürgel 2005: 284.

302 Andrews 1985: 93.

303 J524:8, 980:6.

304 See Andrews and Kalpaklı 2005: 264–269; Kennedy 2005: 50–51.

305 H19:1, 43:5, 66:4, 120:12, 153:5, 185:1, 249:6, 260:6, 325:7, 407:4; U17:4, 39:5; J27:6, 28:11, 90:7, 97:7, 168:1, 241:3, 281:11, 410:15, 643:4, 765:7, 1131:8, 1174:5, 1212:7. See also Sa'di Shirazi 2007: 323; Ridgeon 2010: 10–12.

306 Khurramshahi 1987: 350–351.

307 Aigle 2005: 190–191.

308 See Zarrinkub 1975: 2–4.

309 Shafi'i-Kadkani 2002: 165.

310 'Ubayd Zakani 1999: 281, 283, 289, 293, 312. See also Meneghini 2010; Brookshaw 2012: 47–50.

311 H422:4.

312 U12:5, 140:1; H86:4.

313 U59:1; J66:5, 1070:4.

314 U75:1, 120:1; J1286:2, 1351:4.

315 U57:1, 70:5; J640:7.

316 U125:6; J651:6.

317 U25:3, 85:1, 119:6; J268:6, 422:7, 609:1.

318 Seyed-Gohrab 2008.

319 Lewis 1995: 448. See also Sharlet 2011: 59.

320 See Kamal Isfahani 1969: 46; Hamgar 1996: 322; Shams-i Fakhri 1887: 14; Khvaju Kirmani 1957: 581, 610–611; Salman Savaji 1957: 351–352, 475–476, 481; 'Imad Kirmani 1969: 11, 32, 237–238; Jalal Yazdi 1987: 243.

321   Andrews 1985: 92. See also Meisami 1987: 68; Shahbazi 2017: 26.

322   Bashir 2011: 124–125, 137.

323   See Ilahi Ghomshei 2010: 83–86; de Fouchécour 2010: 151–152.

324   Davis 1999: 284.

325   Moayyad 1988: 137.

326   Rami Tabrizi 1946: 6–7, 11–12, 18, 22, 27–28, 30, 32, 34–35, 37, 43, 48–52, 55, 57, 59, 62.

327   H4:5, 51:2, 110:3, 127:5, 165:1, 181:5, 193:8, 322:7, 409:2; J1222:2.

328   H24:5, 26:2, 76:5, 167:3, 195:1, 271:6, 276:6, 306:2, 370:1, 395:4, 433:10; U6:1, 13:8, 15:4, 21:2, 22:8; J3:7, 28:8, 61:8, 63:9, 290:2, 464:5, 686:3, 964:9.

329   See also ♂53:2; Bauer 1998: 281–282.

330   H314:1, 354:1; U17:1, 134:2; J168:2, 964:9.

331   H395:4; J451:1.

332   H24:5, 195:1, 276:6, 338:1, 370:1; U6:1, 10:6, 13:8, 19:4, 79:1, 127:1, 138:3, 139:3; J25:2, 27:4, 28:8, 63:9, 686:3.

333   U123:4; J1251:2.

334   U17:1, 47:2, 119:4.

335   J11:6.

336   H433:10; J61:8, 464:5, 514:5.

337   JH26:2.

338   H339:7; U3:1.

339   H36:2, 55:2, 95:1, 170:7, 210:4, 306:2, 365:6, 394:2, 443:2; U10:7, 14:1, 22:4, 34:7, 38:7, 45:7, 79:8, 93:7, 139:3; J63:9, 642:1.

340   H55:3, 171:7; J57:7, 61:8, 115:4, 156:4, 464:5, 504:3, 540:5, 638:9, 673:8, 1009:2, 1259:2, 1362:8, 1394:6; U123:2.

341   H271:6; U15:4.

342   H306:2; U22:8; J3:7.

343   H62:2; U78:4; J141:1, 880:6, 887:7.

344   H145:8.

345   U70:2.

346   J77:5, 872:5, 1202:6, 1248:5, 1249:5.

347   U13:1, 14:1.

348   U131:4.

349   U5:1; J121:6, 595:6, 604:5, 606:5, 618:4, 867:2, 1323:4, 1370:8.

350   H29:6, 112:1, 239:5, 401:2, 452:9, 459:1, 484:7; U2:1, 13:3, 22:1, 86:3; J10:6, 50:1, 63:6, 91:5, 150:11, 270:7, 321:2, 410:6, 422:8, 536:6, 851:1, 909:4, 1109:2, 1147:2, 1190:5, 1236:7, 1256:5.

351   H167:3.

352   H107:1, 234:1; U13:3, 95:6; J943:1, 1256:6.

353   H149:3, 268:1, 288:1; J126:6, 246:1, 667:8, 768:6, 1147:2, 1188:1, 1245:7, 1258:4, 1322:4.

354 ♂344:2.

355 ♂307:2.

356 ♂237:4.

357 ♂387:2.

358 ♂304:2.

359 J536:2.

360 J802:7.

361 U10:1.

362 J852:1.

363 H411:8; J90:2.

364 H412:2; U17:6.

365 H63:1, 86:1, 137:1, 144:7, 181:2, 196:3, 342:1, 390:9, 395:1, 441:5; U10:5, 16:1; J952:3.

366 ♂364:3, 226:6.

367 ♂87:1.

368 ♂267:3.

369 J340:5.

370 U16:1, 21:1, 22:1; J25:7, 61:4, 289:9, 534:1, 673:6, 719:3, 767:4, 1173:2, 1205:1. See also Awhadi Maragha'i 1961: 420.

371 U20:8; J50:3.

372 H206:6, 266:2, 385:3, 402:1, 446:7; J46:3, 62:8, 158:1, 842:4, 1399:2 and 1403:2.

373 H4:5 and 410:2.

374 H85:1.

375 H394:1 and U34:4.

376 J293:4.

377 J59:1.

378 H30:3, 406:1.

379 J67:3, 220:1, 906:1.

380 J722:5.

381 J43:1.

382 U34:1; J107:5, 411:1.

383 H9:9, 394:3; U20:1, 22:1, 53:2, 63:2, 67:2, 70:1, 75:5, 128:2, 134:1, 140:2; J131:8.

384 H167:1 and 171:5.

385 U10:5, 15:3, 42:2, 67:3, 87:3; J33:7, 53:1, 54:1, 271:8, 585:1; H38:1.

386 J778:4.

387 J31:8, 32:2.

388 J1395:1.

389 ♂16:2 and 20:5.

390 ♂95:7, 196:7 and 342:2.

391 ♂149:4.

392 ♂160:1.

393 ♂52:2, 55:12, 107:4, 136:1, 170:8, 307:4–5, 366:3.

394 H348:4.

395 U4:6, 10:1, 18:2, 47:1; J437:2.

396 H260:4, 335:3, 427:1, 433:4; J989:1.

397 H452:5; J1326:5, 1327:3.

398 H316:6; U138:5; J1176:9.

399 U75:5, 82:1; J696:6.

400 See 'Attar Nishaburi 1960: 106, 141, 149, 158, 167, 189, 218, 223, 239, 250.

401 H2:6, 23:3, 239:3; U5:1; J941:6. See also ♂50:3, 227:2, 276:3, 333:2, 350:3; ♀4, 5, 6, 7, 185.

402 H12:1, 31:3, 275:4, 280:6, 298:7, 494:1; U121:4, 123:5.

403 H31:3, 118:9.

404 H95:2, 310:9, 402:7, 412:7, 413:2; J270:6, 685:5, 763:3, 846:2, 1005:6, 1076:2.

405 H91:3, 131:5, 173:1, 400:3, 480:7; U95:7; J14:5, 113:5, 430:6, 642:4, 780:6, 784:6, 1058:4, 1067:2, 1087:5, 1152:7.

406 J316:2.

407 H98:3, 117:2, 314:6, 334:6, 412:1, 428:4, 473:11, 491:2; U12:6, 137:4, 140:3; J18:9, 93:10, 98:4, 161:4, 502:2 and 1410:4.

408 H397:3; J235:3, 846:2, 1076:2, 1087:5.

409 H238:1, 408:7; J116:1, 226:3, 302:5, 310:4, 585:5.

410 U12:4; J112:6, 119:5, 127:2, 233:2, 886:2, 931:5, 956:3, 1067:2.

411 H334:6, 399:5; U105:6.

412 H6:3, 341:6.

413 H407:6, 408:1; U8:1, 33:2, 54:2, 63:6; J157:7, 1012:1, 1394:2.

414 H14:4.

415 H3:1, 83:1, 95:3, 304:5, 402:5; U5:2, 52:3; J478:8.

416 U1:5, 5:2.

417 ♂51:14, 239:4. See Bauer 1998: 248–251.

418 J220:1.

419 H36:3, 368:5; J412:5, 450:3. See Sprachman 2012: 84–86.

420 H310:6, 394:5, 427:6, 448:4; U51:7, 61:5, 103:1; J220:1.

421 H85:1, 121:3, 265:8, 270:5, 325:9; U63:1, 98:5, 105:6, 134:1; J13:5, 28:8, 39:7, 46:4, 55:12, 57:4, 580:4, 688:2, 855:3, 1151:4, 1173:4, 1224:1.

422 H314:7.

423 H459:4; J688:3.

424 U13:6. See also ♂92:1, 294:8.

425 H322:4.

426 H81:3, 265:1; J62:4, 408:4, 561:8, 855:3.

427 J43:7, 100:4, 102:1, 361:7, 745:3, 907:2, 952:5.

428 J656:4, 1075:5, 1096:5.

429 J1239:1.

430 H301:5; J318:5, 886:3.

431 H98:5; U13:7, 19:1, 79:2; J26:4, 220:3, 245:3, 844:6.

432 H97:7; U82:4; J437:1, 535:2. See Zipoli 2009: 203–204.

433 H33:9; U14:9, 17:3, 79:3.

434 H476:3; U34:1, 82:4; J1057:6.

435 H50:3, 57:2, 121:3, 193:4, 387:1, 473:6, 481:5; U114:4; J652:2, 764:9.

436 H46:6, 224:2; U33:2, 52:3; J69:5, 115:4, 139:2, 492:4, 594:8, 641:4–5, 700:5, 701:7, 741:4, 1032:3, 1053:8, 1094:5, 1186:1, 1296:7.

437 H104:6, 198:7; J591:2, 626:8, 1229:2.

438 H3:6, 4:2, 204:2, 287:1; J125:7, 534:4, 1039:2, 1207:1.

439 H12:10.

440 H249:8; J466:5.

441 J598:8, 749:4, 802:8.

442 J101:8, 641:4, 696:7, 1296:7, 1328:4.

443 Floor 2009.

444 Tsugitaka 2004.

445 H57:1, 109:5, 155:3, 356:4, 397:10, 455:2; U34:1, 34:9, 47:3, 137:7; J492:1–3, 615:4, 618:1, 619:4, 637:6, 641:5, 807:5, 886:3, 1037:10, 1151:4, 1263:6.

446 H86:4, 105:5, 368:6, 397:10.

447 H97:4, 279:5; U34:9, 78:4, 86:2; J156:7, 265:2, 649:2, 771:5, 985:5, 1249:6.

448 H73:7, 206:2; U13:2, 15:1, 17:3 and 87:1; J274:7.

449 U20:4, 34:3, 122:2.

450 H120:12; U82:5; J612:5, 952:6.

451 H3:3, 34:7, 421:6, 452:4.

452 H336:5. See also Shams-i Fakhri 1887: 36.

453 H97:3, 98:2, 445:4; U121:7.

454 ♂50:2; K383:3.

455 ♂294:12.

456 ♂386:2.

457 ♂308:1.

458 H97:7.

459 H178:5.

460 H389:5.

461 H192:8, 206:8.

462 H8:8, 467:2; J221:4, 582:5, 900:5, 1147:2, 1175:7, 1209:4, 1222:6; Haydar Shirazi 2004: 72.

463 U50:7; J142:7, 367:7; see Khvaju Kirmani 1957: 459, 504.

464 J315:1, 359:7, 1217:4; Khvaju Kirmani 1957: 416.

465 H389:5, 450:9; J1023:7, 1265:2; see 'Attar Shirazi 1990: 69.

466 H282:1; U6:3.

467 H387:3; J535:7, J857:2, 1138:1, 1347:5, 1389:2.

468 H8:8.

469 U52:4; J677:1, 799:2.

470 J466:2, 953:6.

471 See Melikian-Chirvani 1986.

472 H276:5, 388:4; J58:6, 226:3, 614:6, 763:3, 776:4, 872:6, 1175:1.

473 ♂26:1.

474 ♂78:6.

475 ♂26:3.

476 ♂47:18.

477 ♂297:1.

478 ♂168:3.

479 ♂294:3.

480 ♂386:3.

481 ♂356:4–5.

482 ♂153:2.

483 See 'Ubayd Zakani 1999: 331–340.

484 H159:4, 393:8, 320:1, 413:1, 445:4; U47:1. See Bauer 1998: 255–278; Shamisa 2002: 51–53.

485 H14:6, 121:4, 314:2, 433:1; U17:3; J628:5.

486 H66:5; U131:1.

487 H157:1, 308:2.

488 H452:9; U18:3, 54:4, 88:7; J5:7, 105:7, 158:1, 241:6, 316:4, 450:1, 500:1, 519:3, 642:2, 853:6, 988:4, 1210:2, 1249:5, 1389:3, 1408:1.

489 H1:2, 36:4, 83:1, 181:7, 265:4, 406:3; U53:2, 47:1, 85:3; J20:1, 52:3, 54:4, 179:2, 246:5, 247:2, 338:6, 357:1, 504:1, 575:2, 676:4, 733:2.

490 H9:4, 61:1, 250:3, 260:3, 399:6; U42:3, 76:4; J316:4, 734:4.

491 J734:4.

492 H27:5, 124:1, 414:3; U76:4. See also King 2017: 157.

493 H411:1.

494 H415:2; J118:8.

495 H281:4, 414:3, 495:7; J583:5.

496 H58:5, 280:1.

497 J915:3.

498 H281:5.

499 U21:9.

500 See King 2017: 278, 281.

501 See Esin 1983.

502 H23:1, 30:2, 95:1, 441:2, 474:6; J775:1.

503 H287:4; J44:5, 351:3, 1105:7.

504 H112:2, 127:9, 195:4, 240:7; U134:4; J404:4.

505 H23:4, 334:2, 422:1; U95:6 113:3; J642:3, 779:1, 1103:2, 1135:1.

506 U46:6.

507 J26:7, 287:3.

508 H237:8, 271:1, 281:4, 325:5; U45:6; J139:8, 293:5, 582:3, 766:3, 1135:1, 1350:5; Khvaju Kirmani 1957: 214.

509 H14:7; U92:1; J112:7, 338:6, 552:7, 691:4, 880:5, 924:9, 1172:1.

510 H443:2; U2:1, 16:7, 22:4, 45:7, 60:4, 79:4, 120:2, 132:7; J32:7, 100:5, 628:2, 682:5, 1046:2, 1167:3, 1184:9.

511 H99:2, 210:5, 213:7, 340:3, 365:3, 406:3; U17:4, 79:7, 93:7, 131:5; J411:5.

512 J282:10, 577:7.

513 ♂207:6, 222:2, 241:1, 294:6.

514 H26:1, 408:5, 463:5; U16:8, 134:2; J30:3, 522:3, 807:2, 1337:7.

515 H12:8, 59:8, 273:2, 319:5; U47:7, 63:3, 75:4, 85:3, 131:4, 132:6; J89:6, 121:3, 220:2, 543:1, 545:1, 592:7, 1080:2.

516 J408:1.

517 H394:2; U4:4, 35:7, 48:2; J167:1, 360:1.

518 J30:3.

519 H14:4, 323:2, 347:2, 360:5, 402:1, 433:11, 463:5; U3:5, 13:4, 16:8, 35:1, 88:5, 123:1; J331:6, 650:8, 893:5–6, 1060:6.

520 U6:1; J507:6.

521 H31:2; U2:3, 3:6, 9:5, 10:6, 16:7, 127:2, 132:6, 138:3; J506:3.

522 J341:5, 457:3, 469:6, 682:5, 1247:6; Khvaju Kirmani 1957: 266.

523 J656:5, 1095:2, 1096:5, 1097:4. See ♀41; ♂85:2, 303:6, 314:3.

524 J575:7, 730:3, 764:1, 832:2, 1053:5, 1101:3, 1171:9, 1255:3. See ♂71:3.

525 H26:7, 32:5, 324:1; U12:2.

526 H40:5; U18:8, 70:2.

527 U31:7, 98:6, 127:2; J56:1, 61:4.

528 U98:6, 127:2; J56:1, 61:4, 161:3, 682:5, 762:4, 1103:2.

529 H408:5; U15:3, 42:3; J92:7, 161:4.

530 H40:5, 192:6; U51:5, 122:4; J1245:4.

531 H473:12; U98:6; J1104:2, 1210:1, 1226:1.

532 H94:4, 98:3, 433:11; U38:2, 137:3, 140:3; J157:1, 161:4, 293:5.

533 H50:1, 55:1, 352:6, 394:5, 415:9, 448:4; U13:4, 61:5, 98:6, 103:1; J1133:2.

534 U45:6.

535 U138:3; J27:6, 35:8, 615:1, 887:1, 1133:2, 1167:1.

536 See Pancaroğlu 2016.

537 U2:2, 29:5, 41:4, 113:3, 121:5, 137:3, 138:1, 140:3; J27:5, 38:7, 46:5, 70:1, 900:4.

538 H21:6, 197:3; U17:6, 22:2, 128:2; J109:4, 115:1. See Tekin 1997; Bauer 1998: 318.

539 H8:8.

540 J33:3, 244:3, 263:9, 286:6, 1142:4.

541 J548:4, 595:2, 732:4.

542 H11:4, 27:2; J66:4, 101:4, 1407:6.

543 H387:1, 493:7; Khvaju Kirmani 1957: 289. See also van Ruymbeke 2007: 62–63.

544 H11:4, 192:1, 223:1, 322:2, 385:1, 443:1, 493:7; U2:2, 75:6, 87:2, 140:2.

545 H345:1; J13:1, 18:8, 19:4, 23:3, 50:2, 94:3, 101:4.

546 J416:1.

547 H76:5; U10:2, 13:7, 54:4; J33:4, 83:4, 87:1, 101:1, 101:5, 297:4, 580:3, 1276:1, 1401:4.

548 U122:4, 137:5. See also Aʻlam 1993: 506.

549 H133:8; J1057:9.

550 U5:3, 122:5.

551 ♂40:11, 124:5, 134:5, 227:1 and 237:3.

552 ♂134:5.

553 ♂187:2.

554 ♂268:2.

555 H92:1, 425:5; J1041:6.

556 Bauer 1998: 309.

557 ♂8:7.

558 ♂27:6.

559 ♂309:4, 359:7.

560 ♂51:7.

561 ♂62:3.

562 ♂98:7.

563 ♂151:1.

564 ♂223:2.

565 ♂234:7.

566 H358:8, 445:3; U57:4; J371:6, 535:7, 858:5, 1102:5; Haydar Shirazi 2004: 88.

567 U137:4; J1118:1.

568 Zipoli 2009: 172.

569 See Seyed-Gohrab 2012: 4.

570 Seyed-Gohrab 2008.

Chapter 4

1 See Sims 2006; Simpson 2006; Wright 2012: 17, 286.

2 See Pucci 1998: 28.

3 See Wickens 1974: 171–178.

4 See Shamisa 1987: 33, 38; Losensky 1998: 68–69.

5 See Aigle 2014: 19.

6 See Shafi'i-Kadkani 2014: 238–239.

7 See Hamgar 1996: 311, 386; Kutubi 1985: 40–41, 98.

8 See Hanaoka 2016: 209.

9 See Gumbrecht 2012: 1105.

10 See Clarke 2012: 88.

11 Meisami 1990a: 142.

12 Meisami 1993: 263–264.

13 See Manuchihri Damghani 1996: 10, 71; Farrukhi Sistani 1999: 35, 41, 89, 107. See also Tetley 2009: 5, 59, 96.

14 See Clinton 1988: 94–95.

15 Bosworth 1978: 11.

16 See Peacock 2012: 61–69.

17 al-Mas'udi 1966a: 269–274, 285–327. See also Bosworth 1978: 21.

18 See Savant 2013: 40–43, 57.

19 Brinner 2002: xx. See also Bal'ami 1974: 595–602; Bayzavi 2003: 24.

20 Savant 2013: 140.

21 Nora 1989: 7.

22 Ibid: 9, 22.

23 Ibid: 18–19.

24 See Kamal Isfahani 1969: 50; Sa'di 2007: 30, 33, 713, 745, 758; Shams-i Fakhri 1887: 5, 10, 29, 36, 93, 124, 137, 143; Jalal Yazdi 1987: 207; Bayzavi 2003: 103; Zarkub Shirazi 1931: 85. See also Bosworth 1962: 211, 221; Madelung 1969; Donohue 1973: 77–80; Treadwell 2003.

25 See Babayan 2002: 71.

26 See al-Istakhri 1961: 76–77; Ibn al-Balkhi 1921: 32, 125–127, 129; Hamdullah Mustawfi 1957: 136–137, 142, 144–145, 147, 149–151, 154–157; Zarkub Shirazi 1931: 16–19, 26; Daryaee 2002: 20.

27 See Hamdullah Mustawfi 1957: 136–137; Aigle 2005: 71–72.

28 Tusi 1996: 411, 420, 467.

29   Savant 2013: 57.

30   See Sperl 1977: 24; Marsham 2009: 124, 138; Weitzman 2011: 85.

31   See Tusi 1996: 426. See also Soucek 1993: 112, 116; Weitzman 2011: 84–85; Mottahedeh 2013: 248.

32   See Brookshaw 2015.

33   Melikian-Chirvani 1996: 96.

34   See Tuan 1974: 99.

35   See Clarke 2012: 97–98, 101.

36   Canepa 2010: 585.

37   Mozaffari 2014: 45.

38   Canepa 2010: 564. See also Shahbazi 1977: 200.

39   Firdawsi 1987: 51. See also Skjærvø 2008: 504.

40   Shahbazi 1977: 202.

41   See Zarkub Shirazi 1931: 17. See also Shahbazi 1977: 201.

42   See Bayzavi 2003: 18; Hamdullah Mustawfi 1957: 145; Zarkub Shirazi 1931: 17; *Haft kishvar* 1974: 58; Barbaro 1873: 81; Coste and Flandin 1851: 92.

43   See Bayzavi 2003: 17–18; Ibn al-Balkhi 1921: 32; Hamdullah Mustawfi 1957: 144–145.

44   Tusi 1996: 144, 218, 219.

45   al-Qazwini 1984: 148.

46   Streck 2006.

47   See al-Mas'udi 1966b: 399; al-Istakhri 1961: 76, 90; Tusi 1996: 401; al-Qazwini 1984: 147; Hamdullah Mustawfi 1957: 145.

48   Zarkub Shirazi 1931: 20.

49   Skjærvø 2008: 510.

50   Streck 2006.

51   Tusi 1996: 426.

52   Zarkub Shirazi 1931: 17.

53   Sa'di Shirazi 2007: 726. See also Zarkub Shirazi 1931: 4, 83.

54   Tusi 1996: 410, 467.

55   See al-Qazwini 1984: 147.

56   Mottahedeh 2013: 251. See also Soucek 1993: 112.

57   Mottahedeh 2013: 263.

58   Barbaro 1873: 80–81.

59   Melikian-Chirvani 1971: 1–3.

60   Donohue 1973.

61   Basiri 1946: 41–42.

62   See Donohue 1973: 77; Bosworth 1978: 19; Peacock 2012: 60.

63   Mustafavi 1964: 339, 346–347.

64   Sa'di Shirazi 2007: 35–36, 226, 236–237.

65 Nizami Ganjavi 2001: 82–84.

66 Mustafavi 1964: 346. See also 'Ubayd Zakani 1999: 149.

67 Zarkub Shirazi 1931: 85, 151. See also Shams-i Fakhri 1887: 81.

68 Zarkub Shirazi 1931: 79.

69 See Ghani 2001: 126.

70 Zarkub Shirazi 1931: 150.

71 See Mahallati 1962: 76–78.

72 Tusi 1996: 218.

73 See Coste and Flandin 1851: 81. See also Mozaffari 2014: 47.

74 al-Mas'udi 1966b: 399–400; Qazvini 1938: 79. See also Melikian-Chirvani 1971: 10; Ghani 1987: 126.

75 Coste and Flandin 1851: 79.

76 See Ibn al-Balkhi 1921: 154–155; Barbaro 1873: 81; Coste and Flandin 1851: 82; Stronach 2010: 1.

77 See Stronach 1963: 27; Sami 1971: 86–95; Stronach 2010: 2; al-Nisaburi 1961: 283.

78 See Qazvini 1988: 270–272; Hamgar 1996: 227, 304, 550; Vassaf al-Hazrat 1959: 147, 624; Hafiz Shirazi 1999: 384. See also Q2:102.

79 See Vassaf al-Hazrat 1959: 155, 222; Zarkub Shirazi 1931: 85; Shams-i Fakhri 1887: 4.

80 Q27:16.

81 See Melikian-Chirvani 1971: 7, 11–13.

82 Stronach 2010: 3.

83 Sami 1971: 129. See also Aigle 2005: 71.

84 See Melikian-Chirvani 1971: 5.

85 Sami 1971: 132.

86 Whitcomb 1985: 37.

87 Ibid: 38.

88 See Zarkub Shirazi 1931: 26; Coste and Flandin 1851: 233–234. See also Mustafavi 1964: 78; Wilkinson 1965: 341; Whitcomb 1985: 16, 32.

89 Whitcomb 1985: 34–36.

90 Ibid: 15.

91 H11, 48, 112, 147, 153, 162, 167, 207, 212, 219, 225, 242, 283, 284, 292, 304, 319, 327, 343, 356, 361, 381, 392, 402, 421, 471, 472, 473, 484, 488. See Dashti 1973: 132, 140.

92 H329, 433, 454.

93 Rastigar Fasa'i 2006: 55–56.

94 U87, 95.

95 See J156, 288; 'Imad Kirmani 1969: 10–11, 32–33, 179–180, 199, 238, 256–257, 287; Haydar Shirazi 2004: 56; Nasir Bukhara'i 1974: 221–222.

96 Gruendler 2003: 30.

97 Ibid: 27, 29.

98 Meisami 1987: 46.

99 Ibid: 44.

100 Stetkevych 2002: 34.

101 J124:5, 133:9, 439:9, 441:4, 480:5, 568:10, 667:8, 864:7, 865:5, 912:7, 1094:12, 1110:2, 1149:7, 1266:3, 1269:10, 1365:7.

102 J115:6, 317:1, 441:6, 539:5, 605:6, 617:2, 806:5, 945:8, 985:7, 1111:1, 1167:9, 1359:7

103 J442:3, 729:4, 1286:5, 1328:9.

104 J122:8, 133:9, 148:10, 658:10, 676:9, 699:9, 1169:2, 1356:9, 1360:7, 1378:3.

105 Ghani 2001: 176–177.

106 J1257:5.

107 J740:9.

108 J989:6.

109 J442:3, 729:4, 1286:5, 1328:9.

110 See Ahur 1984: 507–508.

111 J110:2, 125:7, 392:4, 449:5, 466:6, 472:3, 525:7, 541:4, 630:5, 655:1, 713:1, 722:1, 738:8, 787:3, 916:1, 943:3, 972:6, 974:9, 1007:5, 1025:1, 1029:10, 1047:7, 1348:6.

112 See Peacock 2007: 39–40.

113 Aigle 2014: 38.

114 Kamal Isfahani 1969: 53.

115 Hamgar 1996: 346.

116 See Piemontese 2007: 36.

117 Hamgar 1996: 356.

118 'Ubayd Zakani 1999: 126, 135.

119 Ibid: 126.

120 Ibid: 54. See also Jahan-Malik Khatun 1995: 516.

121 Shams-i Fakhri 1887: 5, 7, 8, 16, 19, 37, 55, 64, 142.

122 Khvaju Kirmani 1957: 24, 59.

123 'Imad Kirmani 1969: 339.

124 H167:5, 433:3.

125 Hafiz Shirazi 1999: 73.

126 Sa'di Shirazi 2007: 744.

127 Khvaju Kirmani 1957: 581. See also Shams-i Fakhri 1887: 44, 58.

128 Khvaju Kirmani 1957: 603. See also Hafiz Shirazi 1999: 388.

129 Khvaju Kirmani 1957: 595.

130 Hafiz Shirazi 1999: 71.

131 Hamgar 1996: 572.

132 Sa'di Shirazi 2007: 718.

133 Khvaju Kirmani 1957: 79.

134 'Ubayd Zakani 1999: 17.

135 Ibid: 13.

136 Ibid: 22, 34, 35; see Jalal 1987: 202.

137 Khvaju Kirmani 1957: 110.

138 Ibid: 59.

139 'Imad Kirmani 1969: 317.

140 Hafiz Shirazi 1999: 71; 'Ubayd Zakani 1999: 16, 25; 'Imad Kirmani 1969: 317.

141 Haydar Shirazi 2004: 56.

142 H153:10. See also H147:7.

143 Kamal Isfahani 1969: 50; Hamgar 1996: 344.

144 Hamgar 1996: 572.

145 Kamal Isfahani 1969: 42.

146 Khvaju Kirmani 1957: 92.

147 'Ubayd Zakani 1999: 135. See ibid. 39, 54, 149.

148 Ibid: 46.

149 Ibid: 32, 34. See also Khvaju Kirmani 1957: 266.

150 Ibid: 35.

151 Ibid: 24.

152 Shams-i Fakhri 1887: 16, 18, 26, 102.

153 'Ubayd Zakani 1999: 50.

154 Ibid: 37.

155 Khvaju Kirmani 1957: 603.

156 Shams-i Fakhri 1887: 5, 65.

157 'Ubayd Zakani 1999: 37.

158 Khvaju Kirmani 1957: 106.

159 'Imad Kirmani 1969: 335.

160 Salman Savaji 1957: 611.

161 'Imad Kirmani 1969: 318.

162 Salman Savaji 1957: 611.

163 'Ubayd Zakani 1999: 48.

164 Hafiz Shirazi 1999: 71. See also Ahur 1984: 334.

165 H433:9.

166 Yazdi 2007: 22.

167 Kamal Isfahani 1969: 42.

168 'Ubayd Zakani 1999: 54.

169 See Tafazzoli 1994.

170 'Ubayd Zakani 1999: 34. See ibid. 149.

171 See Khvaju Kirmani 1957: 603; Shams-i Fakhri 1887: 19.

172 See 'Ubayd Zakani 1999: 37, 46, 50; Shams-i Fakhri 1887: 48.

173 Khvaju Kirmani 1957: 59, 592.

174 Hafiz Shirazi 1999: 71.

175 Salman Savaji 1957: 611.

176 H304:1.

177 See Kamal Isfahani 1969: 42; Sa'di Shirazi 2007: 169.

178 Kamal Isfahani 1969: 48, 50.

179 Ibid: 52.

180 Hamgar 1996: 550.

181 Sa'di Shirazi 2007: 30.

182 Ibid: 33.

183 Ibid: 718.

184 Ibid: 713.

185 Shams-i Fakhri 1887: 108.

186 'Ubayd Zakani 1999: 58.

187 Shams-i Fakhri 1887: 31, 37, 49, 75.

188 Khvaju Kirmani 1957: 603.

189 Shams-i Fakhri 1887: 17.

190 Khvaju Kirmani 1957: 582.

191 'Imad Kirmani 1969: 257.

192 'Ubayd Zakani 1999: 50, 54, 135.

193 Hafiz Shirazi 1999: 73; Salman Savaji 1957: 476.

194 'Imad Kirmani 1969: 341.

195 Salman Savaji 1957: 611. See Ahur 1984: 472.

196 Haydar Shirazi 2004: 57–58.

197 Khvaju Kirmani 1957: 92.

198 'Ubayd Zakani 1999: 11, 49.

199 Ibid: 54.

200 Ibid: 51.

201 Shams-i Fakhri 1887: 63.

202 'Ubayd Zakani 1999: 57.

203 Hafiz Shirazi 1999: 83.

204 Khvaju Kirmani 1957: 109.

205 Ibid: 59.

206 'Ubayd Zakani 1999: 48.

207 Berlekamp 2011: 93.

208 See Hillenbrand 2014: 40, 43–44; Pancaroğlu 2016: 199–201.

209 Meisami 2003: 418–419. See also Sa'di Shirazi 2007: 629.

210 Firdawsi 1987: 44.

211 See al-Nisaburi 1961: 281–282; Tusi 1996: 280.

212 See Tusi 1996: 9.

213 Firdawsi 1987: 44. See also Bal'ami 1974: 131; Bayzavi 2003: 18.

214 Firdawsi 1987: 45.

215 See Nasir Bukhara'i 1974: 235; Salman Savaji 1957: 500.

216 'Ubayd Zakani 1999: 24, 32, 34, 35, 37, 39, 46, 48, 50, 54, 56.

217 Firdawsi 1992: 344–345. See also Murtazavi 1965: 182–184; Burumand 1988: 102–116.

218 See Khvaju Kirmani 1957: 198, 266, 308, 595, 755; Nasir Bukhara'i 1974: 147, 176, 196, 249, 390; Salman Savaji 1957: 294, 509, 532, 564, 570, 615. See also Simpson 2013: 353–354.

219 See Awhadi Maragha'i 1928: 28.

220 Ibn al-Balkhi 1921: 47.

221 Hafiz Shirazi 1999: 377.

222 Nasir Bukhara'i 1974: 390.

223 Hafiz Shirazi 1999: 377–379.

224 Hafiz Shirazi 1996: 248.

225 See 'Iraqi 1998: 151; Nasir Bukhara'i 1974: 176.

226 'Iraqi 1998: 68.

227 Zarkub Shirazi 1931: 4.

228 See Grigor 2015: 219–233.

229 Khurramshahi 1987: 1119.

230 See Zarkub Shirazi 1931: 30. See also Bosworth 1978: 14–24; Simidchieva 2004: 110–111; Meisami 2004: 74.

231 Hanaoka 2016: 125–126.

232 See Haydar Shirazi 2004: 59.

233 Ibid: 57, 58.

234 H81:6, 372:3, 430:4.

235 See Sa'di Shirazi 2007: 733; Khvaju Kirmani 1957: 59, 592, 603–664; Shams-i Fakhri 1887: 10, 15, 93, 97, 102; Jahan-Malik Khatun 1995: 6; Jalal Yazdi 1987: 219.

236 See Wright 2012: 17, 286.

237 H390:5. See also Sa'di Shirazi 2007: 724.

238 See Ahur 1984: 501–502; Purnamdarian 2003: 216–217. See also Tetley 2009: 17–18.

239 Omidsalar 2011: 153–157.

240 Ibid: 133–134.

241 Davidson 1994: 132.

242 Firdawsi 1992: 381.

243 See Lescot 1944: 67–69.

244 See Shafi'i-Kadkani 2006: 149.

245 See Omidsalar 2011: 149–151. See also Haydar Shirazi 2004: 83.

246 Firdawsi 1990: 123.

247 J1345:5.

248 See 'Adi b. Zayd 1965: 87.

249 K8:14, 25:17, 43:5, 45:1, 52:6, 111:5, 122:5, 124:2, 126:4, 129:8, 150:8–10, 191:8–9, 242:3, 276:3, 278:14, 296:4, 310:2, 398:13, 404:6.

250 Meisami 1998: 65, 69–70; Sumi 2004: 96–100.

251 Shayegan 2013: 807–808.

252 See Khaleghi-Motlagh 1988.

253 See Riyahi 1989: 36.

254 Meisami 1993: 253.

255 Lescot 1944: 64.

256 See Daryaee 1995: 141; Mokhtarian 2010: 135–136.

257 See Savant 2013: 234–235.

258 Aigle 2014: 19.

259 See Hooke 1963: 11.

260 See Shafi'i-Kadkani 2014: 237–238.

261 See Isti'lami 2003: 1095–1096.

262 See Firdawsi 1987: 44–45; Bal'ami 1974: 131–132.

263 See Ibn al-Balkhi 1921: 127; Hamdullah Mustawfi 1957: 145.

264 Meisami 1987: 291.

265 See H40, 41, 202, 283, 284.

266 See Ghani 2001: 214–215; Valavi 2016: 86–88.

267 See Isti'lami 2003: 101.

268 Zipoli 2009: 229.

269 Khayyam 1942: 72.

270 Hafiz Shirazi 1996: 562.

271 See Nizami Ganjavi 2005: 318.

272 Firdawsi 1987: 356–357. See also Shahbazi 1977: 200–201.

273 See Davis 1992: 123–128.

274 See Shamisa 2002: 44–51; Brookshaw 2009: 725–729.

275 See Haydar Shirazi 2004: 98.

276 See Lescot 1944: 65–66; Purnamdarian 2003: 216–223, 287.

277 Awhadi Maragha'i 1961: 384.

278 'Ubayd Zakani 1999: 13, 20, 21, 47; Jahan-Malik Khatun 1995: 515. See also Tetley 2009: 164.

279 Jahan-Malik Khatun 1995: 3–4.

280 See Brookshaw 2003: 200–201.

281 See Kay-Ka'us b. Iskandar 1951: 40; Nizam al-Mulk 1955: 129.

282 See Nizam al-Mulk 1955: 128.

283 See Manuchihri Damghani 1996: 14, 17, 19, 47, 99.

284 Berlekamp 2011: 31.

285 See Melikian-Chirvani 1992: 104.

286 Khvaju Kirmani 1957: 211, 397, 401, 404, 406, 407, 439, 637, 653, 724, 725, 754, 755; 'Imad Kirmani 1969: 231, 239. See also Melikian-Chirvani 1992: 105.

287 See Bal'ami 1974: 130–131.

288 See Tusi 1996: 144, 449.

289 Ibid: 353, 458. See also Le Strange 1930: 224.

290 See Zaryab 1989: 129–130; Purnamdarian 2003: 145.

291 Sudi 1995: 865–866, 873. See also Ahur 1984: 209–210.

292 See Vassaf al-Hazrat 1959: 122.

293 H26:5.

294 Q7:172. See also Zipoli 2009: 223–224.

295 Hafiz Shirazi 1999: 377.

296 See Karamustafa 1994: 17–23, 32–34; Bashir 2011: 64–68.

297 H5:1, 196:7, 402:3; Hafiz Shirazi 1999: 379.

298 See de Fouchécour 2010: 153.

299 See Tusi 1996: 210.

300 Omidsalar 2008: 526.

301 See Hanaoka 2016: 208.

302 Savant 2013: 58–59.

303 Tusi 1996: 195.

304 Huart 1965: 439.

305 See al-Istakhri 1961: 76.

306 See Shafi'i-Kadkani 2006: 198; Shafi'i-Kadkani 2014: 240.

307 See Murtazavi 1965: 207, 225–232.

308 See Manuchihri Damghani 1996: 71.

309 Firdawsi 1987: 51.

310 See 'Unsuri Balkhi 1984: 203, 299.

311 See al-Nisaburi 1961: 305.

312 Meisami 1987: 288.

313 H362:10.

314 Khvaju Kirmani 1957: 122.

315 Ibid: 122, 308; 'Ubayd Zakani 1999: 56.

316 'Ubayd Zakani 1999: 15, 49.

317 Khvaju Kirmani 1957: 29.

318 H363:9, 454:12; see Hafiz Shirazi 1999: 391; 'Attar Shirazi 1990: 99.

319 H49:13, 219:9, 355:8, 359:9, 462:7, 467:8. See also Hafiz Shirazi 1999: 383.

320 H48:9, 356:8, 473:13; Hafiz Shirazi 1999: 77; 'Ubayd Zakani 1999: 49.

321 Khvaju Kirmani 1957: 366; 'Imad Kirmani 1969: 322, 324.

322 Hafiz Shirazi 1999: 77.

323 H228:3.

324 See Jalal Yazdi 1987: 266.

325 Hafiz Shirazi 1999: 71.

326 See Ahur 1984: 209.

327 See Shaked 1986: 86.

328 See Murtazavi 1965: 162–165, 171.

329 Sudi Busnavi 1995: 743.

330 Q4:163.

331 See U99:5.

332 Q21:81. See also al-Nisaburi 1961: 284.

333 See Sa'di Shirazi 2007: 441.

334 Ibid: 761.

335 See Shafi'i-Kadkani 2006: 187.

336 Kamal Khujandi 1958: 247.

337 Khvaju 1957: 704, 706.

338 Hafiz Shirazi 1996: 192.

339 Q113:4.

340 See also Khvaju Kirmani 1957: 271, 457.

341 H121:3.

342 See also Nasir Bukhara'i 1974: 346.

343 Q27: 18–19. See also al-Nisaburi 1961: 287–288.

344 J716:4, 717:2, 718:3.

345 H278:6.

346 See Khvaju Kirmani 1957: 181, 422, 439, 709, 744, 750.

347 Lescot 1944: 78.

348 Salman Savaji 1957: 527. See Wing 2016: 141.

349 Salman Savaji 1957: 503. See also Jalal Yazdi 1987: 231–233.

350 Salman Savaji 1957: 362, 598. See also Rami Tabrizi 1997: 124.

351 Vassaf al-Hazrat 1959: 623, 627.

352 Ibid: 222. See also Limbert 2004a: 22.

353 See Zipoli 2009: 198. See also H145:5.

354 See Sudi Busnavi 1995: 1030–1031.

355 See Q18:83–97; Ibn al-Balkhi 1921: 16, 56; Wheeler 1998: 199–204.

356 Shayegan 2011: 303–304.

357 See Barletta 2010: 184–186.

358 Shayegan 2011: 297, 307.

359 See Rubanovich 2015: 204.

360 al-Dinawari 1960: 29.

361 Firdawsi 1997: 521–524.

362 Firdawsi 2005: 4–6.

363 Ibn al-Balkhi 1921: 56–57.

364 See Southgate 1978; Yamamoto 2003: 25–26.

365 Rubanovich 2016b: 210.

366 See Southgate 1977: 279, 283–284.

367 Askari 2016: 36.

368 Nizami Ganjavi 1966: 141.

369 Ibid: 166. See also al-Dinawari 1960: 34; Firdawsi 2005: 48–49.

370 Nizami Ganjavi 1966: 203.

371 Ibid: 203. See also Tusi 1996: 86.

372 Venetis 2006: 177–178.

373 Piemontese 2007: 37. See also Rubanovich 2016b: 226–227.

374 See Krasnowolska 2009.

375 al-Nisaburi 1961: 338–339.

376 Q18:60–82, 83–98.

377 See Babayan 2002: 368; Krasnowolska 2009.

378 See Firdawsi 2005: 92–93; al-Nisaburi 1961: 331–333; Nizami Ganjavi 1966: 328–330.

379 Le Strange 1930: 263.

380 See Franke 2011: 107–108.

381 Hafiz Shirazi 1996: 342.

382 H39:8, 279:2.

383 See Khvaju Kirmani 1957: 207, 246, 279, 415, 640, 671, 674, 699, 701, 703.

384 al-Nisaburi 1961: 330.

385 H97:4, 437:2.

386 H97:7, 124:6.

387 J259:3. See also J1013:8.

388 J873:9.

389 Rubanovich 2016b: 218.

390 Nizami Ganjavi 1966: 29.

391 H129:4.

392 H488:6.

393 H169:2, 313:7, 351:6.

394 See also J858:6.

395 See Murtazavi 1965: 197–198; Berlekamp 2011: 92.

396 See Zaryab 1989: 61–67.

397 See Murtazavi 1965: 197–198, 218–222.

398 See Tusi 1996: 487.

399 Rastigar Fasa'i 2006: 119–120.

400 Sudi Busnavi 1995: 45.

401 See Mawla'i 1989.

Chapter 5

1 See H344:3; Khvaju Kirmani 1957: 410, 473, 620, 739. See also Riyahi 1989: 113–114.

2 See Wright 2012: 61.

3 Ibid: 285–286.

4 Gabbay 2010: 41.

5 Khvaju Kirmani 1957: 439.

6 See Seyed-Gohrab 2003: 69–73; Rypka 1968: 631.

7 de Bruijn 1986: 1104.

8 See Krackovskij 1955; Khairallah 1980; Miquel and Kemp 1984; Leder 1990.

9 Seyed-Gohrab 2009.

10 See Sa'di Shirazi 2007: 141–142.

11 See Seyed-Gohrab 2003: 74–78.

12 See Feuillebois-Pierunek 2002: 296; Anvar 2011: 57.

13 Anvar 2011: 58.

14 de Bruijn 1986: 1104.

15 Ghazali 1942: 42, 45–46.

16 Anvar 2011: 56.

17 See Sa'di Shirazi 2007: 688.

18 Anvar 2011: 53.

19 See Salman Savaji 1957: 60; Khvaju Kirmani 1957: 403, 644.

20 Sa'di Shirazi 2007: 512.

21 See Zaryab 1989: 279–280.

22 Khvaju Kirmani 1957: 717.

23 See Sa'di Shirazi 2007: 587.

24 Ibid: 429.

25 Jacobi 2010: 633–635.

26 See Manuchihri Damghani 1996: 6, 78.

27 Amir Mu'izzi 1983: 545.

28 J1046, 1047, 1048, 1049.

29 Anvar 2011: 55.

30 Mahsati Ganjavi 2003: 63–64, 145, 164, 171.

31 Jahan-Malik Khatun 1995: 3–4.

32 Seyed-Gohrab 2009.

33 See Anvar 2011: 67–71.

34 U38:1.

35 Sa'di Shirazi 2007: 539.

36 Ibid: 642.

37 Ibid: 502.

38 Ibid: 146.

39 'Attar Shirazi 1990: 13.

40 Kamal Khujandi 1958: 93.

41 See Jalal Yazdi 1987: 202.

42 Khvaju Kirmani 1957: 278.

43 Ibid: 236, 316, 329, 427, 445, 447, 472, 688, 709. See also Qatran Tabrizi 1983: 331.

44 See Davis 2002: 38.

45 See Sa'di Shirazi 2007: 525.

46 See Haydar Shirazi 2004: 75.

47 Sa'di Shirazi 2007: 439. See also Kamal Khujandi 1958: 56.

48 See Shafi'i-Kadkani 2006: 256.

49 See Haydar Shirazi 2004: 86.

50 Khvaju Kirmani 1957: 336; Salman Savaji 1957: 7; 'Attar Shirazi 1990: 32; Sa'di Shirazi 2007: 559.

51 J494:8, 1103:1 and 1185:4. See also Khvaju Kirmani 1957: 223, 437, 741.

52 See J1164:5.

53 See also Sa'di Shirazi 2007: 563.

54 See Orsatti 2006; Howard-Johnston 2010.

55 Orsatti 2006.

56 Meisami 1987: 112.

57 Meisami 1995: xi.

58 Firdawsi 2008: 260–272. See van Ruymbeke 2006: 125.

59 van Ruymbeke 2006: 140–141.

60 Ibid: 125; Rubanovich 2016a: 79.

61 Nizami Ganjavi 2006: 45.

62 Talattof 2000: 54.

63 Moayyad 1999: 257–258.

64   Nizam al-Mulk 1955: 186.

65   *Mujmal al-tavarikh* 2000: 63–64.

66   Bal'ami 1974: 1090–1091.

67   Tusi 1996: 96, 435.

68   Ibid: 96, 179, 435.

69   Ibid: 179.

70   Ibid: 179.

71   Ahmad b. Husayn 1966: 206.

72   Ibid: 203.

73   See Bal'ami 1974: 1090; *Mujmal al-tavarikh* 2000: 64–65; Ibn al-Balkhi 1921: 107–108; Qatran Tabrizi 1983: 284; Nizami Ganjavi 2006: 28; Tusi 1996: 178, 179, 369, 435; Kamal Khujandi 1958: 11, 76, 168, 311; Salman Savaji 1957: 390; Nasir Bukhara'i 1974: 207, 236; Khvaju Kirmani 1957: 420, 536, 685.

74   Khvaju Kirmani 1957: 701.

75   Le Strange 1930: 63, 188.

76   Khvaju Kirmani 1957: 611.

77   Markus-Takeshita 2007: 72; Khaleghi-Motlagh 2012: 64.

78   Nizami Ganjavi 2006: 42–43, 48.

79   van Ruymbeke 2006: 145.

80   Orsatti 2006.

81   See Howard-Johnston 2010; Payne 2015: 172–173, 185.

82   Nizami Ganjavi 2006: 233–237.

83   Orsatti 2006.

84   See Khvaju Kirmani 1957: 603.

85   Meisami 1995: x.

86   Meisami 1987: 80.

87   Kamal Khujandi 1958: 128.

88   Nizami Ganjavi 2006: 209–215.

89   Spuler 1982: 210.

90   Sa'di Shirazi 2007: 713.

91   Jahan-Malik Khatun 1995: 6.

92   Khvaju Kirmani 1957: 557.

93   H423:4; Khvaju Kirmani 1957: 641; Kamal Isfahani 1969: 46; 'Iraqi 1998: 124.

94   Lescot 1944: 65; Ahur 1984: 137–139, 300, 919.

95   Lescot 1944: 66.

96   See Sedgwick 1985.

97   See also Haydar Shirazi 2004: 91.

98   See also Khvaju Kirmani 1957: 321, 410, 685, 755; 'Imad Kirmani 1969: 74, 134, 249, 292.

99 Sa'di Shirazi 2007: 565.

100 Ibid: 566.

101 Khvaju Kirmani 1957: 317, 745.

102 Sa'di Shirazi 2007: 582. See also Khvaju Kirmani 1957: 726.

103 Firdawsi 1990: 191–192.

104 See also Sa'di Shirazi 2007: 431.

105 Junayd Shirazi 1941: 17.

106 Haydar Shirazi 2004: 71.

107 See H393:1.

108 See also Jalal Yazdi 1987: 85.

109 Haydar Shirazi 2004: 95.

110 See Khvaju Kirmani 1957: 707.

111 Ibid: 375, 387, 745.

112 See Nizami Ganjavi 2006: 214–215.

113 'Imad Kirmani 1969: 135.

114 Kamal Khujandi 1958: 127.

115 Ibid: 77.

116 Ibid: 311.

117 Ibid: 114, 110.

118 Awhadi Maragha'i 1961: 654.

119 Jalal Yazdi 1987: 25.

120 Salman Savaji 1957: 225.

121 See also H225:3.

122 Salman Savaji 1957: 225.

123 Ibid: 458.

124 Meisami 2003: 187.

125 'Imad Kirmani 1969: 249. See also Khvaju Kirmani 1957: 321, 410, 643; 'Attar Shirazi 1990: 25.

126 Hamgar 1996: 348.

127 'Imad Kirmani 1969: 110.

128 See Nizami Ganjavi 2006: 228–237. See also Sa'di 2007: 469.

129 Zarrinkub 1993: 98, 105–106; Orsatti 2006.

130 See also 'Imad Kirmani 1969: 296; Jalal Yazdi 1987: 82.

131 Sharlet 2011: 22–28.

132 J492:5.

133 J701:7.

134 J1374:6.

135 J1048:6.

136 Nizami Ganjavi 2006: 55.

137 See Khvaju Kirmani 1957: 660.

138 Kamal Khujandi 1958: 135.

139 Ibid: 370.

140 H469:10.

141 Nizami Ganjavi 2006: 28.

142 Sa'di Shirazi 2007: 790.

143 Hafiz Shirazi 1999: 386.

144 See Khvaju Kirmani 1957: 387; 557; Junayd Shirazi 1941: 36.

145 See Bayhaqi 1971: 328–329. See also Shamisa 2002: 40–44.

146 See Yaghoobi 2017: 72.

147 Farrukhi Sistani 1999: 161–162.

148 Matini 1987: 134.

149 Meisami 1987: 248. See also Kugle 2002.

150 Schimmel 1992: 130.

151 See Ghazali 1942: 62–65, 87–89. See also Sa'di Shirazi 2007: 128–129, 288–289; 'Ubayd Zakani 1999: 281, 295, 303.

152 See Bosworth 1966; van den Berg 1998.

153 Ghazali 1942: 88.

154 Kamal Khujandi 1958: 54.

155 See Yaghoobi 2017: 82–83, 85.

156 Nasir Bukhara'i 1974: 303.

157 Jalal Yazdi 1987: 110.

158 Khvaju Kirmani 1957: 461; Kamal Khujandi 1958: 28, 133.

159 H258:8.

160 Q17:79. See Schimmel 1992: 130.

161 See Lumbard 2016: 151.

162 Khvaju Kirmani 1957: 445.

163 Kamal Khujandi 1958: 125.

164 Lane 1984: 638.

165 See 'Imad Kirmani 1969: 227; Jalal Yazdi 1987: 71; Khvaju Kirmani 1957: 238, 276, 426.

166 Kamal Khujandi 1958: 116.

167 'Imad Kirmani 1969: 292.

168 See Khvaju Kirmani 1957: 24; Shams-i Fakhri 1887: 7.

169 Rubanovich 2016a: 68.

170 Khvaju Kirmani 1957: 181, 278, 329, 439, 445, 472, 477, 479, 499, 619, 661, 709, 739, 740, 744, 752, 754.

171 Haydar Shirazi 2004: 73, 94; Salman Savaji 1957: 458; Jalal Yazdi 1987: 123.

172 See Riyahi 1989: 200–201.

173   Hägg and Utas 2003: 10–16; Davis 2002: 29–36.

174   See Melikian-Chirvani 1970: 6–10; Davis 2002: 41, 72–75; Shafi'i-Kadkani 2014: 471–474.

175   Rypka 1968: 177–179.

176   Davis 2002: 37.

177   Ibid: 37–38.

178   Schimmel 1992: 134.

179   Davis 2008: xxxi–xxxii.

180   Meisami 1987: 111.

181   Rubanovich 2016a: 75.

182   Davis 2008: xxxi.

183   'Ubayd Zakani 1999: 329.

184   Meisami 2003: 302.

185   Sa'di Shirazi 2007: 468.

186   See 'Attar Shirazi 1990: 74.

187   See Sa'di Shirazi 2007: 468, 469, 507, 515, 688; Kamal Isfahani 1969: 712.

188   'Ubayd Zakani 1999: 149–182. See also Halabi 1998: 87–88.

189   'Iraqi 1998: 298–357. See also Chittick 1998: 540.

190   'Ubayd Zakani 1999: 159.

191   'Iraqi 1998: 323–324.

192   Haydar Shirazi 2004: 102.

193   See Khvaju Kirmani 1957: 100.

194   Sa'di Shirazi 2007: 521.

195   Hamgar 1996: 477.

196   Ibid: 433.

197   Ibid: 434, 561.

Chapter 6

1   Brinner 2002: xi.

2   Brinner 2010: 466.

3   See Schwarzbaum 1982.

4   Lowin 2006: 28, 32.

5   Ibid: 38.

6   Yeroushalmi 2002: 77. See also Yamauchi 1990: 458–466.

7   See Mokhtarian 2015: 22–25.

8   Gregg 2015: xiii.

9   Kugel 1990: 3–4. See also Lassner 1993: 42.

10 Lowin 2006: 254.

11 Ibid: 33.

12 Gregg 2015: xiii.

13 Purnamdarian 1990: 8–12.

14 See Rudaki Samarqandi 2014: 73, 99, 102, 113, 121; 'Unsuri Balkhi 1984: 33, 45, 62, 65, 75, 106, 115, 139, 140, 193, 202, 214, 287, 288, 293, 295, 302, 347.

15 Nwiya 1970: 178.

16 Purnamdarian 1990: 7.

17 See Rami Tabrizi 1997: 144.

18 Renard 1994: 151.

19 See Bürgel 1991: 32–33.

20 Khvaju Kirmani 1957: 23, 305, 484, 671, 704, 747; 'Imad Kirmani 1969: 37, 73, 228, 231, 232, 300, 378.

21 Salman Savaji 1957: 486, 566, 574, 582.

22 See Marsham 2009: 124, 178.

23 See Rumi 1962: 4, 11, 14, 47, 57, 80, 97, 137, 185, 197, 230, 255, 257, 258, 276, 307, 354, 426, 463, 464, 489, 497, 507, 538, 548. See also Sa'di Shirazi 2007: 714–715.

24 al-Istakhri 1961: 84.

25 Shahbazi 2004.

26 Yavari 2002: 51; Limbert 2004a: 51–52; Khanbaghi 2006: 83.

27 Moreen 2000: 26–119, 290–292; Yeroushalmi 2002: 82–86.

28 See Marsham 2009: 127–128, 171–172, 178.

29 K238:2, 401:9.

30 H184:1.

31 H206:10.

32 Sa'di Shirazi 2007: 541.

33 J948:5.

34 See Shafi'i-Kadkani 2006: 329.

35 K237:2, 278:8, 401:9.

36 See Imami 1974: 422–423.

37 Tusi 1996: 483.

38 See Hanaoka 2016: 206–207.

39 See Meisami 2003: 53.

40 See Zaryab 1989: 156–157.

41 Renard 1994: 154.

42 See Sa'di Shirazi 2007: 29.

43 Hafiz Shirazi 1996: 54.

44 See Melikian-Chirvani 1992: 110–112.

45 Sa'di Shirazi 2007: 796.

46 J1234:3.

47 Sa'di Shirazi 2007: 29.

48 H307:7.

49 Q4:125.

50 Renard 1994: 53.

51 See Imami 1974: 426.

52 See Savant 2013: 47–49.

53 Netzer 1997: 62. See also Shams-i Fakhri 1887: 27.

54 See Netzer 1997: 62.

55 Q21:68–69.

56 Q21:57–64.

57 See Shams-i Fakhri 1887: 67, 104.

58 See Sa'di Shirazi 2007: 425.

59 Q12:3.

60 Goldman 2003: 55. See also Renard 1994: 59.

61 Ritter 2003: 414.

62 See Lowin 2014: 231.

63 Schimmel 1999: 45. See also Sa'di Shirazi 2007: 134.

64 Renard 1994: 60, 62. See also Rumi 1962: 138, 143, 158.

65 de Bruijn 2002: 361.

66 Renard 1994: 60.

67 See Salman Savaji 1957: 39, 377; Kamal Khujandi 1958: 360.

68 Rumi 1962: 4, 20, 27, 34, 43, 61, 62, 74, 88, 110, 134, 138, 143, 151, 158, 167, 175, 185, 196, 206, 215, 234, 246, 249, 251. See also Renard 1994: 59–66.

69 Sa'di Shirazi 2007: 489. See also Khvaju Kirmani 1957: 723.

70 J828:4. See also J826:3.

71 Q12:93.

72 Q12:96.

73 See Renard 1994: 65–66.

74 See Nasir Bukhara'i 1974: 104; Shams-i Fakhri 1887: 58.

75 See Ahur 1984: 510, 920.

76 See Lescot 1944: 69.

77 See Schimmel 1999: 47; Renard 1994: 152.

78 Lescot 1944: 66–67.

79 J494:1, 1175:8.

80 Q12:96.

81 J827:5, 1176:8.

82 Q12:18.

83 J1176:10.

84 H255:1.

85 J533:8.

86 See Lescot 1944: 78–79.

87 H212, 304, 433.

88 H242, 245, 329, 381, 402.

89 See Rumi 1962: 110, 206.

90 Q12:25.

91 de Bruijn 2002: 361.

92 Rypka 1968: 155–157, 235.

93 de Bruijn 2002: 360.

94 Q12:20.

95 Q12:24.

96 Kugel 1990: 28–35.

97 Q12:31.

98 See Goldman 1995.

99 Tusi 1996: 96.

100 Spellberg 1994: 147.

101 Ibid.

102 Stowasser 1994: 52.

103 Q12:28.

104 Malti-Douglas 1991: 50.

105 Merguerian and Najmabadi 1997: 489.

106 See Mahmood 2017: 23–27.

107 Merguerian and Najmabadi 1997: 497.

108 de Bruijn 2002: 361.

109 Jami 1958: 723–730. See Feuillebois-Pierunek 2002: 297.

110 Gregg 2015: 225.

111 Renard 1994: 64.

112 See Malti-Douglas 1991: 54.

113 See Khvaju Kirmani 1957: 248; Qatran Tabrizi 1983: 158.

114 Khvaju Kirmani 1957: 439.

115 Sa'di Shirazi 2007: 707.

116 Awhadi Maragha'i 1961: 420.

117 Merguerian and Najmabadi 1997: 496.

118 Khvaju Kirmani 1957: 278.

119 'Imad Kirmani 1969: 147, 154.

120 Ibid: 46.

121 Salman Savaji 1957: 182.

122 Kamal Khujandi 1958: 112.

123 See Jami 1958: 727–728.

124 Kugel 1990: 75–76.

125 Gurgani 1959: 111.

126 Merguerian and Najmabadi 1997: 491.

127 Meisami 1990c: 136–137.

128 See Loloi 2004: 22–48.

129 H349:7. See also J1047.

130 'Attar Shirazi 1990: 32.

131 See Mahmood 2017: 32–33.

132 Ghani 2001: 375–376.

133 See Khvaju Kirmani 1957: 581; Kamal Isfahani 1969: 46.

134 See Hamgar 1996: 322; Qatran Tabrizi 1983: 4, 73, 225, 287, 342, 373. See also Browne 1920: 263.

135 Farrukhi Sistani 1999: 139–141, 204–205, 208.

136 'Ubayd Zakani 1999: 26.

137 See Kutubi 1985: 81–82; Yazdi 1947: 11, 15.

138 Meisami 1990c: 142.

139 Dadbeh 2009: 30.

140 See Kutubi 1985: 156.

141 See Ghani 2001: 352, 355.

142 See also Kamal Isfahani 1969: 721; 'Attar Shirazi 1990: 27.

143 See also Sa'di Shirazi 2007: 487.

144 J1167:7.

145 Jami 1958: 713–714, 725–728.

146 'Imad Kirmani 1969: 147.

147 Khvaju Kirmani 1957: 653.

148 Sa'di Shirazi 2007: 461.

149 J1266:5.

150 See Kamal Khujandi 1958: 348; Haydar Shirazi 2004: 79.

151 See Bürgel 2005: 294.

152 Haydar Shirazi 2004: 85.

153 H475:2.

154 See Gurgani 1959: 111; Nizami Ganjavi 2006: 52–55.

155 Najmabadi 2000: 161.

156 Ibid: 155.

157 See U16:1; Kamal Khujandi 1958: 32.

158 See Awhadi Maragha'i 1961: 185.

159 Khvaju Kirmani 1957: 661, 682.

160 Ibid: 752.

161 Ibid: 677.

162 Ibid: 610–613; Jalal Yazdi 1987: 231.

163 See also Awhadi Maragha'i 1961: 185.

164 Q12:18.

165 Sa'di Shirazi 2007: 594.

166 Ibid: 413.

167 See Schimmel 1999: 53–58; Khvaju Kirmani 1957: 728; Qatran Tabrizi 1983: 3.

168 Qatran Tabrizi 1983: 158. See also Purnamdarian 1990: 10–12.

169 Khvaju Kirmani 1957: 447.

170 Sa'di Shirazi 2007: 603.

171 Hamgar 1996: 457.

172 J494:1, 1176:8; see also Bashari 2009: 759; Qatran Tabrizi 1983: 230, 373.

173 See Islami Nudushan 2003: 264–267.

174 See also Khvaju Kirmani 1957: 231.

175 Ibid: 707; Haydar Shirazi 2004: 97.

176 Rajabzadeh 2009.

177 See Hope 2016: 119–120; Ravalde 2016: 60, 63, 65–66, 73.

178 See Khurramshahi 1987: 826–827; Schimmel 1988: 216; Lane 2003: 10, 199–200.

179 See Nafisi 1942: 133–135; Amuli 1957: 252.

180 Baba Kuhi 1953: 61. See also Kasheff 1988.

181 See 'Iraqi 1998: 146.

182 See Zipoli 1993; Lewis 1994: 199–200, 221; Losensky 1994: 229–232; Losensky 1998: 108–114;.

183 See Dawlatabadi 1988: 41–80.

184 Salman Savaji 1957: 184–185; Ghani 1987: 29–30.

185 See Sa'di Shirazi 2007: 286; Kamal Isfahani 1969: 700; Nasir Bukhara'i 1974: 300.

186 Lowin 2014: 18.

187 See Lewis 1995: 108.

188 See Lescot 1944: 78–79.

189 Ibid: 77; Ghani 2001: 24.

190 Q12:20.

191 See Sa'di Shirazi 2007: 518.

192 Salman Savaji 1957: 228.

193 Hamgar 1996: 359.

194 H486:2.

195 Q7:143–147.

196 Khvaju Kirmani 1957: 271, 490, 505.

197 Q28:29–30. See also H188:6, 345:6.

198 Q7:143.

199 See Moreen 2000: 27.

200 Tusi 1996: 195.

201 Renard 1994: 90–91.

202 Khvaju Kirmani 1957: 339, 343, 453. See also Nasir Bukhara'i 1974: 114.

203 Q36:78. See Shafi'i-Kadkani 2006: 294.

204 H367:5.

205 H186:8.

206 H437:2. See also Khvaju Kirmani 1957.

207 Khvaju Kirmani 1957: 230, 653.

208 H175:2; Jalal Yazdi 1987: 248.

209 H93:8.

210 Q7:65–79.

211 See Khvaju Kirmani 1957: 278; Nasir Bukhara'i 1974: 175.

212 See Montgomery 1996; Lewis 2009; Brookshaw 2014: 7–9.

213 J1343:4.

214 J534:5.

215 H86:5.

216 See Qazvini 1988: 281–283.

217 See also Nasir Bukhara'i 1974: 398.

218 See also Awhadi Maragha'i 1961: 253; Jalal Yazdi 1987: 127.

219 See Purnamdarian 2003: 413; Nazari 2007: 65–66, 69–70.

220 Hafiz Shirazi 1999: 377.

221 Khvaju Kirmani 1957: 400. See Melikian-Chirvani 1992: 109; 1996: 95.

222 Choksy 2015.

223 See Tusi 1996: 412, 415.

224 Soroudi 2010: 120.

225 J110:1, 1361:4. See Pello 2013: 252–254, 259.

Bibliography

Primary sources

Abu Nuwas, al-Hasan b. Hani (2003a), *Diwan Abi Nuwas* vol. III, ed. Ewald Wagner, Damascus: al-Mada.

Abu Nuwas, al-Hasan (2003b), *Diwan Abi Nuwas* vol. IV, ed. Gregor Schoeler, Damascus: al-Mada.

Adi b. Zayd al-'Ibadi (1965), *Diwan*, ed. Muhammad Jabbar al-Mu'aybid, Baghdad: Dar al-Jumhuriya.

Ahmad b. Husayn Katib (1966), *Tarikh-i jadid-i Yazd*, ed. Iraj Afshar, Tehran: Ibn Sina.

Amir Mu'izzi (1983), *Kulliyat-i divan-i Mu'izzi*, ed. Nasir Hayyiri, Tehran: Nashr-i Marzban.

Amuli, Shams al-Din Muhammad (1957), *Nafa'is al-funun fi 'ara'is al-'uyun*, ed. Abu'l-Hasan Sha'rani, Tehran: Islamiya.

Ansari, Khvaja 'Abdullah (1987), *Munajat*, ed. 'Ali Panah, Tehran: Furughi.

'Attar Nishaburi (1960), *Divan*, ed. Sa'id Nafisi, Tehran: Sana'i.

'Attar Shirazi, Ruh-i 'Attar (1990), *Divan*, ed. Ahmad Karami, Tehran: Intisharat-i Ma.

Awhadi Maragha'i, Rukn al-Din (1928), *Jam-i jam*, Tehran: Firdawsi.

Awhadi Maragha'i (1961), *Kulliyat*, ed. Sa'id Nafisi, Tehran: Amir Kabir.

Baba Kuhi (1953), *Divan-i Shaykh 'Ali mashhur bi-Baba Kuhi*, Shiraz: Ma'rifat.

Bal'ami, Abu 'Ali Muhammad (1974), *Tarikh-i Bal'ami*, eds. Muhammad-Taqi Bahar and Muhammad Parvin Gunabadi, Tehran: Zavvar.

Bayhaqi, Abu'l-Fazl Muhammad (1971), *Tarikh-i Bayhaqi*, ed. 'Ali-Akbar Fayyaz, Mashhad: Danishgah-i Mashhad.

Bayzavi, Nasir al-Din (2003), *Nizam al-tavarikh*, ed. Mir-Hashim Muhaddith, Tehran: Bunyad-i Mawqufat-i Mahmud Afshar.

Bushaq Shirazi (2014), *Vasf-i ta'am: divan-i at'ima-yi mawlana Abu Ishaq-i Hallaj-i Shirazi*, ed. Muhsin Azarm, Tehran: Chishma.

al-Dinawari, Abu Hanifa (1960), *al-Akhbar al-tiwal*, ed. 'Abd al-Mun'im 'Amir, Cairo: Wazarat al-Thaqafa.

Dawlatshah Samarqandi, b. 'Ala' al-Dawla (1901), *Tadhkirat al-shu'ara'*, ed. Edward G. Browne, Leiden: Brill.

Fakhri Hiravi (1968), *Javahir al-'aja'ib*, ed. Hisam al-Din Rashidi, Haydarabad: Sindhi Adabi Burd.

Farrukhi Sistani (1999), *Divan*, ed. Muhammad Dabir-Siyaqi, Tehran: Zavvar.

Firdawsi, Abu'l-Qasim (1987), *Shahnama* vol. I, ed. Jalal Khaliqi-Mutlaq, New York: Bibliotheca Persica.

Firdawsi, Abu'l-Qasim (1990), *Shahnama* vol. II, ed. Jalal Khaliqi-Mutlaq, New York: Bibliotheca Persica.

Firdawsi, Abu'l-Qasim (1992), *Shahnama* vol. III, ed. Jalal Khaliqi-Mutlaq, New York: Bibliotheca Persica.

Firdawsi, Abu'l-Qasim (1997), *Shahnama* vol. V, ed. Jalal Khaliqi-Mutlaq, New York: Bibliotheca Persica.

Firdawsi, Abu'l-Qasim (2005), *Shahnama* vol. VI, eds. Jalal Khaliqi-Mutlaq and Mahmud Umidsalar, New York: Bibliotheca Persica.

Firdawsi, Abu'l-Qasim (2008), *Shahnama* vol. VIII, ed. Jalal Khaliqi-Mutlaq, New York: Bibliotheca Persica.

Ghazali, Ahmad (1942), *Savanih*, ed. Hellmut Ritter, Istanbul: Matba'a-yi Ma'arif.

Gurgani, Fakhr al-Din (1959), *Vis u Ramin*, ed. Muhammad-Ja'far Mahjub, Tehran: Ibn Sina.

Hafiz Abru (1999), *Jughrafiya-yi Hafiz-i Abru*, ed. Sadiq Sajjadi, Tehran: Bunyan.

Hafiz Shirazi, Shams al-Din Muhammad (1996), *Divan*, ed. Parviz Natil Khanlari, Tehran: Khvarazmi.

Hafiz Shirazi (1999), *Divan*, eds. Qasim Ghani and Muhammad Qazvini, Tehran: Quqnus.

Hafiz Shirazi (2000), *Divan*, eds. Sadiq Sajjadi, 'Ali Bahramian and Kazim Barg-Naysi, Tehran: Fikr-i ruz.

Haft kishvar ya Suvar al-aqalim (1974), ed. Manuchihr Sutuda, Tehran: Bunyad-i Farhang-i Iran.

Hamdullah Mustawfi (1957), *Nuzhat al-qulub*, ed. Muhammad Dabir-Siyaqi, Tehran: Tahuri.

Hamdullah Mustawfi (1960), *Tarikh-i Guzida*, ed. 'Abd al-Husayn Nava'i, Tehran: Amir Kabir.

Hamgar, Majd al-Din (1996), *Divan*, ed. Ahmad Karami, Tehran: Intisharat-i Ma.

Haydar Shirazi (2004), *Divan*, ed. 'Ali Mir-Afzali, Tehran: Kaziruniya.

Ibn al-Balkhi (1921), *Farsnama*, eds. Guy Le Strange and Reynold A. Nicholson. Cambridge: Cambridge University Press.

Ibn Battuta (1975), *Rihlat Ibn Battuta*, ed. Muhammad al-Muntasir al-Kattani, Beirut: Mu'assasat al-Risala.

'Imad Kirmani, 'Imad al-Din Faqih (1969), *Divan*, ed. Rukn al-Din Humayun-Farrukh, Tehran: Ibn Sina.

'Iraqi, Fakhr al-Din Ibrahim (1998), *Kulliyat*, ed. Mahmud 'Ilmi. Tehran: 'Ilmi.

'Isa b. Junayd Shirazi (1985), *tadhkira-yi Hizar mazar*, ed. Nurani Visal, Shiraz: Ahmadi.

al-Istakhri, Abu Ishaq Ibrahim b. Muhammad (1961), *Al-Masalik wa l-mamalik*, ed. Muhammad Jabir 'Abd al-'Al, Cairo: Dar al-Qalam.

Ja'far b. Muhammad (1960), *Tarikh-i Yazd*, ed. Iraj Afshar, Tehran: Bungah-i Tarjuma va Nashr-i Kitab.

Jahan-Malik Khatun (1995), *Divan-i kamil*, eds. Kamil Ahmadnizhad and Purandukht Kashani-Rad, Tehran: Zavvar.

Jalal Yazdi, Jalal al-Din 'Azud (1987), *Divan*, ed. Ahmad Karami, Tehran: Intisharat-i Ma.

Jami, 'Abd al-Rahman (1958), *Mathnavi-yi Haft awrang*, ed. Murtaza Mudarris Gilani, Tehran: Sa'di.

Jami, 'Abd al-Rahman (1962), *Divan-i kamil*, ed. Hashim Razi, Tehran: Piruz.

Jami, 'Abd al-Rahman (1988), *Baharistan*, ed. Isma'il Hakimi, Tehran: Ittila'at.

Jami, 'Abd al-Rahman (1991), *Nafahat al-uns min hazarat al-quds*, ed. Mahmud 'Abidi, Tehran: Ittila'at.

Junayd Shirazi, Mu'in al-Din (1949), *Shadd al-izar fi hatt al-awzar 'an zavvar al-mazar*, eds.Muhammad Qazvini and 'Abbas Iqbal, Tehran: Markazi.

Junayd Shirazi, Mu'in al-Din (1941), *Divan*, ed. Sa'id Nafisi, Tehran: Markazi.

Kamal Isfahani, Kamal al-Din Isma'il (1969), *Divan*, ed. Husayn Bahr al-'Ulumi, Tehran: Dihkhuda.

Kamal Khujandi, Kamal al-Din Mas'ud (1958), *Divan*, ed. 'Aziz Dawlatabadi, Tehran: Kitab-furushi-yi Tehran.

Kay-Ka'us b. Iskandar (1951), *Qabusnama*, ed. Reuben Levy, London: Cresset Press.

Khayyam, 'Umar (1942), *Ruba'iyat*, ed. Muhammad-'Ali Furughi, Tehran: Sami.

Khvaju Kirmani, Kamal al-Din Mahmud (1957), *Divan*, ed. Ahmad Suhayli Khvansari, Tehran: Mahmudi.

Khvand Mir (2001), *Habib al-siyar fi akhbar al-bashar* vol. III, ed. Muhammad Dabir-Siyaqi, Tehran: Khayyam.

Kitab al-Taj fi akhlaq al-muluk (1914), ed. Zaki Ahmad, Cairo: al-Matba'a al-Amiriya.

Kushajim, Mahmud b. al-Husayn (1999), *Adab al-nadim*, ed. al-Nabawi Sha'lan, Cairo: al-Khanji.

Kutubi, Mahmud (1985), *Tarikh-i Al-i Muzaffar*, ed. 'Abd al-Husayn Nava'i, Tehran: Amir Kabir.

al-Mafarrukhi, Mufaddal b. Sa'd (1933), *Kitab mahasin Isfahan*, ed. Jalal al-Din al-Husayni al-Tihrani, Tehran: Matba'a-yi Majlis.

Mahsati Ganjavi (2003), *Mahsati-yi Ganja'i: buzurg-tarin zan-i sha'ir-i ruba'i-sara*, ed. Mu'in al-Din Mihrabi, Tehran: Tus.

Manuchihri Damghani (1996), *Divan*, ed. Muhammad Dabir-Siyaqi, Tehran: Zavvar.

al-Mas'udi (1966a), *Muruj al-dhahab wa ma'adin al-jawhar* vol. I, ed. Charles Pellat, Beirut: al-Jami'a al-Lubnaniya.

al-Mas'udi (1966b), *Muruj al-dhahab wa ma'adin al-jawhar* vol. II, ed. Charles Pellat, Beirut: al-Jami'a al-Lubnaniya.

Mujmal al-tawarikh wa'l-qisas (2000), eds. Seyfeddin Najmabadi and Siegfried Weber. Neckharhausen: Deux Mondes.

Munshi Kirmani, Nasir al-Din (1983), *Simt al-'ula li'l-hazrat al-'ulya dar tarikh-i Qarakhita'iyan-i Kirman*, ed. 'Abbas Iqbal, Tehran: Asatir.

Nasir Bukhara'i (1974), *Divan*, ed. Mihdi Dirakhshan, Tehran: Nuriyani.

Natanzi, Mu'in al-Din (1957), *Muntakhab al-tavarikh-i Mu'ini*, ed. Jean Aubin, Tehran: Khayyam.

Nava'i, Nizam al-Din 'Ali-Shir (1944), *Majalis al-nafa'is dar tadhkira-yi shu'ara-yi qarn-i nuhum-i hijri*, ed. 'Ali-Asghar Hikmat, Tehran: Bank Milli Iran.

al-Nisaburi, Abu Ishaq Ibrahim b. Mansur (1961), *Qisas al-anbiya'*, ed. Habib Yaghma'i, Tehran: Bungah-i Tarjuma va Nashr-i Kitab.

Nizam al-Mulk, Husayn b. 'Ali (1955), *Siyasatnama*, eds. Muhammad Qazvini and Murtaza Mudarrisi-Chahardihi, Tehran: Tahuri.

Nizami 'Aruzi, Ahmad b. 'Umar (1920), *Chahar maqala*, ed. Muhammad Qazvini, Leiden: Brill.

Nizami Ganjavi (1966), *Sharafnama*, ed. Pizhman Bakhtiyari, Tehran: Ibn Sina.

Nizami Ganjavi (2001), *Makhzan al-asrar*, ed. Vahid Dastgirdi and Sa'id Hamidian, Tehran: Qatra.

Nizami Ganjavi (2005), *Haft Paykar*, ed. Vahid Dastgirdi, Tehran: Zavvar.

Nizami Ganjavi (2006), *Khusraw va Shirin*, ed. Vahid Dastgirdi, Tehran: Zavvar.

Nizari Quhistani (1992), *Divan*, ed. Mazahir Musaffa, Tehran: 'Ilmi.

Qatran Tabrizi (1983), *Divan*, ed. Muhammad Nakhjavani, Tehran: Quqnus.

al-Qazwini, Zakariya b. Muhammad (1984), *Athar al-bilad wa akhbar al-'ibad*, Beirut: Dar Bayrut.

Rami Tabrizi, Sharaf al-Din (1946), *Anis al-'Ushshaq*, ed. 'Abbas Iqbal, Tehran: Shirkat-i Sahami-yi Chap.

Rami Tabrizi, Sharaf al-Din (1997), *Anis al-'Ushshaq va chand athar-i digar*, ed. Muhsin Kiyani, Tehran: Rawzana.

Rudaki Samarqandi (2014), *Divan*, ed. Sa'id Nafisi, Tehran: Nigah.

Rumi, Jalal al-Din (1962), *Kulliyat-i Shams-i Tabrizi*, ed. M. Darvish, Tehran: Javidan.

Rumi, Jalal al-Din (1998), *Mathnavi-yi ma'navi*, ed. Mihdi Adhar Yazdi, Tehran: Pazhuhish.

Sa'di Shirazi, Musharrif al-Din Muslih (2007), *Kulliyat*, ed. Muhammad-'Ali Furughi, Tehran: Amir Kabir.

Salman Savaji (1957), *Divan*, ed. Mansur Mushfiq, Tehran: Bungah-i Safi-'Ali Shah.

Shabankara'i, Muhammad b. 'Ali (1984), *Majma' al-ansab*, ed. Mir-Hashim Muhaddith, Tehran: Amir Kabir.

Shams-i Fakhri, Shams al-Din Muhammad (1887), *Mi'yar-i Jamali va miftah-i Abu Ishaqi*, ed. Carolus Salemann, Kazan: ex typ. Imperialis Literarum Universitatis.

Shams-i Qays Razi (2009), *al-Mu'jam fi ma'ayir ash'ar al-'ajam*, ed. Sirus Shamisa, Tehran: 'Ilm.

Sudi Busnavi, Muhammad (1995), *Sharh-i Sudi bar Hafiz*, trans. 'Ismat Sattarzada, Tehran: Zarrin.

Tarikh-i Sistan (1994), ed. Ja'far Mudarris-Sadiqi, Tehran: Markaz.

Tusi, Muhammad b. Mahmud (1996), '*Aja'ibnama*, ed. Ja'far Mudarris-Sadiqi, Tehran: Nashr-i Markaz.

'Ubayd Zakani, Nizam al-Din (1999), *Kulliyat*, ed. Muhammad-Ja'far Mahjub, New York: Bibliotheca Persica Press.

'Unsuri Balkhi (1984), *Divan*, ed. Muhammad Dabir-Siyaqi, Tehran: Sana'i.

Vassaf al-Hazrat, 'Abdullah b. Fazlullah (1959), *Kitab-i mustatab-i Vassaf al-Hazrat*, Tehran: Ibn Sina.

Yazdi, Mu'in al-Din (1947), *Mavahib-i ilahi dar tarikh-i Al-i Muzaffar*, ed. Sa'id Nafisi, Tehran: Iqbal.

Yazdi, Sharaf al-Din (2007), *Manzumat*, ed. Iraj Afshar, Tehran: Thuraya.

Zarkub Shirazi, Ahmad b. Abi'l-khayr (1931), *Shiraznama*, ed. Bahman Karimi, Tehran: Rawshana'i.

Secondary sources

Adamova, Adel T. and Manijeh Bayani (2016), *Persian Painting: The Arts of the Book and Portraiture*, London: Thames and Hudson.

Afsar, K. (1988), 'Bag-e Eram', *Encyclopaedia Iranica* III: 399.

Ahur, Parviz (1984), *Kilk-i khayal-angiz ya farhang-i jami'-i divan-i Hafiz*, Tehran: Zavvar.

Aigle, Denise (2005), *Le Fars sous la domination mongole: politique et fiscalité (XIIIe-XIVe S.)*, Paris: Association pour l'avancement des études iraniennes.

Aigle, Denise (2014), *The Mongol Empire between Myth and Reality: Studies in Anthropological History*, Leiden: Brill.

A'lam, H. (1993), 'Cypress', *Encyclopaedia Iranica* VI: 505–508.

Alemi, Mahvash (2008), 'Shiraz: The City of Gardens and Poets', in Salma K. Jayyusi, *The City in the Islamic World*, vol. I, 525–554, Leiden: Brill.

Ali, Samer M. (2010), *Arabic Literary Salons in the Islamic Middle Ages: Poetry, Public Performance, and the Presentation of the Past*, Notre Dame: University of Notre Dame Press.

Andrews, Walter G. (1985), *Poetry's Voice, Society's Song: Ottoman Lyric Poetry*, Seattle: University of Washington Press.

Andrews, Walter G. and Mehmet Kalpaklı (2005), *The Age of Beloveds: Love and the Beloved in Early-modern Ottoman and European Culture and Society*, Durham: Duke University Press.

Anvar, Leili (2011), 'The Hidden Pearls of Wisdom: Desire and Initiation in *Layli u Majnun*', in Johann-Christoph Bürgel and Christine van Ruymbeke (eds), *A Key to the Treasury of the Hakim: Artistic and Humanistic Aspects of Nizami Ganjavi's* Khamsa, 53–76, Leiden: Leiden University Press.

Arberry, Arthur J. (1960), *Shiraz: Persian City of Saints and Poets*, Norman: University of Oklahoma Press.

Aryanpur, 'Ali-Riza (1986), *Pazhuhishi dar shinakht-i bagh-ha-yi Iran va bagh-ha-yi tarikhi-yi Shiraz*, Tehran: Farhangsara.

Askari, Nasrin (2016), *The Medieval Reception of the* Shahnama *as a Mirror for Princes*, Leiden: Brill.

Aubin, Jean (1970), 'Elements pour l'étude des agglomorations urbaines dans l'Iran medieval', in A. H. Hourani and S. M. Stern (eds), *The Islamic City: A Colloquium*, 49–75, Oxford: Bruno Cassirer.

Avery, Peter and John Heath-Stubbs (1952), *Hafiz of Shiraz: Thirty Poems*, London: John Murray.

Avery, Peter (2007), *The Collected Lyrics of Hafiz of Shiraz*, Cambridge: Archetype.

Azarnouche, Samra (2013), *Husraw i Kawadan ud Redag-e Khosrow fils de Kawad et un page*, Paris: Association pour l'avancement des études iraniennes.

Babaie, Sussan (2008), *Isfahan and its Palaces: Statecraft, Shi'ism, and the Architecture of Conviviality in Early Modern Iran*, Edinburgh: Edinburgh University Press.

Babayan, Kathryn (2002), *Mystics, Monarchs, and Messiahs: Cultural Landscapes of Early Modern Iran*, Cambridge: Center for Middle Eastern Studies of Harvard University.

Bağci, Serpil (1995), 'A New Theme of the Shirazi Frontispiece Miniatures: The *Divan* of Solomon', *Muqarnas* 12: 101–111.

Barbaro, Josafa and Ambrogio Contarini (1873), *Travels to Tana and Persia*, trans. William Thomas, ed. Lord Stanley of Alderley, London: The Hakluyt Society.

Barletta, Vincent (2005), *Covert Gestures: Crypto-Islamic Literature as Cultural Practice in Early Modern Spain*, Minneapolis: University of Minnesota Press.

Barletta, Vincent (2010), *Death in Babylon: Alexander the Great & Iberian Empire in the Muslim Orient*, Chicago: University of Chicago Press.

Bashari, Javad (2009), 'Ash'ari naw-yafta az Jahan-Malik Khatun, sha'ir-i sada-yi hashtum-i hijri'. *Payam-i Baharistan* 1: 740–766.

Bashir, Shahzad (2011), *Sufi Bodies: Religion and Society in Medieval Islam*, New York: Columbia University Press.

Basiri, Husayn (1946), *Rahnama-yi Takht-i Jamshid*, Tehran: Vizarat-i Farhang.

Bauer, Thomas (1998), *Liebe und Liebesdichtung in der arabischen Welt des 9. 10. Jahrhunderts*, Wiesbaden: Harrassowitz Verlag.

Bauman, Richard (1975), 'Verbal Art as Performance', *American Anthropologist* n.s. 77: 290–311.

Bauman, Richard and Charles L. Briggs (1990), 'Poetics and Performance as Critical Perspectives on Language and Social Life', *Annual Review of Anthropology* 19: 59–88.

Bausani, Alessandro (1965), 'Ghazal ii in Persian Literature'. *Encyclopaedia of Islam, New Edition* II: 1033–1036.

Bausani, Alessandro (2000), *Religion in Iran: From Zoroaster to Baha'ullah*, trans. J. M. Marchesi, New York: Bibliotheca Persica.

Bayani, Shirin (1966), *Tarikh-i Al-i Jalayir*, Tehran: Tehran University.

Bednarz, James P. (2001), *Shakespeare and the Poets' War*, New York: Columbia University Press.

Beelaert, A. L. F. A. (2000), *A Cure for the Grieving: Studies on the Poetry of the 12th-century Persian Court Poet Khaqani Širwani*, Leiden: Nederlands Instituut voor het Nabije Oosten.

Berlekamp, Persis (2011), *Wonder, Image, and Cosmos in Medieval Islam*, New Haven: Yale University Press.

Bier, Lionel (1986), *Sarvistan: A Study in Early Iranian Architecture*, University Park: Pennsylvania State University Press.

Blachère, R. (1965), 'i. The Ghazal in Arabic Poetry', *Encyclopaedia of Islam, New Edition* II: 1028–1033.

Blair, Sheila S. (1993), 'The Ilkhanid Palace', *Ars Orientalis* 23: 239–248.

Blair, Sheila S. (2014), *Text and Image in Medieval Persian Art*, Edinburgh: Edinburgh University Press.

Blochet, Edgar (1928), *Catalogue des manuscrits persans de la Bibliothèque nationale* vol. III, Paris: E. Leroux.

Bombaci, Alessio (1966), *The Kufic Inscription in Persian Verses at the Court of the Royal Palace of Mas'ud III at Ghazni*, Rome: Istituto italiano per il Medio ed Estremo Oriente.

Bosworth, C. E. (1962), 'The Titulature of the Early Ghaznavids', *Oriens* 15: 210–233.

Bosworth, C. (1966), 'Mahmud of Ghazna in Contemporary Eyes and in Later Persian Literature', *Iran* 7: 85–92.

Bosworth, C. (1978), 'The Heritage of Rulership in Early Islamic Iran and the Search for Dynastic Connections with the Past', *Iranian Studies* 11: 7–34.

Bosworth, C. (1996), *The New Islamic Dynasties: A Chronological and Genealogical Manual*. Edinburgh: Edinburgh University Press.

Boyce, Mary (1957), 'The Parthian Gosan and the Iranian Minstrel Tradition', *Journal of the Royal Asiatic Society* 18: 10–45.

Brinner, William M. (2002), *'Ara'is al-Majalis fi Qisas al-Anbiya' or 'Lives of the Prophets' as recounted by Abu Ishaq Ahmad ibn Muhammad ibn Ibrahim al-Tha'labi*, Leiden: Brill.

Brinner, William M. (2010), 'Legends of the Prophets (*Qisas al-anbiya*)', in Julie Scott Meisami and Paul Starkey (eds), *The Routledge Encyclopedia of Arabic Literaure*, 465–466. Abingdon: Routledge.

Britland, K. (2012), 'Patronage', in Roland Greene et al. (eds), *The Princeton Encyclopedia of Poetry and Poetics*, 4th edn, 1010–1013, Princeton: Princeton University Press.

Brookshaw, Dominic Parviz (2003), 'Palaces, Pavilions and Pleasure-Gardens: The Context and Setting of the Medieval *Majlis*', *Middle Eastern Literatures* 6: 199–223.

Brookshaw, Dominic Parviz (2005), 'Odes of a Poet-Princess: The *Ghazals* of Jahan-Malik Khatun', *Iran* 43: 173–195.

Brookshaw, Dominic Parviz (2008), 'Jahan-Malek Khatun', *Encyclopaedia Iranica* XIV: 383–385.

Brookshaw, Dominic Parviz (2009), 'To be Feared and Desired: Turks in the Collected Works of 'Ubayd-i Zakani', *Iranian Studies* 42: 725–744.

Brookshaw, Dominic Parviz (2012), 'Have You Heard the One about the Man from Qazvin? Regionalist Humor in the Works of 'Ubayd-i Zakani,' in Dominic Parviz Brookshaw (ed.), *Ruse and Wit: The Humorous in Arabic, Persian, and Turkish Narrative*, 44–69, Boston: Ilex Foundation.

Brookshaw, Dominic Parviz (2014), 'Lascivious Vines, Corrupted Virgins, and Crimes of Honour: Variations on the Wine Production Myth as Narrated in Early Persian Poetry', *Iranian Studies* 47: 87–129.

Brookshaw, Dominic Parviz (2015), 'Mytho-Political Remakings of Ferdowsi's Jamshid in the Lyric Poetry of Injuid and Mozaffarid Shiraz', *Iranian Studies* 48: 463–487.

Browne, Edward G. (1920), *A History of Persian Literature under Tartar Dominion (A.D. 1265–1502)*, Cambridge: Cambridge University Press.

Browne, Edward G. (1932), *A Descriptive Catalogue of the Oriental Mss. Belonging to the Late E.G. Browne*, ed. Reynold A. Nicholson, Cambridge: Cambridge University Press.

Bürgel, Johan Christoph (1991), 'Ambiguity: A Study in the Use of Religious Terminology in the Poetry of Hafiz', in Michael Glünz and J. Christoph Bürgel (eds), *Intoxication, Earthly and Heavenly: Seven Studies on the Poet Hafiz of Shiraz*, 7–39, Bern: Peter Lang.

Bürgel, Johan Christoph (2005), 'The Mighty Beloved: Images and Structures of Power in the Ghazal from Arabic to Urdu', in Thomas Bauer and Angelika Neuwirth (eds), *Ghazal as World Literature I: Transformations of a Literary Genre*, 283–309, Beirut: Ergon Verlag.

Burumand, Javad (1988), *Hafiz va jam-i Jam*, Tehran: Pazhang.

Busch, Allison (2011), *Poetry of Kings: The Classical Hindi Literature of Mughal India*, Oxford: Oxford University Press.

Canepa, Matthew P. (2010), 'Technologies of Memory in Early Sasanian Iran: Achaemenid Sites and Sasanian Identity', *American Journal of Archaeology* 114: 563–596.

Caton, Steven C. (1990), *'Peaks of Yemen I Summon': Poetry as Cultural Practice in a North Yemeni Tribe*, Berkeley: University of California Press.

Chejne, Anwar G. (1965), 'The Boon-Companion in Early 'Abbasid Times', *Journal of the American Oriental Society* 85: 327–335.

Chittick, William C. (1998), 'Eraqi, Fakr-al-Din Ebrahim', *Encyclopaedia Iranica* VIII: 538–540.

Choksy, Jamsheed K. (2015), 'Zoroastrianism ii. Historical Review: from the Arab Conquest to Modern Times', *Encyclopaedia Iranica*, online edition.

Clarke, Nicola (2012), *The Muslim Conquest of Iberia: Medieval Arabic Narratives*. Abingdon: Routledge.

Clavijo, Ruy González de (1928), *Embassy to Tamerlane, 1403–1406*, trans. Guy Le Strange, London: G. Routledge.

Clinton, Jerome W. (1972), *The Divan of Manuchihri Damghani: A Critical Study*, Minneapolis: Bibliotheca Islamica.

Clinton, Jerome W. (1988), 'Court Poetry at the Beginning of the Classical
    Period', in Ehsan Yarshater (ed.), *Persian Literature*, 75–95, Albany:
    Bibliotheca Persica.
Coste, Pascal and Eugène Flandin (1851), *Voyage en Perse de MM. Eugène
    Flandin, peintre, et Pascal Coste, architecte attachés a l'ambassade de France
    en Perse pendant les années 1840 et 1841*, Paris: Gide et Jule Bardry.
Culler, Jonathan (2015), *Theory of the Lyric*, Cambridge MA: Harvard University
    Press.
Dadbeh, Asghar (2009), 'Joseph i in Persian Literature', *Encyclopaedia Iranica* XV:
    30–34.
Danner, Victor (1975), 'Arabic Literature in Iran', in R. N. Frye (ed.), *The Cambridge
    History of Iran, Volume 4: The Period from the Arab Invasion to the Saljuqs*,
    566–594, Cambridge: Cambridge University Press.
Daryaee, Touraj (1995), 'National History or Keyanid History? The Nature of
    Sasanid Zoroastrian Historiography', *Iranian Studies* 28: 129–141.
Daryaee, Touraj (2002), *Šahristaniha i Eranšahr: A Middle Persian Text on Late
    Antique Geography, Epic, and History*, Costa Mesa: Mazda Publishers.
Daryaee, Touraj (2017), '*Sur Saxwan*', *Encyclopaedia Iranica*, online edition.
Dashti, 'Ali (1973), *Kakh-i ibda'*, Tehran: Intisharat-i Majalla-yi Yaghma.
Dashti, 'Ali (2011), *Naqshi az Hafiz*, ed. M. Mahuzi, Tehran: Zavvar.
Davidson, Olga M. (1994), *Poet and Hero in the Persian Book of Kings*, Ithaca:
    Cornell University Press.
Davis, Dick (1992), *Epic and Sedition: The Case of Ferdowsi's Shahnameh*,
    Fayetteville: University of Arkansas Press.
Davis, Dick (1999), 'Sufism and Poetry: A Marriage of Convenience?' *Edebiyat* 10:
    279–292.
Davis, Dick (2002), *Panthea's Children: Hellenistic Novels and Medieval Persian
    Romances*, New York: Bibliotheca Persica.
Davis, Dick (2008), *Vis and Ramin*, Washington DC: Mage.
Davis, Dick (2012), *Faces of Love: Hafez and the Poets of Shiraz*, Washington DC:
    Mage.
Dawlatabadi, Parvin (1988), *Manzur-i khiradmand: bar-rasi-yi ahval va guzida-yi
    ash'ar-i Jahan-Malik Khatun*, Tehran: Guhar.
de Bruijn, J. T. P. (1983), *Of Piety and Poetry: The Interaction of Religion and
    Literature in the Life and Works of Hakim Sana'i of Ghazna*, Leiden: Brill.
de Bruijn, J. T. P. (1986), 'Madjnun Layla 2. In Persian, Kurdish, and Pashto
    Literature', *Encyclopaedia of Islam, New Edition* V: 1103–1105.
de Bruijn, J. T. P. (1987), 'Poets and Minstrels in Early Persian Literature', *Studia
    Iranica* 5: 15–23.
de Bruijn, J. T. P. (1997), *Persian Sufi Poetry: An Introduction to the Mystical Use
    of Classical Poems*, Richmond: Curzon.
de Bruijn, J. T. P. (2000), 'Gazal i. History', *Encyclopaedia Iranica* X: 354–358.
de Bruijn, J. T. P. (2002), 'Yusuf and Zulaykha', *Encyclopaedia of Islam, New
    Edition* XI: 360–361.
de Bruijn, J. T. P. (2003), 'Hafez's Poetic Art', *Encyclopaedia Iranica* XI: 469–474.
de Bruijn, J. T. P. (2006), 'Anvari and the *gazal*: An Exploration', *Eurasiatica* 74: 9–34.
de Bruijn, J. T. P. (2009), 'Kvaju Kermani', *Encyclopaedia Iranica*, online edition.
de Fouchécour, Charles-Henri (2006), *Hafez de Chiraz, Le Divan: Oeuvre lyrique
    d'un spirituel en Perse au XIVe siècle*, Paris: Éditions Verdier.

de Fouchécour, Charles-Henri (2010), 'Hafiz and the Sufi', in Leonard Lewisohn (ed.), *Hafiz and the Religion of Love in Classical Persian Poetry*, 143–157, London: I.B. Tauris.

De Nicola, Bruno (2014), 'Patrons or *Murids*? Mongol Women and Shaykhs in Ilkhanid Iran and Anatolia', *Iran* 52: 142–156.

De Nicola, Bruno (2017), *Women in Mongol Iran: The Khatuns, 1206–1335*, Edinburgh: Edinburgh University Press.

Digard, Jean-Pierre (2002), 'Gypsy i. Gypsies of Persia', *Encyclopaedia Iranica* XI: 412–415.

Donohue, John J. (1973), 'Three Buwayhid Inscriptions', *Arabica* 20: 74–80.

Durand-Guédy, David (2013), 'The Tents of the Saljuqs', in David Durand-Guédy (ed.), *Turko-Mongol Rulers, Cities and City Life*, 149–189, Leiden: Brill.

Duranti, Alessandro (1986), 'The Audience as Co-author: An Introduction', *Text* 6: 239–247.

During, Jean (1988), *Musique et extase: l'audition mystique dans la tradition soufie*, Paris: Albin Michel.

Elias, Norbert (1983), *The Court Society*, New York: Pantheon Books.

El-Rouayheb, Khaled (2005), *Before Homosexuality in the Arab-Islamic World, 1500–1800*, Chicago: University of Chicago Press.

Esin, Emel (1970), 'Ay-Bitigi: The Court Attendants in Turkish Iconography', *Central Asiatic Journal* 14: 78–117.

Esin, Emel (1979), 'Turk-i Mah Chihrah (the Turkish Norm of Beauty in Iran)', in *Akten des VII. Internationalen Kongresses für Iranische Kunst und Archäologie: München, 7–10 September 1976*, 449–460. Berlin: D. Reimer.

Esin, Emel (1983), 'Descriptions of Turks and 'Tatars' (Mongols) of the Thirteenth Century in Some Anatolian Sources', in Klaus Sagaster and Michael Weiers (eds), *Documenta Barbarorum: Festschrift für Walther Heissig zum 70. Geburtstag*, 81–87, Wiesbaden: Harrassowitz.

Fallahzadeh, Mehrdad (2005), *Persian Writing on Music: A Study of Persian Musical Literature from 1000 to 1500 AD*, Uppsala: Uppsala Universitet.

Feeney, Denis (2016), *Beyond Greek: The Beginnings of Latin Literature*, Cambridge MA: Harvard University Press.

Fehévári, Geza and Mehrdad Shokoohy (1980), 'Archaeological Notes on Lashkari Bazar', *Wiener Zeitschrift für die Kunde des Morgenlandes* 72: 83–95.

Feuillebois-Pierunek, Ève (2002), *A la croisée des voies célestes: Faxr al-Din 'Eraqi poésie mystique et expression poétique en Perse médiévale*, Tehran: Institut Français de Recherche en Iran.

Firdawsi, 'Ali (2008), 'Dibacha', in 'Ali Firdawsi (ed.), *Ghazal-ha-yi Hafiz: nakhustin nuskha-yi yaft-shuda az zaman-i hayat-i sha'ir*, 10–60, Tehran: Dibaya.

Fitzherbert, Teresa (1991), 'Khwaju Kirmani (689–753/1290–1352): An *Éminence Grise* of Fourteenth Century Persian Painting', *Iran* 29: 137–151.

Floor, Willem (2009), 'Sugar', *Encyclopaedia Iranica*, online edition.

Franke, Patrick (2011), 'Drinking from the Water of Life – Nizami, Khizr and the Symbolism of Poetical Inspiration in Later Persianate Literature', in Johann-Christoph Bürgel and Christine van Ruymbeke (eds), *A Key to the Treasury of the Hakim: Artistic and Humanistic Aspects of Nizami Ganjavi's Khamsa*, 107–125, Leiden: Leiden University Press.

Gabbay, Alyssa (2010), *Islamic Tolerance: Amir Khusraw and Pluralism*, Abingdon: Routledge.

Galvez, Marisa (2012), *Songbook: How Lyrics Became Poetry in Medieval Europe*, Chicago: University of Chicago Press.

Ghani, Qasim (1987), *Yad-dasht-ha-yi duktur Qasim-i Ghani dar havashi-yi divan-i Hafiz*, ed. Isma'il Sarimi, Tehran: 'Ilmi.

Ghani, Qasim (2001), *Bahth dar athar u afkar u ahval-i Hafiz* vol. I, Tehran: Zavvar.

Ghazi, M. F. (1959), 'Un Group Social: 'Les raffinés' (*zurafa*')', *Studia Islamica* 11: 39–71.

Gignoux, Philippe (1999), 'Matériaux pour une histoire du vin dans l'Iran ancien', *Cahiers de Studia Iranica* 21: 35–50.

Glassen, Erika (1991), 'The Reception of Hafiz: Textual Transmission in a Historical Perspective', in Michael Glünz and J. Christoph Bürgel (eds), *Intoxication, Earthly and Heavenly: Seven Studies on the Poet Hafiz of Shiraz*, 41–52, Bern: Peter Lang.

Glünz, Michael (1986), 'Safis Šahrangiz: ein persisches Matnawi über die schönen Berufsleute von Istanbul', *Asiatische Studien* 40: 133–145.

Goldman, S. (1995), *The Wiles of Women/The Wiles of Men: Joseph and Potiphar's Wife in Ancient Near Eastern, Jewish, and Islamic Folklore*, Albany: SUNY Press.

Goldman, S. (2003), 'Joseph', *Encyclopaedia of the Qur'an* III: 55–57.

Golombek, Lisa and Donald Wilber (1988), *The Timurid Architecture of Iran and Turan*, Princeton: Princeton University Press.

Green, Richard Firth (1980), *Poets and Princepleasers: Literature and the English Court in the Late Middle Ages*, Toronto: Toronto University Press.

Greenblatt, Stephen (1997), 'The Touch of the Real', *Representations* 59: 14–29.

Greenblatt, Stephen (2010), *Shakespeare's Freedom*, Chicago: University of Chicago Press.

Gregg, Robert C. (2015), *Shared Stories, Rival Tellings: Early Encounters of Jews, Christians, and Muslims*, Oxford: Oxford University Press.

Grigor, Talinn (2015), 'Kingship Hybridized, Kingship Homogenized: Revivalism under the Qajar and the Pahlavi Dynasties', in Sussan Babaie and Talinn Grigor (eds), *Persian Kingship and Architecture: Strategies of Power in Iran from the Achaemenids to the Pahlavis*, 219–254, London: I.B. Tauris.

Gronke, Monika (1992), 'The Persian Court between Palace and Tent: from Timur to 'Abbas I', in Lisa Golombek and Maria Subtelny (eds), *Timurid Art and Culture: Iran and Central Asia in the Fifteenth Century*, 18–22, Leiden: Brill.

Gruendler, Beatrice (2003), *Medieval Arabic Praise Poetry: Ibn al-Rumi and the Patron's Redemption*, Abingdon: Routledge.

Gruendler, Beatrice (2008), '*Qasida*: Its Reconstruction in Performance', in Beatrice Gruendler (ed.), *Classical Arabic Humanities in their Own Terms*, 325–389, Leiden: Brill.

Gruendler, Beatrice and Louise Marlow (2004), 'Preface', in Beatrice Gruendler and Louise Marlow (eds), *Writers and Rulers: Perspectives on Their Relationship from Abbasid to Safavid Times*, v–xi, Wiesbaden: Reichert Verlag.

Gumbrecht, H. U. (2012), 'Presence', in Roland Greene et al. (eds), *The Princeton Encyclopedia of Poetry and Poetics*, 4th edn, 1105–1107, Princeton: Princeton University Press.

Hägg, Thomas and Bo Utas (2003), *The Virgin and Her Lover: Fragments of an Ancient Greek Novel and a Persian Epic Poem*, Leiden: Brill.

Halabi, 'Ali-Asghar (1998), '*Ubayd-i Zakani*, Tehran: Tarh-i naw.

Halat, Abu l-Qasim (1967), *Shahan-i sha'ir: ahvalat-i shahan va shahzadagan-i sukhanvar va ba'z-i shu'ara-yi darbar-i anan va barguzida-yi ash'ar-i anan*, Tehran: 'Ilmi.

Hämeen-Anttila, Jaakko (2000), 'Wine and Love in Early 'Abbasid Literature', *Edebiyat* 11: 131–140.

Hämeen-Anttila, Jaakko (2008), 'Building an Identity: Place as an Image of Self in Classical Arabic Literature', *Quaderni di Studi Arabi* n.s. 3: 25–38.

Hammond, Marlé (2003), 'Literature: 9th to 15th Century', *Encyclopaedia of Women & Islamic Cultures* I: 42–50.

Hammond, Marlé (2010), *Beyond Elegy: Classical Arabic Women's Poetry in Context*, Oxford: Oxford University Press.

Hanaoka, Mimi (2016), *Authority and Identity in Medieval Islamic Historiography: Persian Histories from the Peripheries*, Cambridge: Cambridge University Press.

Hanaway, W. L. (1988), 'Bag iii in Persian Literature', *Encyclopaedia Iranica* III: 395–396.

Hansen, Mogens Herman (2006), *Polis: An Introduction to the Ancient Greek City-State*, Oxford: Oxford University Press.

Hasuri, 'Ali (2016), *Hafiz az nigahi digar*, Tehran: Nashr-i Chishma.

Havlioğlu, Didem (2017), *Mihri Hatun: Performance, Gender Bending, and Subversion in Ottoman Intellectual History*, Syracuse: Syracuse University Press.

Hillenbrand, Carole (2003), 'Women in the Seljuq Period', in Guity Nashat and Lois Beck (eds), *Women in Iran from the Rise of Islam to 1800*, 103–120, Urbana: University of Illinois Press.

Hillenbrand, Robert (2014), 'Wine in Islamic Art and Society', in Rachel Ward (ed.), *Court and Craft: A Masterpiece from Northern Iraq*, 38–45, London: Paul Holberton Publishing.

Hillmann, Michael C. (1976), *Unity in the Ghazals of Hafez*, Minneapolis: Bibliotheca Islamica.

Hooke, S. H. (1963), *Middle Eastern Mythology*, London: Penguin Books.

Hope, Michael (2016), *Power, Politics, and Tradition in the Mongol Empire and the Ilkhanate of Iran*, Oxford: Oxford University Press.

Hourani, A. H. (1970), 'The Islamic City in the Light of Recent Research', in A. H. Hourani and S. M. Stern (eds), *The Islamic City: A Colloquium*, 9–24, Oxford: Bruno Cassirer.

Howard-Johnston, James (2010), 'Kosrow II', *Encyclopaedia Iranica*, online edition.

Huart, C. (1965), 'Djamshid', *Enclyclopaedia of Islam, New Edition* II: 438–439.

Husaynian, Ruhullah (1995), *Ghina va musiqi dar fiqh-i Islami*, Tehran: Surush.

Ilahi-Ghomshei, Husayn (2010), 'Of Scent and Sweetness: 'Attar and his Legacy in Rumi, Shabistari and Hafiz', in Leonard Lewisohn and Christopher Shackle (eds), *Attar and the Persian Sufi Tradition: The Art of Spiritual Flight*, 27–56, London: I.B. Tauris.

Imami, Nasrullah (1974), 'Isra'iliyat va asatir Irani', *Nashriya-yi Danishkada-yi Adabiyat-i Danishgah-i Tabriz*, 421–431.

Ingenito, Domenico (2014), '"Tabrizis in Shiraz are Worth Less than a Dog": Sa'di and Humam, a Lyrical Encounter', in Judith Pfeiffer (ed.), *Politics, Patronage and the Transmission of Knowledge in 13th–15th Century Tabriz*, 77–127, Leiden: Brill.

Ingenito, Domenico (2018), 'Jahan Malik Khatun: Gender, Canon, and Persona in the Poems of a Premodern Persian Princess', in Alireza Korangy, Hanadi al-Samman and Michael Beard (eds), *The Beloved in Middle Eastern Literatures: The Culture of Love and Languishing*, 177–212, London: I.B. Tauris.

Islami Nudushan, Muhammad-'Ali (2003), *Ta'ammul dar Hafiz*, Tehran: Athar.

Isti'lami, Muhammad (2003), *Dars-i Hafiz: naqd va sharh-i ghazal-ha-yi Khvaja Shams al-Din Hafiz*, Tehran: Sukhan.

Jackson, Peter (2008a), 'Jalayerids', *Encyclopaedia Iranica* XIV: 415–419.

Jackson, Peter (2008b), 'Muzaffarids', *Encyclopaedia of Islam, new edition* VII: 820–822.

Jacobi, Renate (2010), '*qasida (pl. qasa'id)*', in Julie Scott Meisami and Paul Starkey (eds), *The Routledge Encyclopedia of Arabic Literaure*, 630–633, Abingdon: Routledge.

Jamalzada, Muhammad-'Ali (2005), *Ashna'i ba Hafiz*, ed. 'Ali Dihbashi, Tehran: Sukhan.

Johnston, John H. (1984), *The Poet and the City: A Study in Urban Perspectives*, Athens: University of Georgia Press.

Kamens, Edward (1997), *Utamakura, Allusion, and Intertextuality in Traditional Japanese Poetry*, New Haven: Yale University Press.

Karamustafa, Ahmet T. (1994), *God's Unruly Friends: Dervish Groups in the Islamic Middle Persia, 1200–1550*, Salt Lake City: University of Utah Press.

Karatay, Fehmi (1961), *Topkapı Sarayı Müzesi Kütüphanesi Farsça yazmalar kataloğu: no. 1-940*, Istabnul: Topkapı Sarayı Müzesi.

Kasheff, M. (1988), 'Baba Kuhi', *Encyclopaedia Iranica* III: 293–294.

Katouzian, Homa (2006), *Sa'di: The Poet of Life, Love and Compassion*, Oxford: Oneworld.

Keen, Catherine (2003), *Dante and the City*, Stroud: Tempus.

Kennedy, Philip F. (1997), *The Wine Song in Classical Arabic Poetry: Abu Nuwas and the Literary Tradition*, Oxford: Clarendon Press.

Kennedy, Philip F. (2005), *Abu Nuwas: A Genius of Poetry*, Oxford: Oneworld.

Keshavarz, Fatemeh (2015), *Lyrics of Life: Sa'di on Love, Cosmopolitanism and Care of Self*, Edinburgh: Edinburgh University Press.

Khairallah, As'ad E. (1980), *Love, Madness, and Poetry: An Interpretation of the Maǧnun Legend*, Beirut: Orient-Institut der Deutschen Morgenländischen Gesellschaft.

Khaleghi-Motlagh, Djalal (1988), 'Bahman (2) Son of Esfandiar', *Encyclopaedia Iranica* III: 489–490.

Khaleghi-Motlagh, Djalal (2012), *Women in the Shahnameh: Their History and Social Status within the Framework of Ancient and Medieval Sources*, ed. Nahid Pirnazar, trans. Brigitte Neuenschwander, Costa Mesa: Mazda Publishers.

Khanbaghi, Aptin (2006), *Fire, the Star and the Cross: The Minority Religions in Medieval and Early Modern Iran*, London: I.B. Tauris.

Khurramshahi, Baha' al-Din (1983), *Zihn u zaban-i Hafiz*, Tehran: Nashr-i Naw.

Khurramshahi, Baha' al-Din (1987), *Hafiznama: sharh-i alfaz, a'lam, mafahim-i kalidi va abyat-i dushvar-i Hafiz*, Tehran: Surush.

Khurramshahi, Baha' al-Din (2003), 'Hafez's Life and Times', *Encyclopaedia Iranica* XI: 465–469.

Kilito, Abdelfattah (2001), *The Author and His Doubles: Essays on Classical Arabic Culture*, trans. Michael Cooperson, Syracuse: Syracuse University Press.

King, Anya H. (2017), *Scent from the Garden of Paradise: Musk and the Medieval Islamic World*, Leiden: Brill.

Klein, Yaron (2014), 'Music, Rapture and Pragmatics: Ghazali on *Sama'* and *Wajd*', in Alireza Korangy and Daniel J. Sheffield (eds), *No Tapping around Philology: A Festschrift in Honor of Wheeler McIntosh Thackston Jr.'s 70th Birthday*, 215–241, Wiesbaden: Harrassowitz Verlag.

Kračkovskij, I. J. (1955), 'Die Frühgeschichte der Erzählung von Macnun und Laila in der arabischen Literatur', *Oriens* 8: 1–50.

Kraemer, Joel L. (1986), *Humanism in the Renaissance of Islam: The Cultural Revival During the Buyid Age*, Leiden: Brill.

Krasnowolska, Anna (2009), 'Kezr,' *Encyclopaedia Iranica*, online edition.

Kugel, James L. (1990), *In Potiphar's House: The Interpretive Life of Biblical Texts*, San Francisco: Harper.

Kugle, Scott (2002), 'Sultan Mahmud's Makeover: Colonial Homophobia and the Persian-Urdu Literary Tradition', in Ruth Vanita (ed.), *Queering India: Same-Sex Love and Eroticism in Indian Culture and Society*, 30–46, London: Routledge.

Lambton, Ann K. S. (1988), *Continuity and Change in Medieval Persia: Aspects of Administrative, Economic and Social History, 11th–14th Century*, New York: Bibliotheca Persica.

Lane, Edward William (1984), *Arabic-English Lexicon*, Cambridge: Islamic Texts Society.

Lane, George (2003), *Early Mongol Rule in Thirteenth-Century Iran: A Persian Renaissance*, Abingdon: Routledge.

Lassner, Jacob (1993), *Demonizing the Queen of Sheba: Boundaries of Gender and Culture in Postbiblical Judaism and Medieval Islam*, Chicago: University of Chicago Press.

Leder, Stefan (1990), 'Frühe Erzählungen zu Maǧnun – Maǧnun als Figur one Lebensgeschichte', *Zeitschrift der Deutschen Morgenländischen Gesellschaft* Supplement 8: 150–161.

Lefèvre, Corinne (2014), 'The Court of 'Abd-ur-Rahim Khan-i Khanan as a Bridge Between Iranian and Indian Cultural Traditions', in Thomas de Bruijn and Allison Busch (eds), *Culture and Circulation: Literature in Motion in Early Modern India*, 75–106, Leiden: Brill.

Lescot, Roger (1944), 'Essai d'une chronologie de l'oeuvre de Hafiz', *Bulletin d'Études Orientales* 19: 57–100.

Le Strange, Guy (1930), *The Lands of the Eastern Caliphate: Mesopotamia, Persia, and Central Asia from the Moslem Conquest to the Time of Timur*, Cambridge: Cambridge University Press.

Lewis, Franklin (1994), 'The Rise and Fall of a Persian Refrain: The *Radif "Atash u Ab"*', in Suzanne Pinckney Stetkevych (ed.), *Reorientations/Arabic and Persian Poetry*, 199–226, Bloomington: Indiana University Press.

Lewis, Franklin (1995), *Reading, Writing and Recitation: Sana'i and the Origins of the Persian Ghazal*. PhD thesis, University of Chicago.

Lewis, Franklin (2001), 'The Modes of Literary Production: Remarks on the Composition, Revision and "Publication" of Persian Texts in the Medieval Period', *Persica* 17: 69–83.

Lewis, Franklin (2003a), 'Hafez and *Rendi*', *Encyclopaedia Iranica* XI: 483–491.

Lewis, Franklin (2003b), 'Hafez and Music', *Encyclopaedia Iranica* XI: 491–498.

Lewis, Franklin (2006), 'The Transformation of the Persian *ghazal*: From Amatory Mood to Fixed Form', in Angelika Neuwirth et al. (eds), *Ghazal as World*

Literature II: From a Literary Genre to a Great Tradition, 121–139, Beirut: Ergon Verlag.

Lewis, Franklin (2009), 'Sexual Occidentation: the Politics of Boy-love and Christian-love in "Attar"', *Iranian Studies* 42: 693–723.

Lewis, Franklin (2010), 'The Semiotics of Dawn in the Poetry of Hafiz', in Leonard Lewisohn (ed.), *Hafiz and the Religion of Love in Classical Persian Poetry*, 251–278, London: I.B. Tauris.

Lewis, Franklin (2012), 'Ghazal', in Roland Greene et al., *The Princeton Encyclopedia* of *Poetry and Poetics*, 4th edn, 570–572, Princeton: Princeton University Press.

Lewis, Franklin (2014), 'Ut Pictura Poesis: Verbal and Visual Depictions of the Practice of Poetry in the Medieval Period', in Alireza Korangy and Daniel J. Sheffield (eds), *No Tapping around Philology: A Festschrift in Honor of Wheeler McIntosh Thackston Jr.'s 70th Birthday*, 53–70, Wiesbaden: Harrassowitz Verlag.

Lewisohn, Leonard (2010), 'Prolegomenon to the Study of Hafiz', in Leonard Lewisohn (ed.), *Hafiz and the Religion of Love in Classical Persian Poetry*, 3–73, London: I.B. Tauris.

Limbert, John (2004a), *Shiraz in the Age of Hafez: The Glory of a Medieval Persian City*, Seattle: University of Washington Press.

Limbert, John (2004b), 'Inju Dynasty', *Encyclopaedia Iranica* XIII: 143–147.

Loloi, Parvin (2004), *Hafiz, Master of Persian Poetry: A Critical Bibliography*, London: I.B. Tauris.

Loloi, Parvin and William Oxley (2013), *Poems from the* Divan *of Hafez*, Brixham: Acumen Publications.

Losensky, Paul E. (1994), '"The Allusive Field of Drunkenness": the Safavid-Moghul Responses to a Lyric by Baba Fighani', in Suzanne Pinckney Stetkevych (ed.), *Reorientations/Arabic and Persian Poetry*, 227–262, Bloomington: Indiana University Press.

Losensky, Paul E. (1998), *Welcoming Fighani: Imitation and Poetic Individuality in the Safavid-Mughal Ghazal*, Costa Mesa: Mazda Publishers.

Losensky, Paul E. (2004), '"The Equal of Heaven's Vault": The Design, Ceremony, and Poetry of the Hasanabad Bridge', in Beatrice Gruendler and Louise Marlow (eds), *Writers and Rulers: Perspectives on Their Relationship from Abbasid to Safavid Times*, 95–216, Wiesbaden: Reichert Verlag.

Losensky, Paul E. (2008), 'Jami i. Life and Works', *Encyclopaedia Iranica* XIV: 469–475.

Losensky, Paul E. (2011), 'Kamal Kojandi', *Encyclopaedia Iranica* XV: 412–414.

Lowin, Shari (2006), *The Making of a Forefather: Abraham in Islamic and Jewish Exegetical Narratives*, Leiden: Brill.

Lowin, Shari (2014), *Arabic and Hebrew Love Poems in al-Andalus*, Abingdon: Routledge.

Lumbard, Joseph E. B. (2016), *Ahmad al-Ghazali, Remembrance, and the Metaphysics of Love*, Albany: SUNY Press.

Madelung, Wilferd (1969), 'The Assumption of the Title *Shahanshah* by the Buyids and the "Reign of the Daylam (Dawlat al-Daylam)"', *Journal of Near Eastern Studies* 28: 84–108.

Mahallati, Sadr al-Din (1962), *Dar al-'ilm-i Shiraz*, Shiraz: Ma'rifat.

Mahjub, Muhammad-Ja'far (1999), 'Bar-rasi-yi athar-i 'Ubayd-i Zakani', in *Kulliyat-i 'Ubayd-i Zakani*, ed. Muhammad-Ja'far Mahjub, xviii–lvii, New York: Bibliotheca Persica Press.

Mahmood, Zainab (2017), 'The Wiles of Women, the Guile of Men: Re-reading *Kayd* in *Surat Yusuf*', in Joseph E. Lowry and Shawkat M. Toorawa (eds), *Arabic Humanities, Islamic Thought: Essays in Honor of Everett K. Rowson*, 22–34, Leiden: Brill.

Mallah, Husayn-'Ali (1984), *Hafiz va musiqi*, Tehran: Hunar va Farhang.

Mallah, Husayn-'Ali (1990), 'Čagana', *Encyclopaedia Iranica* IV: 613.

Malti-Douglas, Fedwa (1991), *Woman's Body, Woman's Word: Gender and Discourse in Arabo-Islamic Writing*, Princeton: Princeton University Press.

Manoukian, Setrag (2012), *City of Knowledge in Twentieth Century Iran: Shiraz, History and Poetry*, Abingdon: Routledge.

Manz, Beatrice Forbes (2003), 'Women in Timurid Dynastic Politics', in Guity Nashat and Lois Beck (eds), *Women in Iran from the Rise of Islam to 1800*, 121–139, Urbana: University of Illinois Press.

Manz, Beatrice Forbes (2007), *Power, Politics and Religion in Timurid Iran*. Cambridge: Cambridge University Press.

Marefat, Roya (1993), 'Timurid Women: Patronage and Power', *Asian Art* 6: 29–49.

Markus-Takeshita, Kinga Ilona (2007), 'Shirin and Other Female Archetypes in Firdausi's *Shahnamah*', in Franklin Lewis and Sunil Sharma (eds), *The Necklace of the Pleiades: Studies in Persian Literature Presented to Heshmat Moayyad on his 80th Birthday*, 69–75, Amsterdam: Rozenberg Publishers.

Marsham, Andrew (2009), *Rituals of Islamic Monarchy: Accession and Succession in the First Muslim Empire*, Edinburgh: Edinburgh University Press.

Martines, Lauro (1988), *Power and Imagination: City-states in Renaissance Italy*, Baltimore: Johns Hopkins University Press.

Massé, Henri (1972), 'Le divan de la princesse Djehane', in Parimarz Naficy (ed.), *Mélange d'iranologie en mémoire de feu Said Naficy*, 1–42, Tehran: Tehran University Press.

Matini, J. (1987), 'Ayaz, Abu'l-Najm', *Encyclopaedia Iranica* III: 133–134.

Matthee, Rudi (2005), *The Pursuit of Pleasure: Drugs and Stimulants in Iranian History, 1500–1900*. Princeton: Princeton University Press.

Mawla'i, Muhammad Sarvar (1989), *Tajalli-yi ustura dar shi'r-i Hafiz*, Tehran: Tus.

Meisami, Julie Scott (1985), 'Allegorical Gardens in the Persian Poetic Tradition: Nezami, Rumi, Hafez', *International Journal of Middle East Studies* 17: 229–260.

Meisami, Julie Scott (1987), *Medieval Persian Court Poetry*, Princeton: Princeton University Press.

Meisami, Julie Scott (1990a), 'Allusion in Hafiz: Joseph and His Brothers', in Charles Melville (ed.), *Persian and Islamic Studies in Honour of P.W. Avery*, 141–158, Cambridge: University of Cambridge, Centre of Middle Eastern Studies.

Meisami, Julie Scott (1990b), 'Medieval Persian Panegyric: Ethical Values and Rhetorical Strategies', in Keith Busby and Erik Kooper (eds), *Courtly Literature: Culture and Context*, 439–458, Amsterdam: John Benjamins.

Meisami, Julie Scott (1990c), 'Persona and Generic Conventions in Medieval
    Persian Lyric', *Comparative Criticism* 12: 125–151.
Meisami, Julie Scott (1993), 'The Past in Service of the Present: Attitudes
    Towards History in 11th-Century Persia', *Poetics Today* 14: 247–275.
Meisami, Julie Scott (1995), 'The Body as Garden: Nature and Sexuality in Persian
    Poetry', *Edebiyat* 6: 245–274.
Meisami, Julie Scott (1996), 'Poetic Microcosms: The Persian *Qasida* to the End
    of the Twelfth Century', in Stefan Sperl and Christopher Shackle (eds), *Qasida
    Poetry in Islamic Asia and Africa* vol. I, 137–182, Leiden: Brill.
Meisami, Julie Scott (1998), 'Places in the Past: The Poetics/Politics of Nostalgia',
    Edebiyat 8: 63–106.
Meisami, Julie Scott (2001a), 'The Palace-Complex as Emblem', in C. F. Robinson
    (ed.), *A Medieval Islamic City Reconsidered: An Interdisciplinary Approach to
    Samarra*, 69–78, Oxford: Oxford University Press.
Meisami, Julie Scott (2001b), 'Palaces and Paradises: Palace Description in
    Medieval Persian Poetry', in Oleg Grabar and Cynthia Robinson (eds), *Seeing
    Things: Textuality and Visuality in the Islamic World*, 21–54, Princeton:
    Princeton University Press.
Meisami, Julie Scott (2001c), 'The Poet and His Patrons: Two Ghaznavid
    Panegyrists', *Persica* 17: 91–105.
Meisami, Julie Scott (2003), *Structure and Meaning in Medieval Arabic and
    Persian Poetry: Orient Pearls*, London: RoutledgeCurzon.
Meisami, Julie Scott (2004), 'Rulers and the Writing of History', in Beatrice
    Gruendler and Louise Marlow (eds), *Writers and Rulers: Perspectives on Their
    Relationship from Abbasid to Safavid Times*, 73–95, Wiesbaden: Reichert
    Verlag.
Meisami, Julie Scott (2005), 'The Persian Ghazal between Love Song and
    Panegyric', in Thomas Bauer and Angelika Neuwirth (eds), *Ghazal as World
    Literature I: Transformations of a Literary Genre*, 327–342, Beirut: Ergon Verlag.
Meisami, Julie Scott (2007), 'A Life in Poetry: Hafiz's First Ghazal', in Thomas
    Bauer and Angelika Neuwirth (eds), *The Necklace of the Pleiades: Studies
    in Persian Literature Presented to Heshmat Moayyad on his 80th Birthday*,
    163–181, Amsterdam: Rozenberg Publishers.
Melikian-Chirvani, Assadullah Souren (1970), *Le roman de Varqe et Golšah: essai
    sur les rapports de l'esthétique littéraire et de l'esthétique plastique dans
    l'Iran pré-mongol, suivi de la traduction du poème*, Paris: Maisonneuve.
Melikian-Chirvani, Assadullah Souren (1971), 'Le Royaume de Salomon: les
    inscriptions persanes de sites achéménides', *Le monde iranien et l'Islam* 1:
    1–41.
Melikian-Chirvani, Assadullah Souren (1973), *Le bronze iranien*, Paris: Musée des
    arts décoratifs.
Melikian-Chirvani, Assadullah Souren (1974), 'L'évocation littéraire du bouddhisme
    dans l'Iran musulman', *Le monde iranien et l'Islam* 2: 1–74.
Melikian-Chirvani, Assadullah Souren (1986), 'Silver in Islamic Iran: The
    Evidence from Literature and Epigraphy', in M. Vickers (ed.), *Pots and Pans:
    A Colloquium on Precious Metals and Ceramics in the Muslim, Chinese and
    Graeco-Roman Worlds*, 89–106, Oxford: Oxford University Press.
Melikian-Chirvani, Assadullah Souren (1992), 'The Wine-bull and the Magian
    Master', *Cahiers de Studia Iranica* 11: 101–132.

Melikian-Chirvani, Assadullah Souren (1996), *Les frises du Shāh Nāme dans l'architecture iranienne sous les Ilkhān*, Paris: Association pour l'avancement des études iraniennes.

Melikian-Chirvani, Assadullah Souren (1997), 'The Iranian Wine Leg from Prehistory to Mongol Times', *Bulletin of the Asia Institute* n. s. 11: 65–91.

Melville, Charles (2016), 'The End of the Ilkhanate and After: Observations on the Collapse of the Mongol World Empire', in Bruno De Nicola and Charles Melville (eds), *The Mongols' Middle East*, 307–335, Leiden: Brill.

Meneghini, Daniela (2010), ''Obayd Zakani', *Encyclopaedia Iranica*, online edition.

Merguerian, Gayane Karen and Afsaneh Najmabadi (1997), 'Zulaykha and Yusuf: Whose "Best Story"?', *International Journal of Middle East Studies* 29: 485–508.

Mernissi, Fatima (1993), *The Forgotten Queens of Islam*, Cambridge: Polity Press.

Miller, Isabel A. M. (1989), 'Local History in Ninth/Fifteenth Century Yazd: The *Tarikh-i Jadid-i Yazd*', *Iran* 27: 75–79.

Miller, Isabel A. M. (1990), *The Social and Economic History of Yazd (c. AH 736/AD 1335–c. AH 906/AD 1500)*, PhD thesis, University of London.

Minuvi, Mujtaba (1954), 'yikki az Farsiyat-i Abu Nuwas', *Majalla-yi danishkada-yi adabiyat* 3: 62–77.

Miquel, André and Percy Kemp (1984), *Majnun et Layla: l'amour fou*, Paris: Sindbad.

Moayyad, Heshmat (1988), 'Lyric Poetry', in Ehsan Yarshater (ed.), *Persian Literature*, 120–146, Albany: Bibliotheca Persica.

Moayyad, Heshmat (1989), 'Boshaq At'ema', *Encyclopaedia Iranica* IV: 382–383.

Moayyad, Heshmat (1999), 'Farhad', *Encyclopaedia Iranica* IX: 257–258.

Mokhtarian, Jason Sion (2010), 'Rabbinic Depictions of the Achaemenid King Cyrus the Great: The *Babylonian Esther Midrash* (bMeg. 10b–17a) in its Iranian Context', in Carol Bakhos and M. Rahim Shayegan (eds), *The Talmud in its Iranian Context*, 112–139, Tübingen: Mohr Siebeck.

Mokhtarian, Jason Sion (2015), *Rabbis, Sorcerers, Kings, and Priests: The Culture of the Talmud in Ancient Iran*, Berkeley: University of California Press.

Montgomery, James E. (1996), 'For the Love of a Christian Boy: A Song by Abu Nuwas', *Journal of Arabic Literature* 27: 115–124.

Moreen, Vera Basch, trans. (2000), *In Queen Esther's Garden: An Anthology of Judeo-Persian Literature*, New Haven: Yale University Press.

Mottahedeh, Roy P. (2013), 'The Eastern Travels of Solomon: Reimagining Persepolis and the Iranian Past', in Michael Cook et al., *Law and Tradition in Classical Islamic Thought: Studies in Honor of Professor Hossein Modarressi*, 247–267.

Moynihan, Elizabeth B. (1980), *Paradise as a Garden in Persia and Mughal India*, London: Scolar Press.

Mozaffari, Ali (2014), *Forming National Identity in Iran: The Idea of Homeland Derived from Ancient Persian and Islamic Imaginations of Place*, London: I.B. Tauris.

Mu'in, Muhammad (1991), *Hafiz-i shirin-sukhan*, ed. Mahdukht Mu'in, Tehran: Mu'in.

Murtazavi, Manuchihr (1965), *Maktab-i Hafiz ya muqaddama bar Hafiz-shinasi*, Tehran: Ibn Sina.

Mustafavi, Muhammad-Taqi (1964), *Iqlim-i Pars*, Tehran: Anjuman-i Athar-i Milli.

Nafisi, Parimarz (1971), 'Divan u sharh-i hal-i shai'ra-yi qarn-i haftum, Jahan-Malik Khatun-i Injuy', in Hamid Zarkub (ed.), *Majmu'a-yi sukhanrani-ha-yi duvvumin kungira-yi tahqiqat-i Irani*, 137–146. Mashhad: Mashhad University Press.

Nafisi, Sa'id (1942), *Dar piramun-i ash'ar u ahval-i Hafiz*, Tehran: Iqbal.

Nafisi, Sa'id (1968), 'Hafiz va Jahan-Malik Khatun', *Rahnama-yi kitab* 7: 369–372.

Naim, C. M. (1979), 'The Theme of Homosexual (Pederastic) Love in Pre-Modern Urdu Poetry', in M. U. Memon (ed.), *Studies in the Urdu Gazal and Prose Fiction*, 120–141, Madison: University of Wisconsin Press.

Najmabadi, Afsaneh (2000), 'Reading "Wiles of Women" Stories as Fictions of Masculinity', in Mai Ghoussoub and Emma Sinclair-Webb (eds), *Imagined Masculinities: Male Identity and Culture in the Modern Middle East*, 147–168, London: Saqi Books.

Natiq, Huma (2004), *Hafiz, khunyagari, may u shadi*, Los Angeles: Shirkat-i Kitab.

Nazari, Jalil (2007), *Mughbachchagan-i bada-furush dar shi'r-i Hafiz*, Tehran: Asim.

Netzer, Amnon (1997), 'Ebrahim', *Encyclopaedia Iranica* VIII: 61–62.

Nora, Pierre (1989), 'Between Memory and History: *Les Lieux de Mémoire*', *Representations* 26: 7–25.

Nwiya, Paul (1970), *Exégèse coranique et langage mystique: Nouvel essai sur le lexique technique des mystiques musulmans*, Beirut: Dar el-Machreq.

O'Kane, Bernard (2006), 'Persian Poetry on Ilkhanid Art and Architecture', in Linda Komaroff (ed.), *Beyond the Legacy of Genghis Khan*, 346–354, Leiden: Brill.

Omidsalar, Mahmoud (2008), 'Jamšid ii. Jamšid in Persian Literature', *Encyclopaedia Iranica* XIV: 522–528.

Omidsalar, Mahmoud (2011), *Poetics and Politics of Iran's National Epic, the Shahnameh*, New York: Palgrave Macmillan.

Orsatti, Paola (2006), 'Kosrow o Širin', *Encyclopaedia Iranica*, online edition.

Pancaroğlu, Oya (2016), 'Ornament, Form, and Vision in Ceramics from Medieval Iran: Reflections on the Human Image', in Gülru Necipoğlu and Alina Payne (eds), *Histories of Ornament: From Global to Local*, 192–203, Princeton: Princeton University Press.

Payne, Richard E. (2015), *A State of Mixture: Christians, Zoroastrians, and Iranian Political Culture in Late Antiquity*, Berkeley: University of California Press.

Peacock, Andrew (2007), *Mediaeval Islamic Historiography and Political Legitimacy: Bal'ami's Tarikhnama*, Abingdon: Routledge.

Peacock, Andrew (2012), 'Early Persian Historians and the Heritage of Pre-Islamic Iran', in Edmund Herzig and Sarah Stewart (eds), *Early Islamic Iran*, 59–75, London: I.B. Tauris.

Pellò, Stefano (2013), 'A Paper Temple: Mani's *Arzhang* in and around Persian Lexicography', in *Sogdians, their Precursors, Contemporaries and Heirs*, 252–265. St Petersburg: The State Hermitage Publishers.

Pfeiffer, Judith (2014), '"Not Every Head that Wears a Crown Deserves to Rule": Women in Il-Khanid Political Life and Court Culture', in Rachel Ward (ed.), *Court and Craft: A Masterpiece from Northern Iraq*, 23–29, London: Paul Holberton Publishing.

Piemontese, A. M. (2007), 'Sources and Art of Amir Khosrou's "The Alexandrine Mirror"', in Franklin Lewis and Sunil Sharma (eds), *The Necklace of the Pleiades: Studies in Persian Literature Presented to Heshmat Moayyad on his 80th Birthday*, 31–45, Amsterdam: Rozenberg Publishers.

Pucci, Joseph (1998), *The Full-knowing Reader: Allusion and the Power of the Reader in the Western Literary Tradition*, New Haven: Yale University Press.

Purnamdarian, Taqi (1990), *Dastan-i payambaran dar kulliyat-i Shams*, Tehran: Mu'assasa-yi Mutali'at u Tahqiqat-i Farhangi.

Purnamdarian, Taqi (2003), *Gum-shuda-yi lab-i darya*, Tehran: Sukhan.

Qazvini, Muhammad (1938), *Mamduhin-i Shaykh Sa'di*, Tehran: Chapkhana-yi khudkar va Iran.

Qazvini, Muhammad (1988), *Hafiz az didgah-i 'allama Muhammad-i Qazvini*, ed. Isma'il Sarimi, Tehran: 'Ilmi.

Quade-Reutter, Karin (2003), ' ... *denn sie haben einen unvollkommenen Verstand': Herrschaftliche Damen im Grossraum Iran in der Mongolen- und Timuridenzeit (ca. 1250–1507)*, Aachen: Shaker Verlag.

Rajabzadeh, Hashem (2009), 'Jovayni Family', *Encyclopaedia Iranica* XV: 61–63.

Rastigar Fasa'i, Mansur (2006), *Hafiz va payda u pinhan-i zindagi: mururi dar shi'r, zindagi va andisha-ha-yi Hafiz*, Tehran: Sukhan.

Ravalde, Esther (2016), 'Shams al-Din Juwayni, Vizier and Patron: Mediation between Ruler and Ruled in the Ilkhanate', in Bruno De Nicola and Charles Melville (eds), *The Mongols' Middle East*, 55–78, Leiden: Brill.

Redford, Scott (2000), 'Just Landscape in Medieval Anatolia', *Studies in the History of Gardens and Designed Landscapes* 20: 313–324.

Rehder, Robert M. (1974), 'The Text of Hafiz', *Journal of the American Oriental Society* 94: 145–156.

Renard, John (1994), *All the King's Falcons: Rumi on Prophets and Revelation*, Albany: SUNY Press.

Ridgeon, Lloyd (2010), *Morals and Mysticism in Persian Sufism: A History of Sufi-futuwwat in Iran*, Abingdon: Routledge.

Ridgeon, Lloyd (2012), 'The Controversy of Shaykh Awhad al-Din Kirmani and Handsome, Moon-faced Youths: A Case Study of *Shahid-bazi* in Medieval Sufism', *Journal of Sufi Studies* 1: 3–30.

Ritter, Hellmut (2003), *The Ocean of the Soul: Man, the World and God in the Stories of Farid al-Din 'Attar*, trans. John O'Kane, Leiden: Brill.

Riyahi, Muhammad-Amin (1989), *Gulgasht dar shi'r u andisha-yi Hafiz*, Tehran: 'Ilmi.

Robinson, Cynthia (1997), 'Seeing Paradise: Metaphor and Vision in taifa Palace Architecture', *Gesta* 36: 145–155.

Roemer, H. R. (1986a), 'The Jalayirids, Muzaffarids and Sarbadarids', in Peter Jackson and Laurence Lockhart (eds), *The Cambridge History of Iran vol. VI: The Timurid and Safavid Periods*, 1–40, Cambridge: Cambridge University Press.

Roemer, H. R. (1986b), 'Timur in Iran', in Peter Jackson and Laurence Lockhart (eds), *The Cambridge History of Iran vol. VI: The Timurid and Safavid Periods*, 42–97, Cambridge: Cambridge University Press.

Rollason, David (2016), *The Power of Place: Rulers and their Palaces, Landscapes, Cities, and Holy Places*, Princeton: Princeton University Press.

Rubanovich, Julia (2015), 'Why So Many Stories? Untangling the Versions of Iskandar's Birth and Upbringing', in Julia Rubanovich (ed.), *Orality and Textuality in the Iranian World: Patterns of Interaction across the Centuries*, 202–240, Leiden: Brill.

Rubanovich, Julia (2016a), 'In the Mood of Love: Love Romances in Medieval Persian Poetry and their Sources', in Carolina Cupane and Bettina Krönung (eds), *Fictional Storytelling in the Medieval Eastern Mediterranean and Beyond*, 67–94, Leiden: Brill.

Rubanovich, Julia (2016b), 'A Hero Without Borders: Alexander the Great in the Medieval Persian Tradition', in Carolina Cupane and Bettina Krönung (eds), *Fictional Storytelling in the Medieval Eastern Mediterranean and Beyond*, 210–233, Leiden: Brill.

Rypka, Jan (1968), *History of Iranian Literature*, Dordrecht: D. Reidel.

Sami, Ali (1971), *Pasargadae: The Oldest Imperial Capital of Iran*, trans. R. N. Sharp, Shiraz: Musavi.

Savant, Sarah Bowen (2013), *The New Muslims of Post-Conquest Iran: Tradition, Memory, and Conversion*, Cambridge: Cambridge University Press.

Sedgwick, Eve Kosofsky (1985), *Between Men: English Literature and Male Homosocial Desire*, New York: Columbia University Press.

Schimmel, Annemarie (1973), *Islamic Literatures of India*, Wiesbaden: Harrassowitz.

Schimmel, Annemarie (1975), 'Turk and Hindu: A Poetical Image and Its Application to Historical Fact', in Speros Vryonis (ed.), *Islam and Cultural Changes in the Middle Ages*, 107–126, Wiesbaden: Harrassowitz.

Schimmel, Annemarie (1986), 'Hafiz and His Contemporaries', in Peter Jackson and Laurence Lockhart (eds), *The Cambridge History of Iran Volume IV: The Timurid and Safavid Periods*, 929–947, Cambridge: Cambridge University Press.

Schimmel, Annemarie (1988), 'The Genius of Shiraz: Sa'di and Hafez', in Ehsan Yarshater (ed.), *Persian Literature*, 214–225, Albany: Bibliotheca Persica.

Schimmel, Annemarie (1992), *A Two-Colored Brocade: The Imagery of Persian Poetry*, Chapel Hill: University of North Carolina Press.

Schimmel, Annemarie (1999), 'Yusuf in Mawlana Rumi's Poetry', in Leonard Lewisohn (ed.), *The Heritage of Sufism: Volume II The Legacy of Medieval Persian Sufism (1150–1500)*, 45–59, Oxford: Oneworld.

Schlumberger, Daniel (1952), 'Le palais Ghaznévide de Lashkari Bazar', *Syria* 29: 251–270.

Schlumberger, Daniel (1978), *Lashkari Bazar: Une residence royale Ghaznévide et Ghoride*, Paris: Diffusion de Boccard.

Schoeler, G. (1990), 'Bashshar ibn Burd, Abu'l-'Atahiya, Abu Nuwas', in Julia Ashtiany et al., *Abbasid Belles-Lettres*, 275–299, Camnbridge: Cambridge University Press.

Schwarzbaum, Haim (1982), *Biblical and Extra-Biblical Legends in Islamic Folk-Literature*, Walldorf-Hessen: Verlag für Orientkunde Dr. H. Vorndran.

Seyed-Gohrab, Ali Asghar (2003), *Love, Madness and Mystic Longing in Nizami's Epic Romance*, Leiden: Brill.

Seyed-Gohrab, Ali Asghar (2007), '"My Heart is the Ball, Your Lock the Polo-stick": Development of the Ball and Polo-stick Metaphors in Classical Persian Poetry', in Franklin Lewis and Sunil Sharma (eds), *The Necklace of the Pleiades: Studies in Persian Literature Presented to Heshmat Moayyad on his 80th Birthday*, 183–205, Amsterdam: Rozenberg Publishers.

Seyed-Gohrab, Ali Asghar (2008), 'Wasf', *Encyclopaedia Iranica*, online edition.

Seyed-Gohrab, Ali Asghar (2009), 'Leyli o Majnun', *Encyclopaedia Iranica*, online edition.

Seyed-Gohrab, Ali Asghar (2012), 'Waxing Eloquent: The Masterful Variations on Candle Metaphors in the Poetry of Hafiz and His Predecessors', in Ali Asghar

Seyed-Gohrab (ed.), *Metaphor and Imagery in Persian Poetry*, 81–124, Leiden: Brill.

Shafi'i-Kadkani, Muhammad-Riza (1989), *Musiqi-yi shi'r*, Tehran: Agah.

Shafi'i-Kadkani, Muhammad-Riza (2002), 'Rah-ha-yi intishar-i yik shi'r, dar qadim', in Muhammad Dabir-Siyaqi (ed.), *Ishraqinama*, Qazvin: Hadith-i Imruz.

Shafi'i-Kadkani, Muhammad-Riza (2006), *In Kimiya-yi hasti*, Tehran: Intisharat-i Aydin.

Shafi'i-Kadkani, Muhammad-Riza (2014), *Suvar-i khayal dar shi'r-i Farsi*, Tehran: Nashr-i Agah.

Shahbazi, A. Shapur (1977), 'From *Parsa* to *Taxt-e Jamsid*', in *Archaeologische Mitteilungen aus Iran* vol. 10, 197–207, Berlin: Dietrich Reimer.

Shahbazi, A. Shapur (2002), 'Haft Kešvar', *Encyclopaedia Iranica* XI: 519–522.

Shahbazi, A. Shapur (2004), 'Shiraz i. History to 1940', *Encyclopaedia Iranica*, online edition.

Shahbazi, Iraj (2017), *Sukhan-i ashna: bist u panj ghazal az Hafiz*, Tehran: Rawzana.

Shaked, Shaul (1986), 'From Iran to Islam: On Some Symbols of Royalty', *Jerusalem Studies in Arabic and Islam* 7: 75–91.

Shamisa, Sirus (1983), *Sayr-i ghazal dar shi'r-i Farsi*, Tehran: Firdawsi.

Shamisa, Sirus (1987), *Farhang-i talmihat: isharat-i asatiri, dastani, tarikhi, madhhabi dar adabiyat-i Farsi*, Tehran: Firdaws.

Shamisa, Sirus (2000), *Sabk-shinasi-yi shi'r*, Tehran: Firdaws.

Shamisa, Sirus (2002), *Shahid-bazi dar adabiyat-i Farsi*, Tehran: Firdaws.

Sharlet, Jocelyn (2011), *Patronage and Poetry in the Islamic World: Social Mobility and Status in the Medieval Middle East and Central Asia*, London: I.B. Tauris.

Sharma, Sunil (2000), *Persian Poetry at the Indian Frontier: Mas'ud Sa'd Salman of Lahore*, Delhi: Permanent Black.

Sharma, Sunil (2004), 'The City of Beauties in Indo-Persian Poetic Landscapes', *Comparative Studies of South Asia, Africa and the Middle East* 24: 73–81.

Sharma, Sunil (2009), 'From 'A'esha to Nur Jahan: The Shaping of a Classical Persian Poetic Canon of Women', *Journal of Persianate Studies* 2: 148–164.

Sharma, Sunil (2011), '"If There is a Paradise on Earth, It Is Here"': Urban Ethnography in Indo-Persian Poetic and Historical Texts', in Sheldon Pollock (ed.), *Forms of Knowledge in Early Modern Asia: Explorations in the Intellectual History of India and Tibet, 1500–1800*, 240–256, Durham: Duke University Press.

Sharma, Sunil (2017), *Mughal Arcadia: Persian Literature in an Indian Court*, Cambridge MA: Harvard University Press.

Shayegan, M. Rahim (2011), *Arsacids and Sasanians: Political Ideology in Post-Hellenistic and Late Antique Persia*, Cambridge: Cambridge University Press.

Shayegan, M. Rahim (2013), 'Sasanian Political Ideology', in Daniel T. Potts (ed.), *The Oxford Handbook of Ancient Iran*, 806–813, Oxford: Oxford University Press.

Shehadi, Fadlou (1995), *Philosophies of Music in Medieval Islam*, Leiden: Brill.

Simidchieva, Marta (2004), 'Kingship and Legitimacy in Nizam al-Mulk's Siyasat-Nama, Fifth/Eleventh Century', in Beatrice Gruendler and Louise Marlow (eds), *Writers and Rulers: Perspectives on Their Relationship from Abbasid to Safavid Times*, 97–131, Wiesbaden: Reichert Verlag.

Simpson, Marianna Shreve (2006), 'In the Beginning: Frontispieces and Front Matter in Ilkhanid and Injuid Manuscripts', in Linda Komaroff (ed.), *Beyond the Legacy of Genghis Khan*, 213–247, Leiden: Brill.

Simpson, Marianna Shreve (2013), 'Shahnama Images and Shahnama Settings in Medieval Iran', in Olga M. Davidson and Marianna Shreve Simpson (eds), *Ferdowsi's* Shanama: *Millenial Perspectives*, 72–85, Boston: Ilex Foundation.

Sims, Eleanor (2006), 'Thoughts on a *Shahnama* Legacy of the Fourteenth Century: Four Inju Manuscripts and the Great Mongol *Shahnama*', in Linda Komaroff (ed.), *Beyond the Legacy of Genghis Khan*, 269–286, Leiden: Brill.

Skjærvø, Prods Oktor (2008), 'Jamšid i. Myth of Jamšid', *Encyclopaedia Iranica* XIV: 501–522.

Snir, Reuven (2013), *Baghdad: The City in Verse*, Cambridge MA: Harvard University Press.

Soroudi, Sorour S. (2010), *Persian Literature and Judeo-Persian Culture*, ed. H. E. Chehabi. Boston: Ilex Foundation.

Soucek, Priscilla (1993), 'Solomon's Throne/Solomon's Bath: Model or Metaphor?' *Art Orientalis* 23: 109–134.

Soucek, Priscilla (2003), 'Interpreting the Ghazals of Hafiz', *Anthropology and Aesthetics* 43: 146–163.

Southgate, Minoo S. (1977), 'Portrait of Alexander in Persian Alexander-Romances of the Islamic Era', *Journal of the American Oriental Society* 97: 278–284.

Southgate, Minoo S. (1978), *Iskandarnamah: A Persian Medieval Alexander-Romance*, New York: Columbia University Press.

Southgate, Minoo S. (1984), 'Men, Women, and Boys: Love and Sex in the Works of Sa'di', *Iranian Studies* 17: 413–451.

Spellberg, Denise A. (1994), *Politics, Gender, and the Islamic Past: the Legacy of 'A'isha bint Abi Bakr*, New York: Columbia University Press.

Sperl, Stefan (1977), 'Islamic Kingship and Arabic Panegyric Poetry in the Early 9th Century', *Journal of Arabic Literature* 8: 20–35.

Spiegel, Gabrielle M. (1990), 'History, Historicism, and the Social Logic of the Text in the Middle Ages', *Speculum* 65: 59–86.

Spiegel, Gabrielle M. (1997), *The Past as Text: The Theory and Practice of Medieval Historiography*, Baltimore: The Johns Hopkins University Press.

Sprachman, Paul (1988), 'Persian Satire, Parody and Burlesque: A General Notion of Genre', in Ehsan Yarshater (ed.), *Persian Literature*, 226–248, Albany: Bibliotheca Persica.

Sprachman, Paul (1995), *Suppressed Persian: An Anthology of Forbidden Literature*, Costa Mesa: Mazda Publishers.

Sprachman, Paul (2012), *Licensed Fool: The Damnable, Foul-mouthed Obeyd-e Zakani*, Costa Mesa: Mazda Publishers.

Spuler, B. (1982), 'Abeš Katun', *Encyclopaedia Iranica* I: 210.

Squires, Geoffrey (2014), *Hafez: Translations and Interpretations of the Ghazals*, Oxford OH: Miami University Press.

Stetkevych, Jaroslav (1993), *The Zephyrs of Najd: The Poetics of Nostalgia in the Classical Arabic Nasib*, Chicago: University of Chicago Press.

Stetkevych, Jaroslav (2016), *The Hunt in Arabic Poetry: From Heroic to Lyric to Metapoetic*, Notre Dame: University of Notre Dame Press.

Stetkevych, Suzanne Pinckney (2002), *The Poetics of Islamic Legitimacy: Myth, Gender, and Ceremony in the Classical Arabic Ode*, Bloomington: Indiana University Press.

Stowasser, Barbara F. (1994), *Women in the Qur'an, Traditions, and Interpretation*, Oxford: Oxford University Press.

Streck, M. (2006), 'Istakhr', *Encyclopaedia of Islam, New Edition* IV: 219–222.

Stronach, David (1963), 'Excavations at Pasargadae, First Preliminary Report', *Iran* I: 19–42.

Stronach, David (2010), 'Solomon at Pasargadae: Some New Perspectives', *Bulletin of the Asia Institute* 24: 1–14.

Stroumsa, Sarah (1999), 'Ibn al-Rawandi's *su' adab al-mujadala*: The Role of Bad Manners in Medieval Disputations', in Hava Lazarus-Yafeh et al. (eds), *The Majlis: Inter-religious Encounters in Medieval Islam*, 66–83, Wiesbaden: Harrassowitz.

Subtelny, Maria E. (1984), 'Scenes from the Literary Life of Timurid Herat', in Roger M. Savory and Dionisius A. Agius (eds), *Logos Islamikos*, 137–155, Toronto: Pontifical Institute of Mediaeval Studies.

Subtelny, Maria E. (2002), *Le Monde est un jardin: Aspects de l'histoire culturelle de l'Iran medieval*, Paris: Association pour l'avancement des études iraniennes.

Sumi, Akiko Motoyoshi (2004), *Description in Classical Arabic Poetry: Wasf, Ekphrasis, and Interarts Theory*, Leiden: Brill.

Suvorova, Anna (2011), *Lahore: Topophilia of Space and Place*, Karachi: Oxford University Press.

Swietochowski, Marie Lukens and Stefano Carboni (1994), *Illustrated Poetry and Epic Images: Persian Painting of the 1330s and 1340s*, New York: Metropolitan Museum of Art.

Szuppe, Maria (1998), 'The "Jewels of Wonder": Learned Ladies and Princesses in the Provinces of Early Safavid Iran', in Gavin Hambly (ed.), *Women in the Medieval World: Power, Patronage, and Piety*, Basingstoke: Macmillan: 325–347.

Tafazzoli, Ahmad (1994), 'Dara(b) (1)', *Encyclopaedia Iranica* VII: 1–2.

Tajdini, Muhammad-Riza (2012), *Darya-yi shi'r-i Farsi, kashti-yi shi'r-i Hafiz*, Tehran: Quqnus.

Talattof, Kamran (2000), 'Nizami's Unlikely Heroines: A Study of the Characterizations of Women in Classical Persian Literature', in Jerome W. Clinton and Kamran Talattof (eds), *The Poetry of Nizami Ganjavi: Knowledge, Love and Rhetoric*, New York: Palgrave.

Tekin, Gönül (1997), 'The Motif of the "Cypress-River-Beloved One-Garden" in Neva'i's and Ahmed Paşa's Poetry and Its Archetype', *Oriente Moderno* 15/16: 463–483.

Tetley, G. E. (2009), *The Ghaznavid and Seljuq Turks: Poetry as a Source for Iranian History*, Abingdon: Routledge.

Toorawa, Shawkat M. (1997), 'Language and Male Homosocial Desire in the Autobiography of 'Abd al-Latif Baghdadi (d. 629/1231)', *Edebiyat* 7: 251–265.

Toorawa, Shawkat M. (2010), 'Patronage', in Julie Scott Meisami and Paul Starkey (eds), *The Routledge Encyclopedia of Arabic Literaure*, 598–599. Abingdon: Routledge.

Treadwell, Luke (2003), '*Shahanshah* and *Malik al-Mu'ayyad*: The Legitimation of Power in Samanid and Buyid Iran', in Farhad Daftary and Josef W. Meri (eds), *Culture and Memory in Medieval Islam: Essays in Honour of Wilferd Madelung*, 318–337, London: I.B. Tauris.

Tsugitaka, Saro (2004), 'Sugar in the Economic Life of Mamluk Egypt', *Mamluk Studies Review* 8: 87–107.

Tuan, Yi-Fu (1974), *Topophilia: A Study of Environmental Perception, Attitudes, and Values*, Englewood: Prentice-Hall Inc.

Valavi, Mir-Husayn (2016), *Tarhi az Hafiz: zindagi-yi Hafiz bar asas-i tavarikh u tazkira-ha*, Tehran: Zavvar.

van den Berg, Gabrielle (1998), 'The *Nasib*s in the *Divan* of Farrukhi Sistani: Poetical Speech versus the Reflection of Reality', *Edebiyat* 9: 17–34.

van Gelder, Geert Jan (2001), 'Mudrik al-Shaybani's Poem on a Christian Boy: Bad Taste or Harmless Wit?' in Gert Borg and Ed de Moor (eds), *Representations of the Divine in Arabic Poetry*, 49–70, Amsterdam: Rodopi.

van Gelder, Geert Jan (2008), 'The *Hammam*: A Space between Heaven and Hell', *Quaderni di Studi Arabi* n. s. 3: 9–24.

van Ruymbeke, Christine (2006), 'Firdausi's Dastan-i Khusrau va Shirin: Not Much of a Love Story!' in Charles Melville and Gabrielle van Den Berg (eds), *Shahnama Studies*, 125–47, Cambridge: University of Cambridge, Centre of Middle Eastern and Islamic Studies.

van Ruymbeke, Christine (2007), *Science and Poetry in Medieval Persia: the Botany of Nizami's Khamsa*, Cambridge: Cambridge University Press.

Venetis, Evangelos (2006), *The Iskandarnama: An Analysis of an Anonymous Medieval Persian Prose Romance*, PhD thesis, University of Edinburgh.

von Grunebaum, Gustave E. (1944a), 'Observations on City Panegyrics in Arabic Prose', *Journal of the American Oriental Society* 64: 61–65.

von Grunebaum, Gustave E. (1944b), 'The Concept of Plagiarism in Arabic Theory', *Journal of Near Eastern Studies* 3: 234–253.

von Grunebaum, Gustave E. (1969), 'Aspects of Arabic Urban Literature Mostly in Ninth and Tenth Centuries', *Islamic Studies* 8: 281–300.

Weitzman, Steven (2011), *Solomon: The Lure of Wisdom*, New Haven: Yale University Press.

Wetzsteon, R. (2012), 'Allusion', in Roland Greene et al. (eds), *The Princeton Encyclopedia of Poetry and Poetics*, 42–43, Princeton: Princeton University Press.

Wheeler, Brannon M. (1998), 'Moses or Alexander? Early Islamic Exegesis of Qur'an 18:60–5', *Journal of Near Eastern Studies* 57: 191–215.

Whitcomb, Donald S. (1985), *Before the Roses and Nightingales: Excavations at Qasr-i Abu Nasr, Old Shiraz*, New York: The Metropolitan Museum of Art.

Wickens, G. M. (1971), 'Hafiz', *Encyclopaedia of Islam, new edition* III: 55–57.

Wickens, G. M. (1974), 'The Frozen Periphery of Allusion in Classical Persian Literature', *Literature East and West* 18: 171–190.

Wilber, Donald N. (1979), 'The Timurid Court Life in Gardens and Tents', *Iran* 17: 127–133.

Wilkinson, Charles K. (1965), 'The Achaemenian Remains at Qasr-i Abu Nasr', *Journal of Near East Studies* 24: 341–345.

Wing, Patrick (2014), 'Mozaffarids', *Encyclopaedia Iranica*, online edition.

Wing, Patrick (2016), *The Jalayirids: Dynastic State Formation in the Mongol Middle East*, Edinburgh: Edinburgh University Press.

Wright, Elaine (2006), 'Patronage of the Arts of the Book under the Injuids of Shiraz', in Linda Komaroff (ed.), *Beyond the Legacy of Genghis Khan*, 248–268, Leiden: Brill.

Wright, Elaine (2012), *The Look of the Book: Manuscript Production in Shiraz, 1303–1452*, Seattle: University of Washington Press.

Wright, J. W. (1997), 'Masculine Allusion and the Structure of Satire in Early 'Abbasid Poetry', in J. W. Wright and Everett K. Rowson (eds), *Homoeroticism in Classical Arabic Literature*, 1–23, New York: Columbia University Press.

Wright, Owen (2010), 'Music and Poetry, Medieval', in Julie Scott Meisami and
    Paul Starkey (eds), *The Routledge Encyclopedia of Arabic Literaure*, 555–556,
    Abingdon: Routledge.
Yaghoobi, Claudia (2017), *Subjectivity in 'Attar, Persian Sufism, and European
    Mysticism*, West Lafayette: Purdue University Press.
Yamamoto, Kumiko (2003), *The Oral Background of Persian Epics: Storytelling
    and Poetry*, Leiden: Brill.
Yamauchi, Edwin M. (1990), *Persia and the Bible*, Grand Rapids: Baker Book
    House.
Yarshater, Ehsan (1960), 'The Theme of Wine-Drinking and the Concept of the
    Beloved in Early Persian Poetry', *Studia Islamica* 13: 43–53.
Yarshater, Ehsan (1986), 'Persian Poetry in the Timuird and Safavid Periods', in
    Peter Jackson and Laurence Lockhart (eds), *The Cambridge History of Iran
    Volume IV: The Timurid and Safavid Periods*, 965–994, Cambridge: Cambridge
    University Press.
Yarshater, Ehsan (2003), 'Hafez: An Overview', *Encyclopaedia Iranica* XI: 461–465.
Yarshater, Ehsan (2006), 'Gazal ii. Characteristics and Conventions',
    Encyclopaedia Iranica, online edition.
Yavari, Neguin (2002), 'Jewish-Muslim Interaction in Medieval Iran', in Houman
    Sarshar (ed.), *Esther's Children: A Portrait of Iranian Jews*, 51–59, Philadelphia:
    Jewish Publication Society.
Yeroushalmi, David (2002), 'Judeo-Persian Literature', in Houman Sarshar (ed.),
    Esther's Children: A Portrait of Iranian Jews, 77–93, Philadelphia: Jewish
    Publication Society.
Yoch, James J. (1978), 'Architecture as Virtue: The Luminous Palace from Homeric
    Dream to Stuart Propaganda', *Studies in Philology* 75: 403–429.
Yohannan, John D. (1987), *The Poet Sa'di: A Persian Humanist*, Lanham:
    University Press of America.
Zakavati, 'Ali-Riza (1991), *Hafiziyat*, Hamadan: Intisharat-i Muslim.
Zakeri, Mohsen (2015), 'The Literary Use of Proverbs and Myths in Nasir-i
    Khusraw's *Divan*', in Julia Rubanovich (ed.), *Orality and Textuality in the Iranian
    World: Patterns of Interaction across the Centuries*, 287–306. Leiden: Brill.
Zarrinkub, 'Abd al-Husayn (1975), *Az kucha-yi rindan: dar-bara-yi zindagi u andisha-
    yi Hafiz*, Tehran: Franklin.
Zarrinkub, 'Abd al-Husayn (1993), *Pir-i Ganja: dar justuju-yi nakuja-abad*, Tehran: 'Ilmi.
Zaryab, 'Abbas (1989), *A'ina-yi jam: sharh-i mushkilat-i divan-i Hafiz*, Tehran: 'Ilmi.
Ze'evi, Dror (2006), *Producing Desire: Changing Sexual Discourse in the Ottoman
    Middle East, 1500–1900*, Berkeley: University of California Press.
Zeikowitz, Richard E. (2003), *Homoeroticism and Chivalry: Discourses of Male
    Same-Sex Desire in the Fourteenth Century*, New York: Palgrave Macmillan.
Zipoli, Riccardo (1993), *The Technique of the Ǧawab: Replies by Nawa'i to Hafiz
    and Ǧami*, Venice: Cafoscarina.
Zipoli, Riccardo (1994), 'Oscenità poetiche neopersiane: due tarji'-band sulla
    masturbazione', *Annali di Ca' Foscari* 33: 249–291.
Zipoli, Riccardo (2001), 'The Obscene Sana'i, *Persica* 17: 173–194.
Zipoli, Riccardo (2006), 'Anvari, a Master of Obscene Verse', *Euroasiatica* 74:
    149–172.
Zipoli, Riccardo (2009), 'Poetic Imagery', in J. T. P. de Bruijn (ed.), *General
    Introduction to Persian Literature*, 172–232.

Index

www.ingramcontent.com/pod-product-compliance
Lightning Source LLC
Chambersburg PA
CBHW071146100726
47908CB00002B/266